REFLECTING CHRIST

REFLECTING CHRIST

ELLEN G. WHITE

This book is published in collaboration with
the Youth Department
as an enrichment of the Morning Watch devotional plan.

REVIEW AND HERALD PUBLISHING ASSOCIATION
Washington, DC 20039-0555
Hagerstown, MD 21740

Book design by Richard Steadham
Cover photo by Comstock, Inc.

Printed in U.S.A.

Texts credited to A.R.V. are from the American Revised Version of the Bible, Thomas Nelson and Sons, 1901.

Texts credited to N.E.B. are from *The New English Bible.* © The Delegates of the Oxford University Press and the Syndics of the Cambridge University Press 1961, 1970. Reprinted by permission.

Texts credited to N.I.V. are from *The Holy Bible: New International Version.* Copyright © 1973, 1978, International Bible Society. Used by permission of Zondervan Bible Publishers.

Texts credited to N.K.J.V. are from the New King James Version. Copyright © 1979, 1980, 1982, Thomas Nelson, Inc., Publishers.

Texts credited to R.S.V. are from the Revised Standard Version of the Bible, copyrighted 1946, 1952 © 1971, 1973.

Texts credited to R.V. are from the Revised Version of the Bible, Oxford University Press, 1911.

Library of Congress Cataloging in Publication Data

White, Ellen Gould Harmon, 1827-1915.
    Reflecting Christ.

    ''This book is published in collaboration with the
Youth Department as an enrichment of the Morning Watch
devotional plan.''
    Includes index.
    1. Devotional calendars—Seventh-day Adventists.
2. Seventh-day Adventists—Prayer books and devotions—
English. 3. Adventists—Prayer books and devotions—
English. I. General Conference of Seventh-day
Adventists. Youth Dept. II. Title.
BV4811.W49   1985   242'.2   85-11809

ISBN 0-8280-0305-X

FOREWORD

This volume is the fourteenth book of day-by-day devotional readings to be published from the pen of Ellen G. White. This establishes a new record in the Seventh-day Adventist Church, and probably is a record also in the Christian world at large. Ellen White's writings are at once so voluminous, so Christ-centered, and so practical that they continue to provide an almost endless source of materials that are admirably suited for devotional reading.

During her seventy-year ministry the author spoke, through her pen, to young people, to church members, and to the world in the *Youth's Instructor, Review and Herald,* and *Signs of the Times*. Selections for this book have been drawn from these three periodicals as well as from her books and previously unpublished manuscripts and letters.

In order to bring each reading within the compass of a single page, frequent deletions have been necessary. Such omissions are indicated by marks of ellipsis. In every instance great care has been exercised to preserve without distortion the thought and intent of the writer. *Reflecting Christ*—the title of this book—is a theme that recurs constantly through the writings of Ellen White. Loving the Lord deeply, the author earnestly endeavored to walk in His footsteps herself, and she ever encouraged others to look to Christ as their example. Underlining the theme of this book, she wrote: ''When those who profess to serve God follow Christ's example, practicing the principles of the law in their daily life; when every act bears witness that they love God supremely and their neighbor as themselves, then will the church have power to move the world.''—*Christ's Object Lessons,* p. 340.

Reflecting Christ—this should be every Christian's highest goal. The pursuit of this objective, under the impetus of the indwelling Spirit of God and the grace of Christ, can bring with it only peace and true happiness.

That the meditations in this book may aid and encourage each reader in his or her walk with the Lord is the fervent prayer of

The Trustees of the Ellen G. White Estate
Washington, D.C.

The Author

Ellen Gould (Harmon) White, cofounder of the Seventh-day Adventist Church, writer, lecturer, and counselor, and one upon whom Seventh-day Adventists believe the gift of prophecy was bestowed, was born in Gorham, Maine, November 26, 1827, one of eight children of Robert and Eunice Harmon.

During her seventy years of active service to the church, she found time to write voluminously. She is credited with having written 100,000 manuscript pages. This remarkable legacy to the church could alone have occupied Ellen White's entire life, had she dedicated her time to little else but writing.

However, her service for the church embraces much more than writing. Her diaries tell of her public work, her travels, her personal labor, hostessing, contacts with neighbors, as well as of her being a mother and housewife. God blessed her abundantly in these activities. Her ambitions and concerns, her satisfactions and joys, her sorrows—her whole life—were for the advancement of the cause she loved.

Ellen G. White is reputed to be the most translated woman author and the most translated author in American history. For example, her little book *Steps to Christ* is available in more than 100 languages.

After a full life dedicated to the service of God and others, she died on July 16, 1915, confidently trusting in Him whom she had believed.

BIOGRAPHICAL NOTES

Ellen G. White, 1827-1915

The Early Years, 1827-1860

Born on a late fall day in a farmhouse near Gorham, Maine, Ellen Harmon spent her childhood and youth in nearby Portland. She married James White in 1846, and the struggling young couple lived in a variety of New England locations as they sought to encourage and instruct fellow Advent believers by their preaching, visiting, and publishing. After eleven irregular issues of *The Present Truth,* they launched the *Second Advent Review and Sabbath Herald** in Paris, Maine, in 1850. Thereafter they followed a steadily westward course—to Saratoga Springs, New York, and then Rochester, New York, in the early 1850s, and finally, in 1855, to Battle Creek, Michigan, where they resided for the next twenty years.

1827, November 26	Born at Gorham, Maine.
1836 (c.)	Broken nose and concussion at Portland, Maine.
1840, March	First heard William Miller present the Advent message.
1842, June 26	Baptized and accepted into Methodist Church.
1844, October 22	Disappointed when Christ did not come.
1844, December	First vision.
1845, Spring	Trip to eastern Maine to visit believers; met James White.
1846, August 30	Married James White.
1846, Autumn	Accepted seventh-day Sabbath.
1847-1848	Set up housekeeping at Topsham, Maine.
1847, August 26	Birth of first son, Henry Nichols.
1848, April 20-24	Attended first conference of Sabbathkeeping Adventists at Rocky Hill, Connecticut.
1848, November 18	Vision to begin publishing work—"Streams of Light."
1849, July	First of eleven numbers of *The Present Truth,* published as a result of the vision of November, 1848.
1849, July 28	Birth of James Edson, second son.
1849-1852	Moved from place to place with her publisher-husband.

1851, July	First book published, *A Sketch of Experience and Views*.
1852-1855	In Rochester, New York, where husband published *Review and Herald* and *Youth's Instructor*.
1854, August 29	Third son, William Clarence, born.
1855, November	Moved with the publishing plant to Battle Creek, Michigan.
1855, December	"Testimony for the Church," number 1, a sixteen-page pamphlet, published.
1856, Spring	Moved into their own cottage on Wood Street.
1858, March 14	"Great Controversy" vision at Lovett's Grove, Ohio.
1860, September 20	Fourth son, John Herbert, born.
1860, December 14	Death of John Herbert at three months.

Years of Church Development, 1860-1868

The 1860s saw Ellen White and her husband in the forefront of the struggle to organize the Seventh-day Adventist Church into a stable institution. The decade was also crucial in that it encompassed the beginnings of Adventist health emphasis. Responding to Mrs. White's appeal, the church as a body began to see the importance of healthful living in the Christian life. In response to her "Christmas Vision" of 1865, our first health institution, the Western Health Reform Institute, was opened in 1866. The institute later grew into the Battle Creek Sanitarium.

1860, September 29	Name Seventh-day Adventist chosen.
1861, October 8	Michigan Conference organized.
1863, May	Organization of General Conference of Seventh-day Adventists.
1863, June 6	Health reform vision at Otsego, Michigan.
1863, December 8	Death of eldest son, Henry Nichols, at Topsham, Maine.
1864, Summer	Publication of *Spiritual Gifts,* volume 4, with thirty-page article on health.
1864, August-September	Visit to James C. Jackson's medical institution, Our Home on the Hillside, Dansville, New York, en route to Boston, Massachusetts.
1865	Publication of six pamphlets, *Health: or How to Live*.
1865, August 16	James White stricken with paralysis.
1865, December 25	Vision calling for a medical institution.

1865, December	Mrs. White takes James White to northern Michigan as an aid to his recovery.
1866, September 5	Opening of Western Health Reform Institute, forerunner of Battle Creek Sanitarium.
1867	Purchased a farm at Greenville, Michigan, and built a home and engaged in farming and writing.

The Camp Meeting Years, 1868-1881

Residing at Greenville and Battle Creek, Michigan, respectively, until late 1872, and then dividing her time between Michigan and California, Ellen White spent her winters writing and publishing. During the summer she attended camp meetings, some years as many as twenty-eight! *Testimonies,* numbers 14-30, now found in *Testimonies,* volumes 2-4, were published during these years.

1868, September 1-7	Attended first SDA camp meeting, held in Brother Root's maple grove at Wright, Michigan.
1870, July 28	Second son, James Edson, married on his 21st birthday.
1870	*The Spirit of Prophecy,* volume 1, published; forerunner of *Patriarchs and Prophets.*
1872, July-September	In Rocky Mountains resting and writing en route to California.
1873-1874	Divided time between Battle Creek and California, attended camp meetings, and spent some months in 1873 in Colorado resting and writing.
1874, April 1	Comprehensive vision of the advance of the cause in California, Oregon, and overseas.
1874, June	With James White in Oakland, California, as he founded the Pacific Press Publishing Association and the *Signs of the Times.*
1875, January 3	At Battle Creek for dedication of Battle Creek College. Vision of publishing houses in other countries.
1876, February 11	William Clarence, third son and manager of the Pacific Press, married at the age of 21.
1876, August	Spoke to 20,000 at Groveland, Massachusetts, camp meeting.
1877	*The Spirit of Prophecy,* volume 2, published; forerunner of *The Desire of Ages.*
1877, July 1	Spoke to 5,000 at Battle Creek on temperance.
1878	*The Spirit of Prophecy,* volume 3, published; forerunner of last part of *The Desire of Ages,* and

	The Acts of the Apostles.
1878, November	Spent the winter in Texas.
1879, April	Left Texas to engage in the summer camp meeting work.
1881, August 1	With husband in Battle Creek when he was taken ill.
1881, August 6	Death of James White.
1881, August 13	Spoke for ten minutes at James White's funeral at Battle Creek.

The 1880s, 1881-1891

Following James White's death in August, 1881, Ellen White resided in California, at times in Healdsburg and at times in Oakland. She labored there, writing and speaking, until she left for Europe in August, 1885, in response to the call of the General Conference. During the two years in Europe she resided in Basel, Switzerland, except for three extended visits to the Scandinavian countries, England, and Italy. Returning to the United States in August, 1887, she soon made her way west to her Healdsburg home. She attended the 1888 General Conference session at Minneapolis in October and November; following the conference, while residing in Battle Creek, she worked among the churches in the Midwest and the East. After a year in the East she returned to California, but was called back to attend the General Conference session at Battle Creek in October, 1889. She remained in the vicinity of Battle Creek until she left for Australia in September, 1891.

1881, November	Attended the California camp meeting at Sacramento and participated in planning for a college in the West, which opened in 1882 at Healdsburg.
1882	*Early Writings* published, incorporating three of her early books.
1884	Last recorded public vision, at Portland, Oregon, camp meeting.
1884	*The Spirit of Prophecy,* volume 4, published; forerunner of *The Great Controversy.*
1885, Summer	Left California for trip to Europe.
1887, Summer	*The Great Controversy* published.
1888, October-November	Attended Minneapolis General Conference.
1889	*Testimonies,* volume 5, published, embodying *Testimonies,* numbers 31-33—746 pages.
1890	*Patriarchs and Prophets* published.
1891, September 12	Sailed to Australia via Honolulu.

The Australian Years, 1891-1900

Responding to the call of the General Conference to visit Australia to aid in establishing an educational work, Ellen White arrived in Sydney, December 8, 1891. She accepted the invitation somewhat reluctantly, for she had wanted to get on with her writing of a larger book on the life of Christ. Soon after her arrival she was stricken with inflammatory rheumatism, which confined her to her bed for some eight months. Although suffering intensely, she persisted in writing. In early 1893 she went to New Zealand, where she worked until the end of the year. Returning to Australia in late December, she attended the first Australian camp meeting. At this camp meeting, plans for a rural school were developed that resulted in the establishment of what became Avondale College at Cooranbong, 90 miles north of Sydney. Ellen White purchased land nearby and built her Sunnyside home late in 1895. Here she resided, giving her attention to her writing and traveling among the churches until she returned to the United States in August, 1900.

1892, June	Spoke at opening of Australian Bible School in two rented buildings in Melbourne.
1892	*Steps to Christ* and *Gospel Workers* published.
1894, January	Joined in planning for a permanent school in Australia.
1894, May 23	Visited the Cooranbong site.
1895, December	Moved to her Sunnyside home at Cooranbong, where much of *The Desire of Ages* was written.
1896	*Thoughts From the Mount of Blessing* published.
1898	*The Desire of Ages* published.
1899-1900	Encouraged the establishment of Sydney Sanitarium.
1900	*Christ's Object Lessons* published.
1900, August	Left Australia and returned to United States.

The Elmshaven Years, 1900-1915

When Ellen White settled at Elmshaven, her new home near St. Helena in northern California, she hoped to give most of her time to writing her books. She was 72 and still had a number of volumes that she wished to complete. She little realized how much traveling, counseling, and speaking she would also be called upon to do. The crisis created by the controversies in Battle Creek would also make heavy demands on her time and strength. Even so, by writing early in the morning, she was able to produce nine books during her Elmshaven years.

1900, October	Settled at Elmshaven.

1901, April	Attended the General Conference session at Battle Creek.
1902, February 18	Battle Creek Sanitarium fire.
1902, December 30	Review and Herald fire.
1903, October	Met the pantheism crisis.
1904, April-September	Journeyed east to assist in the beginning of the work in Washington, D.C., to visit her son Edson in Nashville, and to attend important meetings.
1904, November-December	Involved in securing and establishing Paradise Valley Sanitarium.
1905, May	Attended General Conference session in Washington, D.C.
1905	*The Ministry of Healing* published.
1905, June-December	Involved in securing and starting Loma Linda Sanitarium.
1906-1908	Busy at Elmshaven with literary work.
1909, April-September	At the age of 81 traveled to Washington, D.C., to attend the General Conference session. This was her last trip east.
1910, January	Took a prominent part in the establishment of the College of Medical Evangelists at Loma Linda.
1910	Gave attention to finishing *The Acts of the Apostles* and the reissuance of *The Great Controversy,* a work extending into 1911.
1911-1915	With advancing age, made only a few trips to southern California. At Elmshaven engaged in her book work, finishing *Prophets and Kings* and *Counsels to Parents and Teachers.*
1915, February 13	Fell in her Elmshaven home and broke her hip.
1915, July 16	Closed her fruitful life at the age of 87. Her last words were "I know in whom I have believed." *Testimonies,* volumes 6-9, were also published in the Elmshaven years.

---

* Now known as the *Adventist Review,* it is one of the oldest continuously published religious journals in the United States.

TOPICS

CHRIST—ONE WITH THE FATHER

"The virgin . . . will give birth to a son, and they will call him Immanuel"—which means, "God with us." Matt. 1:23, N.I.V.

"The light of the knowledge of the glory of God" is seen "in the face of Jesus Christ." From the days of eternity the Lord Jesus Christ was one with the Father; He was "the image of God," the image of His greatness and majesty, "the outshining of his glory." It was to manifest this glory that He came to our world. To this sin-darkened earth He came to reveal the light of God's love—to be "God with us." Therefore it was prophesied of Him, "His name shall be called Immanuel."

By coming to dwell with us, Jesus was to reveal God both to men and to angels. He was the Word of God—God's thought made audible. In His prayer for His disciples He says, "I have declared unto them thy name"—"merciful and gracious, longsuffering, and abundant in goodness and truth"—"that the love wherewith Thou hast loved Me may be in them, and I in them."

But not alone for His earthborn children was this revelation given. Our little world is the lesson book of the universe. God's wonderful purpose of grace, the mystery of redeeming love, is the theme into which "angels desire to look," and it will be their study throughout endless ages. Both the redeemed and the unfallen beings will find in the cross of Christ their science and their song. It will be seen that the glory shining in the face of Jesus is the glory of self-sacrificing love. In the light from Calvary it will be seen that the law of self-renouncing love is the law of life for earth and heaven; that the love which "seeketh not her own" has its source in the heart of God; and that in the meek and lowly One is manifested the character of Him who dwelleth in the light which no man can approach unto. . . .

We behold God in Jesus. Looking unto Jesus we see that it is the glory of our God to give. "I do nothing of myself," said Christ; "the living Father hath sent me, and I live by the Father." "I seek not mine own glory," but the glory of Him that sent Me (John 8:28; 6:57; 8:50; 7:18). In these words is set forth the great principle which is the law of life for the universe. All things Christ received from God, but He took to give. So in the heavenly courts, in His ministry for all created beings: through the beloved Son, the Father's life flows out to all; through the Son it returns, in praise and joyous service, a tide of love, to the great Source of all. And thus through Christ the circuit of beneficence is complete, representing the character of the great Giver, the law of life.—*The Desire of Ages,* pp. 19-21.

A TEACHER SENT FROM GOD

But when the fulness of the time was come, God sent forth his Son . . . to redeem them that were under the law, that we might receive the adoption of sons. Gal. 4:4, 5.

At the time of Christ's first advent darkness had covered the earth, and gross darkness the people. Truth looked down from heaven, and nowhere could discern the reflection of her image. Spiritual darkness had settled down over the religious world, and this darkness was almost universal and complete. . . .

All things proclaimed the urgent necessity on the earth of a Teacher sent from God—a Teacher in whom divinity and humanity would be united. It was essential that Christ should appear in human form, and stand at the head of the human race, to uplift fallen human beings. Thus only could God be revealed to the world.

Christ volunteered to lay aside His royal robe and kingly crown, and come to this earth to show to human beings what they may be in cooperation with God. He came to shine amidst the darkness, to dispel the darkness by the brightness of His presence. . . .

The Father and the Son in consultation decided that Christ must come to the world as a babe, and live the life that human beings must live from childhood to manhood, bearing the trials that they must bear, and at the same time living a sinless life, that men might see in Him an example of what they can become, and that He might know by experience how to help them in their struggles with sin. He was tried as man is tried, tempted as man is tempted. The life that He lived in this world, men can live, through His power and under His instruction. . . .

Patriarchs and prophets have predicted the coming of a distinguished Teacher, whose words were to be clothed with invincible power and authority. He was to preach the gospel to the poor, and proclaim the acceptable year of the Lord. He was to set judgment in the earth; the isles were to wait for His law; the Gentiles were to come to His light, and kings to the brightness of His rising. He was "the messenger of the covenant," and "the Sun of righteousness." . . .

And "when the fulness of time was come, God sent forth his Son." . . . The heavenly Teacher had come. Who was He? No less a being than the Son of God Himself. He appeared as God, and at the same time as the Elder Brother of the human race.—*Signs of the Times,* May 17, 1905.

What He taught, He lived. . . . What He taught, He was. His words were the expression, not only of His own life experience, but of His own character. Not only did He teach the truth, but He was the truth. It was this that gave His teaching power.—*Education,* pp. 78, 79.

CHRIST SACRIFICED HIMSELF FOR US

We see Jesus, who was made a little lower than the angels for the suffering of death, crowned with glory and honour; that he by the grace of God should taste death for every man. Heb. 2:9.

The Lord created man pure and holy. But Satan led him astray, perverting his principles and corrupting his mind, turning his thoughts into a wrong channel. His purpose was to make the world wholly corrupt.

Christ saw man's fearful danger, and He determined to save him by the sacrifice of Himself. That He might accomplish His purpose of love for the fallen race, He became bone of our bone and flesh of our flesh. "As the children are partakers of flesh and blood, he also himself likewise took part of the same; that through death he might destroy him that had the power of death, that is, the devil; and deliver them who through fear of death were all their lifetime subject to bondage. . . . Wherefore in all things it behoved him to be made like unto his brethren, that he might be a merciful and faithful high priest in things pertaining to God, to make reconciliation for the sins of the people. For in that he himself hath suffered being tempted, he is able to succor them that are tempted." . . .

Through the agency of the Holy Spirit, a new principle of mental and spiritual power was to be brought to man, who, through association with divinity, was to become one with God. Christ, the redeemer and restorer, was to sanctify and purify man's mind, making it a power that would draw other minds to Himself. It is His purpose, by the elevating, sanctifying power of the truth, to give men nobility and dignity. He desires His children to reveal His character, to exert His influence, that other minds may be drawn into harmony with His mind. . . .

Christ might, because of our guilt, have moved far away from us. But instead of moving farther away, He came and dwelt among us, filled with all the fullness of the Godhead, to be one with us, that through His grace we might attain perfection. By a death of shame and suffering He paid our ransom. From the highest excellency He came, His divinity clothed with humanity, descending step by step to the lowest depths of humiliation. No line can measure the depth of His love. . . .

I marvel that professing Christians do not grasp the divine resources, that they do not see the cross more clearly as the medium of forgiveness and pardon, the means of bringing the proud, selfish heart of man into direct contact with the Holy Spirit, that the riches of Christ may be poured into the mind, and the human agent be adorned with the graces of the Spirit, that Christ may be commended to those who know Him not.—*Signs of the Times,* Sept. 24, 1902.

CHRIST SUPPLIES US WITH LIVING WATER

On the last and greatest day of the Feast, Jesus stood and said in a loud voice, "If a man is thirsty, let him come to me, and drink. Whoever believes in me, as the Scripture has said, streams of living water will flow from within him." John 7:37, 38, N.I.V.

The priest . . . performed the ceremony which commemorated the smiting of the rock in the wilderness. That rock was a symbol of Him who by His death would cause living streams of salvation to flow to all who are athirst. Christ's words were the water of life. There in the presence of the assembled multitude He set Himself apart to be smitten, that the water of life might flow to the world. In smiting Christ, Satan thought to destroy the Prince of life; but from the smitten rock there flowed living water. As Jesus thus spoke to the people, their hearts thrilled with a strange awe, and many were ready to exclaim, with the woman of Samaria, "Give me this water, that I thirst not" (John 4:15).

Jesus knew the wants of the soul. Pomp, riches, and honor cannot satisfy the heart. "If any man thirst, let him come unto me." The rich, the poor, the high, the low, are alike welcome. He promises to relieve the burdened mind, to comfort the sorrowing, and to give hope to the despondent. Many of those who heard Jesus were mourners over disappointed hopes, many were nourishing a secret grief, many were seeking to satisfy their restless longing with the things of the world and the praise of men; but when all was gained, they found that they had toiled only to reach a broken cistern, from which they could not quench their thirst. Amid the glitter of the joyous scene they stood, dissatisfied and sad. That sudden cry, "If any man thirst," startled them from their sorrowful meditation, and as they listened to the words that followed, their minds kindled with a new hope. The Holy Spirit presented the symbol before them until they saw in it the offer of the priceless gift of salvation.

The cry of Christ to the thirsty soul is still going forth, and it appeals to us with even greater power than to those who heard it in the temple on the last day of the feast. The fountain is open for all. The weary and exhausted ones are offered the refreshing draught of eternal life. Jesus is still crying, "If any man thirst, let him come unto me, and drink." "Let him that is athirst come. And whosoever will, let him take the water of life freely" (Rev. 22:17). "Whosoever drinketh of the water that I shall give him shall never thirst; but the water that I shall give him shall be in him a well of water springing up into everlasting life" (John 4:14).—*The Desire of Ages,* p. 454.

CHRIST'S COMPASSION KNEW NO LIMIT

This was to fulfil what was spoken by the prophet Isaiah, "He took our infirmities and bore our diseases." Matt. 8:17, R.S.V.

Our Lord Jesus Christ came to this world as the unwearied servant of man's necessity. He "took our infirmities, and bare our sicknesses," that He might minister to every need of humanity. The burden of disease and wretchedness and sin He came to remove. It was His mission to bring to men complete restoration; He came to give them health and peace and perfection of character.

Varied were the circumstances and needs of those who besought His aid, and none who came to Him went away unhelped. From Him flowed a stream of healing power, and in body and mind and soul men were made whole.

The Saviour's work was not restricted to any time or place. His compassion knew no limit. On so large a scale did He conduct His work of healing and teaching that there was no building in Palestine large enough to receive the multitudes that thronged to Him. On the green hillslopes of Galilee, in the thoroughfares of travel, by the seashore, in the synagogues, and in every place where the sick could be brought to Him was to be found His hospital. In every city, every town, every village through which He passed, He laid His hands upon the afflicted ones, and healed them. Wherever there were hearts ready to receive His message, He comforted them with the assurance of their heavenly Father's love. All day He ministered to those who came to Him; in the evening He gave attention to such as through the day must toil to earn a pittance for the support of their families.

Jesus carried the awful weight of responsibility for the salvation of men. He knew that unless there was a decided change in the principles and purposes of the human race, all would be lost. This was the burden of His soul, and none could appreciate the weight that rested upon Him. Through childhood, youth, and manhood, He walked alone. . . .

Day by day He met trials and temptations; day by day He was brought into contact with evil, and witnessed its power upon those whom He was seeking to bless and to save. Yet He did not fail nor become discouraged. . . .

He was always patient and cheerful, and the afflicted hailed Him as a messenger of life and peace. He saw the needs of men and women, children and youth, and to all He gave the invitation, "Come unto me." . . .

As He passed through the towns and cities, He was like a vital current, diffusing life and joy.—*Gospel Workers,* pp. 41-43.

CHANGED INTO HIS IMAGE

But we all, with open face beholding as in a glass the glory of the Lord, are changed into the same image from glory to glory even as by the Spirit of the Lord. 2 Cor. 3:18.

Sin-burdened, struggling souls, Jesus in His glorified humanity has ascended into the heavens to make intercession for us. "For we have not an high priest which cannot be touched with the feeling of our infirmities; but was in all points tempted like as we are, yet without sin. Let us therefore come boldly unto the throne of grace." We should be continually looking unto Jesus, the author and finisher of our faith; for by beholding Him we shall be changed into His image, our character will be made like His. We should rejoice that all judgment is given to the Son, because in His humanity He has become acquainted with all the difficulties that beset humanity.

To be sanctified is to become a partaker of the divine nature, catching the spirit and mind of Jesus, ever learning in the school of Christ. "But we all, with open face beholding as in a glass the glory of the Lord, are changed into the same image from glory to glory even as by the Spirit of the Lord." It is impossible for any of us by our own power or our own efforts to work this change in ourselves. It is the Holy Spirit, the Comforter, which Jesus said He would send into the world, that changes our character into the image of Christ; and when this is accomplished, we reflect, as in a mirror, the glory of the Lord. That is, the character of the one who thus beholds Christ is so like His, that one looking at him sees Christ's own character shining out as from a mirror. Imperceptibly to ourselves, we are changed day by day from our ways and will into the ways and will of Christ, into the loveliness of His character. Thus we grow up into Christ, and unconsciously reflect His image.

Professed Christians keep altogether too near the lowlands of earth. Their eyes are trained to see only commonplace things, and their minds dwell upon the things their eyes behold. Their religious experience is often shallow and unsatisfying, and their words are light and valueless. How can such reflect the image of Christ? How can they send forth the bright beams of the Sun of Righteousness into all the dark places of the earth? To be a Christian is to be Christlike. . . .

[Enoch] was ever under the influence of Jesus. He reflected Christ's character, exhibiting the same qualities in goodness, mercy, tender compassion, sympathy, forbearance, meekness, humility and love. His association with Christ day by day transformed him into the image of Him with whom he was so intimately connected.—*Review and Herald,* Dec. 5, 1912.

CHRIST INSPIRES SOULS WITH CONFIDENCE IN GOD

Whatsoever is born of God overcometh the world: and this is the victory that overcometh the world, even our faith. 1 John 5:4.

What kind of faith is it that overcomes the world? It is that faith which makes Christ your own personal Saviour—that faith which, recognizing your helplessness, your utter inability to save yourself, takes hold of the Helper who is mighty to save, as your only hope. It is faith that will not be discouraged, that hears the voice of Christ saying, ''Be of good cheer, I have overcome the world, and My divine strength is yours.'' It is the faith that hears Him say, ''Lo, I am with you alway, even unto the end of the world.''

The reason why the churches are weak and sickly and ready to die is that the enemy has brought influences of a discouraging nature to bear upon trembling souls. He has sought to shut Jesus from their view as the Comforter, as one who reproves, who warns, who admonishes them, saying, ''This is the way, walk ye in it.'' Christ has all power in heaven and in earth, and He can strengthen the wavering, and set right the erring. He can inspire with confidence, with hope in God; and confidence in God always results in creating confidence in one another.

Every soul must have a realization that Christ is his personal Saviour; then love and zeal and steadfastness will be manifest in the Christian life. However clear and convincing the truth is, it will fail to sanctify the soul, fail to strengthen and fortify it in its conflicts, unless it is brought in constant contact with life. Satan has achieved his greatest success through interposing himself between the soul and the Saviour.

Christ should never be out of the mind. The angels said concerning Him, ''Thou shalt call his name Jesus: for he shall save his people from their sins.'' Jesus, precious Saviour! Assurance, helpfulness, security, and peace are all in Him. He is the dispeller of all our doubts, the earnest of all our hopes. How precious is the thought that we may indeed become partakers of the divine nature, whereby we may overcome as Christ overcame! Jesus is the fullness of our expectation. He is the melody of our songs, the shadow of a great rock in a weary land. He is living water to the thirsty soul. He is our refuge in the storm. He is our righteousness, our sanctification, our redemption. When Christ is our personal Saviour, we shall show forth the praises of Him who hath called us out of darkness into His marvelous light. . . .

Christ died because the law was transgressed, that guilty man might be saved from the penalty of his enormous guilt. But history has proved that it is easier to destroy the world than to reform it; for men crucified the Lord of Glory, who came to unite earth with heaven, and man with God.—*Review and Herald,* Aug. 26, 1890.

BY THE EYE OF FAITH CHRIST IS PRESENT EVER

Nevertheless I tell you the truth; It is expedient for you that I go away: for if I go not away, the Comforter will not come unto you; but if I depart, I will send him unto you. John 16:7.

Christ said, ''It is expedient for you that I go away.'' No one could then have any preference because of his location or personal contact with Christ. The Saviour would be accessible to all alike, spiritually, and in this sense He would be nearer to us all than if He had not ascended on high. Now all may be equally favored by beholding Him and reflecting His character. The eye of faith sees Him ever present, in all His goodness, grace, forbearance, courtesy, and love, those spiritual and divine attributes. And as we behold, we are changed into His likeness.

Christ is soon coming in the clouds of heaven, and we must be prepared to meet Him, not having spot or wrinkle or any such thing. We are now to accept the invitation of Christ. He says, ''Come unto me, all ye that labour and are heavy laden, and I will give you rest. Take my yoke upon you, and learn of me; for I am meek and lowly in heart: and ye shall find rest unto your souls.'' The words of Christ to Nicodemus are of practical value to us today: ''Except a man be born of water and of the Spirit, he cannot enter into the kingdom of God. That which is born of the flesh is flesh; and that which is born of the Spirit is spirit. Marvel not that I said unto thee, Ye must be born again. The wind bloweth where it listeth, and thou hearest the sound thereof, but canst not tell whence it cometh, and whither it goeth: so is every one that is born of the Spirit.''

The converting power of God must be upon our hearts. We must study the life of Christ, and imitate the divine Pattern. We must dwell upon the perfection of His character, and be changed into His image. No one will enter the kingdom of God unless his will is brought into captivity to the will of Christ.

Heaven is free from all sin, from all defilement and impurity; and if we would live in its atmosphere, if we would behold the glory of Christ, we must be pure in heart, perfect in character through His grace and righteousness. We must not be taken up with pleasure and amusement, but be fitting up for the glorious mansions Christ has gone to prepare for us. If we are faithful, seeking to bless others, patient in well- doing, at His coming Christ will crown us with glory, honor, and immortality.— *Review and Herald,* Dec. 5, 1912.

CHRIST BRIDGED THE GULF
CAUSED BY SIN

For God so loved the world, that he gave his only begotten Son, that whosoever believeth in him should not perish, but have everlasting life. John 3:16.

Sin originated in self-seeking. Lucifer, the covering cherub, desired to be first in heaven. He sought to gain control of heavenly beings, to draw them away from their Creator, and to win their homage to himself. Therefore he misrepresented God, attributing to Him the desire for self-exaltation. With his own evil characteristics he sought to invest the loving Creator. Thus he deceived angels. Thus he deceived men. He led them to doubt the word of God, and to distrust His goodness. Because God is a God of justice and terrible majesty, Satan caused them to look upon Him as severe and unforgiving. Thus he drew men to join him in rebellion against God, and the night of woe settled down upon the world.

The earth was dark through misapprehension of God. That the gloomy shadows might be lightened, that the world might be brought back to God, Satan's deceptive power was to be broken. This could not be done by force. The exercise of force is contrary to the principles of God's government; He desires only the service of love; and love cannot be commanded; it cannot be won by force or authority. Only by love is love awakened. To know God is to love Him; His character must be manifested in contrast to the character of Satan. This work only one Being in all the universe could do. Only He who knew the height and depth of the love of God could make it known. Upon the world's dark night the Sun of Righteousness must rise, "with healing in his wings" (Mal. 4:2).

The plan for our redemption was not an afterthought, a plan formulated after the fall of Adam. It was a revelation of "the mystery which hath been kept in silence through times eternal" (Rom. 16:25, R.V.). It was an unfolding of the principles that from eternal ages have been the foundation of God's throne. From the beginning, God and Christ knew of the apostasy of Satan, and of the fall of man through the deceptive power of the apostate. God did not ordain that sin should exist, but He foresaw its existence, and made provision to meet the terrible emergency. . . .

Since Jesus came to dwell with us, we know that God is acquainted with our trials, and sympathizes with our griefs. Every son and daughter of Adam may understand that our Creator is the friend of sinners. For in every doctrine of grace, every promise of joy, every deed of love, every divine attraction presented in the Saviour's life on earth, we see "God with us."—*The Desire of Ages,* pp. 21-24.

THE IMAGE OF THE DIVINE TO SHINE THROUGH

Be ye therefore perfect, even as your Father which is in heaven is perfect. Matt. 5:48.

The ideal of Christian character is Christlikeness. As the Son of man was perfect in His life, so His followers are to be perfect in their life. Jesus was in all things made like unto His brethren. He became flesh, even as we are. He was hungry and thirsty and weary. He was sustained by food and refreshed by sleep. He shared the lot of man; yet He was the blameless Son of God. He was God in the flesh. His character is to be ours. . . .

Christ is the ladder that Jacob saw, the base resting on the earth, and the topmost round reaching to the gate of heaven, to the very threshold of glory. If that ladder had failed by a single step of reaching the earth, we should have been lost. But Christ reaches us where we are. He took our nature and overcame, that we through taking His nature might overcome. Made "in the likeness of sinful flesh" (Rom. 8:3), He lived a sinless life. Now by His divinity He lays hold upon the throne of heaven, while by His humanity He reaches us. He bids us by faith in Him attain to the glory of the character of God. Therefore are we to be perfect, even as our "Father which is in heaven is perfect."

Jesus had shown in what righteousness consists, and had pointed to God as its source. Now He turned to practical duties. In almsgiving, in prayer, in fasting, He said, let nothing be done to attract attention or win praise to self. Give in sincerity, for the benefit of the suffering poor. In prayer, let the soul commune with God. In fasting, go not with the head bowed down, and heart filled with thoughts of self. . . . It is he who yields himself most unreservedly to God that will render Him the most acceptable service. For through fellowship with God men become workers together with Him in presenting His character in humanity.

The service rendered in sincerity of heart has great recompense. "Thy Father which seeth in secret himself shall reward thee openly." By the life we live through the grace of Christ the character is formed. The original loveliness begins to be restored to the soul. The attributes of the character of Christ are imparted, and the image of the Divine begins to shine forth. The faces of men and women who walk and work with God express the peace of heaven. They are surrounded with the atmosphere of heaven. For these souls the kingdom of God has begun. They have Christ's joy, the joy of being a blessing to humanity. They have the honor of being accepted for the Master's use; they are trusted to do His work in His name.—*The Desire of Ages,* pp. 311-312.

CHRIST BROUGHT SPIRITUAL AND PHYSICAL HEALING

Bless the Lord, O my soul, and forget not all his benefits: who forgiveth all thine iniquities; who healeth all thy diseases. Ps. 103:2, 3.

Christ bade the paralytic arise and walk, "that ye may know," He said, "that the Son of man hath power on earth to forgive sins."

The paralytic found in Christ healing for both the soul and the body. The spiritual healing was followed by physical restoration. This lesson should not be overlooked. There are today thousands suffering from physical disease, who, like the paralytic, are longing for the message, "Thy sins are forgiven." The burden of sin, with its unrest and unsatisfied desires, is the foundation of their maladies. They can find no relief until they come to the Healer of the soul. The peace which He alone can give would impart vigor to the mind, and health to the body.

Jesus came to "destroy the works of the devil." "In him was life," and He says, "I am come that they might have life, and that they might have it more abundantly." He is "a quickening spirit." And He still has the same life-giving power as when on earth He healed the sick and spoke forgiveness to the sinner. He "forgiveth all thine iniquities," He "healeth all thy diseases."

The effect produced upon the people by the healing of the paralytic was as if heaven had opened, and revealed the glories of the better world. As the man who had been cured passed through the multitude, blessing God at every step, and bearing his burden as if it were a feather's weight, the people fell back to give him room, and with awe-stricken faces gazed upon him, whispering softly among themselves, "We have seen strange things to day." . . .

In the home of the healed paralytic there was great rejoicing. . . . He stood before them in the full vigor of manhood. Those arms that they had seen lifeless were quick to obey his will. The flesh that had been shrunken and leaden-hued was now fresh and ruddy. He walked with a firm, free step. Joy and hope were written in every lineament of his countenance; and an expression of purity and peace had taken the place of marks of sin and suffering. Glad thanksgiving went up from that home, and God was glorified through His Son, who had restored hope to the hopeless, and strength to the stricken one. This man and his family were ready to lay down their lives for Jesus. No doubt dimmed their faith, no unbelief marred their fealty to Him who had brought light into their darkened home.—*The Desire of Ages,* pp. 270, 271.

CHRIST'S WORDS CARRIED IMPELLING POWER

Behold the Lamb of God, which taketh away the sin of the world. John 1:29.

"Jesus, walking by the sea of Galilee, saw two brethren, Simon called Peter, and Andrew his brother. . . . And he saith unto them, Follow me, and I will make you fishers of men. And they straightway left their nets, and followed him." . . .

The prompt, unquestioning obedience of these men, with no promise of wages, seems remarkable; but the words of Christ were an invitation that carried with it an impelling power. Christ would make these humble fishermen, in connection with Himself, the means of taking men out of the service of Satan, and placing them in the service of God. In this work they would become His witnesses, bearing to the world His truth unmingled with the traditions and sophistries of men. By practicing His virtues, by walking and working with Him, they were to be qualified to be fishers of men. . . .

For three years they labored in connection with the Saviour, and by His teaching, His works of healing, His example, they were prepared to carry on the work that He began. By the simplicity of faith, by pure, humble service, the disciples were taught to carry responsibilities in God's cause.

There are lessons for us to learn from the experience of the apostles. These men were as true as steel to principle. They were men who would not fail nor be discouraged. They were full of reverence and zeal for God, full of noble purposes and aspirations. They were by nature as weak and helpless as any of those now engaged in the work, but they put their whole trust in the Lord. Wealth they had, but it consisted of mind and soul culture; and this every one may have who will make God first and last and best in everything. They toiled long to learn the lessons given them in the school of Christ, and they did not toil in vain. They bound themselves up with the mightiest of all powers, and were ever longing for a deeper, higher, broader comprehension of eternal realities, that they might successfully present the treasures of truth to a needy world. . . .

Everywhere the light of truth is to shine forth, that hearts may be awakened and converted. In all countries the gospel is to be proclaimed. God's servants are to labor in places nigh and afar off, enlarging the cultivated portions of the vineyard, and going to the regions beyond. They are to work while the day lasts; for the night cometh, in which no man can work.—*Gospel Workers,* pp. 24-26.

CHRIST RECOGNIZED THE DIGNITY OF HUMANITY

But now in Christ Jesus ye who sometimes were far off are made nigh by the blood of Christ. For he is our peace, who hath made both one, and hath broken down the middle wall of partition between us. Eph. 2:13, 14.

Christ recognized no distinction of nationality or rank or creed. The scribes and Pharisees desired to make a local and a national benefit of the gifts of heaven, and to exclude the rest of God's family in the world. But Christ came to break down every wall of partition. He came to show that His gift of mercy and love is as unconfined as the air, the light, or the showers of rain that refresh the earth.

The life of Christ established a religion in which there is no caste, a religion by which Jew and Gentile, free and bond, are linked in a common brotherhood, equal before God. No question of policy influenced His movements. He made no difference between neighbors and strangers, friends and enemies. That which appealed to His heart was a soul thirsting for the waters of life.

He passed by no human being as worthless, but sought to apply the healing remedy to every soul. In whatever company He found Himself, He presented a lesson appropriate to the time and the circumstances. Every neglect or insult shown by men to their fellow men only made Him more conscious of their need of His divine-human sympathy. He sought to inspire with hope the roughest and most unpromising, setting before them the assurance that they might become blameless and harmless, attaining such a character as would make them manifest as the children of God.

Often He met those who had drifted under Satan's control, and who had no power to break from his snare. To such a one, discouraged, sick, tempted, fallen, Jesus would speak words of tenderest pity, words that were needed and could be understood. Others He met who were fighting a hand-to-hand battle with the adversary of souls. These He encouraged to persevere, assuring them that they would win; for angels of God were on their side, and would give them the victory.

At the table of the publicans He sat as an honored guest, by His sympathy and social kindliness showing that He recognized the dignity of humanity; and men longed to become worthy of His confidence. Upon their thirsty hearts His words fell with blessed, life-giving power. New impulses were awakened, and to these outcasts of society there opened the possibility of a new life.

Though He was a Jew, Jesus mingled freely with the Samaritans. . . . And while He drew their hearts to Him by the tie of human sympathy, His divine grace brought to them the salvation which the Jews rejected.—*The Ministry of Healing,* pp. 25, 26.

CHRIST ACKNOWLEDGED THE RIGHTS OF EVERYONE

In every nation he that feareth him, and worketh righteousness, is accepted with him. Acts 10:35.

The Lord Jesus demands our acknowledgment of the rights of every man. Men's social rights, and their rights as Christians, are to be taken into consideration. All are to be treated with refinement and delicacy, as the sons and daughters of God.

Christianity will make a man a gentleman. Christ was courteous, even to His persecutors; and His true followers will manifest the same spirit. Look at Paul when brought before rulers. His speech before Agrippa is an illustration of true courtesy as well as persuasive eloquence. The gospel does not encourage the formal politeness current with the world, but the courtesy that springs from real kindness of heart.

The most careful attention to the outward proprieties of life is not sufficient to shut out all fretfulness, harsh judgment, and unbecoming speech. True refinement will never be revealed so long as self is considered the supreme object. Love must dwell in the heart. A thoroughgoing Christian draws his motives of action from his deep heart-love for the Master. Up through the roots of his affection for Christ springs an unselfish interest in his brethren. Love imparts to its possessor grace, propriety, and comeliness of deportment. It illuminates the countenance and subdues the voice; it refines and elevates the entire being.—*Gospel Workers,* p. 123.

Some with whom you are brought in contact may be rough and uncourteous, but do not, because of this, be less courteous yourself. He who wishes to preserve his own self-respect must be careful not to wound needlessly the self-respect of others. This rule should be sacredly observed toward the dullest, the most blundering. What God intends to do with these apparently unpromising ones, you do not know. He has in the past accepted persons no more promising or attractive to do a great work for Him. His Spirit, moving upon the heart, has roused every faculty to vigorous action. The Lord saw in these rough, unhewn stones precious material, which would stand the test of storm and heat and pressure.—*Ibid,* p. 122.

Be polite to those with whom you come in contact; thus you will be polite to God. Praise Him for His goodness. Thus you are witnesses for Him, and you are preparing for the society of the angels. You are learning in this world how to conduct yourselves in the family of Christ in heaven.—Manuscript 31, 1903.

CHRIST WAS NO RESPECTER OF PERSONS

Then Peter opened his mouth, and said, Of a truth I perceive that God is no respecter of persons. Acts 10:34.

The religion of Christ uplifts the receiver to a higher plane of thought and action, while at the same time it presents the whole human race as alike the objects of the love of God, being purchased by the sacrifice of His Son. At the feet of Jesus, the rich and the poor, the learned and the ignorant, meet together, with no thought of caste or worldly preeminence. All earthly distinctions are forgotten as we look upon Him whom our sins have pierced. The self-denial, the condescension, the infinite compassion of Him who was highly exalted in heaven, puts to shame human pride, self-esteem, and social caste. Pure, undefiled religion manifests its heaven-born principles in bringing into oneness all who are sanctified through the truth. All meet as blood-bought souls, alike dependent upon Him who has redeemed them to God.

The Lord has lent men talents to improve. Those whom He has entrusted with money are to bring their talent of means to the Master. Men and women of influence are to use that which God has given them. The ones whom He has endowed with wisdom are to bring to the cross of Christ this gift to be used to His glory.

And the poor have their talent, which perhaps may be larger than any other mentioned. It may be simplicity of character, humility, tried virtue, confidence in God. Through patient toil, through their entire dependence upon God, they are pointing those with whom they associate to Jesus, their Redeemer. They have a heart full of sympathy for the poor, a home for the needy and oppressed, and their testimony is clear and decided as to what Jesus is to them. They seek for glory, honor, and immortality, and their reward will be eternal life.

In the human brotherhood it takes all kinds of talents to make a perfect whole; and the church of Christ is composed of men and women of varied talents, and of all ranks and all classes. God never designed that the pride of men should dissolve that which His own wisdom had ordained—the combination of all classes of minds, of all the varied talents that make a complete whole. There should be no depreciating of any part of God's great work, whether the agencies are high or lowly. All have their part to act in diffusing light in different degrees. . . . We are all woven together in the great web of humanity, and we cannot, without loss, withdraw our sympathies from one another.—*Gospel Workers,* pp. 330, 331.

CHRIST OUR EXAMPLE IN TRUE COURTESY

Be ye all of one mind, having compassion one of another, love as brethren, be pitiful, be courteous. 1 Peter 3:8.

Those who work for Christ are to be upright and trustworthy, firm as a rock to principle, and at the same time kind and courteous. Courtesy is one of the graces of the Spirit. To deal with human minds is the greatest work ever given to man; and he who would find access to hearts must heed the injunction, "Be pitiful, be courteous." Love will do that which argument will fail to accomplish. But a moment's petulance, a single gruff answer, a lack of Christian politeness and courtesy in some small matter, may result in the loss of both friends and influence.

What Christ was on this earth, the Christian worker should strive to be. He is our example, not only in His spotless purity, but in His patience, gentleness, and winsomeness of disposition. His life is an illustration of true courtesy. He had ever a kind look and a word of comfort for the needy and the oppressed. His presence brought a purer atmosphere into the home. His life was as leaven working amid the elements of society. Pure and undefiled, He walked among the thoughtless, the rude, the uncourteous; among unjust publicans, unrighteous Samaritans, heathen soldiers, rough peasants, and the mixed multitude. He spoke a word of sympathy here and a word there. As He saw men weary, and compelled to bear heavy burdens, He shared their burdens, and repeated to them the lessons He had learned from nature, of the love, the kindness, the goodness of God. He sought to inspire with hope the most rough and unpromising, setting before them the assurance that they might attain such a character as would make them manifest as children of God.

The religion of Jesus softens whatever is hard and rough in the temper, and smooths whatever is rugged and sharp in the manners. It makes the words gentle and the demeanor winning. Let us learn from Christ how to combine a high sense of purity and integrity with sunniness of disposition. A kind, courteous Christian is the most powerful argument that can be produced in favor of Christianity.

Kind words are as dew and gentle showers to the soul. The Scripture says of Christ, that grace was poured into His lips, that He might "know how to speak a word in season to him that is weary." And the Lord bids us, "Let your speech be alway with grace" "that it may minister grace unto the hearers."—*Gospel Workers,* pp. 121, 122.

The essence of true politeness is consideration for others.—*Education,* p. 241.

CHRIST AN EXAMPLE IN SOCIAL POWER

And it came to pass, that, as Jesus sat at meat in his house, many publicans and sinners sat also together with Jesus and his disciples: for there were many, and they followed him. Mark 2:15.

All who profess to be children of God should bear in mind that as missionaries they will be brought into contact with all classes of minds. There are the refined and the coarse, the humble and the proud, the religious and the skeptical, the educated and the ignorant, the rich and the poor. These varied minds cannot be treated alike; yet all need kindness and sympathy. By mutual contact our minds should receive polish and refinement. We are dependent upon one another, closely bound together by the ties of human brotherhood. . . .

It is through the social relations that Christianity comes in contact with the world. Every man or woman who has received the divine illumination is to shed light on the dark pathway of those who are unacquainted with the better way. Social power, sanctified by the Spirit of Christ, must be improved in bringing souls to the Saviour. Christ is not to be hid away in the heart as a coveted treasure, sacred and sweet, to be enjoyed solely by the possessor. We are to have Christ in us a well of water, springing up into everlasting life, refreshing all who come in contact with us.—*The Ministry of Healing,* pp. 495, 496.

Christ did not refuse to mingle with others in friendly intercourse. When invited to a feast by Pharisee or publican, He accepted the invitation. On such occasions every word that He uttered was a savor of life unto life to His hearers; for He made the dinner hour an occasion of imparting many precious lessons adapted to their needs. Christ thus taught His disciples how to conduct themselves when in the company of those who were not religious as well as of those who were. By His own example He taught them that, [in] any public gathering, their conversation need not be of the same character as that usually indulged in on such occasions. . . .

If Christ is abiding in the soul there will come forth from the treasure house of the heart words which are pure and uplifting; if Christ is not abiding there, a satisfaction will be found in frivolity, in jesting and joking, which is a hindrance to spiritual growth and a cause of grief to the angels of God. The tongue is an unruly member, but it should not be so. It should be converted; for the talent of speech is a very precious talent. Christ is ever ready to impart of His riches, and we should gather the jewels that come from Him, that, when we speak, these jewels may drop from our lips.—*Testimonies,* vol. 6, pp. 173, 174.

ALL TO REVEAL CHRIST'S SPIRIT AND POWER

The officers answered, Never man spake like this man. John 7:46.

When Jesus delivered the Sermon on the Mount, His disciples were gathered close about Him, and the multitude, filled with intense curiosity, also pressed as near as possible. Something more than usual was expected. Eager faces and listening attitudes gave evidence of the deep interest. The attention of all seemed riveted upon the speaker. His eyes were lighted up with unutterable love, and the heavenly expression upon His countenance gave meaning to every word uttered. Angels of heaven were in that listening throng. There, too, was the adversary of souls with his evil angels, prepared to counteract, as far as possible, the influence of the heavenly Teacher.

The truths there uttered have come down through the ages and have been a light amid the general darkness of error. Many have found in them that which the soul most needed—a sure foundation of faith and practice. But in these words spoken by the greatest Teacher the world has ever known there is no parade of human eloquence. The language is plain, and the thoughts and sentiments are marked with the greatest simplicity. The poor, the unlearned, the most simple-minded, can understand them. The Lord of heaven was in mercy and kindness addressing the souls He came to save. He taught them as one having authority, speaking the words of eternal life.

All should copy the Pattern as closely as possible. While they cannot possess the consciousness of power which Jesus had, they can so connect with the Source of strength that Jesus can abide in them and they in Him, and so His spirit and His power will be revealed in them.

"Walk in the light, as he is in the light." It is earthliness and selfishness that separate from God. The messages from heaven are of a character to arouse opposition. The faithful witnesses for Christ and the truth will reprove sin. Their words will be like a hammer to break the flinty heart, like a fire to consume the dross. There is constant need of earnest, decided messages of warning. God will have men who are true to duty. At the right time He sends His faithful messengers to do a work similar to that of Elijah.—*Testimonies,* vol. 5, pp. 253, 254.

Men of the highest education in the arts and sciences have learned precious lessons from Christians in humble life who were designated by the world as unlearned. But these obscure disciples had obtained an education in the highest of all schools. They had sat at the feet of Him who spoke as "never man spake."—*The Desire of Ages,* p. 251.

THE REVELATION OF GOD'S LOVE IN THE CROSS

It is Christ that died, yea rather, that is risen again, who is even at the right hand of God. Rom. 8:34.

The revelation of God's love to man centers in the cross. Its full significance tongue cannot utter, pen cannot portray, the mind of man cannot comprehend. Looking upon the cross of Calvary, we can only say, "God so loved the world that he gave his only begotten Son, that whosoever believeth in him should not perish, but have everlasting life" (John 3:16).

Christ crucified for our sins, Christ risen from the dead, Christ ascended on high, is the science of salvation that we are to learn and to teach. . . .

"It is Christ that died, yea rather, that is risen again, who is even at the right hand of God" (Rom. 8:34). "Wherefore he is able also to save them to the uttermost that come unto God by him, seeing he ever liveth to make intercession for them" (Heb. 7:25). . . .

It is through the gift of Christ that we receive every blessing. Through that gift there comes to us day by day the unfailing flow of Jehovah's goodness. Every flower, with its delicate tints and its fragrance, is given for our enjoyment through that one Gift. The sun and the moon were made by Him. There is not a star which beautifies the heavens that He did not make. Every drop of rain that falls, every ray of light shed upon our unthankful world, testifies to the love of God in Christ. Everything is supplied to us through the one unspeakable Gift, God's only-begotten Son. He was nailed to the cross that all these bounties might flow to God's workmanship.

"Behold, what manner of love the Father hath bestowed upon us, that we should be called the sons of God" (1 John 3:1). . . .

The knowledge of God as revealed in Christ is the knowledge that all who are saved must have. It is the knowledge that works transformation of character. This knowledge, received, will re-create the soul in the image of God. It will impart to the whole being a spiritual power that is divine. . . .

Of His own life the Saviour said, "I have kept my Father's commandments" (John 15:10). "The Father hath not left me alone; for I do always those things that please him" (chap. 8:29). As Jesus was in human nature, so God means His followers to be. In His strength we are to live the life of purity and nobility which the Saviour lived.—*The Ministry of Healing*, pp. 423-426.

In the rock Christ Jesus is our only safety.—*The Upward Look*, p. 293.

CHRIST'S GLORY SHINES ON THE THIEF

Lord, remember me when thou comest into thy kingdom. Luke 23:42.

To Jesus in His agony on the cross there came one gleam of comfort. It was the prayer of the penitent thief. Both the men who were crucified with Jesus had at first railed upon Him; and one under his suffering only became more desperate and defiant.

But not so with his companion. This man was not a hardened criminal; he had been led astray by evil associations, but he was less guilty than many of those who stood beside the cross reviling the Saviour. He had seen and heard Jesus, and had been convicted by His teaching, but he had been turned away from Him by the priests and rulers. Seeking to stifle conviction, he had plunged deeper and deeper into sin, until he was arrested, tried as a criminal, and condemned to die on the cross.

In the judgment hall and on the way to Calvary he had been in company with Jesus. He had heard Pilate declare, ''I find no fault in Him'' (John 19:4). He had marked His Godlike bearing, and His pitying forgiveness of His tormentors. On the cross he sees the many great religionists shoot out the tongue with scorn, and ridicule the Lord Jesus. He sees the wagging heads. He hears the upbraiding speeches taken up by his companion in guilt: ''If thou be Christ, save thyself and us.''

Among the passersby he hears many defending Jesus. He hears them repeat His words, and tell of His works. The conviction comes back to him that this is the Christ. . . . And now, all sin-polluted as it is, his life history is about to close. ''And we indeed justly,'' he moans; ''for we receive the due reward of our deeds: but this man hath done nothing amiss.'' . . .

Strange, tender thoughts now spring up. He calls to mind all he has heard of Jesus, how He has healed the sick and pardoned sin. . . . The Holy Spirit illuminates his mind, and little by little the chain of evidence is joined together. In Jesus, bruised, mocked, and hanging upon the cross, he sees the Lamb of God, that taketh away the sin of the world. Hope is mingled with anguish in his voice as the helpless, dying soul casts himself upon a dying Saviour. ''Lord, remember me,'' he cries, ''when thou comest into thy kingdom.''

Quickly the answer came. Soft and melodious the tone, full of love, compassion, and power the words: Verily I say unto thee today, Thou shalt be with Me in paradise. . . .

With longing heart He has listened for some expression of faith from His disciples. . . . How grateful then to the Saviour was the utterance of faith and love from the dying thief!—*The Desire of Ages,* pp. 749, 750.

AS OUR EXAMPLE CHRIST IS ALL AND IN ALL

In him was life; and the life was the light of men. John 1:4.

The ethics inculcated by the gospel acknowledge no standard but the perfection of God's mind, God's will. God requires from His creatures conformity to His will. Imperfection of character is sin, and sin is the transgression of the law. All righteous attributes of character dwell in God as a perfect, harmonious whole. Everyone who receives Christ as his personal Saviour is privileged to possess these attributes. This is the science of holiness.

How glorious are the possibilities set before the fallen race! Through His Son, God has revealed the excellency to which man is capable of attaining. Through the merits of Christ, man is lifted from his depraved state, purified, and made more precious than the golden wedge of Ophir. It is possible for him to become a companion of the angels in glory, and to reflect the image of Jesus Christ, shining even in the bright splendor of the eternal throne. It is his privilege to have faith that through the power of Christ he shall be made immortal. Yet how seldom he realizes to what heights he could attain if he would allow God to direct his every step!

God permits every human being to exercise his individuality. He desires no one to submerge his mind in the mind of a fellow mortal. Those who desire to be transformed in mind and character are not to look to men, but to the divine Example. God gives the invitation, "Let *this mind* be in you, which was also in Christ Jesus." By conversion and transformation, men are to receive the mind of Christ. Every one is to stand before God with an individual faith, an individual experience, knowing for himself that Christ is formed within, the hope of glory. For us to imitate the example of any man—even one whom we might regard as nearly perfect in character—would be to put our trust in a defective human being, one who is unable to impart a jot or tittle of perfection.

As our Example, we have One who is all and in all, the chiefest among ten thousand, One whose excellency is beyond comparison. He graciously adapted His life for universal imitation. United in Christ were wealth and poverty; majesty and abasement; unlimited power and meekness and lowliness which in every soul who receives Him will be reflected. In Him, through the qualities and powers of the human mind, the wisdom of the greatest Teacher the world has ever known was revealed.

Before the world, God is developing us as living witnesses to what men and women may become through the grace of Christ.—*Signs of the Times,* Sept. 3, 1902.

CHRIST IS THE TRUTH

Jesus saith unto him, I am the way, the truth, and the life: no man cometh unto the Father, but by me. John 14:6.

Christ is the truth. His words are truth, and they have a deeper significance than appears on the surface. All the sayings of Christ have a value beyond their unpretending appearance. Minds that are quickened by the Holy Spirit will discern the value of these sayings. They will discern the precious gems of truth, though these may be buried treasures.

Human theories and speculations will never lead to an understanding of God's Word. Those who suppose that they understand philosophy think that their explanations are necessary to unlock the treasures of knowledge and to prevent heresies from coming into the church. But it is these explanations that have brought in false theories and heresies. Men have made desperate efforts to explain what they thought to be intricate scriptures; but too often their efforts have only darkened that which they tried to make clear.

The priests and Pharisees thought they were doing great things as teachers, by putting their own interpretation upon the Word of God; but Christ said of them, "Ye know not the scriptures, neither the power of God" (Mark 12:24). He charged them with the guilt of "teaching for doctrines the commandments of men" (chap. 7:7). Though they were the teachers of the oracles of God, though they were supposed to understand His Word, they were not doers of the Word. Satan had blinded their eyes that they should not see its true import.

This is the work of many in our day. Many churches are guilty of this sin. There is danger, great danger, that the supposed wise men of today will repeat the experience of the Jewish teachers. They falsely interpret the divine oracles, and souls are brought into perplexity and shrouded in darkness because of their misconception of divine truth.

The Scriptures need not be read by the dim light of tradition or human speculation. As well might we try to give light to the sun with a torch as to explain the Scriptures by human tradition or imagination. God's Holy Word needs not the torchlight glimmer of earth to make its glories distinguishable. It is light in itself—the glory of God revealed, and beside it every other light is dim.—*Christ's Object Lessons,* pp. 110, 111.

It is the truth . . . we all need, the truth that works by love and purifies the soul.—*The Upward Look,* p. 293.

CHRIST A PERFECT EXAMPLE FOR ALL

And Jesus increased in wisdom and stature, and in favour with God and man. Luke 2:52.

Man has fallen. God's image in him is defaced. By disobedience he is depraved in inclination and weakened in power, unable, apparently, to look forward to anything but tribulation and wrath. But God, through Christ, has wrought out a way of escape, and He says to everyone, "Be ye therefore perfect." It is His purpose that man shall stand before Him upright and noble, and He will not be defeated. He sent His Son to this world to bear the penalty of sin, and to show man how to live a sinless life.

Christ is our ideal. He has left a perfect example for childhood, youth, and manhood. He came to this earth, and passed through the different phases of human experience. In His life sin found no place. From the beginning to the close of His earthly life, He preserved unsullied His loyalty to God. The Word says of Him, "The child grew, and waxed strong in spirit, filled with wisdom: and the grace of God was upon Him." He "increased in wisdom and stature, and in favour with God and man."

The Saviour lived not to please Himself. . . . He had no home in this world, only as the kindness of His friends provided Him one, yet it was heaven to be in His presence. Day by day He met trials and temptations, yet He did not fail or become discouraged. He was always patient and cheerful, and the afflicted hailed Him as a messenger of life and peace and health. His life held nothing that was not pure and noble. . . .

God's promise is, "Ye shall be holy; for I am holy." Holiness is the reflection of God's glory. But in order to reflect this glory, we must cooperate with God. Heart and mind must be emptied of all that leads to wrong. The Word of God must be read and studied with a sincere desire to gain from it spiritual strength. This Word is the Bread of heaven. Those who receive it, and make it a part of their lives, grow strong in the strength of God. Our sanctification is God's object in all His dealing with us. He has chosen us from eternity, that we may be holy. Christ declares, "This is the will of God, even your sanctification." Is it your will, also, that your desires and inclinations shall be brought into conformity to the divine will? . . .

Living the life of the Saviour, overcoming every selfish desire, fulfilling bravely and cheerfully our duty to God and to those around us—this makes us more than conquerors. This prepares us to stand before the great white throne free from spot or wrinkle, having washed our robes of character, and made them white in the blood of the Lamb.—*Signs of the Times,* March 30, 1904.

37

CHRIST "THE PRINCE OF PEACE"

Blessed are the peacemakers: for they shall be called the children of God. Matt. 5:9.

Christ is "The Prince of Peace" (Isa. 9:6), and it is His mission to restore to earth and heaven the peace that sin has broken. "Being justified by faith, we have peace with God through our Lord Jesus Christ" (Rom. 5:1). Whoever consents to renounce sin and open his heart to the love of Christ becomes a partaker of this heavenly peace.

There is no other ground of peace than this. The grace of Christ, received into the heart, subdues enmity; it allays strife and fills the soul with love. He who is at peace with God and his fellow men cannot be made miserable. Envy will not be in his heart; evil surmisings will find no room there; hatred cannot exist. The heart that is in harmony with God is a partaker of the peace of heaven and will diffuse its blessed influence on all around. The spirit of peace will rest like dew upon hearts weary and troubled with worldly strife.

Christ's followers are sent to the world with the message of peace. Whoever, by the quiet, unconscious influence of a holy life, shall reveal the love of Christ; whoever, by word or deed, shall lead another to renounce sin and yield his heart to God, is a peacemaker.

And "blessed are the peacemakers: for they shall be called the children of God." The spirit of peace is evidence of their connection with heaven. The sweet savor of Christ surrounds them. The fragrance of the life, the loveliness of the character, reveal to the world the fact that they are children of God. Men take knowledge of them that they have been with Jesus. . . .

"And the remnant of Jacob shall be in the midst of many people as a dew from the Lord, as the showers upon the grass" (Micah 5:7).—*Thoughts From the Mount of Blessing,* pp. 27, 28.

When Isaiah foretold the birth of the Messiah, he ascribed to Him the title, "Prince of Peace." When angels announced to the shepherds that Christ was born, they sang above the plains of Bethlehem: "Glory to God in the highest, and on earth peace, good will toward men" (Luke 2:14).

There is a seeming contradiction between these prophetic declarations and the words of Christ: "I came not to send peace, but a sword" (Matt. 10:34). But, rightly understood, the two are in perfect harmony. The gospel is a message of peace. Christianity is a system which, received and obeyed, would spread peace, harmony, and happiness throughout the earth. The religion of Christ will unite in close brotherhood all who accept its teachings. It was the mission of Jesus to reconcile men to God, and thus to one another.—*The Great Controversy,* pp. 46, 47.

THE PERSONALITY OF GOD REVEALED IN CHRIST

I and my Father are one. John 10:30.

As a personal being, God has revealed Himself in His Son. The outshining of the Father's glory, "and the express image of his person" (Heb. 1:3), Jesus, as a personal Saviour, came to the world. As a personal Saviour He ascended on high. As a personal Saviour He intercedes in the heavenly courts. Before the throne of God in our behalf ministers "one like unto the Son of man" (Rev. 1:13).

Christ, the Light of the world, veiled the dazzling splendor of His divinity and came to live as a man among men, that they might, without being consumed, become acquainted with their Creator. Since sin brought separation between man and his Maker, no man has seen God at any time, except as He is manifested through Christ.

"I and my Father are one," Christ declared (John 10:30). "No man knoweth the Son, but the Father; neither knoweth any man the Father, save the Son and he to whomsoever the Son will reveal Him" (John l0:30; Matt. 11:27).

Christ came to teach human beings what God desires them to know. In the heavens above, in the earth, in the broad waters of the ocean, we see the handiwork of God. All created things testify to His power, His wisdom, His love. Yet not from the stars or the ocean or the cataract can we learn of the personality of God as it was revealed in Christ.

God saw that a clearer revelation than nature was needed to portray both His personality and His character. He sent His Son into the world to manifest, so far as could be endured by human sight, the nature and the attributes of the invisible God. . . .

Taking humanity upon Him, Christ came to be one with humanity, and at the same time to reveal our heavenly Father to sinful human beings. He who had been in the presence of the Father from the beginning, He who was the express image of the invisible God, was alone able to reveal the character of the Deity to mankind. He was in all things made like unto His brethren. He became flesh even as we are. He was hungry and thirsty and weary. He was sustained by food and refreshed by sleep. He shared the lot of men; yet He was the blameless Son of God. . . . Tender, compassionate, sympathetic, ever considerate of others, He represented the character of God, and was constantly engaged in service for God and man.—*The Ministry of Healing*, pp. 418-423.

The theme of redemption will employ the minds and tongues of the redeemed through everlasting ages. The reflection of the glory of God will shine forth forever and ever from the Saviour's face.—*Letter* 280, 1904.

JESUS IS OUR EXAMPLE

In a word, as God's dear children, try to be like him. Eph. 5:1, N.E.B.

God's watchmen must not study how they shall please the people, nor listen to their words and utter them; for they must listen to hear what saith the Lord, what is His word for the people. If they rely upon discourses prepared years before, they may fail to meet the necessities of the occasion. Their hearts should be laid open so that the Lord may impress their minds, and then they will be able to give the people the precious truth warm from heaven. . . .

There is altogether too little of the Spirit and power of God in the labor of the watchmen. The Spirit which characterized that wonderful meeting on the Day of Pentecost is waiting to manifest its power upon the men who are now standing between the living and the dead as ambassadors for God. The power which stirred the people so mightily in the 1844 movement will again be revealed. The third angel's message will go forth, not in whispered tones, but with a loud voice.

Many who profess to have great light are walking in sparks of their own kindling. They need to have their lips touched with a live coal from off the altar, that they may pour forth the truth like men who are inspired. . . .

Had Christ come in the majesty of a king, with the pomp which attends the great men of earth, many would have accepted Him. But Jesus of Nazareth did not dazzle the senses with a display of outward glory and make this the foundation of their reverence. He came as a humble man to be the Teacher and Exemplar as well as the Redeemer of the race. Had he encouraged pomp, had He come followed by a retinue of the great men of earth, how could He have taught humility? how could He have presented such burning truths as in His Sermon upon the Mount? His example was such as He wished all His followers to imitate. Where would have been the hope of the lowly in life had He come in exaltation and dwelt as a king upon the earth?

Jesus knew the needs of the world better than they themselves knew. He did not come as an angel, clothed with the panoply of heaven, but as a man. Yet combined with His humility was an inherent power and grandeur that awed men while they loved Him. Although possessing such loveliness, such an unassuming appearance, He moved among them with the dignity and power of a heaven-born king. The people were amazed, confounded. They tried to reason the matter out; but, unwilling to renounce their own ideas, they yielded to doubts, clinging to the old expectation of a Saviour to come in earthly grandeur.—*Testimonies,* vol. 5, pp. 252, 253.

JESUS PROVIDED A MODEL OF CHARACTER

For ye are dead, and your life is hid with Christ in God. When Christ who is our life, shall appear, then shall ye also appear with him in glory. Col. 3:3, 4.

Let your light shine forth in good works. Said Christ, "Ye are the salt of the earth: but if the salt have lost his savour, wherewith shall it be salted? it is thenceforth good for nothing, but to be cast out, and to be trodden under foot of men." I fear that there are many who are in this condition. All have not the same work to do; different circumstances and talents qualify individuals for different kinds of work in God's vineyard. There are some who fill more responsible positions than do others; but to each one is given his work, and if he does his work with fidelity and zeal, he is a faithful steward of the grace of God.

God does not intend that your light shall so shine that your good words or works shall bring the praise of men to yourself; but that the Author of all good shall be glorified and exalted. Jesus, in His life, gave to men a model of character. How little power did the world have over Him to mold Him according to its standard! All its influence was thrown off. He declared, "My meat is to do the will of him that sent me, and to finish his work!" If we had this devotion to the work of God, doing it with an eye single to His glory, we should be able to say with Christ, "I seek not mine own glory." His life was full of good works, and it is our duty to live as our great Example lived. Our life must be hid with Christ in God, and then the light will be reflected from Jesus to us, and we shall reflect it upon those around us, not in mere talk and profession, but in good works, and by manifesting the character of Christ. Those who are reflecting the light of God will cherish a loving disposition. They will be cheerful, willing, obedient to all the requirements of God. They will be meek and self-sacrificing, and will work with devoted love for the salvation of souls. . . .

All who are true lightbearers will reflect light upon the pathway of others. Let those who have named the name of Christ, depart from all iniquity. If you yield to the claims of God, and become permeated with His love, and filled with His fullness, children, youth, and young disciples will look to you for their impressions of what constitutes practical godliness; and you may thus be the means of leading them in the path of obedience to God. You will then be exerting an influence which will bear the test of God, and your work will be compared to gold, silver, and precious stones, for it will be of an imperishable nature.—*Review and Herald*, Oct. 16, 1888.

CHRIST FILLED HIS DISCIPLES' THOUGHTS

When they saw the boldness of Peter and John, and perceived that they were unlearned and ignorant men, they marvelled; and they took knowledge of them, that they had been with Jesus. Acts 4:13.

Ever since the fall of Adam, Christ had been committing to chosen servants the seed of His Word, to be sown in human hearts. During His life on earth He had sown the seed of truth, and had watered it with His blood. The conversions that took place on the Day of Pentecost were the result of this sowing, the harvest of Christ's work, revealing the power of His teaching. . . .

Under the training of Christ the disciples had been led to feel their need of the Spirit. Under the Spirit's teaching, they received the final qualification, and went forth to their lifework. No longer were they ignorant and uncultured. No longer were they a collection of independent units or discordant, conflicting elements. No longer were their hopes set on worldly greatness. They were of "one accord," "of one heart and of one soul" (Acts 2:46; 4:32). Christ filled their thoughts; the advancement of His kingdom was their aim. In mind and character they had become like their Master, and men "took knowledge of them, that they had been with Jesus."

Pentecost brought them the heavenly illumination. The truths they could not understand while Christ was with them were now unfolded. With a faith and assurance that they had never before known, they accepted the teachings of the Sacred Word. No longer was it a matter of faith with them that Christ was the Son of God. They knew that although clothed with humanity, He was indeed the Messiah, and they told their experience to the world with a confidence which carried with it the conviction that God was with them.

They could speak the name of Jesus with assurance; for was He not their Friend and Elder Brother? Brought into close communion with Christ, they sat with Him in heavenly places. With what burning language they clothed their ideas as they bore witness for Him! Their hearts were surcharged with a benevolence so full, so deep, so far-reaching, that it impelled them to go to the ends of the earth, testifying to the power of Christ. They were filled with an intense longing to carry forward the work He had begun. They realized the greatness of their debt to heaven, and the responsibility of their work. Strengthened by the endowment of the Holy Spirit, they went forth filled with zeal to extend the triumphs of the cross. The Spirit animated them and spoke through them. The peace of Christ shone from their faces. They had consecrated their lives to Him for service, and their very features bore evidence to the surrender they had made.—*The Acts of the Apostles,* pp. 45, 46.

CHRIST REVEALED THE RICHES OF HEAVEN

The Spirit of the Lord God is upon me; because the Lord hath anointed me to preach good tidings unto the meek; he hath sent me to bind up the brokenhearted. Isa. 61:1.

Never was there such an evangelist as Christ. He was the Majesty of heaven, but He humbled Himself to take our nature, that He might meet men where they were. To all people, rich and poor, free and bond, Christ, the Messenger of the covenant, brought the tidings of salvation. His fame as the Great Healer spread throughout Palestine. The sick came to the places through which He would pass, that they might call on Him for help. Hither, too, came many anxious to hear His words and to receive a touch of His hand. Thus He went from city to city, from town to town, preaching the gospel and healing the sick—the King of glory in the lowly garb of humanity.

He attended the great yearly festivals of the nation, and to the multitude absorbed in outward ceremony He spoke of heavenly things, bringing eternity within their view. To all He brought treasures from the storehouse of wisdom. He spoke to them in language so simple that they could not fail of understanding. By methods peculiarly His own, He helped all who were in sorrow and affliction. With tender, courteous grace, He ministered to the sin-sick soul, bringing healing and strength. . . .

What a busy life He led! Day by day He might have been seen entering the humble abodes of want and sorrow, speaking hope to the downcast and peace to the distressed. Gracious, tenderhearted, pitiful, He went about lifting up the bowed-down and comforting the sorrowful. Wherever He went, He carried blessing.

While He ministered to the poor, Jesus studied also to find ways of reaching the rich. He sought the acquaintance of the wealthy and cultured Pharisee, the Jewish nobleman, and the Roman ruler. He accepted their invitations, attended their feasts, made Himself familiar with their interests and occupations, that He might gain access to their hearts, and reveal to them the imperishable riches.

Christ came to this world to show that by receiving power from on high, man can live an unsullied life. With unwearying patience and sympathetic helpfulness, He met men in their necessities. By the gentle touch of grace, He banished from the soul unrest and doubt, changing enmity to love, and unbelief to confidence. . . .

At the sound of His voice the spirit of greed and ambition fled from the heart, and men arose, emancipated, to follow the Saviour.—*The Ministry of Healing,* pp. 22-25.

CHRIST'S FOLLOWERS TO DO GREATER WORKS THAN HE

Verily, verily, I say unto you, He that believeth on me, the works that I do shall he do also; and greater works than these shall he do; because I go unto my Father. John 14:12.

Christ did not mean that the disciples would make more exalted exertions than He had made, but that their work would have greater magnitude. He did not refer merely to miracle working, but to all that would take place under the agency of the Holy Spirit. "When the Comforter is come," He said, "whom I will send unto you from the Father, even the Spirit of truth, which proceedeth from the Father, he shall testify of me: and ye also shall bear witness, because ye have been with me from the beginning" (John 15:26, 27).

Wonderfully were these words fulfilled. After the descent of the Holy Spirit, the disciples were so filled with love for Him and for those for whom He died, that hearts were melted by the words they spoke and the prayers they offered. They spoke in the power of the Spirit; and under the influence of that power, thousands were converted.

As Christ's representatives, the apostles were to make a decided impression on the world. The fact that they were humble men would not diminish their influence, but increase it; for the minds of their hearers would be carried from them to the Saviour, who, though unseen, was still working with them. The wonderful teaching of the apostles, their words of courage and trust, would assure all that it was not in their own power that they worked, but in the power of Christ. Humbling themselves, they would declare that He whom the Jews had crucified was the Prince of life, the Son of the living God, and that in His name they did the works that He had done.

In His parting conversation with His disciples on the night before the crucifixion, the Saviour made no reference to the suffering that He had endured and must yet endure. He did not speak of the humiliation that was before Him, but sought to bring to their minds that which would strengthen their faith, leading them to look forward to the joys that await the overcomer. He rejoiced in the consciousness that He could and would do more for His followers than He had promised; that from Him would flow forth love and compassion, cleansing the soul temple, and making men like Him in character; that His truth, armed with the power of the Spirit, would go forth conquering and to conquer.

"These things I have spoken unto you," He said, "that in me ye might have peace. In the world ye shall have tribulation: but be of good cheer; I have overcome the world" (chap. 16:33).—*The Acts of the Apostles,* pp. 22, 23.

CHRIST THE CHANNEL OF SAVING GRACE

For in him dwelleth all the fulness of the Godhead bodily. Col. 2:9.

By His humanity, Christ touched humanity; by His divinity, He lays hold upon the throne of God. As the Son of man, He gave us an example of obedience; as the Son of God, He gives us power to obey. . . .

In stooping to take upon Himself humanity, Christ revealed a character the opposite of the character of Satan. . . .

Christ was treated as we deserve, that we might be treated as He deserves. He was condemned for our sins, in which He had no share, that we might be justified by His righteousness, in which we had no share. He suffered the death which was ours, that we might receive the life which was His. ''With his stripes we are healed.''

By His life and His death, Christ has achieved even more than recovery from the ruin wrought through sin. It was Satan's purpose to bring about an eternal separation between God and man; but in Christ we become more closely united to God than if we had never fallen. In taking our nature, the Saviour has bound Himself to humanity by a tie that is never to be broken. Through the eternal ages He is linked with us. . . . To assure us of His immutable counsel of peace, God gave His only-begotten Son to become one of the human family, forever to retain His human nature. . . . God has adopted human nature in the person of His Son, and has carried the same into the highest heaven. It is the ''Son of man'' who shares the throne of the universe. It is the ''Son of man'' whose name shall be called, ''Wonderful, Counsellor, The mighty God, The everlasting Father, The Prince of Peace'' (Isa. 9:6). . . . In Christ the family of earth and the family of heaven are bound together. Christ glorified is our brother. Heaven is enshrined in humanity, and humanity is enfolded in the bosom of Infinite Love. . . .

Through Christ's redeeming work the government of God stands justified. The Omnipotent One is made known as the God of love. Satan's charges are refuted, and his character unveiled. Rebellion can never again arise. Sin can never again enter the universe. Through eternal ages all are secure from apostasy. By love's self-sacrifice, the inhabitants of earth and heaven are bound to their Creator in bonds of indissoluble union.

The work of redemption will be complete. In the place where sin abounded, God's grace much more abounds. . . . Our little world, under the curse of sin the one dark blot in His glorious creation, will be honored above all other worlds in the universe of God.—*The Desire of Ages,* pp. 24-26.

Reflecting Christ by Obedience to God's Law

A REVELATION OF GOD'S WILL AND CHARACTER

The law is holy, and the commandment holy, and just, and good. Rom. 7:12.

Many religious teachers assert that Christ by His death abolished the law, and men are henceforth free from its requirements. There are some who represent it as a grievous yoke, and in contrast to the bondage of the law they present the liberty to be enjoyed under the gospel.

But not so did prophets and apostles regard the holy law of God. Said David: "I will walk at liberty: for I seek thy precepts" (Ps. 119:45). The apostle James, who wrote after the death of Christ, refers to the Decalogue as "the royal law" and "the perfect law of liberty" (James 2:8; 1:25). And the revelator, half a century after the crucifixion, pronounces a blessing upon them "that do His commandments, that they may have right to the tree of life, and may enter in through the gates into the city" (Rev. 22:14).

The claim that Christ by His death abolished His Father's law is without foundation. Had it been possible for the law to be changed or set aside, then Christ need not have died to save man from the penalty of sin. The death of Christ, so far from abolishing the law, proves that it is immutable. The Son of God came to "magnify the law, and make it honourable" (Isa. 42:21). . . . And concerning Himself He declares: "I delight to do thy will, O my God: yea, thy law is within my heart" (Ps. 40:8).

The law of God, from its very nature, is unchangeable. It is a revelation of the will and the character of its Author. God is love, and His law is love. Its two great principles are love to God and love to man. "Love is the fulfilling of the law" (Rom. 13:10). The character of God is righteousness and truth; such is the nature of His law. Says the psalmist: "Thy law is the truth"; "all thy commandments are righteousness" (Ps. 119:142, 172). And the apostle Paul declares: "The law is holy, and the commandment holy, and just, and good" (Rom. 7:12). Such a law, being an expression of the mind and will of God, must be as enduring as its Author.

It is the work of conversion and sanctification to reconcile men to God by bringing them into accord with the principles of His law. In the beginning, man was created in the image of God. He was in perfect harmony with the nature and the law of God; the principles of righteousness were written upon his heart. But sin alienated him from his Maker. He no longer reflected the divine image. . . . But "God so loved the world, that He gave His only-begotten Son," that man might be reconciled to God. Through the merits of Christ he can be restored to harmony with his Maker.—*The Great Controversy*, pp. 466, 467.

SINNERS BROUGHT INTO HARMONY WITH THE LAW

For what the law could not do, in that it was weak through the flesh, God sending his own Son in the likeness of sinful flesh, and for sin, condemned sin in the flesh: that the righteousness of the law might be fulfilled in us, who walk not after the flesh, but after the Spirit. Rom. 8:3, 4.

The law reveals to man his sins, but it provides no remedy. While it promises life to the obedient, it declares that death is the portion of the transgressor. The gospel of Christ alone can free him from the condemnation or the defilement of sin. He must exercise repentance toward God, whose law has been transgressed; and faith in Christ, His atoning sacrifice. Thus he obtains "remission of sins that are past" and becomes a partaker of the divine nature. He is a child of God, having received the spirit of adoption, whereby he cries: "Abba, Father"!

Is he now free to transgress God's law? Says Paul: "Do we then make void the law through faith? God forbid: yea, we establish the law" (Rom. 3:31). "How shall we, that are dead to sin, live any longer therein?" (chap. 6:2). And John declares: "This is the love of God, that we keep His commandments: and His commandments are not grievous" (1 John 5:3). In the new birth the heart is brought into harmony with God, as it is brought into accord with His law. When this mighty change has taken place in the sinner, he has passed from death unto life, from sin unto holiness, from transgression and rebellion to obedience and loyalty. The old life of alienation from God has ended; the new life of reconciliation, of faith and love, has begun. Then "the righteousness of the law" will "be fulfilled in us, who walk not after the flesh, but after the Spirit" (Rom. 8:4). And the language of the soul will be: "O how love I thy law! it is my meditation all the day" (Ps. 119:97).

"The law of the Lord is perfect, converting the soul" (Ps. 19:7). Without the law, men have no just conception of the purity and holiness of God or of their own guilt and uncleanness. They have no true conviction of sin and feel no need of repentance. Not seeing their lost condition as violators of God's law, they do not realize their need of the atoning blood of Christ. The hope of salvation is accepted without a radical change of heart or reformation of life. Thus superficial conversions abound, and multitudes are joined to the church who have never been united to Christ. . . . By the Word and the Spirit of God are opened to men the great principles of righteousness embodied in His law.—*The Great Controversy,* pp. 467-469.

GOD'S LAW IS THE STANDARD OF CHARACTER

Thy righteousness is an everlasting righteousness, and thy law is the truth. Psalm 119:142.

Erroneous theories of sanctification . . . have a prominent place in the religious movements of the day. These theories are both false in doctrine and dangerous in practical results; and the fact that they are so generally finding favor renders it doubly essential that all have a clear understanding of what the Scriptures teach upon this point.

True sanctification is a Bible doctrine. The apostle Paul, in his letter to the Thessalonian church, declares: "This is the will of God, even your sanctification." And he prays: "The very God of peace sanctify you wholly" (1 Thess. 4:3; 5:23). The Bible clearly teaches what sanctification is and how it is to be attained. The Saviour prayed for His disciples: "Sanctify them through thy truth: thy word is truth" (John 17:17). And Paul teaches that believers are to be "sanctified by the Holy Ghost" (Rom. 15:16).

What is the work of the Holy Spirit? Jesus told His disciples: "When he, the Spirit of truth, is come, he will guide you into all truth" (John 16:13). And the psalmist says: "Thy law is the truth." . . . And since the law of God is "holy, and just, and good," a transcript of the divine perfection, it follows that a character formed by obedience to that law will be holy.

Christ is a perfect example of such a character. He says: "I have kept my Father's commandments." "I do always those things that please him" (John 15:10; 8:29). The followers of Christ are to become like Him—by the grace of God to form characters in harmony with the principles of His holy law. This is Bible sanctification.

This work can be accomplished only through faith in Christ, by the power of the indwelling Spirit of God. Paul admonishes believers: "Work out your own salvation with fear and trembling. For it is God which worketh in you both to will and to do of his good pleasure" (Phil. 2:12, 13). The Christian will feel the promptings of sin, but he will maintain a constant warfare against it. Here is where Christ's help is needed. Human weakness becomes united to divine strength, and faith exclaims: "Thanks be to God, which giveth us the victory through our Lord Jesus Christ" (1 Cor. 15:57).

The Scriptures plainly show that the work of sanctification is progressive. When in conversion the sinner finds peace with God through the blood of the atonement, the Christian life has but just begun. Now he is to "go on unto perfection"; to grow up "unto the measure of the stature of the fulness of Christ."—*The Great Controversy,* pp. 469, 470.

TRUE FOLLOWERS OBEY GOD'S LAW

Sin is the transgression of the law. 1 John 3:4.

The desire for an easy religion that requires no striving, no self-denial, no divorce from the follies of the world, has made the doctrine of faith, and faith only, a popular doctrine; but what saith the Word of God? Says the apostle James: ''What doth it profit, my brethren, though a man say he hath faith, and have not works? can faith save him? . . . Wilt thou know, O vain man, that faith without works is dead? Was not Abraham our father justified by works, when he had offered Isaac his son upon the altar? Seest thou how faith wrought with his works, and by works was faith made perfect? . . . Ye see then how that by works a man is justified, and not by faith only'' (James 2:14-24).

The testimony of the Word of God is against this ensnaring doctrine of faith without works. It is not faith that claims the favor of Heaven without complying with the conditions upon which mercy is to be granted, it is presumption; for genuine faith has its foundation in the promises and provisions of the Scriptures. . . .

The commission of a known sin silences the witnessing voice of the Spirit and separates the soul from God. ''Sin is the transgression of the law.'' And ''whosoever sinneth [transgresseth the law] hath not seen him, neither known him'' (1 John 3:6). Though John in his Epistles dwells so fully upon love, yet he does not hesitate to reveal the true character of that class who claim to be sanctified while living in transgression of the law of God. ''He that saith, I know him, and keepeth not his commandments, is a liar, and the truth is not in him. But whoso keepeth his word, in him verily is the love of God perfected'' (chap. 2:4, 5).

Here is the test of every man's profession. We cannot accord holiness to any man without bringing him to the measurement of God's only standard of holiness in heaven and in earth. If men feel no weight of the moral law, if they belittle and make light of God's precepts, if they break one of the least of these commandments, and teach men so, they shall be of no esteem in the sight of Heaven, and we may know that their claims are without foundation.

And the claim to be without sin is, in itself, evidence that he who makes this claim is far from holy. It is because he has no true conception of the infinite purity and holiness of God or of what they must become who shall be in harmony with His character; because he has no true conception of the purity and exalted loveliness of Jesus, and the malignity and evil of sin, that man can regard himself as holy.—*The Great Controversy,* pp. 472, 473.

It was the righteousness revealed in His [Christ's] life that distinguished Him from the world.—*The Upward Look,* p. 303.

GOD'S LAW IS CHANGELESS

Now is the judgment of this world: now shall the prince of this world be cast out. And I, if I be lifted up from the earth, will draw all men unto me. John 12:31, 32.

Since the divine law is as sacred as God Himself, only one equal with God could make atonement for its transgression. None but Christ could redeem fallen man from the curse of the law, and bring him again into harmony with Heaven. Christ would take upon Himself the guilt and shame of sin—sin so offensive to a holy God that it must separate the Father and His Son. Christ would reach to the depths of misery to rescue the ruined race.—*Patriarchs and Prophets,* p. 63.

The plan of redemption had a yet broader and deeper purpose than the salvation of man. It was not for this alone that Christ came to the earth; it was not merely that the inhabitants of this little world might regard the law of God as it should be regarded; but it was to vindicate the character of God before the universe. To this result of His great sacrifice—its influence upon the intelligences of other worlds, as well as upon man—the Saviour looked forward when just before His crucifixion He said: "Now is the judgment of this world: now shall the prince of this world be cast out. And I, if I be lifted up from the earth, will draw all men unto me."

The act of Christ in dying for the salvation of man would not only make heaven accessible to men, but before all the universe it would justify God and His Son in their dealing with the rebellion of Satan. It would establish the perpetuity of the law of God, and would reveal the nature and the results of sin.

From the first the great controversy had been upon the law of God. Satan had sought to prove that God was unjust, that His law was faulty, and that the good of the universe required it to be changed. In attacking the law he aimed to overthrow the authority of its Author. In the controversy it was to be shown whether the divine statutes were defective and subject to change, or perfect and immutable. . . .

Heaven marked the insult and mockery that He received, and knew that it was at Satan's instigation. . . . They watched the battle between light and darkness as it waxed stronger. And as Christ in His expiring agony upon the cross cried out, "It is finished" (John 19:30), a shout of triumph rang through every world and through heaven itself. . . . Satan had revealed his true character. . . . The very fact that Christ bore the penalty of man's transgression is a mighty argument to all created intelligences that the law is changeless; that God is righteous, merciful, and self-denying; and that infinite justice and mercy unite in the administration of His government.—*Ibid.,* 68-70.

GOD'S LAW IS THE LAW OF LOVE

" 'Love the Lord your God with all your heart and with all your soul and with all your mind and with all your strength.' The second is this: 'Love your neighbor as yourself.' " Mark 12:30-31, N.I.V.

Love, the basis of creation and of redemption, is the basis of true education. This is made plain in the law that God has given as the guide of life. . . . To love Him, the infinite, the omniscient one, with the whole strength and mind and heart, means the highest development of every power. It means that in the whole being—the body, the mind, as well as the soul—the image of God is to be restored.

Like the first is the second commandment, "Thou shalt love thy neighbour as thyself." The law of love calls for the devotion of body, mind, and soul to the service of God and our fellow men. And this service, while making us a blessing to others, brings the greatest blessing to ourselves. Unselfishness underlies all true development. . . .

Lucifer in heaven desired to be first in power and authority; he wanted to be God, to have the rulership of heaven; and to this end he won many of the angels to his side. When with his rebel host he was cast out from the courts of God, the work of rebellion and self-seeking was continued on earth. Through the temptation to self-indulgence and ambition, Satan accomplished the fall of our first parents; and from that time to the present the gratification of human ambition and the indulgence of selfish hopes and desires have proved the ruin of mankind.

Under God, Adam was to stand at the head of the earthly family, to maintain the principles of the heavenly family. This would have brought peace and happiness. But the law that none "liveth to himself" Satan was determined to oppose. He desired to live for self. He sought to make himself a center of influence. It was this that had incited rebellion in heaven, and it was man's acceptance of this principle that brought sin on earth. When Adam sinned, man broke away from the heaven-ordained center. A demon became the central power in the world. Where God's throne should have been, Satan placed his throne. The world laid its homage, as a willing offering, at the feet of the enemy.

The transgression of God's law brought woe and death in its train. Through disobedience man's powers were perverted, and selfishness took the place of love. His nature became so weakened that it was impossible for him to resist the power of evil. . . . Men had chosen a ruler who chained them to his car as captives. . . . Christ came to the world to show them that He had planted for them the tree of life, the leaves of which are for the healing of the nations.—*Review and Herald,* Jan. 16, 1913.

INDIVIDUAL ACCOUNTABILITY

All thy commandments are righteousness. Ps. 119:172.

The Spirit of God will lead us in the path of the commandments; for the promise is that "when he, the Spirit of truth, is come, he will guide you into all truth." We should try the spirits by the test of God's Word; for there are many spirits in the world. "To the law and to the testimony: if they speak not according to this word, it is because there is no light in them." . . .

God holds every one of us to an individual accountability, and calls upon us to serve Him from principle, to choose Him for ourselves. . . .

God will not lightly esteem the transgression of His law. "The wages of sin is death." The consequences of disobedience prove that the nature of sin is at enmity with the well-being of God's government and the good of His creatures. God is a jealous God, visiting the sins of the fathers upon the children to the third and fourth generations of them that hate Him. The results of transgression follow those who persist in wrongdoing; but He shows mercy unto thousands of them that love Him and keep His commandments. Those who repent and turn to His service find the favor of the Lord; and He forgiveth all their iniquities and healeth all their diseases.

In earthly affairs, the servant who seeks most carefully to fulfill the requirements of his office, and to carry out the will of his master, is most highly valued. A gentleman once wished to employ a trusty coachman. Several men came in answer to his advertisement. He asked each one how near he could drive to the edge of a certain precipice without upsetting the carriage. One and another replied that he could go within a perilous distance; but at last one answered that he would keep as far as possible from such a dangerous undertaking. He was employed to fill the position.

Shall a man be more appreciative of a good servant than is our heavenly Father? Our anxiety should not be to see how far we can depart from the commandments of the Lord, and presume on the mercy of the Lawgiver, and still flatter our souls that we are within the bounds of God's forbearance; but our care should be to keep as far as possible from transgression. We should be determined to be on the side of Christ and our heavenly Father, and run no risks by heady presumption. . . .

We should magnify the precepts of heaven by our words and actions. He who honors the law will be honored by it in the judgment.—*Review and Herald,* June 22, 1911.

CHRIST CAME TO MAGNIFY HIS LAW

The Lord was pleased, for his righteousness' sake, to magnify his law and make it glorious. Isa. 42:21, R.S.V.

Through the devices of the great apostate, man has been led to separate himself from God, and has yielded to the temptations of the adversary of God and man in committing sin and breaking the law of the Most High. God could not alter one jot or tittle of His holy law to meet man in his fallen condition; for this would reflect discredit upon the wisdom of God in making a law by which to govern heaven and earth. But God could give His only-begotten Son to become man's substitute and surety, to suffer the penalty that was merited by the transgressor, and to impart to the repentant soul His perfect righteousness.

Christ became the sinless sacrifice for a guilty race, making men prisoners of hope, so that, through repentance toward God because they had broken His holy law, and through faith in Christ as their substitute, surety, and righteousness, they might be brought back to loyalty to God and to obedience to His holy law. . . .

The life and death of Christ in behalf of sinful man were for the purpose of restoring the sinner to God's favor, through imparting to him the righteousness that would meet the claims of the law, and find acceptance with the Father. But it is ever the purpose of Satan to make void the law of God, and to pervert the true meaning of the plan of salvation. Therefore he has originated the falsehood that the sacrifice of Christ on Calvary's cross was for the purpose of freeing men from the obligation of keeping the commandments of God. He has foisted upon the world the deception that God has abolished His constitution, thrown away His moral standard, and made void His holy and perfect law. Had He done this, at what terrible expense would it have been to Heaven!

Instead of proclaiming the abolition of the law, Calvary's cross proclaims in thunder tones its immutable and eternal character. Could the law have been abolished, and the government of heaven and earth and the unnumbered worlds of God maintained, Christ need not have died. The death of Christ was to forever settle the question of the validity of the law of Jehovah. Having suffered the full penalty for a guilty world, Jesus became the mediator between God and man, to restore the repenting soul to favor with God by giving him grace to keep the law of the Most High.

Christ came not to destroy the law or the prophets, but to fulfill them to the very letter. The atonement of Calvary vindicated the law of God as holy, just, and true, not only before the fallen world, but before heaven and before worlds unfallen.—*Signs of the Times,* June 20, 1895.

HOW WE MAGNIFY THE LAW

"Whoever practices and teaches these commands will be called great in the kingdom of heaven." Matt. 5:19, N.I.V.

What reason have men for thinking that God is not particular whether they obey Him implicitly or take their own course? Adam and Eve lost Eden for one transgression of His command; and how dare we trifle with the law of the Most High, and frame deceitful apologies to our souls? We do this at a terrible peril. We must keep all the law, every jot and tittle; for he that offendeth in one point is guilty of all. Every ray of light must be received and cherished, or we shall become bodies of darkness. The Lord Jesus declares: "Whosoever therefore shall break one of these least commandments, and shall teach men so, he shall be called the least in the kingdom of heaven: but whosoever shall do and teach them, the same shall be called great in the kingdom of heaven." We should magnify the precepts of heaven by our words and actions. . . .

Before the Flood swept upon the world, God sent a message through Noah to warn the people of the coming deluge. There were those who did not believe the warning; but their unbelief did not stay the showers, nor prevent the waters of the great deep from submerging a scoffing world. And today, while the last message is being heralded to bring God's servants in harmony with every precept of His law, there will be scoffers and unbelievers; but every soul must stand in his own integrity. As Noah was faithful in warning the antediluvian world, so we must be faithful to the great trust that God has given us. Although there are scoffers . . . on every side, we must not shrink from presenting the truth of heaven to this generation. . . .

There are those who will be glad to lull you to sleep in your carnal security; but I have a different work. My message is to alarm you, to bid you reform your lives, and cease your rebellion against the God of the universe. . . .

Faith in Jesus does not make void the law, but establishes it, and will work the fruits of obedience in our lives. . . .

The church that Christ presents before the throne of His glory is without "spot, or wrinkle, or any such thing." Do you want to be among those who have washed their robes of character in the blood of the Lamb? then, "cease to do evil; learn to do well' "; walk in the commandments and ordinances of your God blameless. You are not to ask whether it suits your convenience to keep the truth of heaven. You are to take up your cross and follow Jesus, cost what it may. You will find that His yoke is easy, and His burden is light.—*Review and Herald,* June 22, 1911.

THE LAW, AS A MIRROR, REVEALS SIN

Whoso keepeth his word, in him verily is the love of God perfected: hereby know we that we are in him. 1 John 2:5.

God has a standard of righteousness by which He measures character. This standard is His holy law, which is given to us as a rule of life. We are called upon to comply with its requirements, and when we do this we honor both God and Jesus Christ; for God gave the law, and Christ died to magnify it, and make it honorable. He declares: "If ye keep my commandments, ye shall abide in my love; even as I have kept my Father's commandments, and abide in his love." . . . "The world passeth away, and the lust thereof: but he that doeth the will of God abideth for ever."

There are many hearers, but few doers, of the words of Christ. His words may be theoretically accepted, but if they are not stamped upon the soul, and woven into the life, they will have no sanctifying effect upon the character. It is one thing to accept the truth, and another thing to practice it in the daily life. From those who hear only, God's Word calls for no grateful response. The commandment, "Thou shalt love the Lord thy God with all thy heart, and with all thy soul, and with all thy strength," is acknowledged to be just, but its claims are not recognized; its principles are not carried out.

We are all sinful, and of ourselves are unable to do the words of Christ. But God has made provision whereby the condemned sinner may be freed from spot and stain. "If any man sin, we have an advocate with the Father, Jesus Christ the righteous." "If we confess our sins, he is faithful and just to forgive us our sins, and to cleanse us from all unrighteousness." But while Christ saves the sinner, He does not do away with the law which condemns the sinner. . . . The law shows us our sins, as a mirror shows us that our face is not clean. The mirror has no power to cleanse the face; that is not its office.

So it is with the law. It points out our defects, and condemns us, but it has no power to save us. We must come to Christ for pardon. He will take our guilt upon His own soul, and will justify us before God. And not only will He free us from sin, but He will give us power to render obedience to God's will. . . .

Today many erect a standard of their own, thinking to gain heaven, even though they neglect to do God's will. But all such are building upon the sand. They are hearers only. . . . Our salvation cost the life of the Son of God, and God demands of us that we build our characters upon a foundation that will stand the test of the judgment.—*Signs of the Times,* Sept. 24, 1896.

THE LAW OF GOD VERSUS THE LAW OF SELF

For as by one man's disobedience many were made sinners, so by the obedience of one shall many be made righteous. Moreover the law entered, that the offence might abound. But where sin abounded, grace did much more abound. Rom. 5:19, 20.

Adam did not set his mind in defiance against God, nor did he in any way speak against God; he simply went directly contrary to His express command. And how many today are doing the very same thing, and their guilt is of much greater magnitude because they have the example of Adam's experience in disobedience and its terrible results to warn them of the consequences of transgressing the law of God. So they have clear light upon this subject, and no excuse for their guilt in denying and disobeying God's authority. Adam did not stop to calculate the result of his disobedience.

We can stand down here, . . . and with the aftersight we are privileged to have, we can see what it means to disobey God's commandments. Adam yielded to temptation and as we have the matter of sin and its consequences laid so distinctly before us, we can read from cause to effect and see the greatness of the act is not that which constitutes sin; but the disobedience of God's expressed will, which is a virtual denial of God, refusing the laws of His government. The happiness of man is in his obedience to the laws of God. In his obedience to God's law he is surrounded as with a hedge and kept from the evil.

No man can be happy and depart from God's specified requirements, and set up a standard of his own which he decides he can safely follow. Then there would be a variety of standards to suit the different minds, and the government taken out of the Lord's hands and human beings grasp the reins of government. The law of self is erected, the will of man is made supreme; and when the high and holy will of God is presented to be obeyed, respected, and honored the human will wants its own way . . . to do its own promptings, and there is a controversy between the human agent and the divine.

The fall of our first parents broke the golden chain of implicit obedience of the human will to the divine. Obedience has no longer been deemed an absolute necessity. The human agents follow their own imaginations which the Lord said of the inhabitants of the old world were evil and that continually. The Lord Jesus declares, "I have kept my Father's commandments." How? As a man. Lo, I come to do Thy will, O God. To the accusations of the Jews He stood forth in His pure, virtuous, holy character and challenged them, "Which of you convinceth me of sin?"—Manuscript 1, 1892.

NO COMPROMISE WITH EVIL

Let the wicked forsake his way, and the unrighteous man his thoughts: and let him return unto the Lord, and he will have mercy upon him; and to our God, for he will abundantly pardon. Isa. 55:7.

When the book of the law was found in the house of the Lord, in the time of ancient Israel, it was read before Josiah the king. And he rent his garments, and bade the men in holy office to inquire of the Lord for him, and for his people; for they had departed from the statutes of the Lord. He called together all the men of Israel, and the words of the book were read in the hearing of the congregation. The sin of the rulers and the people was pointed out, and the king stood up before them, and confessed his transgression. He manifested his repentance, and made a covenant to keep the statutes of the Lord with his whole heart. Josiah did not rest until the people did all they could to return from their backsliding, and serve the living God.

Is not this our work today? Our fathers have transgressed, and we have followed in their footsteps; but God has opened the book of the law, and backslidden Israel hear the commandments of the Lord. Their transgression stands revealed, and the wrath of God will be upon every soul that does not repent and reform as the light shines upon his pathway.

When Josiah heard the words of warning and condemnation because Israel had trampled upon the precepts of Heaven, he humbled himself. He wept before the Lord. He made a thorough work of repentance and reformation, and God accepted his efforts. The whole congregation of Israel entered into a solemn covenant to keep the commandments of Jehovah. This is our work today. We must repent of the past evil of our doings, and seek God with all our hearts. We must believe that God means just what He says, and make no compromise with evil in any way. We should greatly humble ourselves before God, and consider any loss preferable to the loss of His favor.

Christ left all to save men from the consequence and penalty of the transgression of the law. The way from the manger to Calvary was marked with blood. The Son of God did not deviate from the path of unwavering obedience, even to the death of the cross. He endured all the woe of man's sin. . . . I beseech you, in the name of Christ, that you confess your sins and reform your ways, that your name may not be blotted out of the book of life, but may be confessed before the Father and before His angels. Jesus is pleading His blood before the Father; and now, while mercy lingers and probation is prolonged, seek the approbation of Heaven.—*Review and Herald,* June 29, 1911.

GOD REVEALS HIS JUSTICE AND LOVE

Love is the fulfilling of the law. Rom. 13:10.

After the fall of our first parents, Christ declared that in order to save man from the penalty of sin, He would come to the world to conquer Satan on the enemy's own battlefield. The controversy that began in heaven was to be continued on the earth.

In this controversy much was to be involved. Vast interests were at stake. Before the inhabitants of the heavenly universe were to be answered the questions: ''Is God's law imperfect, in need of amendment or abrogation, or is it immutable? Is God's government in need of change, or is it stable?''

Before Christ's first advent, the sin of refusing to conform to God's law had become widespread. Apparently Satan's power was growing; his warfare against heaven was becoming more and more determined. A crisis had been reached. With an intense interest God's movements were watched by the heavenly angels. Would He come forth from His place to punish the inhabitants of the world for their iniquity? Would He send fire or flood to destroy them? All heaven waited the bidding of their Commander to pour out the vials of wrath upon a rebellious world. One word from Him, one sign, and the world would have been destroyed. The worlds unfallen would have said, ''Amen. Thou art righteous, O God, because Thou hast exterminated rebellion.''

But ''God so loved the world, that he gave his only begotten Son, that whosoever believeth in him should not perish, but have everlasting life.'' God might have sent His Son to condemn, but He sent Him to save. Christ came as a Redeemer. No words can describe the effect of this movement on the heavenly angels. With wonder and admiration they could only exclaim, ''Herein is love!''

Christ entered upon His mission of mercy, and from the manger to the cross was beset by the enemy. Satan contested every inch of ground, exerting his utmost power to overcome Him. Like a tempest temptation after temptation beat upon Him. But the more mercilessly they fell, the more firmly did the Son of God cling to the hand of His Father, and press on in the bloodstained path.

The severity of the conflict through which Christ passed was proportionate to the vastness of the interests involved in His success or failure. . . . Satan sought to overthrow Christ, in order that he himself might continue to reign in this world as supreme. . . . The Father, the Son, and Lucifer have been revealed in their true relation to one another. God has given unmistakable evidence of His justice and His love.—*Signs of the Times,* Aug. 27, 1902.

TRUTH MUST BE PRACTICED IN THE LIFE

Let no man deceive you: he that doeth righteousness is righteous, even as he is righteous. 1 John 3:7.

Those who are looking for the revelation of Christ in the clouds of heaven with power and great glory, as King of kings and Lord of lords, in life and character will seek to represent Him to the world. "And every man that hath this hope in him purifieth himself, even as he is pure." They will hate sin and iniquity, even as Christ hated sin. They will keep the commandments of God, as Christ kept His Father's commandments. They will realize that it is not enough to acquiesce in the doctrines of truth, but that the truth must be applied to the heart, practiced in the life, in order that the followers of Christ may be one with Him, and that men may be as pure in their sphere as God is in His sphere. There have been men in every generation who have claimed to be the sons of God, who paid tithes of mint and anise and cummin, and yet who led a godless life; for they neglected the weightier matters of the law—mercy, justice, and the love of God. . . .

The sons of God will not be like the worldling; for the truth received into the heart will be the means of purifying the soul, and transforming the character, and of making its receiver like-minded with God. Unless a man becomes like-minded with God, he is still in his natural depravity. If Christ is in the heart, He will appear in the home, in the workshop, in the marketplace, in the church. The power of the truth will be felt in elevating, ennobling the mind, and softening and subduing the heart, bringing the whole man into harmony with God. He who is transformed by the truth will shed a light upon the world. He that hath the hope of Christ in him will purify himself even as He is pure. The hope of Christ's appearing is a large hope, a far-reaching hope. It is the hope of seeing the King in His beauty, and of being made like Him. . . .

He that abideth in Christ is perfected in the love of God, and his purposes, thoughts, words, and actions are in harmony with the will of God expressed in the commandments of His law. There is nothing in the heart of the man who abides in Christ that is at war with any precept of God's law. Where the Spirit of Christ is in the heart, the character of Christ will be revealed, and there will be manifested gentleness under provocation, and patience under trial. "Little children, let no man deceive you: he that doeth righteousness is righteous, even as he is righteous." Righteousness can be defined only by God's great moral standard, the Ten Commandments. There is no other rule by which to measure character.—*Signs of the Times,* June 20, 1895.

GOD'S AUTHORITY FOREVER ESTABLISHED

Then saith Jesus unto him, Get thee hence, Satan: for it is written, Thou shalt worship the Lord thy God, and him only shalt thou serve. Matt. 4:10.

Satan sought to make it appear that he was working for the liberty of the universe. He was determined to make his arguments so varied, so deceptive, so insidious, that everyone would be convinced that God's law was tyrannical. Even while hanging on the cross, assailed by Satan with his fiercest temptations, Christ was victorious. . . . With His parting breath He exclaimed, ''It is finished.'' The battle had been won. . . . The blood of the innocent had been shed for the guilty. By the life that He gave, man was ransomed from eternal death, and the doom of him who had the power of death was sealed.

Not until the death of Christ was the character of Satan clearly revealed to the angels or to the unfallen worlds. Then the prevarications and accusations of him who had once been an exalted angel were seen in their true light. It was seen that his professedly spotless character was deceptive. His deeply laid scheme to exalt himself to supremacy was fully discerned. His falsehoods were apparent to all. God's authority was forever established. Truth triumphed over falsehood.

Not merely in the minds of a few finite creatures in this world, but in the minds of all the inhabitants of the heavenly universe, has the immutability of God's law been established. Satan's course against Christ was heralded to every world. When the issue was finally determined, every unfallen being expressed indignation at the rebellion. With one voice they extolled God as righteous, merciful, self-denying, just. . . .

The heavenly universe had witnessed the weapons that were chosen by the Prince of life—the words of Scripture, ''It is written''; and the weapons used by the prince of the world—falsehood and deception. They had seen the Prince of life deal in straightforward lines of truth, honesty, and integrity, while the prince of the world exercised his power of cunning, artful secrecy, intrigue, enmity, and revenge. They had seen the One who bore the banner of truth sacrifice everything, even His life, to maintain truth, while the one who bore the banner of rebellion continued to strengthen his accusations against the God of truth.

The heavenly worlds and heaven itself were amazed at God's long forbearance. . . . The Lord had demonstrated His wisdom and justice in banishing Satan from heaven. . . . All the unfallen beings are now united in regarding God's law as changeless. . . . His law has been proved faultless. His government is forever secure.—*Signs of the Times,* Aug. 27, 1902.

PRINCIPLES THAT UNDERLIE THE LAW OF GOD

Blessed are the poor in spirit: for theirs is the kingdom of heaven. Matt. 5:3.

In Christ's sermon on the mount, light and truth are given, and principles laid down which apply to every condition of life, and to every duty that God requires at our hands. Christ had come to magnify and make honorable the law that He Himself had proclaimed from Mount Sinai to His chosen people during their wilderness wandering. . . .

In all His lessons, Christ sought to impress upon the minds and hearts of His hearers the principles which underlie His great standard of righteousness. He taught them that if they would keep God's commandments, love for God and for their fellow men must be manifested in their daily life. He sought to instill into their hearts the love He felt for humanity. Thus He sowed the seeds of truth, the fruits of which will produce a rich harvest of holiness and beauty of cháracter. The holy influence will not only be far-reaching while time shall last, but its results will be felt throughout eternity. It will sanctify the actions, and have a purifying influence wherever it exists.

Seated upon the mount, surrounded by His disciples and a large . . . gathering, Jesus "opened his mouth, and taught them, saying, Blessed are the poor in spirit: for theirs is the kingdom of heaven." These are not murmurers and complainers, but those who are content with their condition and surroundings in life. They do not cherish the feeling that they deserve a better position than that which Providence has assigned them, but manifest a spirit of gratitude for every favor bestowed upon them. Every proud thought and exalted feeling is banished. . . .

Those who are truly sanctified have a sense of their own weakness. Feeling their need, they will go for light and grace and strength to Jesus, in whom all fullness dwells, and who alone can supply their wants. Conscious of their own imperfections, they seek to become more like Christ, and to live in accordance with the principles of His holy law. This continual sense of inefficiency will lead to such entire dependence upon God, that His Spirit will be exemplified in them. The treasures of heaven will be opened to supply the wants of every hungering, thirsting soul. All of this character have the assurance of one day beholding the glory of that kingdom which as yet the imagination can only faintly grasp. . . .

The standard the Christian is to keep before him is the purity and loveliness of Christ's character. Day by day he may be putting on new beauties, and reflecting to the world more and still more of the divine image.—*Bible Echo,* Feb. 21, 1898.

THE STANDARD IN THE JUDGMENT

So speak ye, and so do, as they that shall be judged by the law of liberty. James 2:12.

The first angel of Revelation 14 calls upon men to "fear God, and give glory to him," and to worship Him as the Creator of the heavens and the earth. In order to do this, they must obey His law. . . . Without obedience to His commandments, no worship can be pleasing to God; for "this is the love of God, that we keep his commandments" (1 John 5:3).

Many religious teachers say that Christ, by His death, freed us from the law; but not all take this view. . . . The law of God, from its very nature, is unchangeable. It is a revelation of the will and character of its Author. God is love, and His law is love. Its two great principles are love to God and man. "Love is the fulfilling of the law." The character of God is righteousness and truth, and such is the nature of His law. The psalmist says, "Thy law is the truth"; "all thy commandments are righteousness." And the apostle Paul declares, "The law is holy, and the commandment holy, and just, and good." Such a law, an expression of the mind and will of God, must be as enduring as its Author.

And this law is the standard by which the lives and characters of men will be tested in the judgment. After pointing out our duty to obey His commandments, Solomon adds: "For God shall bring every work into judgment." The apostle James admonishes his brethren, "So speak ye, and so do, as they that shall be judged by the law of liberty."

Jesus will appear in the judgment as the advocate of His people, to plead in their behalf before God. "If any man sin, we have an advocate with the Father, Jesus Christ the righteous" (1 John 2:1). "For Christ is not entered into the holy places made with hands, which are the figures of the true; but into heaven itself, now to appear in the presence of God for us." "Wherefore he is able also to save them to the uttermost that come unto God by him, seeing he ever liveth to make intercession for them" (Heb. 9:24; 7:25).

In the judgment all who have truly repented of sin, and by faith claimed the blood of Christ as their atoning sacrifice, have had pardon entered against their names in the books of heaven; as they have become partakers of the righteousness of Christ, and their characters are found to be in harmony with the law of God, their sins will be blotted out, and they themselves will be accounted worthy of eternal life. . . . Jesus said, "He that overcometh, the same shall be clothed in white rainment; and I will not blot out his name out of the book of life, but I will confess his name before my Father, and before his angels."—*Southern Watchman,* Oct. 10, 1905.

HOW WE MAY KEEP GOD'S LAW

His work is honourable and glorious: and his righteousness endureth for ever. Ps. 111:3.

One ray of the glory of God, one gleam of the purity of Christ, penetrating the soul, makes every spot of defilement painfully distinct, and lays bare the deformity and defects of the human character. How can anyone who is brought before the holy standard of God's law, which makes apparent the evil motives, the unhallowed desires, the infidelity of the heart, the impurity of the lips, and that lays bare the life, make any boast of holiness? His acts of disloyalty in making void the law of God are exposed to his sight, and his spirit is stricken and afflicted under the searching influences of the Spirit of God. He loathes himself as he views the greatness, the majesty, the pure and spotless character of Jesus Christ.

When the Spirit of Christ stirs the heart with its marvelous awakening power, there is a sense of deficiency in the soul, that leads to contrition of mind, and humiliation of self, rather than to proud boasting of what has been acquired. When Daniel beheld the glory and majesty surrounding the heavenly messenger that was sent unto him, he exclaimed, as he described the wonderful scene, "Therefore I was left alone, and saw this great vision, and there remained no strength in me: for my comeliness was turned in me into corruption, and I retained no strength."

The soul that is thus touched will never wrap itself about with self-righteousness, or a pretentious garb of holiness; but will hate its selfishness, abhor its self-love, and will seek, through Christ's righteousness, for that purity of heart which is in harmony with the law of God and the character of Christ. He will then reflect the character of Christ, the hope of glory. It will be the greatest mystery to him that Jesus should have made so great a sacrifice to redeem him.

He will exclaim, with humble mien and quivering lip, "He loved me. He gave Himself for me. He became poor that I, through His poverty, might be made rich. The Man of Sorrows did not spurn me, but poured out His inexhaustible, redeeming love that my heart might be made clean; and He has brought me back into loyalty and obedience to all His commandments. His condescension, His humiliation, His crucifixion, are the crowning miracles in the marvelous exhibition of the plan of salvation. . . . All this He has done to make it possible to impart to me His own righteousness, that I may keep the law I have transgressed. For this I adore Him. I will proclaim Him to all sinners."—*Review and Herald,* Oct. 16, 1888.

THE MEANING OF GOD'S LAW

The law of the Lord is perfect, converting the soul. Ps. 19:7.

The carnal mind is enmity against God, and it rebels against His will. . . .

I have been shown what man is without a knowledge of the will of God. . . . But when the Spirit of God reveals to him the full meaning of the law, what a change takes place in his heart! Like Belshazzar, he reads intelligently the handwriting of the Almighty, and conviction takes possession of his soul. The thunders of God's word startle him from his lethargy, and he calls for mercy in the name of Jesus. And to that humble plea God always listens with a willing ear. He never turns the penitent away comfortless. . . .

If God's people would recognize His dealings with them and accept His teachings, they would find a straight path for their feet and a light to guide them through darkness and discouragement. David learned wisdom from God's dealings with him and bowed in humility beneath the chastisement of the Most High. The faithful portrayal of his true state by the prophet Nathan made David acquainted with his own sins and aided him to put them away. He accepted counsel meekly and humiliated himself before God. "The law of the Lord," he exclaims, "is perfect, converting the soul."

Repentant sinners have no cause to despair because they are reminded of their transgressions and warned of their danger. These very efforts in their behalf show how much God loves them and desires to save them. They have only to follow His counsel and do His will, to inherit eternal life. God sets the sins of His erring people before them, that they may behold them in all their enormity under the light of divine truth. It is then their duty to renounce them forever.

God is as powerful to save from sin today as He was in the times of the patriarchs, of David, and of the prophets and apostles. The multitude of cases recorded in sacred history where God has delivered His people from their own iniquities should make the Christian of this time eager to receive divine instruction and zealous to perfect a character that will bear the close inspection of the judgment. . . .

The words of inspiration comfort and cheer the erring soul. Although the patriarchs and apostles were subject to human frailties, yet through faith they obtained a good report, fought their battles in the strength of the Lord, and conquered gloriously. Thus may we trust in the virtue of the atoning sacrifice and be overcomers in the name of Jesus. Humanity is humanity the world over from the time of Adam down to the present generation, and the love of God through all ages is without a parallel.—*Testimonies*, vol. 4, pp. 13-15.

STUDY CHRIST'S CHARACTER AND BECOME LIKE HIM

No man can serve two masters: for either he will hate the one, and love the other; or else he will hold to the one, and despise the other. Matt. 6:24.

Halfhearted Christians obscure the glory of God, misinterpret piety, and cause men to receive false ideas as to what constitutes vital godliness. Others think that they, also, can be Christians and yet consult their own tastes and make provision for the flesh, if these falsehearted professors can do so. On many a professed Christian's banner the motto is written, "You can serve God and please self—you can serve God and mammon." They profess to be wise virgins, but not having the oil of grace in their vessels with their lamps, they shed forth no light to the glory of God and for the salvation of men. They seek to do what the world's Redeemer said was impossible to do; He has declared, "Ye cannot serve God and mammon."

Those who profess to be Christians, but do not follow in the footsteps of Christ, make of none effect His words, and obscure the plan of salvation. By their spirit and deportment they virtually say, "Jesus, in Your day You did not understand as well as we do in our day, that man can serve God and mammon." These professors of religion claim to keep the law of God, but they do not keep it. Oh, what would the standard of true manhood have become had it been left in the hands of man! God has lifted His own standard—the commandments of God and the faith of Jesus; and the experience that follows complete surrender to God is righteousness, peace, and joy in the Holy Ghost.—*Review and Herald,* Aug. 19, 1890.

You need not wait to grow good; you need not think that any effort of yours will make your prayers acceptable, and bring you salvation. Let each man and woman pray to God, not to man. Let each one come to Christ in humility.

You should pray to God for yourself, believing that He listens to every word you utter. Lay bare your heart for His inspection, confess your sins, asking Him to forgive you, pleading the merits of the atonement, and then by faith contemplate the great scheme of redemption, and the Comforter will bring all things to your remembrance.

The more you study the character of Christ, the more attractive will He appear to you. He will become as one near you, in close companionship with you; your affections will go out after Him. If the mind is molded by the objects with which it has most to do, then to think of Jesus, to talk of Him, will enable you to become like Him in spirit and character. You will reflect His image in that which is great and pure and spiritual. You will have the mind of Christ, and He will send you forth to the world as His spiritual representative.—*Ibid.,* Aug. 26, 1890.

TRUE CHARITY WILL NOT COMPROMISE WITH EVIL

Whosoever committeth sin transgresseth also the law: for sin is the transgression of the law. And ye know that he was manifested to take away our sins; and in him is no sin. 1 John 3:4, 5.

As the years went by and the number of believers grew, John labored with increasing fidelity and earnestness for his brethren. The times were full of peril for the church. Satanic delusions existed everywhere. By misrepresentation and falsehood the emissaries of Satan sought to arouse opposition against the doctrines of Christ, and in consequence dissensions and heresies were imperiling the church. Some who professed Christ claimed that His love released them from obedience to the law of God. On the other hand, many taught that it was necessary to observe the Jewish customs and ceremonies; that a mere observance of the law, without faith in the blood of Christ, was sufficient for salvation.

Some held that Christ was a good man, but denied His divinity. Some who pretended to be true to the cause of God were deceivers, and in practice they denied Christ and His gospel. Living themselves in transgression, they were bringing heresies into the church. Thus many were being led into the mazes of skepticism and delusion.

John was filled with sadness as he saw these poisonous errors creeping into the church. He saw the dangers to which the church was exposed, and he met the emergency with promptness and decision. The Epistles of John breathe the spirit of love. It seems as if he wrote with a pen dipped in love. But when he came in contact with those who were breaking the law of God, yet claiming that they were living without sin, he did not hesitate to warn them of their fearful deception. . . .

We are authorized to hold in the same estimation as did the beloved disciple those who claim to abide in Christ while living in transgression of God's law. There exist in these last days evils similar to those that threatened the prosperity of the early church; and the teachings of the apostle John on these points should be carefully heeded. "You must have charity" is the cry heard everywhere, especially from those who profess sanctification. But true charity is too pure to cover an unconfessed sin. While we are to love the souls for whom Christ died, we are to make no compromise with evil. We are not to unite with the rebellious and call this charity. God requires His people in this age of the world to stand for the right as unflinchingly as did John in opposition to soul-destroying errors. . . . His testimony in regard to the Saviour's life and death was clear and forcible. Out of the abundance of a heart overflowing with love for the Saviour he spoke; and no power could stay his words.—*The Acts of the Apostles*, pp. 553-555.

THE SPIRITUALITY OF THE LAW

I am not come to destroy the law, but to fulfil. Matt. 5:17.

It was Christ who, amid thunder and flame, had proclaimed the law upon Mount Sinai. The glory of God, like devouring fire, rested upon its summit, and the mountain quaked at the presence of the Lord. The hosts of Israel, lying prostrate upon the earth, had listened in awe to the sacred precepts of the law. . . .

When the law was given, Israel, degraded by the long bondage in Egypt, had need to be impressed with the power and majesty of God; yet He revealed Himself to them no less as a God of love. . . .

The law given upon Sinai was the enunciation of the principle of love, a revelation to earth of the law of heaven. It was ordained in the hand of a Mediator—spoken by Him through whose power the hearts of men could be brought into harmony with its principles. God had revealed the purpose of the law when He declared to Israel, ''Ye shall be holy men unto me'' (Ex. 22:31).

But Israel had not perceived the spiritual nature of the law, and too often their professed obedience was but an observance of forms and ceremonies, rather than a surrender of the heart to the sovereignty of love. As Jesus in His character and work represented to men the holy, benevolent, and paternal attributes of God, and presented the worthlessness of mere ceremonial obedience, the Jewish leaders did not receive or understand His words. They thought that He dwelt too lightly upon the requirements of the law; and when He set before them the very truths that were the soul of their divinely appointed service, they, looking only at the external, accused Him of seeking to overthrow it.

The words of Christ, though calmly spoken, were uttered with an earnestness and power that stirred the hearts of the people. . . . They ''were astonished at his teaching: for he taught them as one having authority, and not as their scribes'' (Matt. 7:28, 29, R.V.). The Pharisees noted the vast difference between their manner of instruction and that of Christ. They saw that the majesty and purity and beauty of the truth, with its deep and gentle influence, was taking firm hold upon many minds. The Saviour's divine love and tenderness drew the hearts of men to Him. . . .

The Saviour said nothing to unsettle faith in the religion and institutions that had been given through Moses; for every ray of divine light that Israel's great leader communicated to his people was received from Christ. While many are saying in their hearts that He has come to do away with the law, Jesus in unmistakable language reveals His attitude toward the divine statutes. ''Think not,'' He said, ''that I am come to destroy the law, or the prophets.''—*Thoughts From the Mount of Blessing,* pp. 45-48.

THE NEW COVENANT PROMISE

This is the covenant that I will make with them after those days, saith the Lord, I will put my laws into their hearts, and in their minds will I write them; and their sins and iniquities will I remember no more. Heb. 10:16, 17.

It is the Creator of men, the Giver of the law, who declares that it is not His purpose to set aside its precepts. Everything in nature, from the mote in the sunbeam to the worlds on high, is under law. And upon obedience to these laws the order and harmony of the natural world depend. So there are great principles of righteousness to control the life of all intelligent beings, and upon conformity to these principles the well-being of the universe depends.

Before this earth was called into being, God's law existed. Angels are governed by its principles, and in order for earth to be in harmony with heaven, man also must obey the divine statutes. To man in Eden Christ made known the precepts of the law "when the morning stars sang together, and all the sons of God shouted for joy" (Job 38:7). The mission of Christ on earth was not to destroy the law, but by His grace to bring man back to obedience to its precepts.

The beloved disciple, who listened to the words of Jesus on the mount, writing long afterward under the inspiration of the Holy Spirit, speaks of the law as of perpetual obligation. He says that "sin is the transgression of the law" and that "whosoever committeth sin transgresseth also the law" (1 John 3:4). He makes it plain that the law to which he refers is "an old commandment which ye had from the beginning" (chap. 2:7). He is speaking of the law that existed at the creation and was reiterated upon Mount Sinai. . . .

He [Jesus] was to show the spiritual nature of the law, to present its far-reaching principles, and to make plain its eternal obligation.

The divine beauty of the character of Christ, of whom the noblest and most gentle among men are but a faint reflection; of whom Solomon by the Spirit of inspiration wrote, He is "the chiefest among ten thousand. . . . Yea, he is altogether lovely" (S. of Sol. 5:10-16); of whom David, seeing Him in prophetic vision, said, "Thou art fairer than the children of men" (Ps. 45:2); Jesus, the express image of the Father's person, the effulgence of His glory; the self-denying Redeemer, throughout His pilgrimage of love on earth, was a living representation of the character of the law of God. In His life it is made manifest that heaven-born love, Christlike principles, underlie the laws of eternal rectitude. . . .

Those principles that were made known to man in Paradise as the great law of life will exist unchanged in Paradise restored.—*Thoughts From the Mount of Blessing,* pp. 48-51.

GOD'S LAW A HEDGE AGAINST EVIL

[His commandments] stand fast for ever and ever, and are done in truth and uprightness. Ps. 111:8.

He who willfully breaks one commandment, does not, in spirit and truth, keep any of them. "Whosoever shall keep the whole law, and yet offend in one point, he is guilty of all" (James 2:10).

It is not the greatness of the act of disobedience that constitutes sin, but the fact of variance from God's expressed will in the least particular; for this shows that there is yet communion between the soul and sin. The heart is divided in its service. There is a virtual denial of God, a rebellion against the laws of His government.

Were men free to depart from the Lord's requirements and to set up a standard of duty for themselves, there would be a variety of standards to suit different minds and the government would be taken out of the Lord's hands. The will of man would be made supreme, and the high and holy will of God—His purpose of love toward His creatures—would be dishonored, disrespected.

Whenever men choose their own way, they place themselves in controversy with God. They will have no place in the kingdom of heaven, for they are at war with the very principles of heaven. In disregarding the will of God, they are placing themselves on the side of Satan, the enemy of God and man. Not by one word, not by many words, but by every word that God has spoken, shall man live. We cannot disregard one word, however trifling it may seem to us, and be safe. There is not a commandment of the law that is not for the good and happiness of man, both in this life and in the life to come.

In obedience to God's law, man is surrounded as with a hedge and kept from the evil. He who breaks down this divinely erected barrier at one point has destroyed its power to protect him; for he has opened a way by which the enemy can enter to waste and ruin.

By venturing to disregard the will of God upon one point, our first parents opened the floodgates of woe upon the world. And every individual who follows their example will reap a similar result. The love of God underlies every precept of His law, and he who departs from the commandment is working his own unhappiness and ruin. . . .

A legal religion is insufficient to bring the soul into harmony with God. . . . The only true faith is that which "worketh by love" (Gal. 5:6) to purify the soul. It is as leaven that transforms the character. . . . Jesus proceeded to show His hearers what it means to keep the commandments of God—that it is a reproduction in themselves of the character of Christ. For in Him, God was daily made manifest before them.—*Thoughts From the Mount of Blessing,* pp. 51-55.

EVERY SOUL TO BE TREATED WITH RESPECT

Thou shalt not hate thy brother in thine heart. . . . Thou shalt not avenge, nor bear any grudge against the children of thy people, but thou shalt love thy neighbour as thyself. Lev. 19:17, 18.

The Saviour's words revealed to His hearers the fact that, while they were condemning others as transgressors, they were themselves equally guilty; for they were cherishing malice and hatred. . . . They cherished the most bitter hatred of their Roman oppressors and felt themselves at liberty to hate and despise all other peoples, and even their own countrymen who did not in all things conform to their ideas. In all this they were violating the law which declares, ''Thou shalt not kill.''

The spirit of hate and revenge originated with Satan, and it led him to put to death the Son of God. Whoever cherishes malice or unkindness is cherishing the same spirit. . . . In the revengeful thought the evil deed lies enfolded, as the plant in the seed. . . . In the gift of His Son for our redemption, God has shown how high a value He places upon every human soul, and He gives to no man liberty to speak contemptuously of another. We shall see faults and weaknesses in those about us, but God claims every soul as His property—His by creation, and doubly His as purchased by the precious blood of Christ. All were created in His image, and even the most degraded are to be treated with respect and tenderness. God will hold us accountable for even a word spoken in contempt of one soul for whom Christ laid down His life. . . .

Jesus says that whoever shall condemn his brother as an apostate or a despiser of God shows that he himself is worthy of the same condemnation.

Christ Himself, when contending with Satan about the body of Moses, ''durst not bring against him a railing accusation'' (Jude 9). Had He done this, He would have placed Himself on Satan's ground, for accusation is the weapon of the evil one. He is called in Scripture, ''the accuser of our brethren'' (Rev. 12:10). Jesus would employ none of Satan's weapons. He met him with the words, ''The Lord rebuke thee'' (Jude 9).

His example is for us. When we are brought in conflict with the enemies of Christ, we should say nothing in a spirit of retaliation or that would bear even the appearance of a railing accusation. He who stands as a mouthpiece for God should not utter words which even the Majesty of heaven would not use when contending with Satan. We are to leave with God the work of judging and condemning.—*Thoughts From the Mount of Blessing,* pp. 55-58.

CHRISTIANS TO BE AS TRANSPARENT AS SUNLIGHT

But I say unto you, Swear not at all; neither by heaven; for it is God's throne: nor by the earth; for it is his footstool: neither by Jerusalem; for it is the city of the great King. Neither shalt thou swear by thy head, because thou canst not make one hair white or black. Matt. 5:34-36.

Everything we possess comes to us stamped with the cross, bought with the blood that is precious above all estimate, because it is the life of God. Hence there is nothing that we have a right to pledge, as if it were our own, for the fulfillment of our word. . . .

Our Saviour did not, however, forbid the use of the judicial oath, in which God is solemnly called to witness that what is said is truth and nothing but the truth. Jesus Himself, at His trial before the Sanhedrin, did not refuse to testify under oath. The high priest said unto Him, "I adjure thee by the living God, that thou tell us whether thou be the Christ, the Son of God." Jesus answered, "Thou hast said" (Matt. 26:63, 64). . . .

If there is anyone who can consistently testify under oath, it is the Christian. He lives constantly as in the presence of God, knowing that every thought is open to the eyes of Him with whom we have to do; and when required to do so in a lawful manner, it is right for him to appeal to God as a witness that what he says is the truth, and nothing but the truth. . . .

Everything that Christians do should be as transparent as the sunlight. Truth is of God; deception, in every one of its myriad forms, is of Satan. . . . It is not a light or an easy thing to speak the exact truth. We cannot speak the truth unless we know the truth, and how often preconceived opinions, mental bias, imperfect knowledge, errors of judgment, prevent a right understanding of matters with which we have to do! We cannot speak the truth unless our minds are continually guided by Him who is truth.

Through the apostle Paul, Christ bids us, "Let your speech be alway with grace" (Col. 4:6). "Let no corrupt communication proceed out of your mouth, but that which is good to the use of edifying, that it may minister grace unto the hearers" (Eph. 4:29). In the light of these scriptures the words of Christ upon the mount are seen to condemn jesting, trifling, and unchaste conversation. They require that our words should be not only truthful, but pure.

Those who have learned of Christ will "have no fellowship with the unfruitful works of darkness" (chap. 5:11). In speech, as in life, they will be simple, straightforward, and true; for they are preparing for the fellowship of those holy ones in whose mouth "was found no guile" (Rev. 14:5).—*Thoughts From the Mount of Blessing,* pp. 66-69.

GOD'S LAW OF FORGIVING LOVE

Love your enemies. Matt. 5:44.

The Saviour's lesson, ''Resist not him that is evil,'' was a hard saying for the revengeful Jews. . . . But Jesus now made a still stronger declaration: . . .

''Love your enemies, bless them that curse you, do good to them that hate you, and pray for them which despitefully use you, and persecute you; that ye may be the children of your Father which is in heaven'' (Matt. 5:44, 45).

Such was the spirit of the law which the rabbis had misinterpreted as a cold and rigid code of exactions. They regarded themselves as better than other men, and as entitled to the special favor of God by virtue of their birth as Israelites; but Jesus pointed to the spirit of forgiving love as that which would give evidence that they were actuated by any higher motives than even the publicans and sinners, whom they despised.

He pointed His hearers to the Ruler of the universe, under the new name, ''Our Father.'' He would have them understand how tenderly the heart of God yearned over them. He teaches . . . that ''like as a father pitieth his children, so the Lord pitieth them that fear him'' (Ps. 103:13). Such a conception of God was never given to the world by any religion but that of the Bible. Heathenism teaches men to look upon the Supreme Being as an object of fear rather than of love—a malign deity to be appeased by sacrifices, rather than a Father pouring upon His children the gift of His love. Even the people of Israel had become so blinded to the precious teaching of the prophets concerning God that this revelation of His paternal love was as an original subject, a new gift to the world. . . .

Every good thing we have, each ray of sunshine and shower of rain, every morsel of food, every moment of life, is a gift of love.

While we were yet unloving and unlovely in character, ''hateful, and hating one another,'' our heavenly Father had mercy on us. . . .

The children of God are those who are partakers of His nature. It is not earthly rank, nor birth, nor nationality, nor religious privilege, which proves that we are members of the family of God; it is love, a love that embraces all humanity. Even sinners whose hearts are not utterly closed to God's Spirit will respond to kindness; while they may give hate for hate, they will also give love for love. But it is only the Spirit of God that gives love for hatred. To be kind to the unthankful and to the evil, to do good hoping for nothing again, is the insignia of the royalty of heaven, the sure token by which the children of the Highest reveal their high estate.—*Thoughts From the Mount of Blessing,* pp. 73-75.

GOD'S LAW OF LOVE PERFECTED IN US

If we love one another, God dwelleth in us, and his love is perfected in us. 1 John 4:12.

The conditions of eternal life, under grace, are just what they were in Eden—perfect righteousness, harmony with God, perfect conformity to the principles of His law. The standard of character presented in the Old Testament is the same that is presented in the New Testament. This standard is not one to which we cannot attain. In every command or injunction that God gives there is a promise, the most positive, underlying the command. God has made provision that we may become like unto Him, and He will accomplish this for all who do not interpose a perverse will and thus frustrate His grace.

With untold love our God has loved us, and our love awakens toward Him as we comprehend something of the length and breadth and depth and height of this love that passeth knowledge. By the revelation of the attractive loveliness of Christ, by the knowledge of His love expressed to us while we were yet sinners, the stubborn heart is melted and subdued, and the sinner is transformed and becomes a child of heaven. God does not employ compulsory measures; love is the agent which He uses to expel sin from the heart. By it He changes pride into humility, and enmity and unbelief into love and faith. . . .

He tells us to be perfect as He is, in the same manner. We are to be centers of light and blessing to our little circle, even as He is to the universe. We have nothing of ourselves, but the light of His love shines upon us, and we are to reflect its brightness. ''In His borrowed goodness good,'' we may be perfect in our sphere, even as God is perfect in His.

Jesus said, Be perfect as *your Father* is perfect. If you are the children of God you are partakers of His nature, and you cannot but be like Him. Every child lives by the life of his father. If you are God's children, begotten by His Spirit, you live by the life of God. In Christ dwells ''all the fullness of the Godhead bodily'' (Col. 2:9); and the life of Jesus is made manifest ''in our mortal flesh'' (2 Cor. 4:11). That life in you will produce the same character and manifest the same works as it did in Him. Thus you will be in harmony with every precept of His law; for ''the law of the Lord is perfect, restoring the soul'' (Ps. 19:7, margin). Through love ''the righteousness of the law'' will be ''fulfilled in us, who walk not after the flesh, but after the Spirit'' (Rom. 8:4).—*Thoughts From the Mount of Blessing,* pp. 76-78.

JUSTIFICATION BY FAITH
—OUR ONLY HOPE

If any man sin, we have an advocate with the Father, Jesus Christ the righteous: and he is the propitiation for our sins: and not for ours only, but also for the sins of the whole world. 1 John 2:1, 2.

As the penitent sinner, contrite before God, discerns Christ's atonement in his behalf, and accepts this atonement as his only hope in this life and the future life, his sins are pardoned. This is justification by faith. Every believing soul is to conform his will entirely to God's will, and keep in a state of repentance and contrition, exercising faith in the atoning merits of the Redeemer and advancing from strength to strength, from glory to glory.

Pardon and justification are one and the same thing. Through faith, the believer passes from the position of a rebel, a child of sin and Satan, to the position of a loyal subject of Christ Jesus, not because of an inherent goodness, but because Christ receives him as His child by adoption. The sinner receives the forgiveness of his sins, because these sins are borne by his Substitute and Surety. The Lord speaks to His heavenly Father, saying: "This is My child. I reprieve him from the condemnation of death, giving him My life insurance policy—eternal life—because I have taken his place and have suffered for his sins. He is even My beloved son." Thus man, pardoned, and clothed with the beautiful garments of Christ's righteousness, stands faultless before God.

The sinner may err, but he is not cast off without mercy. His only hope, however, is repentance toward God and faith in the Lord Jesus Christ. It is the Father's prerogative to forgive our transgressions and sins, because Christ has taken upon Himself our guilt and reprieved us, imputing to us His own righteousness. His sacrifice satisfies fully the demands of justice.

Justification is the opposite of condemnation. God's boundless mercy is exercised toward those who are wholly undeserving. He forgives transgressions and sins for the sake of Jesus, who has become the propitiation for our sins. Through faith in Christ, the guilty transgressor is brought into favor with God and into the strong hope of life eternal.—*The SDA Bible Commentary,* vol. 6, pp. 1070, 1071.

The sinner is justified through the merits of Jesus, and this is God's acknowledgment of the perfection of the ransom paid for man. That Christ was obedient even unto the death of the cross is a pledge of the repenting sinner's acceptance with the Father.—*Signs of the Times,* July 4, 1892.

THE REPENTANT SINNER ACCEPTED IN CHRIST

For Christ is not entered into the holy places made with hands, which are the figures of the true; but into heaven itself, now to appear in the presence of God for us. Heb. 9:24.

Christ is our sacrifice, our substitute, our surety, our divine intercessor; He is made unto us righteousness, sanctification, and redemption. "For Christ is not entered into the holy places made with hands, which are the figures of the true; but into heaven itself, now to appear in the presence of God for us."

The intercession of Christ in our behalf is that of presenting His divine merits in the offering of Himself to the Father as our substitute and surety; for He ascended up on high to make an atonement for our transgressions. . . . "Herein is love, not that we loved God, but that he loved us, and sent his Son to be the propitiation for our sins" (1 John 4:10). "He is able also to save them to the uttermost that come unto God by him, seeing he ever liveth to make intercession for them" (Heb. 7:25).

From these scriptures it is evident that it is not God's will that you should be distrustful, and torture your soul with the fear that God will not accept you because you are sinful and unworthy. . . . Present your case before Him, pleading the merits of the blood shed for you upon Calvary's cross. Satan will accuse you of being a great sinner, and you must admit this, but you can say: "I know I am a sinner, and that is the reason I need a Saviour. Jesus came into the world to save sinners. 'The blood of Jesus Christ his Son cleanseth us from all sin.' . . . I have no merit or goodness whereby I may claim salvation, but I present before God the all-atoning blood of the spotless Lamb of God, which taketh away the sin of the world. This is my only plea. The name of Jesus gives me access to the Father. His ear, His heart, is open to my faintest pleading, and He supplies my deepest necessities."

It is the righteousness of Christ that makes the penitent sinner acceptable to God and works his justification. However sinful has been his life, if he believes in Jesus as his personal Saviour, he stands before God in the spotless robes of Christ's imputed righteousness.

The sinner so recently dead in trespasses and sins is quickened by faith in Christ. He sees by faith that Jesus is his Saviour, and alive forevermore, able to save unto the uttermost all that come unto God by Him. In the atonement made for him the believer sees such breadth, and length, and height, and depth of efficiency, sees such completeness of salvation, purchased at such an infinite cost, that his soul is filled with praise and thanksgiving.—*Signs of the Times,* July 4, 1892.

WE ARE COMPLETE IN CHRIST

If we confess our sins, he is faithful and just to forgive us our sins, and to cleanse us from all unrighteousness. 1 John 1:9.

When the sinner has a view of the matchless charms of Jesus, sin no longer looks attractive to him; for he beholds the Chiefest among ten thousand, the One altogether lovely. He realizes by a personal experience the power of the gospel, whose vastness of design is equaled only by its preciousness of purpose.

We have a living Saviour. He is not in Joseph's new tomb; He is risen from the dead and has ascended on high as a substitute and surety for every believing soul. . . . The sinner is justified through the merits of Jesus, and this is God's acknowledgment of the perfection of the ransom paid for man. That Christ was obedient even unto the death of the cross is a pledge of the repenting sinner's acceptance with the Father. Then shall we permit ourselves to have a vacillating experience of doubting and believing, believing and doubting? Jesus is the pledge of our acceptance with God. We stand in favor before God, not because of any merit in ourselves, but because of our faith "in the Lord our righteousness."

Jesus stands in the holy of holies, now to appear in the presence of God for us. There He ceases not to present His people moment by moment, complete in Himself. But because we are thus represented before the Father, we are not to imagine that we are to presume upon His mercy and become careless, indifferent, and self-indulgent. Christ is not the minister of sin. We are complete in Him, accepted in the Beloved, only as we abide in Him by faith.

Perfection through our own good works we can never attain. The soul who sees Jesus by faith repudiates his own righteousness. He sees himself as incomplete, his repentance insufficient, his strongest faith but feebleness, his most costly sacrifice as meager, and he sinks in humility at the foot of the cross. But a voice speaks to him from the oracles of God's Word. In amazement he hears the message, "Ye are complete in him" (Col 2:10). Now all is at rest in his soul. No longer must he strive to find some worthiness in himself, some meritorious deed by which to gain the favor of God.

Beholding the Lamb of God, which taketh away the sin of the world, he finds the peace of Christ; for pardon is written against his name, and he accepts the word of God, "Ye are complete in him." How hard is it for humanity, long accustomed to cherish doubt, to grasp this great truth! But what peace it brings to the soul, what vital life!—*Signs of the Times,* July 4, 1892.

CHRIST'S BLOOD WAS SHED TO REMIT OUR SINS

Since all have sinned and fall short of the glory of God, they are justified by his grace as a gift, through the redemption which is in Christ Jesus. Rom. 3:23, 24, R.S.V.

We need Jesus every moment. To lose His love from our hearts means much. Yet He Himself says: "I have somewhat against thee, because thou hast left thy first love." . . .

The religion of many is very much like an icicle—freezingly cold. The hearts of not a few are still unmelted, unsubdued. They cannot touch the hearts of others, because their own hearts are not surcharged with the blessed love that flows from the heart of Christ. . . .

Genuine religion is based upon a belief in the Scriptures. God's Word is to be believed without question. No part of it is to be cut and carved to fit certain theories. Men are not to exalt human wisdom by sitting in judgment upon God's Word. The Bible was written by holy men of old, as they were moved upon by the Holy Spirit; and this Book contains all that we know for certain and all that we can ever hope to learn in regard to God and Christ, unless, like Paul, we are taken to the third heaven. . . . This revelation to the apostle did not spoil his humility.

The life of a Christian is a life regulated by the Word of God just as it reads. All the truths of the Old and the New Testaments form a complete whole. These truths we are to cherish, believe, and obey. To the true disciple, faith in God's Word is a living, active principle; for "with the heart man believeth unto righteousness; and with the mouth confession is made unto salvation" (Rom. 10:10). By faith man believes that he receives the righteousness of Christ.

Faith, in itself, is an act of the mind. Jesus Himself is the author and the finisher of our faith. He gave His life for us; and His blood speaks in our behalf better things than spoke the blood of Abel, which cried unto God against Cain the murderer. Christ's blood was shed to remit our sins.

Many commit the error of trying to define minutely the fine points of distinction between justification and sanctification. Into the definitions of these two terms they often bring their own ideas and speculations. Why try to be more minute than is Inspiration on the vital question of righteousness by faith?—Manscript 21, 1891.

Those who are united with Christ through the daily, hourly exercise of the faith which works by love and purifies the soul receive the forgiveness of their sins, and are sanctified unto eternal life.—Manscript 12a, 1901.

JUSTIFIED SOULS WALK IN THE LIGHT

God presented him [Christ Jesus] as a sacrifice of atonement, through faith in his blood. . . . He did it to demonstrate his justice at the present time, so as to be just and the one who justifies the man who has faith in Jesus. Rom. 3:25, 26, N.I.V.

"Being justified freely by his grace," the apostle Paul says, "through the redemption that is in Christ Jesus: whom God hath set forth to be a propitiation through faith in his blood, to declare his righteousness for the remission of sins that are past, through the forbearance of God; to declare, I say, at this time his righteousness: that he might be just, and the justifier of him which believeth in Jesus."

Here the truth is laid out in plain lines. This mercy and goodness is wholly undeserved. The grace of Christ is freely to justify the sinner without merit or claim on his part. Justification is a full, complete pardon of sin. The moment a sinner accepts Christ by faith, that moment he is pardoned. The righteousness of Christ is imputed to him, and he is no more to doubt God's forgiving grace.

There is nothing in faith that makes it our saviour. Faith cannot remove our guilt. Christ is the power of God unto salvation to all them that believe. The justification comes through the merits of Jesus Christ. He has paid the price for the sinner's redemption. Yet it is only through faith in His blood that Jesus can justify the believer.

The sinner cannot depend upon his own good works as a means of justification. He must come to the point where he will renounce all his sin, and embrace one degree of light after another, as it shines upon his pathway. He simply grasps by faith the free and ample provision made in the blood of Christ. He believes the promises of God which through Christ are made unto him sanctification and righteousness and redemption.

And if he follows Jesus, he will walk humbly in the light, rejoicing in the light, and diffusing that light to others. Being justified by faith, he carries cheerfulness with him in his obedience in all his life. Peace with God is the result of what Christ is to him. The souls who are in subordination to God, who honor Him, and are doers of His Word, will receive divine enlightenment. In the precious Word of God, there is purity and loftiness as well as beauty that, unless assisted by God, the highest powers of man cannot attain to. . . .

We are none of us excusable, under any form of trial, for letting our hold upon God become loosened. Although the compassion of man may fail, still God loves and pities, and reaches out His helping hand. God's everlasting arms encircle the soul that turns to Him for aid. . . . God loves to have His children ask Him, and trust Him to do for them those things which they cannot do for themselves.—*Signs of the Times,* May 19, 1898.

FAITH WITHOUT WORKS IS DEAD

Was not Abraham our father justified by works, when he had offered Isaac his son upon the altar? Seest thou how faith wrought with his works, and by works was faith made perfect? James 2:21, 22.

We need to have more of Jesus, and far less of self. We need a childlike simplicity that will lead us to tell the Lord all our wants, and believe that according to His riches and goodness and love He will satisfy our needs. "If ye shall ask any thing in my name," He says, "I will do it." If you love Me, you will show that love by keeping My commandments. "And I will pray the Father, and he shall give you another Comforter, that he may abide with you for ever; even the Spirit of truth." . . .

"He that hath my commandments, and keepeth them, he it is that loveth me: and he that loveth me shall be loved of my Father, and I will love him, and will manifest myself to him." This is the only true test of character. In doing the will of God we give the best evidence that we love God and Jesus Christ whom He has sent. The oft-repeated words of love for God are of no value unless that love is made manifest in the life practice. Love for God is not a mere sentiment; it is a living, working power. The man who does the will of his Father who is in heaven shows to the world that he loves God. The fruit of his love is seen in good works. . . .

The apostle James saw that dangers would arise in presenting the subject of justification by faith, and he labored to show that genuine faith cannot exist without corresponding works. The experience of Abraham is presented. "Seest thou," he says, "how faith wrought with his works, and by works was faith made perfect?" This genuine faith does a genuine work in the believer. Faith and obedience bring a solid, valuable experience.

There is a belief that is not a saving faith. The Word declares that the devils believe and tremble. The so-called faith that does not work by love and purify the soul will not justify any man. "Ye see," says the apostle, "how that by works a man is justified, and not by faith only." Abraham believed God. How do we know that he believed? His works testified to the character of his faith, and his faith was accounted to him for righteousness.

We need the faith of Abraham in our day, to lighten the darkness that gathers around us, shutting out the sweet sunlight of God's love, and dwarfing spiritual growth. Our faith should be prolific of good works; for faith without works is dead. Every duty performed, every sacrifice made in the name of Jesus, brings an exceeding great reward. In the very act of duty, God speaks and gives His blessing.—*Signs of the Times,* May 19, 1898.

SANCTIFICATION CONTINUES AS LONG AS LIFE LASTS

For both he that sanctifieth and they who are sanctified are all of one: for which cause he is not ashamed to call them brethren. Heb. 2:11.

While with penitence and humble trust we meditate upon Jesus, whom our sins have pierced and our sorrows have burdened, we may learn to walk in His footsteps. By beholding Him we become changed into His divine likeness. And when this work is wrought in us, we shall claim no righteousness of our own, but shall exalt Jesus Christ, while we hang our helpless souls upon His merits.

Our Saviour ever condemned self-righteousness. He taught His disciples that the highest type of religion is that which manifests itself in a quiet, unobtrusive manner. He cautioned them to perform their deeds of charity quietly; not for display, not to be praised or honored of men, but for the glory of God, expecting their reward hereafter. If they should perform good deeds to be lauded by men, no reward would be given them by their Father in heaven.

The followers of Christ were instructed not to pray for the purpose of being heard of men. ''But thou, when thou prayest, enter into thy closet, and when thou hast shut thy door, pray to thy Father which is in secret, and thy Father which seeth in secret shall reward thee openly'' (Matt. 6:6). Such expressions as this from the lips of Christ show that He did not regard with approval that kind of piety so prevalent among the Pharisees. His teachings upon the mount show that deeds of benevolence assume a noble form and acts of religious worship shed a most precious fragrance when performed in an unpretending manner, in penitence and humility. The pure motive sanctifies the act.

True sanctification is an entire conformity to the will of God. Rebellious thoughts and feelings are overcome, and the voice of Jesus awakens a new life, which pervades the entire being. Those who are truly sanctified will not set up their own opinion as a standard of right and wrong. . . . True sanctification is a daily work, continuing as long as life shall last. Those who are battling with daily temptations, overcoming their own sinful tendencies, and seeking for holiness of heart and life, make no boastful claims of holiness. They are hungering and thirsting for righteousness. Sin appears to them exceedingly sinful. . . .

The truly righteous, who sincerely love and fear God, wear the robe of Christ's righteousness in prosperity and adversity alike.—*The Sanctified Life,* pp. 8-11.

SANCTIFICATION IS THE RESULT OF LIFELONG OBEDIENCE

He that saith he abideth in him ought himself also so to walk, even as he walked. 1 John 2:6.

John was a teacher of holiness, and in his letters to the church he laid down unerring rules for the conduct of Christians. "Every man that hath this hope in him," he wrote, "purifieth himself, even as he is pure" (1 John 3:3). . . . He taught that the Christian must be pure in heart and life. Never should he be satisfied with an empty profession. As God is holy in His sphere, so fallen man, through faith in Christ, is to be holy in his sphere. . . .

The sanctification of the church is God's object in all His dealings with His people. He has chosen them from eternity, that they might be holy. He gave His Son to die for them, that they might be sanctified through obedience to the truth, divested of all the littleness of self. From them He requires a personal work, a personal surrender. God can be honored by those who profess to believe in Him, only as they are conformed to His image and controlled by His Spirit. Then, as witnesses for the Saviour, they may make known what divine grace has done for them.

True sanctification comes through the working out of the principle of love. "God is love; and he that dwelleth in love dwelleth in God, and God in him" (chap. 4:16). The life of him in whose heart Christ abides, will reveal practical godliness. The character will be purified, elevated, ennobled, and glorified. Pure doctrine will blend with works of righteousness; heavenly precepts will mingle with holy practices. . . .

It is the fragrance of our love for our fellow men that reveals our love for God. It is patience in service that brings rest to the soul. It is through humble, diligent, faithful toil that the welfare of Israel is promoted. God upholds and strengthens the one who is willing to follow in Christ's way.

[Sanctification] is not gained by a happy flight of feeling, but is the result of constantly dying to sin, and constantly living for Christ. Wrongs cannot be righted nor reformations wrought in the character by feeble, intermittent efforts. It is only by long, persevering effort, sore discipline, and stern conflict, that we shall overcome. We know not one day how strong will be our conflict the next. So long as Satan reigns, we shall have self to subdue, besetting sins to overcome; so long as life shall last, there will be no stopping place, no point which we can reach and say, I have fully attained. Sanctification is the result of lifelong obedience.—*The Acts of the Apostles,* pp. 559-561.

MORE ATTENTION TO "THE FAITH OF JESUS"

Without controversy great is the mystery of godliness: God was manifest in the flesh, justified in the Spirit, seen of angels, preached unto the Gentiles, believed on in the world, received up into glory. 1 Tim. 3:16.

Many people seem to be ignorant of what constitutes faith. Many complain of darkness and discouragements. I asked, Are your faces turned toward Jesus? Are you beholding Him, the Sun of Righteousness? You need plainly to define to the churches the matter of faith and entire dependence upon the righteousness of Christ. . . . There has been so little dwelling upon Christ, His matchless love, His great sacrifice made in our behalf, that Satan has nearly eclipsed the views we should have and must have of Jesus Christ. We must trust less in human beings for spiritual help and more, far more, in approaching Jesus Christ as our Redeemer.

We may dwell with a determined purpose on the heavenly attributes of Jesus Christ; we may talk of His love, we may tell and sing of His mercies, we may make Him our own personal Saviour. Then we are one with Christ. We love that which Christ loved, we hate sin, that which Christ hated. These things must be talked of, dwelt upon. . . .

We are to keep before the mind the sin-pardoning Saviour. But we are to present Him in His true position—coming to die to magnify the law of God and make it honorable, and yet to justify the sinner who shall depend wholly upon the merits of the blood of a crucified and risen Saviour. . . .

The soul-saving message, the third angel's message, is the message to be given to the world. The commandments of God and the faith of Jesus are both important, immensely important, and must be given with equal force and power. The first part of the message has been dwelt upon mostly, the last part casually. The faith of Jesus is not comprehended. We must talk it, we must live it, we must pray it, and educate the people to bring this part of the message into their home life. . . .

Why are our lips so silent upon the subject of Christ's righteousness and His love for the world? Why do we not give to the people that which will revive and quicken them into a new life? The apostle Paul is filled with transport and adoration as he declares, "Without controversy great is the mystery of godliness: God was manifest in the flesh, justified in the Spirit, seen of angels, preached unto the Gentiles, believed on in the world, received up into glory.". . .

The character of Christ is an infinitely perfect character, and He must be lifted up, He must be brought prominently into view, for He is the power, the might, the sanctification and righteousness of all who believe in Him.—Manuscript 27, 1889.

TESTING TIME REVEALS FAITH AND LOVE

The foundation of God standeth sure, having this seal, The Lord knoweth them that are his. 2 Tim. 2:19.

Self-denial, self-sacrifice, benevolence, kindness, love, patience, fortitude, and Christian trust are the daily fruits borne by those who are truly connected with God. Their acts may not be published to the world, but they themselves are daily wrestling with evil, and gaining precious victories over temptation and wrong. Solemn vows are renewed, and kept through the strength gained by earnest prayer and constant watching thereunto.

The ardent enthusiast does not discern the struggles of these silent workers; but the eye of Him who seeth the secrets of the heart notices and regards with approval every effort put forth in lowliness and meekness. It requires the testing time to reveal the pure gold of love and faith in the character. When trials and perplexities come upon the church, then the steadfast zeal and warm affections of Christ's true followers are developed. . . .

The humble in heart, who have daily felt the importance of riveting their souls to the eternal Rock, will stand unmoved amid the tempests of trial, because they trusted not to themselves. . . .

A healthy man, who is able to attend to the vocations of life and goes forth day after day to his labor with buoyant spirits and with a healthy current of blood flowing through his veins, does not call the attention of everyone he meets to his soundness of body. Health and vigor are the natural conditions of his life, and therefore he is scarcely conscious that he is in the enjoyment of so rich a boon.

Thus it is with the truly righteous man. He is unconscious of his goodness and piety. Religious principle has become the spring of his life and conduct, and it is just as natural for him to bear the fruits of the Spirit as for the fig tree to bear figs or for the rosebush to yield roses. His nature is so thoroughly imbued with love for God and his fellow men that he works the works of Christ with a willing heart.

All who come within the sphere of his influence perceive the beauty and fragrance of his Christian life, while he himself is unconscious of it, for it is in harmony with his habits and inclinations. He prays for divine light, and loves to walk in that light. It is his meat and drink to do the will of his heavenly Father. His life is hid with Christ in God.—*The Sanctified Life*, pp. 11-13.

SANCTIFICATION EMBRACES THE ENTIRE BEING

And the very God of peace sanctify you wholly; and I pray God your whole spirit and soul and body be preserved blameless unto the coming of our Lord Jesus Christ. 1 Thess. 5:23.

The sanctification set forth in the Scriptures embraces the entire being—spirit, soul, and body. Paul prayed for the Thessalonians that their "whole spirit and soul and body be preserved blameless unto the coming of our Lord Jesus Christ." Again he writes to believers: "I beseech you therefore, brethren, by the mercies of God, that ye present your bodies a living sacrifice, holy, acceptable unto God" (Rom. 12:1).

In the time of ancient Israel, every offering brought as a sacrifice to God was carefully examined. If any defect was discovered in the animal presented, it was refused; for God had commanded that the offering be "without blemish." So Christians are bidden to present their bodies, "a living sacrifice, holy, acceptable unto God."

In order to do this, all their powers must be preserved in the best possible condition. Every practice that weakens physical or mental strength unfits man for the service of his Creator. And will God be pleased with anything less than the best we can offer? Said Christ: "Thou shalt love the Lord thy God with all thy heart."

Those who do love God with all the heart will desire to give Him the best service of their life, and they will be constantly seeking to bring every power of their being into harmony with the laws that will promote their ability to do His will. They will not, by the indulgence of appetite or passion, enfeeble or defile the offering which they present to their heavenly Father.

Peter says: "Abstain from fleshly lusts, which war against the soul" (1 Peter 2:11). Every sinful gratification tends to benumb the faculties and deaden the mental and spiritual perceptions, and the Word or the Spirit of God can make but a feeble impression upon the heart. Paul writes to the Corinthians: "Let us cleanse ourselves from all filthiness of the flesh and spirit, perfecting holiness in the fear of God" (2 Cor. 7:1). And with the fruits of the Spirit—"love, joy, peace, longsuffering, gentleness, goodness, faith, meekness"—he classes "temperance" (Gal. 5:22, 23).

Notwithstanding these inspired declarations, how many professed Christians are enfeebling their powers in the pursuit of gain or the worship of fashion; how many are debasing their godlike manhood by gluttony, by wine drinking, by forbidden pleasure. . . . He whose body is the temple of the Holy Spirit will not be enslaved by a pernicious habit. His powers belong to Christ, who has bought him with the price of blood.—*The Great Controversy,* pp. 473-475.

DANIEL STANDS FIRM WHATEVER THE RESULT

Then the king ordered Ashpenaz . . . to bring in some of the Israelites from the royal family and the nobility—young men without any physical defect, handsome, showing aptitude for every kind of learning, well informed, quick to understand, and qualified to serve in the king's palace. Daniel 1:3, 4, N.I.V.

The prophet Daniel was an illustrious character. He was a bright example of what men may become when united with the God of wisdom. A brief account of the life of this holy man of God is left on record for the encouragement of those who should afterward be called to endure trial and temptation.

When the people of Israel, their king, nobles, and priests were carried into captivity, four of their number were selected to serve in the court of the king of Babylon. One of these was Daniel, who early gave promise of the remarkable ability developed in later years. These youth were all of princely birth, and are described as "children in whom was no blemish, but well favoured, and skilful in all wisdom, and cunning in knowledge, and understanding science, and such as had ability in them" (Dan. 1:4).

Perceiving the superior talents of these youthful captives, King Nebuchadnezzar determined to prepare them to fill important positions in his kingdom. That they might be fully qualified for their life at court, according to Oriental custom, they were to be taught the language of the Chaldeans, and to be subjected for three years to a thorough course of physical and intellectual discipline.

The youth in this school of training were not only to be admitted to the royal palace, but it was provided that they should eat of the meat and drink of the wine which came from the king's table. . . .

Among the viands placed before the king were swine's flesh and other meats which were declared unclean by the law of Moses, and which the Hebrews had been expressly forbidden to eat. Here Daniel was brought to a severe test. Should he adhere to the teachings of his fathers concerning meats and drinks, and offend the king, and probably lose not only his position but his life? or should he disregard the commandment of the Lord and retain the favor of the king, thus securing great intellectual advantages and the most flattering worldly prospects?

Daniel did not long hesitate. He decided to stand firm in his integrity, let the result be what it might. He "purposed in his heart that he would not defile himself with the portion of the king's meat, nor with the wine which he drank" (verse 8). . . . He made God his strength, and the fear of God was continually before him in all the transactions of his life.—*The Sanctified Life*, pp. 18-20.

DANIEL'S LIFE ILLUSTRATES SANCTIFICATION

So Daniel said to the steward whom the chief of the eunuchs had set over Daniel, Hananiah, Mishael, and Azariah, "Please test your servants for ten days, and let them give us vegetables to eat and water to drink." Dan. 1:11, 12, N.K.J.V.

Daniel might have found a plausible excuse to depart from his strictly temperate habits; but the approval of God was dearer to him than the favor of the most powerful earthly potentate—dearer even than life itself. . . .

Daniel requested that the matter be decided by a ten days' trial—the Hebrew youth during this brief period being permitted to eat of simple food, while their companions partook of the king's dainties. . . . The Lord regarded with approval the firmness and self-denial of the Hebrew youth, and His blessing attended them. . . .

The life of Daniel is an inspired illustration of what constitutes a sanctified character. It presents a lesson for all, and especially for the young. A strict compliance with the requirements of God is beneficial to the health of body and mind. In order to reach the highest standard of moral and intellectual attainments, it is necessary to seek wisdom and strength from God and to observe strict temperance in all the habits of life.

In the experience of Daniel and his companions we have an instance of the triumph of principle over temptation to indulge the appetite. It shows us that through religious principle young men may triumph over the lusts of the flesh and remain true to God's requirements, even though it cost them a great sacrifice.

What if Daniel and his companions had made a compromise with those heathen officers and had yielded to the pressure of the occasion by eating and drinking as was customary with the Babylonians? That single instance of departure from principle would have weakened their sense of right and their abhorrence of wrong. Indulgence of appetite would have involved the sacrifice of physical vigor, clearness of intellect, and spiritual power. One wrong step would probably have led to others, until, their connection with Heaven being severed, they would have been swept away by temptation.

God has said, "Them that honour me I will honour" (1 Sam. 2:30). While Daniel clung to his God with unwavering trust, the Spirit of prophetic power came upon him. While he was instructed of man in the duties of court life, he was taught of God to read the mysteries of future ages and to present to coming generations, through figures and similitudes, the wonderful things that would come to pass in the last days.—*The Sanctified Life,* pp. 21-24.

IN THE PRESENCE OF THE INFINITE

Lo, I see four men loose, walking in the midst of the fire, and they have no hurt; and the form of the fourth is like the Son of God. Dan. 3:25.

The fiery furnace had been heated seven times more than it was wont, and into it were cast the Hebrew exiles. So furious were the flames, that the men who cast them in were burned to death.

Suddenly the countenance of the king paled with terror. His eyes were fixed upon the glowing flames, and turning to his lords, he said, "Did not we cast three men bound into the midst of the fire?" (Dan. 3:24). The answer was, "True, O king." And now the monarch exclaimed, "Lo, I see four men loose, walking in the midst of the fire, and they have no hurt; and the form of the fourth is like the Son of God" (verse 25).

When Christ manifests Himself to the children of men, an unseen power speaks to their souls. They feel themselves to be in the presence of the Infinite One. Before His majesty, kings and nobles tremble, and acknowledge that the living God is above every earthly power.

With feelings of remorse and shame, the king exclaimed, "Ye servants of the most high God, come forth" (verse 26). And they obeyed, showing themselves unhurt before that vast multitude, not even the smell of the fire being upon their garments. This miracle produced a striking change in the minds of the people. The great golden image, set up with such display, was forgotten. The king published a decree that anyone speaking against the God of these men should be put to death, "because there is no other God that can deliver after this sort" (verse 29).

These three Hebrews possessed genuine sanctification. True Christian principle will not stop to weigh the consequences. It does not ask, What will people think of me if I do this? or, How will it affect my worldly prospects if I do that? With the most intense longing the children of God desire to know what He would have them do, that their works may glorify Him. The Lord has made ample provision that the hearts and lives of all His followers may be controlled by divine grace, that they may be as burning and shining lights in the world.

These faithful Hebrews possessed great natural ability, they had enjoyed the highest intellectual culture, and now occupied a position of honor; but all this did not lead them to forget God. Their powers were yielded to the sanctifying influence of divine grace. By their steadfast integrity they showed forth the praises of Him who had called them out of darkness into His marvelous light.—*The Sanctified Life*, pp. 38-40.

THREE HEBREWS DISPLAY THE POWER OF GOD

Then Nebuchadnezzar spake, and said, Blessed be the God of Shadrach, Meshach, and Abednego, who hath sent his angel, and delivered his servants that trusted in him. Dan. 3:28.

In their wonderful deliverance were displayed, before that vast assembly, the power and majesty of God. Jesus placed Himself by their side in the fiery furnace, and by the glory of His presence convinced the proud king of Babylon that it could be no other than the Son of God. The light of Heaven had been shining forth from Daniel and his companions, until all their associates understood the faith which ennobled their lives and beautified their characters. By the deliverance of His faithful servants, the Lord declares that He will take His stand with the oppressed and overthrow all earthly powers that would trample upon the authority of the God of heaven.

What a lesson is here given to the fainthearted, the vacillating, the cowardly in the cause of God! What encouragement to those who will not be turned aside from duty by threats or peril! These faithful, steadfast characters exemplify sanctification, while they have no thought of claiming the high honor. The amount of good which may be accomplished by comparatively obscure but devoted Christians cannot be estimated until the life records shall be made known, when the judgment shall sit and the books be opened.

Christ identifies His interest with this class; He is not ashamed to call them brethren. There should be hundreds where there is now one among us, so closely allied to God, their lives in such close conformity to His will, that they would be bright and shining lights, sanctified wholly, in soul, body, and spirit.

The conflict still goes on between the children of light and the children of darkness. Those who name the name of Christ should shake off the lethargy that enfeebles their efforts, and should meet the momentous responsibilities that devolve upon them. All who do this may expect the power of God to be revealed in them. The Son of God, the world's Redeemer, will be represented in their words and in their works, and God's name will be glorified.—*The Sanctified Life,* pp. 40-41.

As in the days of Shadrach, Meshach, and Abednego, so in the closing period of earth's history the Lord will work mightily in behalf of those who stand steadfastly for the right. He who walked with the Hebrew worthies in the fiery furnace will be with His followers wherever they are. . . . His chosen ones will stand unmoved.—*Prophets and Kings,* p. 513.

HOW THE KING RECOGNIZED THE SON OF GOD

Ye servants of the most high God, come forth, and come hither. Dan. 3:26.

How did that heathen king know what the Son of God was like? The Hebrew captives filling positions of trust in Babylon had in life and character represented before him the truth. When asked for a reason of their faith, they had given it without hesitation. Plainly and simply they had presented the principles of righteousness, thus teaching those around them of God whom they worshiped. They had told of Christ, the Redeemer to come; and in the form of the fourth in the midst of the fire the king recognized the Son of God. . . .

Then Shadrach, Meshach, and Abednego came forth before the vast multitude, showing themselves unhurt. The presence of their Saviour had guarded them from harm, and only their fetters had been burned. "And the princes, governors, and captains, and the king's counsellors, being gathered together, saw these men, upon whose bodies the fire had no power, nor was an hair of their head singed, neither were their coats changed, nor the smell of fire had passed on them." . . .

The experiences of that day led Nebuchadnezzar to issue a decree, "That every people, nation, and language, which speak any thing amiss against the God of Shadrach, Meshach, and Abednego, shall be cut in pieces, and their houses shall be made a dunghill." "There is no other God," he urged as the reason for the decree, "that can deliver after this sort."

In these and like words the king of Babylon endeavored to spread abroad before all the peoples of earth his conviction that the power and authority of the God of the Hebrews was worthy of supreme adoration. And God was pleased with the effort of the king to show Him reverence, and to make the royal confession of allegiance as widespread as was the Babylonian realm.

It was right for the king to make public confession, and to seek to exalt the God of heaven above all other gods; but in endeavoring to force his subjects to make a similar confession of faith and to show similar reverence, Nebuchadnezzar was exceeding his right as a temporal sovereign. He had no more right, either civil or moral, to threaten men with death for not worshiping God, than he had to make a decree consigning to the flames all who refused to worship the golden image. God never compels the obedience of man. He leaves all free to choose whom they will serve.—*Prophets and Kings, pp. 509-511.*

GOD ANSWERS DANIEL'S FERVENT PRAYER

O Daniel, a man greatly beloved, . . . for unto thee am I now sent . . . for from the first day that thou didst set thine heart to understand . . . thy words were heard, and I am come for thy words. Dan. 10:11, 12.

"I Daniel alone saw the vision. . . . And there remained no strength in me: for my comeliness was turned in me into corruption" (Dan. 10:7, 8). . . . All who are truly sanctified will have a similar experience. The clearer their views of the greatness, glory, and perfection of Christ, the more vividly will they see their own weakness and imperfection. They will have no disposition to claim a sinless character; that which has appeared right and comely in themselves will, in contrast with Christ's purity and glory, appear only as unworthy and corruptible. It is when men are separated from God, when they have very indistinct views of Christ, that they say, "I am sinless; I am sanctified."

Gabriel now appeared to the prophet, and thus addressed him: "O Daniel, a man greatly beloved, understand the words that I speak unto thee" (verse 11). . . . . What great honor is shown to Daniel by the Majesty of heaven! He comforts His trembling servant and assures him that his prayer has been heard in heaven. In answer to that fervent petition the angel Gabriel was sent to affect the heart of the Persian king. The monarch had resisted the impressions of the Spirit of God during the three weeks while Daniel was fasting and praying, but heaven's Prince, the Archangel, Michael, was sent to turn the heart of the stubborn king to take some decided action to answer the prayer of Daniel.

"And when he had spoken such words unto me, I set my face toward the ground, and I became dumb. And, behold, one like the similitude of the sons of men touched my lips. . . . And said, O man greatly beloved, fear not: peace be unto thee, be strong, yea, be strong. And when he had spoken unto me, I was strengthened, and said, Let my lord speak; for thou hast strengthened me" (verses 15-19).

So great was the divine glory revealed to Daniel that he could not endure the sight. Then the messenger of heaven veiled the brightness of his presence and appeared to the prophet as "one like the similitude of the sons of men" (verse 16). By his divine power he strengthened this man of integrity and of faith, to hear the message sent to him from God.

Daniel was a devoted servant of the Most High. His long life was filled up with noble deeds of service for his Master. His purity of character and unwavering fidelity are equaled only by his humility of heart and his contrition before God. We repeat, the life of Daniel is an inspired illustration of true sanctification.—*The Sanctified Life,* pp. 50-52.

THE TRULY SANCTIFIED FEEL UNWORTHY

We do not present our supplications before thee for our righteousnesses, but for thy great mercies. Dan. 9:18.

Those who experience the sanctification of the Bible will manifest a spirit of humility. Like Moses, they have had a view of the awful majesty of holiness, and they see their own unworthiness in contrast with the purity and exalted perfection of the Infinite One.

The prophet Daniel was an example of true sanctification. His long life was filled with noble service for his Master. He was a man "greatly beloved" (Dan. 10:11) of Heaven. Yet instead of claiming to be pure and holy, this honored prophet identified himself with the really sinful of Israel as he pleaded before God in behalf of his people: "We do not present our supplications before thee for our righteousnesses, but for thy great mercies." "We have sinned, we have done wickedly" (chap. 9:18, 15). . . .

When Job heard the voice of the Lord out of the whirlwind, he exclaimed: "I abhor myself, and repent in dust and ashes" (Job 42:6). It was when Isaiah saw the glory of the Lord, and heard the cherubim crying, "Holy, holy, holy, is the Lord of hosts," that he cried out, "Woe is me! for I am undone" (Isa. 6:3, 5). Paul, after he was caught up into the third heaven and heard things which it was not possible for a man to utter, speaks of himself as "less than the least of all saints" (2 Cor. 12:2-4, margin; Eph. 3:8). . . .

There can be no self-exaltation, no boastful claim to freedom from sin, on the part of those who walk in the shadow of Calvary's cross. They feel that it was their sin which caused the agony that broke the heart of the Son of God, and this thought will lead them to self-abasement. Those who live nearest to Jesus discern most clearly the frailty and sinfulness of humanity, and their only hope is in the merit of a crucified and risen Saviour.

The sanctification now gaining prominence in the religious world carries with it a spirit of self-exaltation and a disregard for the law of God that mark it as foreign to the religion of the Bible. Its advocates teach that sanctification is an instantaneous work, by which, through faith alone, they attain to perfect holiness. "Only believe," say they, "and the blessing is yours." . . . At the same time they deny the authority of the law of God, urging that they are released from obligation to keep the commandments. But is it possible for men to be holy, in accord with the will and character of God, without coming into harmony with the principles which are an expression of His nature and will, and which show what is well pleasing to Him?—*The Great Controversy,* pp. 470, 471.

LOVE WAS THAT OF A REPENTANT SINNER

Beloved, let us love one another: for love is of God; and every one that loveth is born of God, and knoweth God. 1 John 4:7.

The apostle John was distinguished above his brethren as "the disciple whom Jesus loved." While not in the slightest degree cowardly, weak, or vacillating in character, he possessed an amiable disposition and a warm, loving heart. He seemed to have enjoyed, in a preeminent sense, the friendship of Christ, and he received many tokens of the Saviour's confidence and love. He was one of the three permitted to witness Christ's glory upon the mount of transfiguration and His agony in Gethsemane; and to the care of John our Lord confided His mother in those last hours of anguish upon the cross.

The Saviour's affection for the beloved disciple was returned with all the strength of ardent devotion. John clung to Christ as the vine clings to the stately pillar. For his Master's sake he braved the dangers of the judgment hall and lingered about the cross; and at the tidings that Christ had risen, he hastened to the sepulcher, in his zeal outstripping even the impetuous Peter.

John's love for his Master was not a mere human friendship, but it was the love of a repentant sinner, who felt that he had been redeemed by the precious blood of Christ. He esteemed it the highest honor to work and suffer in the service of his Lord. His love for Jesus led him to love all for whom Christ died. His religion was of a practical character. He reasoned that love to God would be manifested in love to His children. "We love him, because he first loved us. If a man say, I love God, and hateth his brother, he is a liar: for he that loveth not his brother whom he hath seen, how can he love God whom he hath not seen?" (1 John 4:19, 20). The apostle's life was in harmony with his teachings.

The love which glowed in his heart for Christ, led him to put forth the most earnest, untiring labor for his fellow men, especially for his brethren in the Christian church. . . .

John desired to become like Jesus, and under the transforming influence of the love of Christ, he became meek and lowly of heart. Self was hid in Jesus. He was closely united to the Living Vine, and thus became a partaker of the divine nature. Such will ever be the result of communion with Christ. This is true sanctification.—*The Sanctified Life,* pp. 53-55.

JOHN LEARNED WELL THE LESSONS JESUS TAUGHT

The Son of man is not come to destroy men's lives, but to save them. Luke 9:56.

Upon one occasion Christ sent messengers before Him unto a village of the Samaritans, requesting the people to prepare refreshments for Himself and His disciples. But when the Saviour approached the town, He appeared to be passing on toward Jerusalem. This aroused the enmity of the Samaritans, and instead of sending messengers to invite and even urge Him to tarry with them, they withheld the courtesies which they would have given to a common wayfarer. Jesus never urges His presence upon any, and the Samaritans lost the blessing which would have been granted them had they solicited Him to be their guest.

We may wonder at this uncourteous treatment of the Majesty of heaven, but how frequently are we who profess to be followers of Christ guilty of similar neglect. Do we urge Jesus to take up His abode in our hearts and in our homes? He is full of love, of grace, of blessing, and stands ready to bestow these gifts upon us; but, like the Samaritans, we are often content without them.

The disciples were aware of the purpose of Christ to bless the Samaritans with His presence; and when they saw the coldness, jealousy, and disrespect shown to their Master, they were filled with surprise and indignation. James and John were especially stirred. That He whom they so highly reverenced should be thus treated seemed to them a crime too great to be passed over without immediate punishment. In their zeal they said, "Lord, wilt thou that we command fire to come down from heaven, and consume them, even as Elias did?" (Luke 9:54). . . .

Jesus rebuked His disciples, saying, "Ye know not what manner of spirit ye are of. For the Son of man is not come to destroy men's lives, but to save them" (verses 55, 56). John and his fellow disciples were in a school in which Christ was teacher. Those who were ready to see their own defects, and were anxious to improve in character, had ample opportunity. John treasured every lesson and constantly sought to bring his life into harmony with the Divine Pattern.

The lessons of Jesus, setting forth meekness, humility, and love as essential to growth in grace, and a fitness for his work, were of the highest value to John. These lessons are addressed to us as individuals and as brethren in the church, as well as to the first disciples of Christ.—*The Sanctified Life,* pp. 57-59.

THE CONTRAST BETWEEN JOHN AND JUDAS

He that hath the Son hath life; and he that hath not the Son of God hath not life. 1 John 5:12.

During the years of his close association with Christ, he [John] was often warned and cautioned by the Saviour; and these reproofs he accepted. As the character of the Divine One was manifested to him, John saw his own deficiencies, and was humbled by the revelation. Day by day, in contrast with his own violent spirit, he beheld the tenderness and forbearance of Jesus, and heard His lessons of humility and patience. Day by day his heart was drawn out to Christ, until he lost sight of self in love for his Master. The power and tenderness, the majesty and meekness, the strength and patience, that he saw in the daily life of the Son of God, filled his soul with admiration. He yielded his resentful, ambitious temper to the molding power of Christ, and divine love wrought in him a transformation of character.

In striking contrast to the sanctification worked out in the life of John is the experience of his fellow disciple, Judas. Like his associate, Judas professed to be a disciple of Christ, but he possessed only a form of godliness. He was not insensible to the beauty of the character of Christ; and often, as he listened to the Saviour's words, conviction came to him, but he would not humble his heart or confess his sins. . . .

John warred earnestly against his faults; but Judas violated his conscience and yielded to temptation, fastening upon himself more securely his habits of evil. The practice of the truths that Christ taught was at variance with his desires and purposes, and he could not bring himself to yield his ideas in order to receive wisdom from heaven. Instead of walking in the light, he chose to walk in darkness. Evil desires, covetousness, revengeful passions, dark and sullen thoughts, were cherished until Satan gained full control of him.

John and Judas are representatives of those who profess to be Christ's followers. Both these disciples had the same opportunities to study and follow the divine Pattern. . . . Each possessed serious defects of character; and each had access to the divine grace that transforms character. But while one in humility was learning of Jesus, the other revealed that he was not a doer of the word, but a hearer only. One, daily dying to self and overcoming sin, was sanctified through the truth; the other, resisting the transforming power of grace and indulging selfish desires, was brought into bondage to Satan. . . .

There may be marked defects in the character of an individual, yet when he becomes a true disciple of Christ, the power of divine grace transforms and sanctifies him.—*The Acts of the Apostles,* pp. 557-559.

AMAZED AT GOD'S LOVE

I was in the Spirit on the Lord's day. Rev. 1:10.

The Lord's day mentioned by John was the Sabbath, the day on which Jehovah rested after the great work of creation, and which He blessed and sanctified because He had rested upon it. The Sabbath was as sacredly observed by John upon the Isle of Patmos as when he was among the people, preaching upon that day. By the barren rocks surrounding him, John was reminded of rocky Horeb, and how, when God spoke His law to the people there, He said, "Remember the sabbath day, to keep it holy" (Ex. 20:8).

The Son of God spoke to Moses from the mountaintop. God made the rocks His sanctuary. His temple was the everlasting hills. The Divine Legislator descended upon the rocky mountain to speak His law in the hearing of all the people, that they might be impressed by the grand and awful exhibition of His power and glory, and fear to transgress His commandments. God spoke His law amid thunders and lightnings and the thick cloud upon the top of the mountain, and His voice was as the voice of a trumpet exceeding loud. The law of Jehovah was unchangeable, and the tablets upon which He wrote that law were solid rock, signifying the immutability of His precepts. Rocky Horeb became a sacred place to all who loved and revered the law of God.

While John was contemplating the scenes of Horeb, the Spirit of Him who sanctified the seventh day came upon him. He contemplated the sin of Adam in transgressing the divine law, and the fearful result of that transgression. The infinite love of God, in giving His Son to redeem a lost race, seemed too great for language to express. As he presents it in his epistle he calls upon the church and the world to behold it. "Behold, what manner of love the Father hath bestowed upon us, that we should be called the sons of God: therefore the world knoweth us not, because it knew him not" (1 John 3:1).

It was a mystery to John that God could give His Son to die for rebellious man. And he was lost in amazement that the plan of salvation, devised at such a cost to Heaven, should be refused by those for whom the infinite sacrifice had been made. . . .

It is no light matter to sin against God, to set the perverse will of man in opposition to the will of his Maker. It is for the best interest of men, even in this world, to obey God's commandments. And it is surely for their eternal interest to submit to God, and be at peace with Him. . . . God made him a free moral agent, to obey or disobey. The reward of everlasting life—an eternal weight of glory—is promised to those who do God's will.—*The Sanctified Life,* pp. 74-76.

LOVE IS SHOWN BY WILLING OBEDIENCE

If ye be willing and obedient, ye shall eat the good of the land. Isa. 1:19.

The character of the Christian is shown by his daily life. Said Christ, "Every good tree bringeth forth good fruit; but a corrupt tree bringeth forth evil fruit" (Matt. 7:17). Our Saviour compares Himself to a vine, of which His followers are the branches. He plainly declares that all who would be His disciples must bring forth fruit; and then He shows how they may become fruitful branches. "Abide in me, and I in you. As the branch cannot bear fruit of itself, except it abide in the vine; no more can ye, except ye abide in me" (John 15:4).

The apostle Paul describes the fruit which the Christian is to bear. He says that it "is in all goodness and righteousness and truth" (Eph. 5:9). And again, "The fruit of the Spirit is love, joy, peace, longsuffering, gentleness, goodness, faith, meekness, temperance" (Gal. 5:22, 23) These precious graces are but the principles of God's law carried out in the life.

The law of God is the only true standard of moral perfection. That law was practically exemplified in the life of Christ. He says of Himself, "I have kept my Father's commandments" (John 15:10). Nothing short of this obedience will meet the requirements of God's Word. "He that saith he abideth in him ought himself also so to walk, even as he walked" (1 John 2:6). We cannot plead that we are unable to do this, for we have the assurance, "My grace is sufficient for thee" (2 Cor. 12:9). As we look into the divine mirror, the law of God, we see the exceeding sinfulness of sin, and our own lost condition as transgressors. But by repentance and faith we are justified before God, and through divine grace enabled to render obedience to His commandments.

Those who have genuine love for God will manifest an earnest desire to know His will and to do it. . . . The child who loves his parents will show that love by willing obedience; but the selfish, ungrateful child seeks to do as little as possible for his parents, while he at the same time desires to enjoy all the privileges granted to the obedient and faithful.

The same difference is seen among those who profess to be children of God. Many who know that they are the objects of His love and care, and who desire to receive His blessing, take no delight in doing His will. They regard God's claims upon them as an unpleasant restraint, His commandments as a grievous yoke. But he who is truly seeking for holiness of heart and life delights in the law of God, and mourns only that he falls so far short of meeting its requirements.—*The Sanctified Life,* pp. 80, 81.

SANCTIFIED BY FAITH AND OBEDIENCE

Herein is my Father glorified, that ye bear much fruit; so shall ye be my disciples. John 15:8.

Many shrink from such a life as our Saviour lived. They feel that it requires too great a sacrifice to imitate the Pattern, to bring forth fruit in good works, and then patiently endure the pruning of God that they may bring forth more fruit. But when the Christian regards himself as only a humble instrument in the hands of Christ, and endeavors to faithfully perform every duty, relying upon the help which God has promised, then he will wear the yoke of Christ and find it easy; then he will bear burdens for Christ, and pronounce them light. He can look up with courage and with confidence, and say, "I know whom I have believed, and am persuaded that he is able to keep that which I have committed unto him" (2 Tim. 1:12).

If we meet obstacles in our path, and faithfully overcome them; if we encounter opposition and reproach, and in Christ's name gain the victory; if we bear responsibilities and discharge our duties in the spirit of our Master—then, indeed, we gain a precious knowledge of His faithfulness and power. We no longer depend upon the experience of others, for we have the witness in ourselves. Like the Samaritans of old, we can say, "We have heard him ourselves, and know that this is indeed the Christ, the Saviour of the world" (John 4:42).

The more we contemplate the character of Christ, and the more we experience of His saving power, the more keenly shall we realize our own weakness and imperfection, and the more earnestly shall we look to Him as our strength and our Redeemer. . . . By faith in Christ and obedience to the law of God we may be sanctified, and thus obtain a fitness for the society of holy angels and the white-robed redeemed ones in the kingdom of glory.

It is not only the privilege but the duty of every Christian to maintain a close union with Christ and to have a rich experience in the things of God. Then his life will be fruitful in good works. . . .

When we read the lives of men who have been eminent for their piety we often regard their experiences and attainments as far beyond our reach. But this is not the case. Christ died for all; and we are assured in His Word that He is more willing to give His Holy Spirit to them that ask than are earthly parents to give good gifts to their children.

The prophets and apostles did not perfect Christian character by a miracle. They used the means which God had placed within their reach; and all who will put forth the same effort will secure the same results.—*The Sanctified Life,* pp. 82-84.

PAUL EMPHASIZES SANCTIFICATION

Ye know what commandments we gave you by the Lord Jesus. For this is the will of God, even your sanctification. 1 Thess. 4:2, 3.

In his letter to the church at Ephesus, Paul sets before them the "mystery of the gospel" (Eph. 6:19), the "unsearchable riches of Christ" (chap. 3:8), and then assures them of his earnest prayers for their spiritual prosperity:

"I bow my knees unto the Father of our Lord Jesus Christ, . . . that he would grant you, according to the riches of his glory, to be strengthened with might by his Spirit in the inner man; that Christ may dwell in your hearts by faith; that ye, being rooted and grounded in love, may be able to comprehend with all saints what is the breadth, and length, and depth, and height; and to know the love of Christ, which passeth knowledge, that ye might be filled with all the fulness of God" (verses 14-19).

He writes to his Corinthian brethren also, "to them that are sanctified in Christ Jesus . . . : Grace be unto you, and peace, from God our Father, and from the Lord Jesus Christ. I thank my God always on your behalf, for the grace of God which is given you by Jesus Christ; that in every thing ye are enriched by him, in all utterance, and in all knowledge; even as the testimony of Christ was confirmed in you: so that ye come behind in no gift; waiting for the coming of our Lord Jesus Christ" (1 Cor. 1:2-7).

These words are addressed not only to the church at Corinth but to all the people of God to the close of time. Every Christian may enjoy the blessing of sanctification.

The apostle continues in these words: "Now I beseech you, brethren, by the name of our Lord Jesus Christ, that ye all speak the same thing, and that there be no divisions among you; but that ye be perfectly joined together in the same mind and in the same judgment" (verse 10). Paul would not have appealed to them to do that which was impossible. Unity is the sure result of Christian perfection. . . .

The apostle himself was endeavoring to reach the same standard of holiness which he set before his brethren. . . . Paul did not hesitate to enforce, upon every suitable occasion, the importance of Bible sanctification. He says: "Ye know what commandments we gave you by the Lord Jesus. For this is the will of God, even your sanctification" (1 Thess. 4:2, 3).

"Wherefore, my beloved, as ye have always obeyed, not as in my presence only, but now much more in my absence, work out your own salvation with fear and trembling. . . . Do all things without murmurings and disputings: that ye may be blameless and harmless, the sons of God, without rebuke, in the midst of a crooked and perverse nation, among whom ye shine as lights in the world" (Phil. 2:12-15).—*The Sanctified Life,* pp. 84-87.

BEHOLDING JESUS WITH THE EYE OF FAITH

Thanks be to God, which giveth us the victory through our Lord Jesus Christ. 1 Cor. 15:57.

By faith look upon the crowns laid up for those who shall overcome; listen to the exultant song of the redeemed, Worthy, worthy is the Lamb that was slain and hast redeemed us to God! Endeavor to regard these scenes as real.

Stephen, the first Christian martyr, in his terrible conflict with principalities and powers and spiritual wickedness in high places exclaimed, "Behold, I see the heavens opened, and the Son of man standing on the right hand of God" (Acts 7:56). The Saviour of the world was revealed to him as looking down from heaven upon him with the deepest interest, and the glorious light of Christ's countenance shone upon Stephen with such brightness that even his enemies saw his face shine like the face of an angel.

If we would permit our minds to dwell more upon Christ and the heavenly world, we should find a powerful stimulus and support in fighting the battles of the Lord. Pride and love of the world will lose their power as we contemplate the glories of that better land so soon to be our home. Beside the loveliness of Christ, all earthly attractions will seem of little worth.

Let none imagine that without earnest effort on their part they can obtain the assurance of God's love. When the mind has been long permitted to dwell only on earthly things, it is a difficult matter to change the habits of thought. That which the eye sees and the ear hears too often attracts the attention and absorbs the interest. But if we would enter the city of God, and look upon Jesus and His glory, we must become accustomed to beholding Him with the eye of faith here. The words and the character of Christ should be often the subject of our thoughts and of our conversation, and each day some time should be especially devoted to prayerful meditation upon these sacred themes.

Sanctification is a daily work. Let none deceive themselves with the belief that God will pardon and bless them while they are trampling upon one of His requirements. The willful commission of a known sin silences the witnessing voice of the Spirit and separates the soul from God.

Whatever may be the ecstasies of religious feeling, Jesus cannot abide in the heart that disregards the divine law. God will honor those only who honor Him. . . . Here is where Christ's help is needed. Human weakness becomes united to divine strength, and faith exclaims, "Thanks be to God, which giveth us the victory through our Lord Jesus Christ" (1 Cor. 15:57)!—*The Sanctified Life,* pp. 91-93.

GOD WORKS ON PLAN OF MULTIPLICATION

Grace and peace be multiplied unto you through the knowledge of God, and of Jesus our Lord. 2 Peter 1:2.

If we would develop a character which God can accept, we must form correct habits in our religious life. Daily prayer is as essential to growth in grace, and even to spiritual life itself, as is temporal food to physical well-being. We should accustom ourselves to lift the thoughts often to God in prayer. If the mind wanders, we must bring it back; by persevering effort, habit will finally make it easy. We cannot for one moment separate ourselves from Christ with safety. We may have His presence to attend us at every step, but only by observing the conditions which He Himself has laid down.

Religion must be made the great business of life. Everything else should be held subordinate to this. All our powers, of soul, body, and spirit, must be engaged in the Christian warfare. We must look to Christ for strength and grace, and we shall gain the victory as surely as Jesus died for us.

We must come nearer to the cross of Christ. Penitence at the foot of the cross is the first lesson of peace we have to learn. The love of Jesus—who can comprehend it? Infinitely more tender and self-denying than a mother's love! If we would know the value of a human soul, we must look in living faith upon the cross, and thus begin the study which shall be the science and the song of the redeemed through all eternity. The value of our time and our talents can be estimated only by the greatness of the ransom paid for our redemption. . . .

Sanctification is a progressive work. The successive steps are set before us in the words of Peter: "Giving all diligence, add to your faith virtue; and to virtue knowledge; and to knowledge temperance; and to temperance patience; and to patience godliness; and to godliness brotherly kindness; and to brotherly kindness charity. For if these things be in you, and abound, they make you that ye shall neither be barren nor unfruitful in the knowledge of our Lord Jesus Christ" (2 Peter 1:5-8). . . .

Here is a course by which we may be assured that we shall never fall. Those who are thus working upon the plan of addition in obtaining the Christian graces have the assurance that God will work upon the plan of multiplication in granting them the gifts of His Spirit. . . . By divine grace, all who will may climb the shining steps from earth to heaven, and at last, "with songs and everlasting joy" (Isa. 35:10), enter through the gates into the city of God.—*The Sanctified Life,* pp. 93-95.

GOD'S WORD THE MEANS OF OUR SANCTIFICATION

And for their sakes I sanctify myself, that they also might be sanctified through the truth. John 17:19.

Before Jesus went forth to His final conflict with the powers of darkness, He lifted up His eyes to heaven, and prayed for His disciples. He said: "I pray not that thou shouldest take them out of the world, but that thou shouldest keep them from the evil. They are not of the world, even as I am not of the world. Sanctify them through thy truth: thy word is truth." . . .

The burden of Jesus' request was that those who believed on Him might be kept from the evil of the world, and be sanctified through the truth. He does not leave us to vague surmising as to what the truth is, but adds, "Thy word is truth." The Word of God is the means by which our sanctification is to be accomplished. It is of the greatest importance, then, that we acquaint ourselves with the sacred instruction of the Bible.

It is as necessary for us to understand the words of life as it was for the early disciples to be informed concerning the plan of salvation. We shall be inexcusable if, through our own negligence, we are ignorant of the claims of God's Word. God has given us His Word, the revelation of His will, and has promised the Holy Spirit to them that ask Him, to guide them into all truth; and every soul who honestly desires to do the will of God shall know of the doctrine. . . .

The mission of Jesus was demonstrated by convincing miracles. His doctrine astonished the people. . . . It was a system of truth that met the wants of the heart. His teaching was plain, clear, and comprehensive. The practical truths He uttered had a convincing power, and arrested the attention of the people. Multitudes lingered at His side, marveling at His wisdom. His manner corresponded with the great truths He proclaimed. There was no apology, no hesitancy, not the shadow of a doubt or uncertainty that it might be other than He declared. He spoke of the earthly and the heavenly, of the human and the divine, with positive authority; and the people "were astonished at his doctrine: for his word was with power." . . .

It is a matter of the highest importance and interest to us that we understand what truth is, and our petitions should go forth with intense earnestness that we may be guided into all truth.

David appreciated the divine enlightenment, and recognized the power of the Word of God. He declared, "The entrance of thy words giveth light; it giveth understanding unto the simple." Let those who desire light search the Scriptures, comparing scripture with scripture, and pleading with God for the illumination of the Holy Spirit. The promise is that those who seek shall find.—*Review and Herald,* July 6, 1911.

THE NEED FOR PERSONAL CONSECRATION

Be ye steadfast, unmoveable, always abounding in the work of the Lord, forasmuch as ye know that your labour is not in vain in the Lord. 1 Cor. 15:58.

There is great need of the Holy Spirit's influence in our midst. There must be an individual work done in the breaking of stubborn hearts. There needs to be deep heart-searching, that will lead to confession of sin. Believers should at this time stand with softened, sanctified, broken hearts, every sin confessed in repentance that needeth not to be repented of. The Holy Spirit is waiting to kindle in the heart the love of God, that His praise may be spoken from lips that are true, unselfish, clean, and honest. When holy principles guide the life, the soul will be beautiful in its simplicity.

The influence of the prayer of faith is as far-reaching as eternity. The Lord will bless all who will seek Him with the whole heart, and who with humble souls and earnest purpose strive to follow the example of Christ. To those who thus seek to become partakers of the divine nature, the words are spoken, "Be not weary in well doing," "always abounding in the work of the Lord." He who labors in faith and humility, holding fast to the promises of God, will prevail. The greatness of the kingdom under the whole heaven will be given to the faithful, believing children of God. . . .

I am instructed to urge the necessity of personal consecration and sanctification of the whole being to God. Let each soul inquire, Lord, what wouldst Thou have me to do, that the vigilance of Christ may be seen in my life, and that His example may be copied by me, and that I may speak sincere words that will help souls who are in darkness and sin? . . .

Every individual is under obligation to give to others the truth he possesses. Nothing should be allowed to keep the servant of Christ from letting his light shine forth to his fellow men. . . . We should be daily increasing in ability to do the precious work of winning souls to Christ. This is such a precious work, such a satisfying work! And all heaven is waiting for channels through which can be poured the heavenly oil to refresh and strengthen needy souls. The Lord will protect and guide those who will let His divine fullness flow from their lips in grateful praise, and who labor, through deeds of charity and love, to bless mankind. Such workers will become consecrated agents for God.

I would say to every believer, Bring the spirit of heavenly grace into your soul, into your experience: this is the impress of the character of Christ. . . . And your reward for service will be found in the reflection of the tender spirit of Christ in your own life.—*Review and Herald,* Feb. 25, 1909.

WITHOUT JESUS WE CAN DO NOTHING

Of him are ye in Christ Jesus, who of God is made unto us wisdom, and righteousness, and sanctification, and redemption. 1 Cor. 1:30.

Many think that it is impossible to love our neighbor as ourselves; but it is the only genuine fruit of Christianity. Love to others is putting on the Lord Jesus Christ; it is walking and working with the invisible world in view. We are thus to keep looking unto Jesus, the author and finisher of our faith.

The solemn warning that was given to the foolish rich man should be a sufficient warning for all men to the close of time. Lesson upon lesson was given by our Lord to take everyone away from selfishness, and to establish close bonds of fellowship and brotherhood between man and man. He desired that the hearts of believers should be closely knit together in strong bonds of sympathy, so that there might be unity in Himself. They are together to rejoice in hope of the glory of God, looking for eternal life through the virtue of Jesus Christ. If Christ is abiding in the heart, His love will diffuse itself to others through its possessor, and will bind heart to heart.

The grace of Christ must be the sole dependence of the Christian, and when it is, he will love his brethren as Christ loved him. Then he can say, "Come," and beseech and woo souls, entreating them to be reconciled to God. His influence will be more and more decided, and he will devote his life to Christ, who was crucified for him.

Where love is perfected, the law is kept, and self finds no place. Those who love God supremely, work, suffer, and live for Him who gave His life for them. We can keep the law only through making the righteousness of Christ our own. Christ says, "Without me ye can do nothing." When we receive the heavenly gift, the righteousness of Christ, we shall find that divine grace has been provided for us, and that human resources are powerless. Jesus gives the Holy Spirit in large measure for great emergencies, to help our infirmities, to give us strong consolation, to illuminate our minds, and purify and ennoble our hearts. Christ becomes unto us wisdom, righteousness, sanctification, and redemption.

From the first to the last of the Christian life, not one successful step can be taken without Christ. He has sent His Spirit to be with us constantly, and by confiding in Christ to the uttermost, surrendering our will to Him, we may follow Him whithersoever He goeth.—*Review and Herald,* June 26, 1894.

The Holy Spirit will work every heart susceptible to its holy influence. Christ's righteousness will go before such an one, and the glory of the Lord will be his rearward.—Letter 192, 1902.

UNITED TO CHRIST, WE OBTAIN HIS MIND

The wisdom that is from above is first pure, then peaceable, gentle and easy to be intreated, full of mercy and good fruits, without partiality, and without hypocrisy. And the fruit of righteousness is sown in peace of them that make peace. James 3:17, 18.

Wherever there is union with Christ there is love. Whatever other fruit we may bear, if love be missing, they profit nothing. Love to God and our neighbor is the very essence of our religion. No one can love Christ and not love His children. When we are united to Christ, we have the mind of Christ. Purity and love shine forth in the character, meekness and truth control the life. The very expression of the countenance is changed.

Christ abiding in the soul exerts a transforming power, and the outward aspect bears witness to the peace and joy that reign within. We drink in the love of Christ, as the branch draws nourishment from the vine. If we are grafted in Christ, if fiber by fiber we have been united with the Living Vine, we shall give evidence of the fact by bearing rich clusters of living fruit. If we are connected with the Light, we shall be channels of light and in our words and works we shall reflect light to the world.

Those who are truly Christians are bound with the chain of love which links earth to heaven, which binds finite man to the infinite God. The light that shines in the face of Jesus Christ shines in the hearts of His followers to the glory of God.

By beholding we are to become changed; and as we meditate upon the perfections of the divine Model, we shall desire to become wholly transformed, and renewed in the image of His purity. It is by faith in the Son of God that transformation takes place in the character, and the child of wrath becomes the child of God. He passes from death unto life; he becomes spiritual and discerns spiritual things. The wisdom of God enlightens his mind, and he beholds wondrous things out of His law. . . . In becoming a man of obedience to God, he has the mind of Christ, and the will of God becomes his will.

He who places himself unreservedly under the guidance of the Spirit of God will find that his mind expands and develops. He obtains an education in the service of God which is not one-sided and deficient developing a one-sided character, but one which results in symmetry and completeness. Weaknesses that have been manifested in a vacillating will and powerless character are overcome, for continual devotion and piety bring the man in such close relation to Christ that he has the mind of Christ. He is one with Christ, having soundness and strength of principle.—*Selected Messages,* book 1, pp. 337-338.

GOD'S ORIGINAL PLAN OF COMMUNICATION

And they heard the voice of the Lord God walking in the garden in the cool of the day. Gen. 3:8.

In a knowledge of God all true knowledge and real development have their source. Wherever we turn, in the physical, the mental, or the spiritual realm; in whatever we behold, apart from the blight of sin, this knowledge is revealed. Whatever line of investigation we pursue, with a sincere purpose to arrive at truth, we are brought in touch with the unseen, mighty Intelligence that is working in and through all. The mind of man is brought into communion with the mind of God, the finite with the Infinite. The effect of such communion on body and mind and soul is beyond estimate.

In this communion is found the highest education. It is God's own method of development. "Acquaint now thyself with him" is His message to mankind. The method outlined in these words was the method followed in the education of the father of our race. When in the glory of sinless manhood Adam stood in holy Eden, it was thus that God instructed him. . . .

When Adam came from the Creator's hand, he bore, in his physical, mental, and spiritual nature, a likeness to his Maker. "God created man in his own image" (Gen. 1:27), and it was His purpose that the longer man lived the more fully he should reveal this image—the more fully reflect the glory of the Creator. All his faculties were capable of development; their capacity and vigor were continually to increase. Vast was the scope offered for their exercise, glorious the field opened to their research. . . . Face-to-face, heart-to-heart communion with his Maker was his high privilege. Had he remained loyal to God, all this would have been his forever. . . . More and more fully would he have fulfilled the object of his creation, more and more fully have reflected the Creator's glory.—*Education,* pp. 14, 15.

The laws and operations of nature, and the great principles of truth that govern the spiritual universe, were opened to their minds by the infinite Author of all. In "the light of the knowledge of the glory of God" (2 Cor. 4:6), their mental and spiritual powers developed, and they realized the highest pleasures of their holy existence. . . .

The Garden of Eden was a representation of what God desired the whole earth to become, and it was His purpose that, as the human family increased in numbers, they should establish other homes and schools like the one He had given. Thus in course of time the whole earth might be occupied with homes and schools where the words and the works of God should be studied, and where the students should thus be fitted more and more fully to reflect, throughout endless ages, the light of the knowledge of His glory.—*Ibid.,* p. 22.

CHRIST OFFERS THE RICHES OF THE UNIVERSE

For God, who commanded the light to shine out of darkness, hath shined in our hearts, to give the light of the knowledge of the glory of God in the face of Jesus Christ. 2 Cor. 4:6.

By sin man was shut out from God. Except for the plan of redemption, eternal separation from God, the darkness of unending night, would have been his. Through the Saviour's sacrifice, communion with God is again made possible. We may not in person approach into His presence; in our sin we may not look upon His face; but we can behold Him and commune with Him in Jesus, the Saviour. "The light of the knowledge of the glory of God" is revealed "in the face of Jesus Christ." God is "in Christ, reconciling the world unto himself" (2 Cor. 4:6; 5:19). . . .

"In him was life; and the life was the light of men" (John 1:4). The life and the death of Christ, the price of our redemption, are not only to us the promise and pledge of life, not only the means of opening again to us the treasures of wisdom: they are a broader, higher revelation of His character than even the holy ones of Eden knew.

And while Christ opens heaven to man, the life which He imparts opens the heart of man to heaven. Sin not only shuts us away from God, but destroys in the human soul both the desire and the capacity for knowing Him. All this work of evil it is Christ's mission to undo. The faculties of the soul, paralyzed by sin, the darkened mind, the perverted will, He has power to invigorate and to restore. He opens to us the riches of the universe, and by Him the power to discern and to appropriate these treasures is imparted.

Christ is the "Light, which lighteth every man that cometh into the world" (verse 9). As through Christ every human being has life, so also through Him every soul receives some ray of divine light. Not only intellectual but spiritual power, a perception of right, a desire for goodness, exists in every heart. But against these principles there is struggling an antagonistic power. The result of the eating of the tree of knowledge of good and evil is manifest in every man's experience. There is in his nature a bent to evil, a force which, unaided, he cannot resist. To withstand this force, to attain that ideal which in his inmost soul he accepts as alone worthy, he can find help in but one power. That power is Christ. Cooperation with that power is man's greatest need.—*Education,* pp. 28, 29.

Christ stands as the representative of the Father, the connecting link between God and man; He is the great teacher of mankind. And He ordained that men and women should be His representatives.—*Ibid.,* p. 33.

SELF IS HIDDEN AND CHRIST IS REVEALED

I am crucified with Christ: nevertheless I live; yet not I, but Christ liveth in me: and the life which I now live in the flesh I live by the faith of the Son of God, who loved me, and gave himself for me. Gal. 2:20.

As a Christian submits to the solemn rite of baptism, the three highest powers in the universe—the Father, the Son, and the Holy Spirit—place Their approval on his act, pledging Themselves to exert Their power in his behalf as he strives to honor God. He is buried in the likeness of Christ's death, and is raised in the likeness of His resurrection. . . .

The three great powers of heaven pledge Themselves to furnish the Christian with all the assistance he requires. The Spirit changes the heart of stone to the heart of flesh. And by partaking of the Word of God, Christians obtain an experience that is after the divine similitude. When Christ abides in the heart by faith, the Christian is the temple of God. Christ does not abide in the heart of the sinner, but in the heart of him who is susceptible to the influences of heaven.

The light that shines forth from the life of the true Christian testifies to his union with Christ. Self is hidden from view, and Christ is revealed. . . . "Now are we the sons of God, and it doth not yet appear what we shall be: but we know that, when he shall appear, we shall be like him; for we shall see him as he is" (1 John 3:2). Then those whose lives have been hidden with Christ, those who on this earth have fought the good fight of faith, will shine forth with the Redeemer's glory in the kingdom of God.

My brother, my sister, God's purpose for you is that you shall live a life that will make others better—a life which will show that Christ is formed within, the hope of glory. It is His purpose that you shall be able to say with the apostle Paul, "I live; yet not I, but Christ liveth in me" (Gal. 2:20). In perfect content, resting in the love of Christ, trusting the Redeemer and Life-giver to work out for you the salvation of your soul, you will know, as you draw nearer and still nearer to Him, what it means to endure the seeing of Him who is invisible. . . . The contentment that Christ bestows is a gift worth infinitely more than gold and silver and precious stones. . . .

Our lives are pure only when we are under the control of God, and happy only when we hold communion with Him. The luster possessed by those who have gained the richest experience is but the reflection of the light of the Sun of Righteousness. He who lives nearest to Jesus shines the brightest.—*Signs of the Times,* Aug. 16, 1905.

WHAT TRUE SURRENDER TO GOD INVOLVES

And this is life eternal, that they might know thee the only true God, and Jesus Christ, whom thou hast sent. John 17:3.

Wait not for some magical change to be wrought in you, without taking the requisite steps yourself. Life must be with you a humble working out your own salvation with fear and trembling, for it is God that worketh in you to will and to do of His good pleasure. Halt not, but escape for your life. . . .

Christ requires that we shall press together, that we shall be one with Him as He is one with the Father. You must depend on God, be disciplined and trained for the higher life. Yes, depend on God; wait His pleasure; follow Him; rely in obedience on the strength of His Word.

To obey when it seems the hardest is true surrender to God. This will quicken your moral nature and subdue your pride. Learn to submit your will to God's will, and you will be made meet for the inheritance of the saints in light.—Manuscript 12, 1888.

A general faith is not enough. We must put on the robe of Christ's righteousness and wear it openly, bravely, decidedly, exhibiting Christ, and not expect too much of finite man, but keep looking unto Jesus, and become ravished with the perfections of His character. Then we shall individually make manifest the character of Jesus, and make it evident that we are invigorated by the truth; because it sanctifies the soul and brings into captivity every thought to the obedience of Christ.—Letter 14, 1891.

Every missionary will have hard battles to fight with self, and these combats will not become fewer. But if we are constantly growing in Christian experience, if we continue to look to Jesus in faith, strength will be given us for every emergency. All the powers and faculties of a regenerated nature must be brought into constant, daily exercise. Every day we shall have occasion to crucify self, to war against inclination and a perverse temperament that would draw the will in a wrong direction. The repose and triumph of victory are not yet ours, except as we by faith enter into the victory that Christ has gained for us.—Letter 4, 1892.

The promises of God accepted in genuine faith have a fragrant influence upon the life and the character, making the human agent to reflect the image of the Divine. . . . God works on His part . . . , imparting grace to the one who imparts in his life the graces given him in representing genuine sanctification to the world in his own character.—Manuscript 45, 1900.

CHRIST'S LOVE IS A SATISFYING FOUNTAIN

Whosoever drinketh of the water that I shall give him shall never thirst. John 4:14.

What said Christ to the Samaritan woman at Jacob's well? . . . "Whosoever drinketh of this water shall thirst again: but whosoever drinketh of the water that I shall give him shall never thirst; but the water that I shall give him shall be in him a well of water springing up into everlasting life" (John 4:13, 14).

The water to which Christ referred was the revelation of His grace in His Word. His spirit, His teaching, His love is as a satisfying fountain to every soul. Every other source to which men resort proves unsatisfying; but the Word of truth is as cool streams, represented as the waters of Lebanon, which are always satisfying. In Christ is fullness of joy forevermore. The pleasures and amusements of the world are never satisfying, or healing to the soul. But Jesus says, "Whoso eateth my flesh, and drinketh my blood, hath eternal life."

Christ's gracious presence in His Word ever speaks to the soul, representing Him as the well of living water to refresh the thirsting. It is our privilege to have a living, abiding Saviour. He is the source of spiritual power in us, and His influence will flow forth in words and actions that will refresh all within the sphere of our influence, begetting in them desires and aspirations for strength and purity, for holiness and peace, for that joy which brings no sorrow with it. Such an experience will be the result of having Christ as an indwelling Saviour.

[Jesus] walked once a man on earth, His divinity clothed with humanity, a suffering, tempted man, beset with Satan's devices. . . . Now He is at the right hand of God, He is in heaven as our advocate, making intercession for us. We must always take comfort and hope as we think of this. He is thinking of those who are subject to temptations in this world. He thinks of us individually, and knows our every necessity. When tempted, just say, He cares for me, He makes intercession for me, He loves me, He has died for me. I will give myself unreservedly to Him.

We grieve the heart of Christ when we go mourning over ourselves as though we were our own saviour. No; we must commit the keeping of our souls to God as unto a faithful Creator. He ever lives to make intercession for the tried, tempted ones. Open your heart to the bright beams of the Sun of Righteousness, and let not one breath of doubt, one word of unbelief, escape your lips, lest you sow the seeds of doubt. There are rich blessings for us; let us grasp them by faith. I entreat you to have courage in the Lord. Divine strength is ours, and let us talk courage and strength and faith.—*Signs of the Times,* Sept. 3, 1896.

WE CAN BEAR THE FRUITS OF RIGHTEOUSNESS

That they might be called trees of righteousness, the planting of the Lord, that he might be glorified. Isa. 61:3.

Christians must be like Christ. They should have the same spirit, exert the same influence, and have the same moral excellence that He possessed. The idolatrous and corrupt in heart must repent and turn to God. Those who are proud and self-righteous must abase self and become penitent and meek and lowly in heart. The worldly-minded must have the tendrils of the heart removed from the rubbish of the world, around which they are clinging, and entwined about God; they must become spiritually minded. The dishonest and untruthful must become just and true. The ambitious and covetous must be hid in Jesus and seek His glory, not their own. They must despise their own holiness and lay up their treasure above. The prayerless must feel the need of both secret and family prayer, and must make their supplications to God with great earnestness.

As the worshipers of the true and living God we should bear fruit corresponding to the light and privileges we enjoy. Many are worshiping idols instead of the Lord of heaven and earth. Anything that men love and trust in instead of loving the Lord and trusting wholly in Him becomes an idol and is thus registered in the books of heaven. Even blessings are often turned into a curse.

The sympathies of the human heart, strengthened by exercise, are sometimes perverted until they become a snare. If one is reproved, there are always some who will sympathize with him. They entirely overlook the harm that has been done to God's cause by the wrong influence of one whose life and character do not in any way resemble those of the Pattern. God sends His servants with a message to the people professing to be followers of Christ; but some are children of God only in name, and they reject the warning.

God has in a wonderful manner endowed man with reasoning powers. He who fitted the tree to bear its burden of goodly fruit has made man capable of bearing the precious fruits of righteousness. He has planted man in His garden and tenderly cared for him, and He expected him to bear fruit. In the parable of the fig tree Christ says: ''Behold, these three years I come seeking fruit.'' . . .

How anxiously we watch a favorite tree or plant, expecting it to reward our care by producing buds, blossoms, and fruit; and how disappointed we are to find upon it nothing but leaves. With how much more anxiety and tender interest does the heavenly Father watch the spiritual growth of those whom He has made in His own image and for whom He condescended to give His Son that they may be elevated, ennobled, and glorified.—*Testimonies,* vol. 5, pp. 249-251.

THE WORD OF GOD IS STRONG AND POWERFUL

For the word of God is quick, and powerful, and sharper than any twoedged sword. Heb. 4:12.

The Word of God is to be our spiritual food. "I am that bread of life" (John 6:48), Christ said. . . . The world is perishing for want of pure, unadulterated truth. Christ is the truth. His words are truth, and they have a deeper significance than appears on the surface, and a value beyond their unpretending appearance. Minds that are quickened by the Holy Spirit will discern the value of these words. When our eyes are anointed with the holy eyesalve, we shall be able to detect the precious gems of truth, even though they may be buried beneath the surface.

Truth is delicate, refined, elevated. When it molds the character, the soul grows under its divine influence. Every day the truth is to be received into the heart. Thus we eat Christ's words, which He declares are spirit and life. The acceptance of truth will make every receiver a child of God, an heir of heaven. Truth that is cherished in the heart is not a cold, dead letter, but a living power.

Truth is sacred, divine. It is stronger and more powerful than anything else in the formation of a character after the likeness of Christ. In it there is fullness of joy. When it is cherished in the heart, the love of Christ is preferred to the love of any human being. This is Christianity. This is the love of God in the soul. Thus pure, unadulterated truth occupies the citadel of the being. The words are fulfilled, "A new heart also will I give you, and a new spirit will I put within you." There is a nobleness in the life of the one who lives and works under the vivifying influence of the truth. . . .

Many are supposed to be converted who will not stand the stress of trial and temptation. . . . They have no depth of spiritual experience. They do not apply the truth to the heart and conscience. . . . There is a lack of pure-toned piety; and this lack makes them weaklings in the army of the Lord, when they might be giants if they were but willing to be truly converted. . . .

We are living in perilous times. In the fear of God I tell you that the true exposition of the Scriptures is necessary for the correct moral development of our characters. When mind and heart are controlled by the Holy Spirit, when self is dead, the truth is capable of constant expansion and development. When the truth as it is in Jesus molds our characters, it will be seen to be truth indeed. As it is contemplated by the believer, it will grow brighter, shining with its original beauty. It will increase in value, quickening and vivifying the mind. . . . It will elevate our aspirations, enabling us to reach the perfect standard of holiness.—*Review and Herald,* Feb. 14, 1899.

TRUTH MUST BE STAMPED UPON THE HEART

Every word of God is pure: he is a shield unto them that put their trust in him. Prov. 30:5.

God gives to every man his work, and with the imparted commission He gives to His messengers a measure of power proportionate to their faith. He is constantly unfolding to the heart the riches of His grace. Light will shine forth in clear rays from those who receive light from the Word of God. . . .

Those who support the truth, not only by argument, but in their lives, range themselves on the side of righteousness. By a converted life they give evidence that they bear a solemn message of warning, which is a savor of life unto life, or of death unto death. When men are really converted, controversy and debate will be ended. The plain, searching truth will be proclaimed by lips touched with a live coal from the altar of God. . . .

The Old Testament is the ground where the seeds of practical godliness were first sown. This was repeated in Christ's words to His disciples. We have yet to learn that the whole Jewish economy is a compacted prophecy of the gospel. It is the gospel in figures. From the pillar of cloud, Christ presented man's duty to God and to his fellow men. His words to His appointed agencies, both in the Old Testament and in the New, point out plainly the Christian virtues. Through all His teaching He scattered the precious grains of truth. All will find these to be precious pearls, rich in value, if they will practice the principles laid down.

We have the truth. Shall we not practice it? Selfishness is the great evil that makes of none effect the preaching of the cross of Christ. . . . Make a practical application of the truth. Urge the truth home with sanctified assurance and directness, presenting the high standard God sets before His people. Truth must become truth to the receiver to all intents and purposes. It must be stamped upon the heart. . . .

"Thou shalt love the Lord thy God with all thy heart, and with all thy soul, and with all thy strength, and with all thy mind." This is the service that God requires. Nothing short of this is pure and undefiled religion. The heart is the citadel of the being; and until that is wholly on the Lord's side, the enemy will gain constant victories over us by his subtle temptations.

If the life is given into its control, the power of the truth is unlimited. The thoughts are brought into captivity to Christ. From the treasure of the heart are brought forth appropriate and fitting words. Especially will our words be guarded.—*Review and Herald,* Feb. 21, 1899.

THE LIGHT OF SCRIPTURES
TO BE CHERISHED

O send out thy light and thy truth: let them lead me; let them bring me unto thy holy hill, and to thy tabernacles. Ps. 43:3.

The Holy Spirit must work on the hearts of the teachers of God's Word, that they may give the truth to the people in the clear, pure way that Christ Himself gave the truth. He revealed it, not only in His words, but in His life. . . .

Men in this age of the world act as if they were at liberty to question the words of the Infinite, to review His decisions and statutes, endorsing, revising, reshaping, and annulling, at their pleasure. If they cannot misconstrue, misinterpret, or alter God's plain decision, or bend it to please the multitude and themselves, they break it. We are never safe while we are guided by human opinions; but we are safe when we are guided by a ''Thus saith the Lord.'' We cannot trust the salvation of our souls to any lower standard than the decision of an infallible Judge. Those who make God their guide, and His Word their counselor, follow the lamp of life. God's living oracles guide their feet in straight paths.

Those who are thus led do not dare judge the Word of God, but ever hold that His Word judges them. They get their faith and religion from His Word. It is the guide that directs their path. It is a light to their feet, and a lamp to their path. They walk under the direction of the Father of light, with whom is no variableness, neither shadow of turning. He whose tender mercies are over all His works, makes the path of the just as a shining light, which shines more and more unto the perfect day.—*Review and Herald*, Feb. 21, 1899.

We have light on the Scriptures, and we shall be held accountable for all the light not cherished. The works of many do not harmonize with the truth they have received. There is far too much of the human element brought into our plans. We do not depend upon the Holy Spirit to work with its transforming energy upon the heart and life. We are deficient in faith, which is invincible and mysterious. The efficacy of truth is weakened by the course of those who do not purify their souls by obeying the truth.

The secrets of the Lord are with them that fear Him and keep His covenant. We need faith in God, that under the sanctifying power of God's Word, the principles of human brotherhood may be manifested. We need the Holy Spirit's guidance. Its power upon mind and heart will enable us to present the truths of God's Holy Word. Sound doctrines brought into actual contact with human souls will result in sound and elevating practices. The truth as it is in Jesus must be cherished. Then Christians will not be Christians in name only. The love of Christ will pervade their lives.—*Ibid.*, Feb. 28, 1899.

THE TRUTH MAKES US FREE

Stand fast therefore in the liberty wherewith Christ hath made us free, and be not entangled again with the yoke of bondage. Gal. 5:1.

I am afraid for our churches. I tremble before God on their account. We have light on the Scriptures, and we shall be held accountable for all the light not cherished. . . .

The power of the Holy Spirit is needed to chase away our unbelief and unchristlike attributes. We must see our need of a physician. We are sick, and do not know it. May the Lord convert the hearts of His workmen! When there is a converted ministry, then look for results. But we cannot convert our own hearts. This work can be done only by the power of the Holy Spirit. In every stage of the work let this be remembered: ''Not by might, nor by power, but by my spirit, saith the Lord of hosts.'' . . .

Christ has promised to send us the Comforter, whose work is to establish the kingdom of God in the soul. When such abundant provisions of mercy, grace, and peace have been made, why do human beings act as if they regarded the truth as a yoke of bondage? It is because the heart has never tasted and seen that the Lord is good. The truth of the Word of God is thought by some to be a fetter. But it is the truth that makes men free. If the truth therefore shall make you free, ye shall be free indeed. The truth separates man from his sins, from his hereditary and cultivated tendencies to wrongdoing. The soul that cherishes the love of Christ is full of freedom, light, and joy. In such a soul there are no divided thoughts. The whole man yearns after God. He does not go to men to know his duty, but to Christ, the source of all wisdom. He searches the Word of God, that he may find out what standard he must reach.

Can we ever find a surer guide than Jesus? True religion consists in being under the guidance of the Holy One in thought, word, and deed. He, who is the Way, the Truth, and the Life, takes the humble, earnest, wholehearted seeker, and says, Follow Me. He leads him in the narrow way to holiness and heaven. Christ has opened this path for us at great cost to Himself, and we are not left to stumble our way along in the darkness. Jesus is at our right hand, proclaiming, I am the way; and all who decide to follow the Lord will be led in the royal path cast up for the ransomed of the Lord to walk in. . . .

What kind of vessels are meet for the Master's use? Empty vessels. When we empty the soul of every defilement, we are ready for use. . . . When mind and heart are worked by the Spirit, when self is dead, the truth is capable of constant expansion and new development.—*Review and Herald,* Feb. 28, 1899.

THE IMPRESS OF DEITY SEEN IN HIS WORD

Let the word of Christ dwell in you richly in all wisdom. Col. 3:16.

In God's Word we behold the power that laid the foundation of the earth and that stretched out the heavens. Here only can we find a history of our race unsullied by human prejudice or human pride. Here are recorded the struggles, the defeats, and the victories of the greatest men this world has ever known. Here the great problems of duty and destiny are unfolded. The curtain that separates the visible from the invisible world is lifted, and we behold the conflict of the opposing forces of good and evil, from the first entrance of sin to the final triumph of righteousness and truth; and all is but a revelation of the character of God. In the reverent contemplation of the truths presented in His Word the mind . . . is brought into communion with the infinite mind. Such a study will not only refine and ennoble the character, but it cannot fail to expand and invigorate the mental powers.

The teaching of the Bible has a vital bearing upon man's prosperity in all the relations of this life. It unfolds the principles that are the cornerstone of a nation's prosperity—principles with which is bound up the well being of society, and which are the safeguard of the family—principles without which no man can attain usefulness, happiness, and honor in this life, or can hope to secure the future, immortal life. There is no position in life, no phase of human experience, for which the teaching of the Bible is not an essential preparation. Studied and obeyed, the Word of God would give to the world men of stronger and more active intellect than will the closest application to all the subjects that human philosophy embraces. It would give men of strength and solidity of character, of keen perception and sound judgment—men who would be an honor to God and a blessing to the world.

In the study of the sciences also we are to obtain a knowledge of the Creator. All true science is but an interpretation of the handwriting of God in the material world. Science brings from her research only fresh evidences of the wisdom and power of God. Rightly understood, both the book of nature and the Written Word make us acquainted with God by teaching us something of the wise and beneficent laws through which He works. . . .

The impress of Deity, manifest in the pages of revelation, is seen upon the lofty mountains, the fruitful valleys, the broad, deep ocean. The things of nature speak to man of his Creator's love.—*Patriarchs and Prophets,* pp. 596-600.

MEETING SATAN WITH SCRIPTURE WEAPONS

Thy word have I hid in mine heart, that I might not sin against thee. Ps. 119:11.

It is the first and highest duty of every rational being to learn from the Scriptures what is truth, and then to walk in the light and encourage others to follow his example. We should day by day study the Bible diligently, weighing every thought and comparing scripture with scripture. With divine help we are to form our opinions for ourselves as we are to answer for ourselves before God. . . .

An understanding of Bible truth depends not so much on the power of intellect brought to the search as on the singleness of purpose, the earnest longing after righteousness.

The Bible should never be studied without prayer. The Holy Spirit alone can cause us to feel the importance of those things easy to be understood, or prevent us from wresting truths difficult of comprehension. It is the office of heavenly angels to prepare the heart so to comprehend God's Word that we shall be charmed with its beauty, admonished by its warnings, or animated and strengthened by its promises. We should make the psalmist's petition our own, "Open thou mine eyes, that I may behold wondrous things out of thy law" (Ps. 119:18).

Temptations often appear irresistible because, through neglect of prayer and the study of the Bible, the tempted one cannot readily remember God's promises and meet Satan with the Scripture weapons. But angels are round about those who are willing to be taught in divine things; and in the time of great necessity they will bring to their remembrance the very truths which are needed. Thus "when the enemy shall come in like a flood, the Spirit of the Lord shall lift up a standard against him" (Isa. 59:19).

Jesus promised His disciples: "The Comforter, which is the Holy Ghost, whom the Father will send in my name, he shall teach you all things, and bring all things to your remembrance, whatsoever I have said unto you" (John 14:26). But the teachings of Christ must previously have been stored in the mind in order for the Spirit of God to bring them to our remembrance in the time of peril. . . .

We are living in the most solemn period of this world's history. The destiny of earth's teeming multitudes is about to be decided. Our own future well-being and also the salvation of other souls depend upon the course which we now pursue. We need to be guided by the Spirit of truth. . . . We should now seek a deep and living experience in the things of God. We have not a moment to lose. Events of vital importance are taking place around us. We are on Satan's enchanted ground. Sleep not.—*The Great Controversy,* pp. 598-601.

THE REWARD OF SEARCHING

If thou criest after knowledge, and liftest up thy voice for understanding; if thou seekest for her as silver, and searchest for her as for hid treasures; then shalt thou understand the fear of the Lord, and find the knowledge of God. Prov. 2:3-5.

There must be earnest study and close investigation. Sharp, clear perceptions of truth will never be the reward of indolence. No earthly blessing can be obtained without earnest, patient, persevering effort. If men attain success in business, they must have a will to do and a faith to look for results. And we cannot expect to gain spiritual knowledge without earnest toil. Those who desire to find the treasures of truth must dig for them as the miner digs for the treasure hidden in the earth. No halfhearted, indifferent work will avail. It is essential for old and young, not only to read God's Word, but to study it with wholehearted earnestness, praying and searching for truth as for hidden treasure. Those who do this will be rewarded, for Christ will quicken the understanding. . . .

No one can search the Scriptures in the spirit of Christ without being rewarded. When man is willing to be instructed as a little child, when he submits wholly to God, he will find the truth in His Word. If men would be obedient, they would understand the plan of God's government. The heavenly world would open its chambers of grace and glory for exploration. Human beings would be altogether different from what they now are, for by exploring the mines of truth men would be ennobled. The mystery of redemption, the incarnation of Christ, His atoning sacrifice, would not be as they are now, vague in our minds. They would be not only better understood, but altogether more highly appreciated.

In His prayer to the Father, Christ gave to the world a lesson which should be graven on mind and soul. "This is life eternal," He said, "that they might know thee the only true God, and Jesus Christ, whom thou hast sent" (John 17:3). This is true education. It imparts power. The experimental knowledge of God and of Jesus Christ whom He has sent transforms man into the image of God. It gives to man the mastery of himself, bringing every impulse and passion of the lower nature under the control of the higher powers of the mind. It makes its possessor a son of God and an heir of heaven. It brings him into communion with the mind of the Infinite, and opens to him the rich treasures of the universe.

This is the knowledge which is obtained by searching the Word of God. And this treasure may be found by every soul who will give all to obtain it.—*Christ's Object Lessons,* pp. 111-114.

DIVINE POWER OBTAINED THROUGH PRAYER

And in the morning, rising up a great while before day, he went out, and departed into a solitary place, and there prayed. Mark 1:35.

No other life was ever so crowded with labor and responsibility as was that of Jesus; yet how often He was found in prayer! How constant was His communion with God! Again and again in the history of His earthly life are found records such as these: . . . "Great multitudes came together to hear, and to be healed by him of their infirmities. And he withdrew himself into the wilderness, and prayed." "And it came to pass in those days, that he went out into a mountain to pray, and continued all night in prayer to God" (Luke 5:15, 16; 6:12).

In a life wholly devoted to the good of others, the Saviour found it necessary to withdraw from the thoroughfares of travel and from the throng that followed Him day after day. He must turn aside from a life of ceaseless activity and contact with human needs, to seek retirement and unbroken communion with His Father. As one with us, a sharer in our needs and weaknesses, He was wholly dependent upon God, and in the secret place of prayer He sought divine strength, that He might go forth braced for duty and trial. In a world of sin Jesus endured struggles and torture of soul. In communion with God He could unburden the sorrows that were crushing Him. Here He found comfort and joy.

In Christ the cry of humanity reached the Father of infinite pity. As a man He supplicated the throne of God till His humanity was charged with a heavenly current that should connect humanity with divinity. Through continual communion He received life from God, that He might impart life to the world. His experience is to be ours.

"Come ye yourselves apart," He bids us. If we would give heed to His Word, we should be stronger and more useful. . . .

In all who are under the training of God is to be revealed a life that is not in harmony with the world, its customs, or its practices; and everyone needs to have a personal experience in obtaining a knowledge of the will of God. We must individually hear Him speaking to the heart. When every other voice is hushed, and in quietness we wait before Him, the silence of the soul makes more distinct the voice of God. He bids us, "Be still, and know that I am God" (Ps. 46:10).

Here alone can true rest be found. And this is the effectual preparation for all who labor for God. Amid the hurrying throng, and the strain of life's intense activities, the soul that is thus refreshed will be surrounded with an atmosphere of light and peace. The life will breathe out fragrance, and will reveal a divine power that will reach men's hearts.—*The Desire of Ages,* pp. 362-363.

WAIT AND WATCH AND PRAY

Wait on the Lord: be of good courage, and he shall strengthen thine heart: wait, I say, on the Lord. Ps. 27:14.

Wait on the Lord, and again I say, Wait on the Lord. We may ask of the human agents and not receive. We may ask of God and He says, Ye shall receive. Therefore you know to whom to look; you know in whom to trust. You must not trust in man or make flesh your arm. Lean as heavily as you please upon the Mighty One who hath said, "Let him take hold of my strength, that he may make peace with me; and he shall make peace with me." Then wait and watch and pray and work, keeping your face constantly turned to the Sun of Righteousness.

Let the bright beams from the face of Jesus shine into your hearts, to shine upon others through you. "Ye are the light of the world. . . . Let your light so shine before men, that they may see your good works, and glorify your Father which is in heaven" (Matt. 5:14-16). We must lift up Jesus before the people. . . .

Just as sure as you depend on man to be appreciated and to sustain you, you will be wholly disappointed. Your encouragement and sustaining will not come from the very best of men. The Lord has a lesson to teach you, to depend on Him alone, for He is your Redeemer. You are His property—His by creation and by redemption. The way of the Lord is to be chosen, the will of the Lord is to be your will. . . .

The Holy One has given us rules for the guidance of all. These rules form the standard from which there can be no departure. The principles of holiness have yet to be learned daily, and then the will of God will become paramount. In God you can stand, in God you can make aggressive warfare, presenting the truth as it is in Jesus.

Do not feel at all ashamed of the heart softening under the movings of the Holy Spirit. Let Jesus come in as He knocks for entrance and then appreciate Him, rejoice in heart, encourage a constant gratitude that while you felt that there was no arm to save, His arm brought salvation, His love was made apparent to you. Then when in the full joy of that love you presented Jesus to others, the Holy Spirit was working through you . . . to bless others. . . . It is the privilege of everyone who receives the Spirit of truth to represent the truth in its simplicity, to reach the hearts of the perplexed, trembling souls who are really bewildered. . . . He knows how to apply the balm. . . .

Make God your entire trust. Pray, pray, pray, pray in faith. Trust then the keeping of your soul to God. He will keep that which is committed to Him against that day. . . . Trust fully, unwaveringly in God.—Letter 126, 1895.

POWER TO PREVAIL WITH GOD AND MEN

I have seen God face to face, and my life is preserved. Gen. 32:30.

Those who exercise but little faith now, are in the greatest danger of falling under the power of satanic delusions and the decree to compel the conscience. And even if they endure the test they will be plunged into deeper distress and anguish in the time of trouble, because they have never made it a habit to trust in God. The lessons of faith which they have neglected they will be forced to learn under a terrible pressure of discouragement.

We should now acquaint ourselves with God by proving His promises. Angels record every prayer that is earnest and sincere. We should rather dispense with selfish gratifications than neglect communion with God. The deepest poverty, the greatest self-denial, with His approval, is better than riches, honors, ease, and friendship without it. We must take time to pray. If we allow our minds to be absorbed by worldly interests, the Lord may give us time by removing from us our idols of gold, of houses, or of fertile lands.

The young would not be seduced into sin if they would refuse to enter any path save that upon which they could ask God's blessing. If the messengers who bear the last solemn warning to the world would pray for the blessing of God, not in a cold, listless, lazy manner, but fervently and in faith, as did Jacob, they would find many places where they could say "I have seen God face to face, and my life is preserved." They would be accounted of heaven as princes, having power to prevail with God and with men. . . .

Now, while our great High Priest is making the atonement for us, we should seek to become perfect in Christ. Not even by a thought could our Saviour be brought to yield to the power of temptation. . . . Christ declared of Himself: "The prince of this world cometh, and hath nothing in me" (John 14:30).—*The Great Controversy,* pp. 622, 623.

Were not miracles wrought by Christ and His apostles? The same compassionate Saviour lives today, and He is as willing to listen to the prayer of faith as when He walked visibly among men. The natural cooperates with the supernatural. It is a part of God's plan to grant us, in answer to the prayer of faith, that which He would not bestow did we not thus ask.—*Ibid.,* p. 525.

No man is safe for a day or an hour without prayer. . . . While we must constantly guard against the devices of Satan, we should pray in faith continually: "Lead us not into temptation."—*Ibid.,* p. 530.

PRAYING BELIEVERS SHOULD ENCIRCLE THE WORLD

Men ought always to pray, and not to faint. Luke 18:1.

Let our brethren and sisters remember that we are living on the verge of the eternal world. The cases of all are being tried in the heavenly courts, and it is high time to put away sin, and to work earnestly to save as many as possible.

Among God's people there should be, at this time, frequent seasons of sincere, earnest prayer. The mind should constantly be in a prayerful attitude. In the home and in the church, let earnest prayers be offered in behalf of those who have given themselves to the preaching of the Word. Let believers pray as did the disciples after the ascension of Christ.

The members of our churches need to be converted, to become more spiritual-minded. A chain of earnest, praying believers should encircle the world. Let all pray in humility. A few neighbors may meet together to pray for the Holy Spirit. Let those who cannot leave home gather in their children, and unite in learning to pray together. They may claim the promise of the Saviour, ''Where two or three are gathered together in my name, there am I in the midst of them'' (Matt. 18:20). . . .

In response to the prayers of God's people, angels are sent with heavenly blessings. The Lord desires us to be far more successful in our missionary efforts. Through daily prayer and consecration all may so relate themselves to their heavenly Father that He can bestow upon them rich blessings.

Especially do those young in the faith need to be wide awake, and on their guard against the strategies of Satan. They must adhere steadfastly to an unwavering faith in the great atoning sacrifice. They need not continue in sin. Through prayer they may receive grace that will enable them to overcome. . . .

How much more might have been accomplished had the time spent by God's people in faultfinding been spent in encouraging one another, and in active service! How much better for voices to blend in prayer, in holy unison, than to be employed in finding fault!—*Review and Herald,* Jan. 3, 1907.

The greatest victories to the church of Christ or to the individual Christian are not those that are gained by talent or education, by wealth or the favor of men. They are those victories that are gained in the audience chamber with God, when earnest, agonizing faith lays hold upon the mighty arm of power.—*Patriarchs and Prophets,* p. 203.

What we want most is . . . heart power, prayer to God in faith for His converting power. . . . It is not brain power or purse power, but heart power, that the people need now.—Letter 20, 1890.

PRAYER IS APPROPRIATE ANYTIME, ANYWHERE

If ye shall ask any thing in my name, I will do it. John 14:14.

There is no time or place in which it is inappropriate to offer up a petition to God. There is nothing that can prevent us from lifting up our hearts in the spirit of earnest prayer. In the crowds of the street, in the midst of a business engagement, we may send up a petition to God and plead for divine guidance, as did Nehemiah when he made his request before King Artaxerxes. A closet of communion may be found wherever we are. We should have the door of the heart open continually and our invitation going up that Jesus may come and abide as a heavenly guest in the soul.

Although there may be a tainted, corrupted atmosphere around us, we need not breathe its miasma, but may live in the pure air of heaven. We may close every door to impure imaginings and unholy thoughts by lifting the soul into the presence of God through sincere prayer. Those whose hearts are open to receive the support and blessing of God will walk in a holier atmosphere than that of earth and will have constant communion with heaven.

We need to have more distinct views of Jesus and a fuller comprehension of the value of eternal realities. The beauty of holiness is to fill the hearts of God's children; and that this may be accomplished, we should seek for divine disclosures of heavenly things.

Let the soul be drawn out and upward, that God may grant us a breath of the heavenly atmosphere. We may keep so near to God that in every unexpected trial our thoughts will turn to Him as naturally as the flower turns to the sun.

Keep your wants, your joys, your sorrows, your cares, and your fears before God. You cannot burden Him; you cannot weary Him. He who numbers the hairs of your head is not indifferent to the wants of His children. "The Lord is very pitiful, and of tender mercy" (James 5:11). His heart of love is touched by our sorrows and even by our utterances of them. Take to Him everything that perplexes the mind. Nothing is too great for Him to bear, for He holds up worlds. He rules over all the affairs of the universe.

Nothing that in any way concerns our peace is too small for Him to notice. There is no chapter in our experience too dark for Him to read; there is no perplexity too difficult for Him to unravel. . . . The relations between God and each soul are as distinct and full as though there were not another soul upon the earth to share His watchcare, not another soul for whom He gave His beloved Son.—*Steps to Christ,* pp. 99, 100.

FAITH THAT WORKS BY LOVE

Trust in the Lord with all thine heart; and lean not unto thine own understanding. Prov. 3:5.

When we speak of faith, there is a distinction that should be borne in mind. There is a kind of belief that is wholly distinct from faith. The existence and power of God, the truth of His Word, are facts that even Satan and his hosts cannot at heart deny. The Bible says that "the devils also believe, and tremble" (James 2:19); but this is not faith. Where there is not only a belief in God's Word, but a submission of the will to Him; where the heart is yielded to Him, the affections fixed upon Him, there is faith—faith that works by love and purifies the soul.

Through this faith the heart is renewed in the image of God. And the heart that in its unrenewed state is not subject to the law of God, neither indeed can be, now delights in its holy precepts, exclaiming with the psalmist, "O how love I thy law! it is my meditation all the day" (Ps. 119:97). And the righteousness of the law is fulfilled in us, "who walk ⹁ not after the flesh, but after the Spirit" (Rom. 8:1).

There are those who have known the pardoning love of Christ and who really desire to be children of God, yet they realize that their character is imperfect, their life faulty, and they are ready to doubt whether their hearts have been renewed by the Holy Spirit. To such I would say, Do not draw back in despair. We shall often have to bow down and weep at the feet of Jesus because of our shortcomings and mistakes, but we are not to be discouraged. Even if we are overcome by the enemy, we are not cast off, not forsaken and rejected of God. No; Christ is at the right hand of God, who also maketh intercession for us. Said the beloved John, "These things write I unto you, that ye sin not. And if any man sin, we have an advocate with the Father, Jesus Christ the righteous" (1 John 2:1).

And do not forget the words of Christ, "the Father himself loveth you" (John 16:27). He desires to restore you to Himself, to see His own purity and holiness reflected in you. And if you will but yield yourself to Him, He that hath begun a good work in you will carry it forward to the day of Jesus Christ. Pray more fervently; believe more fully. . . .

The less we see to esteem in ourselves, the more we shall see to esteem in the infinite purity and loveliness of our Saviour. A view of our sinfulness drives us to Him who can pardon; and when the soul, realizing its helplessness, reaches out after Christ, He will reveal Himself in power. The more our sense of need drives us to Him and to the Word of God, the more exalted views we shall have of His character, and the more fully we shall reflect His image.—*Steps to Christ,* pp. 63-65.

BY FAITH ALL THINGS ARE OURS

For all things are yours; . . . and ye are Christ's; and Christ is God's. 1 Cor. 3:21-23.

Not only has the Son of God been given as a sacrifice for the guilty, as a Redeemer for the lost, but through Him all things are ours. Those who have faith in Christ, those who are obedient to His instruction, will know by experience the boundlessness of the power that gives us constant witness that we are Christ's, and that Christ is ours. The Saviour has given us the charter of our inheritance, and we stand on vantage ground, because we have chosen Christ as our portion.

Those who are obedient to His Word can receive this evidence—the assurance of the truth as it is in Jesus. If we will accustom our minds to dwell upon the facts of faith that have been given us, we may endure the seeing of Him who is invisible. Those who walk with Jesus may rejoice with joy unspeakable and full of glory. . . .

An abiding faith, a constant obedience, is essential to a continuance in His love. . . . We are to live by every word that proceedeth out of the mouth of God. Then the truth as it is in Jesus, the truth that is exemplified in His character, will be expressed in our lives, in our spirit, our words, our temper. Truth will be the law of the mind. Christ will be formed within, the hope of glory.

There is a peculiarly close union between the transformed soul and God. It is impossible to find words to describe this union. It is a treasure worth infinitely more to the true believer than gold and silver.

The Christian sees the Saviour ever before him, and by beholding, he becomes changed into the same image, from glory to glory. He bears the signature of God. Shall we give this up for the science of sophistry? Never! Truth is full of Godlike richness. He who is a partaker of the divine nature will hold firm to the truth. He will never let go; for the truth holds him.

Let us never forget that by the characters which we are forming day by day, we are deciding our future destiny. Those whose hearts are filled with the love of Christ will find in the heavenly courts a glad reception. . . .

It is the spirituality of the children of God that is their glory in His eyes. This is the distinguishing mark that separates them from the world. . . . We are to hunger and thirst after righteousness, that we may represent Christ to the world. If His love abides in our hearts, it will be distinctly revealed. We shall be lights in the world. Christ calls upon every follower of His to reveal His virtues of character, to represent Him in word and deed, to make known His love.—Manuscript 84, 1905.

BY FAITH EXCELLENCE IS DEVELOPED

Except a man be born again, he cannot see the kingdom of God. John 3:3.

Do you ask, What shall I do to be saved? You must lay your preconceived opinions, your hereditary and cultivated ideas, at the door of investigation. If you search the Scriptures to vindicate your own opinions, you will never reach the truth. Search in order to learn what the Lord says. If conviction comes as you search, if you see that your cherished opinions are not in harmony with the truth, do not misinterpret the truth in order to suit your own belief, but accept the light given. Open mind and heart that you may behold wondrous things out of God's Word.

Faith in Christ as the world's Redeemer calls for an acknowledgment of the enlightened intellect controlled by a heart that can discern and appreciate the heavenly treasure. This faith is inseparable from repentance and transformation of character. To have faith means to find and accept the gospel treasure, with all the obligations which it imposes.

"Except a man be born again, he cannot see the kingdom of God." He may conjecture and imagine, but without the eye of faith he cannot see the treasure. Christ gave His life to secure for us this inestimable treasure; but without regeneration through faith in His blood, there is no remission of sins, no treasure for any perishing soul.

We need the enlightenment of the Holy Spirit in order to discern the truths in God's Word. The lovely things of the natural world are not seen until the sun, dispelling the darkness, floods them with its light. So the treasures in the Word of God are not appreciated until they are revealed by the bright beams of the Sun of Righteousness.

The Holy Spirit, sent from heaven by the benevolence of infinite love, takes the things of God and reveals them to every soul that has an implicit faith in Christ. By His power the vital truths upon which the salvation of the soul depends are impressed upon the mind, and the way of life is made so plain that none need err. . . . As we study the Scriptures, we should pray for the light of God's Holy Spirit to shine upon the Word, that we may see and appreciate its treasures.—*Christ's Object Lessons,* pp. 112, 113.

Through faith in Christ, every deficiency of character may be supplied, every defilement cleansed, every fault corrected, every excellence developed.—*Education,* p. 257.

FAITH IS A SHIELD FOR EVERY SOUL

Above all, taking the shield of faith, wherewith ye shall be able to quench all the fiery darts of the wicked. Eph. 6:16.

Faith is trusting God—believing that He loves us, and knows best what is for our good. Thus, instead of our own, it leads us to choose His way. In place of our ignorance, it accepts His wisdom; in place of our weakness, His strength; in place of our sinfulness, His righteousness. Our lives, ourselves, are already His; faith acknowledges His ownership and accepts its blessing. Truth, uprightness, purity, have been pointed out as secrets of life's success. It is faith that puts us in possession of these principles.

Every good impulse or aspiration is the gift of God; faith receives from God the life that alone can produce true growth and efficiency.

How to exercise faith should be made very plain. To every promise of God there are conditions. If we are willing to do His will, all His strength is ours. Whatever gift He promises is in the promise itself. "The seed is the word of God" (Luke 8:11). As surely as the oak is in the acorn, so surely is the gift of God in His promise. If we receive the promise, we have the gift.

Faith that enables us to receive God's gifts is itself a gift, of which some measure is imparted to every human being. It grows as exercised in appropriating the Word of God. In order to strengthen faith, we must often bring it in contact with the Word. In the study of the Bible the student should be led to see the power of God's Word. In the creation, "he spake and it was done; he commanded, and it stood fast" (Ps. 33:9). . . .

Viewed from its human side, life is to all an untried path. It is a path in which, as regards our deeper experiences, we each walk alone. Into our inner life no other human being can fully enter. As the little child sets forth on that journey in which, sooner or later, he must choose his own course, himself deciding life's issues for eternity, how earnest should be the effort to direct his trust to the sure Guide and Helper!

As a shield from temptation and an inspiration to purity and truth, no other influence can equal the sense of God's presence. "All things are naked and opened unto the eyes of him with whom we have to do." He is "of purer eyes than to behold evil, and canst not look on iniquity" (Heb. 4:13; Hab. 1:13). This thought was Joseph's shield amidst the corruptions of Egypt. To the allurements of temptation his answer was steadfast: "How . . . can I do this great wickedness, and sin against God?" (Gen. 39:9). Such a shield, faith, if cherished, will bring to every soul.—*Education,* pp. 253-255.

FAITH QUALIFIES FOR US THE ROYAL LINE

Now faith is being sure of what we hope for and certain of what we do not see. Heb. 11:1, N.I.V.

How often those who trusted the Word of God, though in themselves utterly helpless, have withstood the power of the whole world—Enoch, pure in heart, holy in life, holding fast his faith in the triumph of righteousness against a corrupt and scoffing generation; Noah and his household against the men of his time, men of the greatest physical and mental strength and the most debased in morals; the children of Israel at the Red Sea, a helpless, terrified multitude of slaves, against the mightiest army of the mightiest nation on the globe; David, a shepherd lad, having God's promise of the throne, against Saul, the established monarch, bent on holding fast his power; Shadrach and his companions in the fire, and Nebuchadnezzar on the throne; Daniel among the lions, his enemies in the high places of the kingdom; Jesus on the cross, and the Jewish priests and rulers forcing even the Roman governor to work their will; Paul in chains led to a criminal's death, Nero the despot of a world empire.

Such examples are not found in the Bible only. They abound in every record of human progress. The Vaudois and the Huguenots, Wycliffe and Huss, Jerome and Luther, Tyndale and Knox, Zinzendorf and Wesley, with multitudes of others, have witnessed to the power of God's Word against human power and policy in support of evil. These are the world's true nobility. This is its royal line. In this line the youth of today are called to take their places.

Faith is needed in the smaller no less than in the greater affairs of life. In all our daily interests and occupations the sustaining strength of God becomes real to us through an abiding trust. . . .

Only the sense of God's presence can banish the fear that, for the timid child, would make life a burden. Let him fix in his memory the promise, "The angel of the Lord encampeth round about them that fear him, and delivereth them." Let him read that wonderful story of Elisha in the mountain city, and, between him and the hosts of armed foemen, a mighty encircling band of heavenly angels. Let him read how to Peter, in prison and condemned to death, God's angel appeared; how, past the armed guards, the massive doors and great iron gateway with their bolts and bars, the angel led God's servant forth in safety. . . .

In no less marked a manner than He wrought then will He work now wherever there are hearts of faith to be channels of His power.—*Education,* pp. 254-256.

HOW TO GAIN SPIRITUAL STRENGTH

Search the scriptures; for in them ye think ye have eternal life: and they are they which testify of me. John 5:39.

The Holy Spirit is beside every true searcher of God's Word, enabling him to discover the hidden gems of truth. Divine illumination comes to his mind, stamping the truth upon him with a new, fresh importance. He is filled with a joy never before felt. The peace of God rests upon him. The preciousness of truth is realized as never before. A heavenly light shines upon the Word, making it appear as though every letter were tinged with gold. God Himself speaks to the heart, making His Word spirit and life.

Eternal life is the receiving of the living elements in the Scriptures, the doing of the will of God. This is what is meant by eating the flesh and drinking the blood of the Son of God. It is the privilege of all to partake of the bread of heaven by studying the Word, and thus gain spiritual sinew and muscle. . . .

A rich banquet is set before those who accept Christ as a personal Saviour. Day by day, as they partake of His Word, they are nourished and strengthened.

Why do God's people pass by the words of the Great Teacher? Why do they rely upon human beings for help and comfort, when they have the great and grand promise, "He that eateth my flesh, and drinketh my blood, dwelleth in me, and I in him. As the living Father hath sent me, and I live by the Father; so he that eateth me, even he shall live by me. . . . He that eateth of this bread shall live for ever"? . . .

Those who partake of the banquet provided for them will gain an experience of the highest value. They will see that in comparison with the Word of God, the word of man is as chaff to the wheat.

In every plan we make, we must act with entire dependence upon God, else we shall be deceived by a semblance instead of the reality. . . .

By reason of the waste in the body, the blood must be constantly renewed by food. So with our spiritual life. The Word must be daily received, believed, and acted upon. Christ must dwell in us, energizing the whole being, renewing the lifeblood of the soul. His example is to be our guide. In our dealing with one another, we must reveal His sympathy. There must be a real working out of Christ's grace in our hearts. Then we can say with the apostle, "I live; yet not I, but Christ liveth in me." Christ's life abiding in the soul is the cause of joy and the pledge of our glory.—*Review and Herald,* Oct. 1, 1901.

THE HOLY SPIRIT, REPRESENTATIVE OF CHRIST

The Comforter, which is the Holy Ghost, whom the Father will send in my name, he shall teach you all things, and bring all things to your remembrance, whatsoever I have said unto you. John 14:26.

That Christ should manifest Himself to them, and yet be invisible to the world, was a mystery to the disciples. They could not understand the words of Christ in their spiritual sense. They were thinking of the outward, visible manifestation. They could not take in the fact that they could have the presence of Christ with them, and yet He be unseen by the world. They did not understand the meaning of a spiritual manifestation.

The Great Teacher longed to give to the disciples all the encouragement and comfort possible; for they were to be sorely tried. But it was difficult for them to comprehend His words. They had yet to learn that the inward spiritual life, all fragrant with the obedience of love, would give them the spiritual power they needed.

The promise of the Comforter presented a rich truth to them. It assured them that they should not lose their faith under the most trying circumstances. The Holy Spirit, sent in the name of Christ, was to teach them all things, and bring all things to their remembrance. The Holy Spirit was to be the representative of Christ, the Advocate who is constantly pleading for the fallen race. He pleads that spiritual power may be given to them, that by the power of One mightier than all the enemies of God and man, they may be able to overcome their spiritual foes.

He who knows the end from the beginning has provided for the attack of satanic agencies. And He will fulfill His word to the faithful in every age. That word is sure and steadfast; not one jot or tittle of it can fail. If men will keep under the protection of God, His banner will be over them as an impregnable fortress. He will give evidence that His word can never fail. He will prove a light which shineth in a dark place until the day dawn. He, the Sun of Righteousness, will arise with healing in His beams. . . .

He has assured you that the Holy Spirit was given to abide with you forever, to be your pleader and your guide. He asks you to trust in Him, and commit yourself into His keeping. The Holy Spirit is constantly at work, teaching, reminding, testifying, coming to the soul as a divine comforter, and convincing of sin as an appointed judge and guide. . . .

Your work is to cooperate with Christ, that you may be complete in Him. In being united to Him by faith, believing and receiving Him, you become part of Himself. Your character is His glory revealed in you. —Manuscript 44, 1897.

IMBUED BY THE POWER OF THE HOLY SPIRIT

Ye shall receive power, after that the Holy Ghost is come upon you and ye shall be witnesses unto me both in Jerusalem, and in al Judaea, and in Samaria, and unto the uttermost part of the earth Acts 1:8.

It is our privilege to preach the Word in the demonstration of the Spirit It is the privilege of every soul to exercise faith in our Lord Jesus Christ But pure spiritual life comes only as the soul surrenders itself to the will o God through Christ, the reconciling Saviour. It is our privilege to be worked by the Holy Spirit. Through exercise of faith we are brought into communion with Christ Jesus, for Christ dwells in the hearts of all who are meek and lowly. Theirs is a faith that works by love and purifies the soul, a faith that brings peace to the heart, and leads in the path o self-denial and self-sacrifice.

The promise is that if we follow on to know the Lord, we shall know that "his going forth is prepared as the morning." It is essential that we have daily the converting grace of God in the heart, that all our words and deeds may give evidence that we are in submission to the mind and will o God. In doing with meekness and humility our appointed service, we are to reveal the converting power of the Holy Spirit in our lives. Then we become the Lord's agencies to do His work.

With humility and meekness and yet with great earnestness we are to render our service to God. Christ is our pattern, our example in all things He was filled with the Spirit, and the Spirit's power was manifested through Him, not by bodily movements, but by a zeal for good works.

Among God's people there is need of deep, thorough heart searching, that we may be able to understand what constitutes true religion. Christ is a wonderful educator. His life and words are based upon sound principles. His manner of teaching was very simple. He was fashioned after the divine similitude, and if we follow Him, we shall make no mistakes. . . .

Our lives must be hid with Christ in God. We must have a personal knowledge of Christ. Then only can we rightly represent Him before the world. Wherever we are, we must let our light shine forth to the glory of God in good works. This is the great, the important work of our lives Those who are really under the influence of the Holy Spirit will reveal its power by a practical application of the eternal principles of truth. They will reveal that the holy oil is emptied from the two olive branches into the chambers of the soul temple. Their words will be imbued with the power of the Holy Spirit to soften and subdue the heart. It will be manifest that the words spoken are spirit and life.—Letter 352, 1908.

WE CANNOT USE THE HOLY SPIRIT, THE SPIRIT IS TO USE US

When he is come, he will reprove the world of sin, and of righteousness, and of judgment. John 16:8.

Christ promised the gift of the Holy Spirit to His church, and the promise belongs as much to us as to the first disciples. But like every other promise, it is given on conditions. There are many who profess to believe and claim the Lord's promises; they talk about Christ and the Holy Spirit; yet they receive no benefit, because they do not surrender their souls to the guidance and control of divine agencies.

We cannot use the Holy Spirit; the Spirit is to use us. Through the Spirit, God works in His people "to will and to do of his good pleasure" (Phil. 2:13). But many will not submit to be led. They want to manage themselves. This is why they do not receive the heavenly gift. Only to those who wait humbly upon God, who watch for His guidance and grace, is the Spirit given. This promised blessing, claimed by faith, brings all other blessings in its train. It is given according to the riches of the grace of Christ, and He is ready to supply every soul according to the capacity to receive.

The impartation of the Spirit is the impartation of the life of Christ. Those only who are thus taught of God, those only who possess the inward working of the Spirit, and in whose life the Christ-life is manifested, can stand as true representatives of the Saviour.

God takes men as they are, and educates them for His service, if they will yield themselves to Him. The Spirit of God, received into the soul, quickens all its faculties. Under the guidance of the Holy Spirit, the mind that is devoted unreservedly to God develops harmoniously, and is strengthened to comprehend and fulfill the requirements of God. The weak, vacillating character becomes changed to one of strength and steadfastness.

Continual devotion establishes so close a relation between Jesus and His disciples that the Christian becomes like his Master in character. He has clearer, broader views. His discernment is more penetrative, his judgment better balanced. So quickened is he by the life-giving power of the Sun of Righteousness, that he is enabled to bear much fruit to the glory of God. . . .

Of what avail would it be to us that the only-begotten Son of God humbled Himself, endured the temptations of the wily foe, and died, the just for the unjust, if the Spirit had not been given as a constant, working, regenerating agent, to make effectual in each individual case what has been wrought out by the world's Redeemer?—*Gospel Workers,* pp. 284-286.

THE HOLY SPIRIT, CHRIST'S SPECIAL GIFT

But grace was given to each of us according to the measure of Christ's gift. Therefore it is said, "When he ascended on high he led a host of captives, and he gave gifts to men." Eph. 4:7, 8, R.S.V.

Jesus the Son of God humbled Himself for us, endured temptation for us, overcame in our behalf, to show us how we may overcome. . . .

The Holy Spirit was promised to be with those who were wrestling for victory, in demonstration of all mightiness, endowing the human agent with supernatural powers, and instructing the ignorant in the mysteries of the kingdom of God. That the Holy Spirit is to be the grand helper is a wonderful promise. . . .

The imparted Holy Spirit enabled His disciples, the apostles, to stand firmly against every species of idolatry and to exalt the Lord and Him alone. Who, but Jesus Christ by His Spirit and divine power, guided the pens of the sacred historians that to the world might be presented the precious record of the sayings and work of Jesus Christ?

The promised Holy Spirit, that He would send after He ascended to His Father, is constantly at work to draw the attention to the great official sacrifice upon the cross of Calvary, and to unfold to the world the love of God to man, and to open to the convicted soul the precious things in the Scriptures, and to open to darkened minds the bright beams of the Sun of Righteousness, the truths that make their hearts burn within them with the awakened intelligence of the truths of eternity.

Who but the Holy Spirit presents before the mind the moral standard of righteousness and convinces of sin, and produces godly sorrow which worketh repentance that needeth not to be repented of, and inspires the exercise of faith in Him who alone can save from all sin? . . .

The life of Christ is to be carefully meditated upon, and to be constantly studied with a desire to understand the reason why He had to come at all. We can only form our conclusions by searching the Scriptures as Christ has enjoined upon us to do, for He says, "They testify of me." We may find by searching the Word the virtues of obedience in contrast with the sinfulness of disobedience. "As by one man's disobedience many were made sinners, so by the obedience of one shall many be made righteous."

The garden of Eden, with its foul blot of disobedience, is to be carefully studied and compared with the garden of Gethsemane, where the world's Redeemer suffered superhuman agony when the sins of the whole world were rolled upon Him.—Manuscript 1, 1892.

THE EFFECT OF RECEIVING THE SPIRIT

Now we have received, not the spirit of the world, but the spirit which is of God; that we might know the things that are freely given to us of God. 1 Cor. 2:12.

The Holy Spirit enabled the disciples to exalt the Lord alone, and guided the pens of the sacred historians, that the record of the words and works of Christ might be given to the world. Today this Spirit is constantly at work, seeking to draw the attention of men to the great sacrifice made upon the cross of Calvary, to unfold to the world the love of God to man, and to open to the convicted soul the promises of the Scriptures.

It is the Spirit that causes to shine into darkened minds the bright beams of the Sun of Righteousness; that makes men's hearts burn within them with an awakened realization of the truths of eternity; that presents before the mind the great standard of righteousness, and convinces of sin, that inspires faith in Him who alone can save from sin; that works to transform character by withdrawing the affections of men from those things that are temporal and perishable, and fixing them upon the eternal inheritance. The Spirit re-creates, refines, and sanctifies human beings, fitting them to become members of the royal family, children of the heavenly King.

When one is fully emptied of self, when every false god is cast out of the soul, the vacuum is filled by the inflowing of the Spirit of Christ. Such a one has the faith that purifies the soul from defilement. He is conformed to the Spirit, and he minds the things of the Spirit. He has no confidence in self. Christ is all and in all. He receives with meekness the truth that is constantly being unfolded, and gives the Lord all the glory, saying, "God hath revealed them unto us by his Spirit." . . .

The Spirit that reveals also works in him the fruits of righteousness. Christ is in him, "a well of water springing up into everlasting life." He is a branch of the True Vine, and bears rich clusters of fruit to the glory of God. What is the character of the fruit borne? The fruit of the Spirit is "love," not hatred; "joy," not discontent and mourning; "peace," not irritation, anxiety, and manufactured trials. It is "longsuffering, gentleness, goodness, faith, meekness, temperance" (Gal. 5:22, 23). Those who have this Spirit are earnest workers together with God. . . . They speak words of solid sense, and from the treasury of the heart bring forth pure, sacred things, after the example of Christ.—*Gospel Workers,* pp. 286-288.

WE ARE TO REVEAL CHRIST'S LOVE AND JOY

Now the God of hope fill you with all joy and peace in believing, that ye may abound in hope, through the power of the Holy Ghost. Rom. 15:13.

In the great and measureless gift of the Holy Spirit are contained all of heaven's resources. It is not because of any restriction on the part of God that the riches of His grace do not flow earthward to men. If all were willing to receive, all would become filled with His Spirit. It is the privilege of every soul to be a living channel through which God can communicate to the world the treasures of His grace, the unsearchable riches of Christ. There is nothing that Christ desires so much as agents who will represent to the world His Spirit and character. There is nothing that the world needs so much as the manifestation through humanity of the Saviour's love. All heaven is waiting for channels through which can be poured the holy oil to be a joy and blessing to human hearts.

Christ has made every provision that His church shall be a transformed body, illumined with the Light of the world, possessing the glory of Emmanuel. It is His purpose that every Christian shall be surrounded with a spiritual atmosphere of light and peace. He desires that we shall reveal His own joy in our lives.

The indwelling of the Spirit will be shown by the outflowing of heavenly love. The divine fullness will flow through the consecrated human agent, to be given forth to others.

The Sun of Righteousness has "healing in his wings" (Mal. 4:2). So from every true disciple is to be diffused an influence for life, courage, helpfulness, and true healing.

The religion of Christ means more than the forgiveness of sin; it means taking away our sins, and filling the vacuum with the graces of the Holy Spirit. It means divine illumination, rejoicing in God. It means a heart emptied of self, and blessed with the abiding presence of Christ. When Christ reigns in the soul, there is purity, freedom from sin. The glory, the fullness, the completeness of the gospel plan is fulfilled in the life. The acceptance of the Saviour brings a glow of perfect peace, perfect love, perfect assurance. The beauty and fragrance of the character of Christ revealed in the life testifies that God has indeed sent His Son into the world to be its Saviour.—*Christ's Object Lessons,* pp. 419, 420.

There is peace in believing, and joy in the Holy Ghost. Believing brings peace, and trusting in God brings joy.—*Testimonies,* vol. 2, pp. 319, 320.

THE GLORIOUS TREE OF LIFE

The Lord God planted a garden eastward in Eden. . . . And out of e ground made the Lord God to grow every tree that is pleasant to e sight, and good for food; the tree of life also in the midst of the rden, and the tree of knowledge of good and evil. Gen. 2:8, 9.

Man was formed in the likeness of God. His nature was in harmony ith the will of God. His mind was capable of comprehending divine ings. His affections were pure; his appetites and passions were under e control of reason. He was holy and happy in bearing the image of God d in perfect obedience to His will. As man came forth from the hand of s Creator, he was of lofty stature and perfect symmetry. His untenance bore the ruddy tint of health, and glowed with the light of life d joy. . . .

Everything that God had made was the perfection of beauty, and thing seemed wanting that could contribute to the happiness of the holy ir; yet the Creator gave them still another token of His love, by eparing a garden especially for their home. In this garden were trees of ery variety, many of them laden with fragrant and delicious fruit. . . . In e midst of the garden stood the tree of life, surpassing in glory all other es. Its fruit appeared like apples of gold and silver, and had the power perpetuate life. . . .

The tree of knowledge, which stood near the tree of life in the midst of e garden, was to be a test of the obedience, faith, and love of our first rents. While permitted to eat freely of every other tree, they were rbidden to taste of this, on pain of death. . . .

They were visited by angels, and were granted communion with their aker, with no obscuring veil between. They were full of the vigor parted by the tree of life, and their intellectual power was but little less an that of the angels.—*Patriarchs and Prophets,* pp. 45-50.

[Our first parents] were to enjoy communion with God and with holy gels; but . . . their loyalty must be tested. . . . Obedience, perfect and rpetual, was the condition of eternal happiness. On this condition he nan] was to have access to the tree of life.—*Ibid.,* pp. 48, 49.

In order to possess an endless existence, man must continue to partake the tree of life. Deprived of this, his vitality would gradually diminish til life should become extinct. . . . He [Satan] hoped that they would eat the tree of life. . . . But after man's fall, holy angels were immediately mmissioned to guard the tree of life. . . . None of the family of Adam ere permitted to pass that barrier to partake of the life-giving fruit; hence ere is not an immortal sinner.—*Ibid.,* p. 60.

THE UNIVERSAL DOMINION OF LAW

The earth is the Lord's, and the fulness thereof; the world, an they that dwell therein. For he hath founded it upon the seas, an established it upon the floods. Ps. 24:1, 2.

Upon all created things is seen the impress of the Deity. Nature testifi of God. The susceptible mind, brought in contact with the miracle a mystery of the universe, cannot but recognize the working of infini power. Not by its own inherent energy does the earth produce i bounties, and year by year continue its motion around the sun. An unsee hand guides the planets in their circuit of the heavens. A mysterious li pervades all nature—a life that sustains the unnumbered worl throughout immensity, that lives in the insect atom which floats in th summer breeze, that wings the flight of the swallow and feeds the your ravens which cry, that brings the bud to blossom, and the flower to fruit

The same power that upholds nature is working also in man. The san great laws that guide alike the star and the atom control human life. Th laws that govern the heart's action, regulating the flow of the current life to the body, are the laws of the mighty Intelligence that has th jurisdiction of the soul. From Him all life proceeds. Only in harmor with Him can be found its true sphere of action. For all the objects of H creation the condition is the same—a life sustained by receiving the life God, a life exercised in harmony with the Creator's will. To transgres His law, physical, mental, or moral, is to place one's self out of harmon with the universe, to introduce discord, anarchy, ruin.

To him who learns thus to interpret its teachings, all nature become illuminated; the world is a lesson book, life a school. The unity of ma with nature and with God, the universal dominion of law, the results transgression, cannot fail of impressing the mind and molding th character. . . .

So far as possible, let the child from his earliest years be placed whe this wonderful lesson book shall be open before him. Let him behold th glorious scenes painted by the great Master Artist upon the shiftin canvas of the heavens, . . . let him watch the unfolding mysteries of th changing seasons, and, in all His works, learn of the Creator.

In no other way can the foundation of a true education be so firmly an surely laid. Yet even the child, as he comes in contact with nature, wi see cause for perplexity. He cannot but recognize the working c antagonistic forces. It is here that nature needs an interpreter. Lookin upon the evil manifest even in the natural world, all have the sam sorrowful lesson to learn—''An enemy hath done this.'' . . . Only in th light that shines from Calvary can nature's teaching be read aright.–*Education,* pp. 99-101.

THE LAWS OF NATURE ARE THE LAWS OF GOD

Attend to my words; incline thine ear unto my sayings. . . . For they are life unto those that find them, and health to all their flesh. Prov. 4:20-22.

Since the mind and the soul find expression through the body, both mental and spiritual vigor are in great degree dependent upon physical strength and activity; whatever promotes physical health promotes the development of a strong mind and a well-balanced character. Without health, no one can as distinctly understand or as completely fulfill his obligations to himself, to his fellow beings, or to his Creator. Therefore the health should be as faithfully guarded as the character. A knowledge of physiology and hygiene should be the basis of all educational effort. . . .

The youth, in the freshness and vigor of life, little realize the value of their abounding energy. A treasure more precious than gold, more essential to advancement than learning or rank or riches—how lightly it is held! how rashly squandered! How many a man, sacrificing health in the struggle for riches or power, has almost reached the object of his desire, only to fall helpless, while another, possessing superior physical endurance, grasped the longed-for prize! Through morbid conditions, the result of neglecting the laws of health, how many have been led into evil practices, to the sacrifice of every hope for this world and the next! . . .

The youth should be taught that the laws of nature are the laws of God—as truly divine as are the precepts of the Decalogue. The laws that govern our physical organism, God has written upon every nerve, muscle, and fiber of the body. Every careless or willful violation of these laws is a sin against our Creator. How necessary, then, that a thorough knowledge of these laws should be imparted! . . .

The influence of the mind on the body, as well as of the body on the mind, should be emphasized. The electric power of the brain, promoted by mental activity, vitalizes the whole system, and is thus an invaluable aid in resisting disease. . . . The power of the will and the importance of self-control, both in the preservation and in the recovery of health, the depressing and even ruinous effect of anger, discontent, selfishness, or impurity, and, on the other hand, the marvelous life-giving power to be found in cheerfulness, unselfishness, gratitude, should also be shown. There is a physiological truth—truth that we need to consider—in the scripture, ''A merry rejoicing heart doeth good like a medicine'' (Prov. 17:22).—*Education,* pp. 195-197.

GLORIFY GOD IN OUR BODY AND SPIRIT

For ye are bought with a price: therefore glorify God in your body, and in your spirit, which are God's. 1 Cor. 6:20.

How shall we follow Him to learn of Him who is our teacher? We can search His Word, and become acquainted with His life and works. His words we are to receive as bread for our souls. In every sphere where man shall be placed, the Lord Jesus has left us His footprints. We do well to follow Him. The Spirit by which He spake, we must cherish; we are to present the truth as it is in Jesus. We are to follow Him especially in heart-purity, in love. Self must be hid with Christ in God; then when Christ who is our life shall appear, we also shall appear with Him in glory. . . .

By the inspiration of the Spirit of God, Paul the apostle writes that "whatsoever ye do," even the natural act of eating or drinking, should be done, not to gratify a perverted appetite, but under a sense of responsibility—"do all to the glory of God." Every part of the man is to be guarded; we are to beware lest that which is taken into the stomach shall banish from the mind high and holy thoughts.

May I not do as I please with myself? ask some, as if we were seeking to deprive them of a great good, when we present before them the necessity of eating intelligently, and conforming all their habits to the laws God has established.

There are rights which belong to every individual. We have an individuality and an identity that is our own. No one can submerge his identity in that of any other. All must act for themselves, according to the dictates of their own conscience. As regards our responsibility and influence, we are amenable to God as deriving our life from Him. This we do not obtain from humanity, but from God only. We are His by creation and by redemption. Our very bodies are not our own, to treat as we please, to cripple by habits that lead to decay, making it impossible to render to God perfect service. Our lives and all our faculties belong to Him. He is caring for us every moment; He keeps the living machinery in action; if we were left to run it for one moment, we should die. We are absolutely dependent upon God.

A great lesson is learned when we understand our relation to God, and His relation to us. The words "Know ye not that . . . ye are not your own? For ye are bought with a price" should be hung in memory's hall, that we may ever recognize God's right to our talents, our property, our influence, our individual selves. We are to learn how to treat this gift of God, in mind, in soul, in body, that as Christ's purchased possession, we may do Him healthful, savory [pleasing] service.—*Special Testimonies, Series A, No. 9, pp. 58, 59.*

WE ARE TO REVEAL THE PRINCIPLES OF HEAVEN

Come out from among them, and be ye separate, saith the Lord, and touch not the unclean things; and I will receive you. 2 Cor. 6:17.

Professed Christians yearly expend an immense sum upon useless and pernicious indulgences, while souls are perishing for the Word of life. God is robbed in tithes and offerings, while they consume upon the altar of destroying lust more than they give to relieve the poor or for the support of the gospel. If all who profess to be followers of Christ were truly sanctified, their means, instead of being spent for needless and even hurtful indulgences, would be turned into the Lord's treasury, and Christians would set an example of temperance, self-denial, and self-sacrifice. Then they would be the light of the world.

The world is given up to self-indulgence. ''The lust of the flesh, and the lust of the eyes, and the pride of life'' control the masses of the people. But Christ's followers have a holier calling. ''Come out from among them, and be ye separate, saith the Lord, and touch not the unclean.'' In the light of God's Word we are justified in declaring that sanctification cannot be genuine which does not work this utter renunciation of the sinful pursuits and gratifications of the world.

To those who comply with the conditions, ''Come out from among them, and be ye separate, . . . and touch not the unclean,'' God's promise is, ''I will receive you, and will be a Father unto you, and ye shall be my sons and daughters, saith the Lord Almighty'' (2 Cor. 6:17, 18). It is the privilege and duty of every Christian to have a rich and abundant experience in the things of God. ''I am the light of the world,'' said Jesus. ''He that followeth me shall not walk in darkness, but shall have the light of life'' (John 8:12). ''The path of the just is as the shining light, that shineth more and more unto the perfect day'' (Prov. 4:18). Every step of faith and obedience brings the soul into closer connection with the Light of the world, in whom there is ''no darkness at all.'' The bright beams of the Sun of Righteousness shine upon the servants of God, and they are to reflect His rays. As the stars tell us that there is a great light in heaven with whose glory they are made bright, so Christians are to make it manifest that there is a God on the throne of the universe whose character is worthy of praise and imitation. The graces of His Spirit, the purity and holiness of His character, will be manifest in His witnesses.—*The Great Controversy,* pp. 475, 476.

Our work in this world is to reveal the pure principles that are current in heaven.—*The Upward Look,* p. 291.

HEALTH IS A BLESSING FEW APPRECIATE

Know ye not that your body is the temple of the Holy Ghost which is in you, which ye have of God, and ye are not your own? 1 Cor. 6:19.

Health is a blessing of which few appreciate the value; yet upon it the efficiency of our mental and physical powers largely depends. Our impulses and passions have their seat in the body, and it must be kept in the best condition physically and under the most spiritual influences in order that our talents may be put to the highest use.

Anything that lessens physical strength enfeebles the mind and makes it less capable of discriminating between right and wrong. We become less capable of choosing the good and have less strength of will to do that which we know to be right.

The misuse of our physical powers shortens the period of time in which our lives can be used for the glory of God. And it unfits us to accomplish the work God has given us to do. By allowing ourselves to form wrong habits, by keeping late hours, by gratifying appetite at the expense of health, we lay the foundation for feebleness. By neglecting physical exercise, by overworking mind or body, we unbalance the nervous system. Those who thus shorten their lives and unfit themselves for service by disregarding nature's laws are guilty of robbery toward God.

And they are robbing their fellow men also. The opportunity of blessing others, the very work for which God sent them into the world, has by their own course of action been cut short. And they have unfitted themselves to do even that which in a briefer period of time they might have accomplished. The Lord holds us guilty when by our injurious habits we thus deprive the world of good.

Transgression of physical law is transgression of the moral law; for God is as truly the author of physical laws as He is the author of the moral law. His law is written with His own finger upon every nerve, every muscle, every faculty, which has been entrusted to man. And every misuse of any part of our organism is a violation of that law.

All should have an intelligent knowledge of the human frame that they may keep their bodies in the condition necessary to do the work of the Lord. The physical life is to be carefully preserved and developed that through humanity the divine nature may be revealed in its fullness. The relation of the physical organism to the spiritual life is one of the most important branches of education. It should receive careful attention in the home and in the school. . . . All should place themselves in the best possible relation to life and health.

Our habits should be brought under the control of a mind that is itself under the control of God.—*Christ's Object Lessons,* pp. 346-348.

NATURE HONORS THOSE WHO OBEY HER LAWS

Daniel purposed in his heart that he would not defile himself with the portion of the king's meat, nor with the wine which he drank: therefore he requested of the prince of the eunuchs that he might not defile himself. Dan. 1:8.

We can have no right understanding of the subject of temperance until we consider it from a Bible standpoint. And nowhere shall we find a more comprehensive and forcible illustration of true temperance and its attendant blessings than is afforded by the history of the prophet Daniel and his associates in the court of Babylon. . . .

It was not their own pride or ambition that had brought these young men into the king's court, into the companionship of those who neither knew nor feared the true God. They were captives in a strange land, and Infinite Wisdom had placed them where they were. They considered their position, with its difficulties and its dangers; and then, in the fear of God, made their decision. Even at the risk of the king's displeasure, they would be true to the religion of their fathers. They obeyed the divine law, both natural and moral, and the blessing of God gave them strength and comeliness, and intellectual power.

These youth had received a right education in early life; and now, when separated from home influences and sacred associations, they honored the instructors of their childhood. With their habits of self-denial were coupled earnestness of purpose, diligence, and steadfastness. They had no time to squander in pleasure, vanity, or folly. They were not actuated by pride or unworthy ambition; but they sought to acquit themselves creditably, for the honor of their own downtrodden people and for His glory whose servants they were.

God always honors the right. The most promising youth of every land subdued by the great conqueror had been gathered at Babylon; yet amid them all, the Hebrew captives were without a rival. The erect form, the firm, elastic step, the fair countenance showing that the blood was uncorrupted, the undimmed senses, the untainted breath—all were so many certificates of good habits, insignia of the nobility with which nature honors those who are obedient to her laws. And when their ability and acquirements were tested by the king at the close of the three years of training, none were found "like Daniel, Hananiah, Mishael, and Azariah." Their keen apprehension, their choice and exact language, their extensive and varied knowledge, testified to the unimpaired strength and vigor of their mental powers.

The history of Daniel and his companions has been recorded on the pages of the Inspired Word for the benefit of all the youth of all succeeding ages.—*Signs of the Times,* Feb. 11, 1886.

THE IMPORTANCE OF STRICT TEMPERANCE

Blessed art thou, O land, when . . . thy princes eat in due season, for strength, and not for drunkenness! Eccl. 10:17.

The lesson from the experience of these [Hebrew] youth is one which we would all do well to ponder. Our danger is not from scarcity, but from abundance. We are constantly tempted to excess. But those who would preserve their powers unimpaired for the service of God must observe strict temperance in the use of all His bounties, as well as total abstinence from every injurious or debasing indulgence.

Right physical habits promote mental superiority. Intellectual power, physical strength, and longevity depend upon immutable laws. There is no happen-so, no chance, about this matter. Heaven will not interfere to preserve men from the consequences of the violation of nature's laws. There is much of truth in the adage that every man is the architect of his own fortune. While parents are responsible for the stamp of character, as well as for the education and training which they give their sons and daughters, it is still true that our position and usefulness in the world depend, to a great degree, upon our own course of action.

Let old and young remember that for every violation of the laws of life, nature will utter her protest. The penalty will fall upon the mental as well as the physical powers. And it does not end with the guilty trifler. The effects of his misdemeanors are seen in his offspring, and thus hereditary evils are passed down, even to the third or fourth generation. . . .

We are suffering for the wrong habits of our fathers, and yet how many take a course every way worse than theirs! Every year millions of gallons of intoxicating liquors are drunk, and millions of dollars are spent for tobacco. Opium, tea, coffee, tobacco, and intoxicating liquors are rapidly extinguishing the spark of vitality still left in the race. . . .

The use of intoxicating liquor dethrones reason, and hardens the heart against every pure and holy influence. . . .

There is need now of men like Daniel—men who have the self-denial and the courage to be radical temperance reformers. Let every Christian see that his example and his influence are on the side of reform. Let ministers of the gospel be faithful in instructing and warning the people. And let all remember that our happiness in two worlds depends upon the right improvement of one.—*Signs of the Times,* Feb. 11, 1886.

ALL OF THE LIVING ORGANISM IS THE LORD'S

In all matters of wisdom and understanding, that the king enquired of them, he found them ten times better than all the magicians and astrologers that were in all his realm. Dan. 1:20.

Why did Daniel and his companions refuse to eat at the king's table? Why did they refuse his meats and wines? Because they had been taught that this class of food would not keep the mind or the physical structure in the very best condition of health to do God's service. These youth urged most earnestly that the one who had charge of their food should not compel them to partake of the king's luxuries, or drink of his wine. They begged him to try them ten days only, and then examine them, and decide by their physical appearance whether their abstemious diet would be to their disadvantage. When they came in for examination, the result was decidedly in their favor.

It was otherwise with the youth who had eaten of the luxuries of the king's table, and drank of his wine. The clear sparkle of the eye was gone; the ruddy, healthful glow had disappeared from the countenance. The four Hebrew captives were thereafter permitted to have the diet they had chosen. What effect did it have upon mind and character? They had conscientiously refused the stimulus of flesh and of wine. They obeyed God's will in self-denial, and He showed His approval. He desired His servants to honor Him by their adherence to steadfast principle in all their habits of life. Their countenances would be a certificate of physical soundness and moral purity.

"And as for these four children, God gave them knowledge and skill in all learning and wisdom: and Daniel had understanding in all visions and dreams." These youth had the Lord as their educator. The golden links of the chain of heaven connected the finite with the infinite. They were partakers of the divine nature. They were very careful to keep themselves in touch with God. They prayed and studied and brought into their practical life strictly conscientious, humble minds. . . . The word of the Lord was their meat and their drink. "And in all matters of wisdom and understanding, that the king enquired of them, he found them ten times better than all the magicians and astrologers." . . .

When the children of faith shall with earnest prayer dedicate themselves to God without reserve, the Lord will honor their faith, and will bless them with a clear mind. . . .

The very flesh in which the soul tabernacles, and through which it works, is the Lord's. We have no right to neglect any part of the living machinery. Every portion of the living organism is the Lord's. The knowledge of our own physical organism should teach us that every member is to do God's service, as an instrument of righteousness.—*Special Testimonies,* Series A, No. 9, pp. 60-62.

THE RELATIONSHIP BETWEEN FLESH AND SPIRIT

For he that soweth to his flesh shall of the flesh reap corruption; but he that soweth to the Spirit shall of the Spirit reap life everlasting. Gal. 6:8.

The lower passions have their seat in the body and work through it. The words "flesh" or "fleshly" or "carnal lusts" embrace the lower, corrupt nature; the flesh of itself cannot act contrary to the will of God. We are commanded to crucify the flesh, with the affections and lusts. How shall we do it? Shall we inflict pain on the body? No; but put to death the temptation to sin. The corrupt thought is to be expelled. Every thought is to be brought into captivity to Jesus Christ. All animal propensities are to be subjected to the higher powers of the soul. The love of God must reign supreme; Christ must occupy an undivided throne. Our bodies are to be regarded as His purchased possession. The members of the body are to become the instruments of righteousness.—*The Adventist Home,* pp. 127, 128.

A strict compliance with the requirements of God is beneficial to the health of body and mind. In order to reach the highest standard of moral and intellectual attainments, it is necessary to seek wisdom and strength from God, and to observe strict temperance in all the habits of life. In the experience of Daniel and his companions we have an instance of the triumph of principle over temptation to indulge the appetite. It shows us that through religious principle young men may triumph over the lusts of the flesh, and remain true to God's requirements, even though it cost them a great sacrifice. . . .

We should consider the words of the apostle in which he appeals to his brethren, by the mercies of God, to present their bodies "a living sacrifice, holy, acceptable unto God." This is true sanctification. It is not merely a theory, an emotion, or a form of words, but a living, active principle, entering into the everyday life. It requires that our habits of eating, drinking, and dressing be such as to secure the preservation of physical, mental, and moral health, that we may present to the Lord our bodies—not an offering corrupted by wrong habits, but—"a living sacrifice, holy, acceptable unto God." . . .

A close sympathy exists between the physical and the moral nature. . . . Wherever they may be, those who are truly sanctified will elevate the moral standard by preserving correct physical habits, and, like Daniel, presenting to others an example of temperance and self-denial. Every depraved appetite becomes a warring lust. Everything that conflicts with natural law creates a diseased condition of the soul. . . .

With what care should Christians regulate their habits, that they may preserve the full vigor of every faculty to give to the service of Christ.—*Review and Herald,* Jan. 25, 1881.

THE HEALTH-GIVING VALUE OF OUTDOOR LIFE

Beloved, I wish above all things that thou mayest prosper and be in health, even as thy soul prospereth. 3 John 2.

The things of nature are God's blessings, provided to give health to body, mind, and soul. They are given to the well to keep them well and to the sick to make them well. Connected with water treatment, they are more effective in restoring health than all the drug medication in the world.

In the country the sick find many things to call their attention away from themselves and their sufferings. Everywhere they can look upon and enjoy the beautiful things of nature—the flowers, the fields, the fruit trees laden with their rich treasure, the forest trees casting their grateful shade, and the hills and valleys with their varied verdure and many forms of life.

And not only are they entertained by these surroundings, but at the same time they learn most precious spiritual lessons. Surrounded by the wonderful works of God, their minds are lifted from the things that are seen to the things that are unseen. The beauty of nature leads them to think of the matchless charms of the earth made new, where there will be nothing to mar the loveliness, nothing to taint or destroy, nothing to cause disease or death.

Nature is God's physician. The pure air, the glad sunshine, the beautiful flowers and trees, the orchards and vineyards, and outdoor exercise amid these surroundings, are health-giving—the elixir of life. Outdoor life is the only medicine that many invalids need. Its influence is powerful to heal sickness caused by fashionable life, a life that weakens and destroys the physical, mental, and spiritual powers.

How grateful to weary invalids accustomed to city life, the glare of many lights, and the noise of the streets are the quiet and freedom of the country! How eagerly do they turn to the scenes of nature! How glad would they be for the advantages of a sanitarium in the country, where they could sit in the open air, rejoice in the sunshine, and breathe the fragrance of tree and flower! There are life-giving properties in the balsam of the pine, in the fragrance of the cedar and the fir. And there are other trees that are health-promoting. Let no such trees be ruthlessly cut down. Cherish them where they are abundant, and plant more where there are but few. . . .

Nothing so tends to restore health and happiness as living amid attractive country surroundings. . . . May God help us to do our utmost to utilize the life-giving power of sunshine and fresh air.—*Testimonies*, vol. 7, pp. 76-79.

EACH YOUTH MUST DECIDE FOR HIMSELF

And every man that striveth for the mastery is temperate in all things. 1 Cor. 9:25.

It rests with us individually to decide whether our lives shall be controlled by the mind or by the body. The youth must, each for himself, make the choice that shapes his life; and no pains should be spared that he may understand the forces with which he has to deal, and the influences which mold character and destiny.

Intemperance is a foe against which all need to be guarded. The rapid increase of this terrible evil should arouse every lover of his race to warfare against it.—*Education,* p. 202.

The observance of temperance and regularity in all things has a wonderful power. It will do more than circumstances or natural endowments in promoting that sweetness and serenity of disposition which count so much in smoothing life's pathway. At the same time the power of self-control thus acquired will be found one of the most valuable of equipments for grappling successfully with the stern duties and realities that await every human being.

Wisdom's "ways are ways of pleasantness, and all her paths are peace" (Prov. 3:17). Let every youth in our land, with the possibilities before him of a destiny higher than that of crowned kings, ponder the lesson conveyed in the words of the wise man, "Blessed art thou, O land, when . . . thy princes eat in due season, for strength, and not for drunkenness!" (Eccl. 10:17).—*Ibid.,* p. 206.

"Let thine heart keep my commandments," God says; "for length of days, and years of life, and peace, shall they add to thee." "They are life unto those that find them, and health to all their flesh." "Pleasant words," the Scriptures declare to be not only "sweet to the soul," but "health to the bones" (Prov. 3:1, 2, margin; 4:22; 16:24).

The youth need to understand the deep truth underlying the Bible statement that with God "is the fountain of life" (Ps. 36:9). Not only is He the originator of all, but He is the life of everything that lives. It is His life that we receive in the sunshine, in the pure, sweet air, in the food which builds up our bodies and sustains our strength. It is by His life that we exist, hour by hour, moment by moment. Except as perverted by sin, all His gifts tend to life, to health and joy.

"He hath made every thing beautiful in its time" (Eccl. 3:11, R.V.) and true beauty will be secured, not in marring God's work, but in coming into harmony with the laws of Him who created all things, and who finds pleasure in their beauty and perfection.—*Ibid.,* pp. 197, 198.

EXERCISE IS INDISPENSABLE TO HEALTH

The glory of young men is their strength. Prov. 20:29.

Attention to health is one of our most important duties. We owe this to ourselves, to society, and to God. Young men and young women are proverbially careless in regard to their health. . . .

Exercise is indispensable to the health of every organ. If one set of muscles is used to the neglect of others, the living machinery is not being worked intelligently.

When physical exercise is taken, the circulation is quickened. The heart receives blood faster and sends it to the lungs faster. The lungs work more vigorously, furnishing a greater amount of blood, which is sent with stronger power through the entire being. Exercise gives new life and strength to every part of the body.

The nerves gain or lose strength in accordance with the way in which they are treated. If used too long and too severely, they are overtaxed and weakened. If used properly, they gain strength.

In order to have health, equilibrium of action must be maintained. The mind must harmonize with this. . . . If physical exercise is regarded as drudgery, if the mind takes no interest in the exercise of the different parts of the body [the benefits will not be realized]. The mind must be interested in exercise of the muscles.

In the education of the youth, physical exercise must be combined with mental taxation.—Letter 6, 1885.

Perfect obedience to God's commands calls for conformity to the laws of the being. . . .

The time spent in physical exercise is not lost. The student who is constantly poring over his books, while he takes but little exercise in the open air, does himself an injury. A proportionate exercise of the various organs and faculties of the body is essential to the best work of each. When the brain is constantly taxed while the other organs are left inactive, there is a loss of physical and mental strength. The physical powers are robbed of their healthy tone, the mind loses its freshness and vigor, and a morbid excitability is the result.

In order for men and women to have well-balanced minds, all the powers of the being should be called into use and developed. . . .

[The Lord] bids us reason from cause to effect, to remember that we are His property, and to unite with Him in keeping the body pure and healthy, and the whole being sanctified to Him.—*Counsels to Parents and Teachers,* pp. 295-300.

APPROPRIATE EXERCISE

Whatsoever thy hand findeth to do, do it with thy might; for there is no work, nor device, nor knowledge, nor wisdom, in the grave, whither thou goest. Eccl. 9:10.

The various trades and occupations have to be learned, and they call into exercise a great variety of mental and physical capabilities; the occupations requiring sedentary habits are the most dangerous, for they take men away from the open air and sunshine, and train one set of faculties, while other organs are becoming weak from inaction. Men carry on their work, perfect their business, and soon lie down in the grave.

Much more favorable is the condition of one whose occupation keeps him in the open air, exercising his muscles, while the brain is equally taxed, and all the organs have the privilege of doing their work. To those who can live outside of the cities, and labor in the open air, beholding the works of the great Master Artist, new scenes are continually unfolding. As they make the book of nature their study, a softening, subduing influence comes over them; for they realize that God's care is over all, from the glorious sun in the heavens to the little brown sparrow or the tiniest insect that has life.

The Majesty of heaven has pointed us to these things of God's creation as an evidence of His love. He who fashioned the flowers has said: "Consider the lilies of the field, how they grow; they toil not, neither do they spin: and yet I say unto you, that even Solomon in all his glory was not arrayed like one of these." . . . The Lord is our teacher, and under His instruction we may learn the most precious lessons from nature.

The world is under the curse of sin, and yet even in its decay it is very beautiful. If it were not defiled by the wicked, corrupt deeds of the men who tread the soil, we could, with the blessing of God, enjoy our world as it is. But ignorance, pleasure loving, and sinful habits, corrupting soul, body, and spirit, make the world full of moral leprosy; a deadly moral malaria is destroying thousands and tens of thousands. What shall be done to save our youth? *We* can do little, but God lives and reigns, and He can do much. . . .

While we shun the false and artificial, discarding horse racing, card playing, lotteries, prize fights, liquor drinking, and tobacco using, we must supply sources of pleasure that are pure and noble and elevating. We should choose a location . . . where the eye will not rest continually upon the dwellings of men, but upon the works of God; where there shall be places of interest for them to visit, other than what the city affords. Let [them] be placed where nature can speak to the senses, and in her voice they may hear the voice of God. Let them be where they can look upon His wondrous works, and through nature behold her Creator.—*Fundamentals of Christian Education*, pp. 319, 320.

THE WONDERS OF THE HUMAN BODY

God hath not given us the spirit of fear; but of power, and of love, and of a sound mind. 2 Tim. 1:7.

We are God's workmanship, and His Word declares that we are "fearfully and wonderfully made." He has prepared this living habitation for the mind; it is "curiously wrought," a temple which the Lord Himself has fitted up for the indwelling of His Holy Spirit. The mind controls the whole man. All our actions, good or bad, have their source in the mind. It is the mind that worships God and allies us to heavenly beings. Yet many spend all their lives without becoming intelligent in regard to the casket [the human body] that contains this treasure.—*Child Guidance,* p. 360.

All the physical organs are the servants of the mind, and the nerves are the messengers that transmit its orders to every part of the body, guiding the motions of the living machinery. Exercise is an important aid to physical development. It quickens the circulation of the blood, and gives tone to the system. If the muscles are allowed to remain unused, it will soon be apparent that the blood does not sufficiently nourish them. Instead of increasing in size and strength, they will lose their firmness and elasticity, and become soft and weak. Inactivity is not the law the Lord has established in the human body. The harmonious action of all the parts—brain, bone, and muscle—is necessary to the full and healthful development of the entire human organism. . . .

The appetites and passions must be controlled, that through them we shall not weaken or defile God's human temple.

Anything that lessens the physical power enfeebles the mind, and makes it less clear to discriminate between good and evil, between right and wrong. This principle is illustrated in the case of Nadab and Abihu. God gave them a most sacred work to perform, permitting them to come near to Himself in their appointed service; but they had a habit of drinking wine, and they entered upon the holy service in the sanctuary with confused minds.

There was the sacred fire, which was kindled by God Himself; but they used the common fire upon their censers, when they offered incense to ascend as a sweet fragrance with the prayers of God's people. Because their minds were clouded by an unholy indulgence, they disregarded the divine requirement; "and there went out fire from the Lord, and devoured them." . . .

It is the duty of each student, of each individual, to do all in his power to present his body to Christ, a cleansed temple, physically perfect as well as morally free from defilement—a fit abode for God's indwelling presence.—*Fundamentals of Christian Education,* pp. 426-428.

MORAL PRINCIPLES SAFEGUARD THE SOUL

Flee fornication. Every sin that a man doeth is without the body; but he that committeth fornication sinneth against his own body. 1 Cor. 6:18.

I have been shown that we live amid the perils of the last days. Because iniquity abounds, the love of many waxes cold. The word "many" refers to the professed followers of Christ. They are affected by the prevailing iniquity and backslide from God, but it is not necessary that they should be thus affected. The cause of this declension is that they do not stand clear from this iniquity. The fact that their love to God is waxing cold because iniquity abounds shows that they are, in some sense, partakers in this iniquity, or it would not affect their love for God and their zeal and fervor in His cause.

A terrible picture of the condition of the world has been presented before me. Immorality abounds everywhere. Licentiousness is the special sin of this age. Never did vice lift its deformed head with such boldness as now. The people seem to be benumbed, and the lovers of virtue and true goodness are nearly discouraged by its boldness, strength, and prevalence. The iniquity which abounds is not merely confined to the unbeliever and the scoffer. Would that this were the case, but it is not.
. . .

Every Christian will have to learn to restrain his passions and be controlled by principle.

The brain nerves which communicate with the entire system are the only medium through which Heaven can communicate to man and affect his inmost life. Whatever disturbs the circulation of the electric currents in the nervous system lessens the strength of the vital powers, and the result is a deadening of the sensibilities of the mind.—*Testimonies,* vol. 2, pp. 346, 347.

Moral principle, strictly carried out, becomes the only safeguard of the soul. If ever there was a time when the diet should be of the most simple kind, it is now. . . . The less feverish the diet, the more easily can the passions be controlled. Gratification of taste should not be consulted irrespective of physical, intellectual, or moral health. . . .

God has given you a habitation to care for and preserve in the best condition for His service and glory. Your bodies are not your own. "What? know ye not that your body is the temple of the Holy Ghost which is in you, which ye have of God, and ye are not your own? For ye are bought with a price; therefore glorify God in your body, and in your spirit, which are God's." "Know ye not that ye are the temple of God, and that the Spirit of God dwelleth in you?"—*Ibid.,* pp. 352, 353.

WRONG PHYSICAL HABITS AFFECT THE BRAIN

Whether therefore ye eat, or drink, or whatsoever ye do, do all to he glory of God. 1 Cor. 10:31.

The character of the food and the manner in which it is eaten exert a owerful influence on the health. Many . . . have never made a etermined effort to control the appetite, or to observe proper rules in egard to eating. Some eat too much at their meals, and some eat between neals whenever the temptation is presented.

The need of carefulness in habits of diet should be impressed on the ninds of all. . . . I appeal to all to refuse to eat those things that will injure ne health. Thus they can serve the Lord by sacrifice.

Those who obey the laws of health will give time and thought to the eeds of the body and to the laws of digestion. And they will be rewarded y clearness of thought and strength of mind. On the other hand it is ossible for one to spoil his Christian experience by abuse of the stomach. hose things that derange the digestion have a benumbing influence on ne finer feelings of the heart. . . . Every habit that injures the health reacts pon the mind. That time is well spent which is directed to the stablishment and preservation of sound physical and mental health. 'irm, quiet nerves and a healthy circulation help men to follow right rinciples and to listen to the promptings of conscience. . . .

The brain is the citadel of the being. Wrong physical habits affect the rain, and prevent the attainment of . . . good mental discipline. Unless ne youth are versed in the science of how to care for the body as well as or the mind, they will not be successful students. Study is not the rincipal cause of breakdown of the mental powers. The main cause is mproper diet, irregular meals, a lack of physical exercise, and careless nattention in other respects to the laws of health. When we do all that we an to preserve the health, then we can ask God in faith to bless our fforts. . . .

The youth should be taught that they are not at liberty to do as they lease with their lives. God will not hold guiltless those who treat lightly lis precious gifts. Men should realize that the greater their endowment of trength, of talent, of means, or of opportunities, the more heavily should ne burden of God's work rest upon them, and the more they should do for lim. The youth who are trained to believe that life is a sacred trust will esitate to plunge into the vortex of dissipation and crime that swallows p so many promising young men of this age.—*Counsels to Parents and 'eachers,* pp. 297-300.

Mental and moral power is dependent upon the physical health.— *1ind, Character, and Personality,* vol. 1, p. 61.

LIFE IS A HOLY TRUST

With thee is the foundation of life: in thy light shall we see the light Ps. 36:9.

We need as workers to keep looking unto Jesus, the author and finishe of our faith. As workers together with God, we are to draw souls t Christ. We are to remember that each has a special part to act in th Master's service. O how much good the members of the church migh accomplish if they realized the responsibility resting upon them to poir those with whom they come in contact to the Redeemer.

When church members shall disinterestedly engage in the work give them of God, a much stronger influence will be exerted in behalf of soul ready to die, and much more earnest efforts will be put forth in medica missionary lines. When every member of the church does his par faithfully, the workers in the field will be helped and encouraged and th cause of God will move forward with power. . . .

When you take time to cultivate your garden, thus gaining the exercis needed to keep the system in good working order, you are just as mucl doing the work of God as in holding meetings. God is our Father, H loves us, and He does not require any of His servants to abuse thei bodies.

Another cause, both of ill health and inefficiency in labor, i indigestion. It is impossible for the brain to do its best work when th digestive powers are abused. Many eat hurriedly of various kinds of food this causes war in the stomach, and confuses the brain. The use o unwholesome food, and overeating of even that which is wholesome should alike be avoided. Many eat at all hours, regardless of the laws o health. Then gloom covers the mind. How can men be honored witl divine enlightenment when they are so reckless in their habits, s inattentive to the light which God has given in regard to these things? . .

Life is a holy trust, which God alone can enable us to keep, and to us to His glory. But He who formed the wonderful structure of the body wil take special care to keep it in order if men do not work at cross-purpose with Him. Every talent entrusted to us He will help us to improve and us in accordance with the will of the Giver. Days, months, and years ar added to our existence that we may improve our opportunities an advantages for working out our individual salvation, and by our unselfis life promote the well-being of others. Thus may we build up the kingdor of Christ, and make manifest the glory of God.—*Review and Herald* June 20, 1912.

TRUE RELIGION PROMOTES HEALTH

[Wisdom's] ways are ways of pleasantness, and all her paths are peace. Prov. 3:17.

This world is not all sorrow and misery. "God is love" is written upon every opening bud, upon the petals of every flower, and upon every spire of grass. Though the curse of sin has caused the earth to bring forth thorns and thistles, there are flowers upon the thistles and the thorns are hidden by roses. All things in nature testify to the tender, fatherly care of our God and to His desire to make His children happy. His prohibitions and injunctions are not intended merely to display His authority, but in all that He does He has the well-being of His children in view. He does not require them to give up anything that it would be for their best interest to retain.

The opinion which prevails in some classes of society, that religion is not conducive to health or to happiness in this life, is one of the most mischievous of errors. The Scripture says: "The fear of the Lord tendeth to life: and he that hath it shall abide satisfied" (Prov. 19:23). "What man is he that desireth life, and loveth many days, that he may see good? Keep thy tongue from evil, and thy lips from speaking guile. Depart from evil, and do good; seek peace, and pursue it" (Ps. 34:12-14). The words of wisdom "are life unto those that find them, and health to all their flesh" (Prov. 4:22).

True religion brings man into harmony with the laws of God, physical, mental, and moral. It teaches self-control, serenity, temperance. Religion ennobles the mind, refines the taste, and sanctifies the judgment. It makes the soul a partaker of the purity of heaven. Faith in God's love and overruling providence lightens the burdens of anxiety and care. It fills the heart with joy and contentment in the highest or the lowliest lot. Religion tends directly to promote health, to lengthen life, and to heighten our enjoyment of all its blessings. It opens to the soul a never-failing fountain of happiness. Would that all who have not chosen Christ might realize that He has something vastly better to offer them than they are seeking for themselves. . . .

There is an intimate relation between the mind and the body, and in order to reach a high standard of moral and intellectual attainment the laws that control our physical being must be heeded. To secure a strong, well-balanced character, both the mental and the physical powers must be exercised and developed. What study can be more important . . . than that which treats of this wonderful organism that God has committed to us, and of the laws by which it may be preserved in health?—*Patriarchs and Prophets,* pp. 600, 601.

WE ARE TO VALUE GOD'S MARVELOUS WORKS

I will praise thee; I am fearfully and wonderfully made: marvellous are thy works; and that my soul knoweth right well. Ps. 139:14.

Every power that God has given us should be employed in the very wisest and highest service to God. The Lord has brought out a people from the world to fit them not only for a pure and holy heaven but to prepare them through the wisdom He shall give them to be colaborers with God in preparing a people to stand in the day of God.

Great light has been given upon health reform, but it is essential for all to treat this subject with candor and to advocate it with wisdom. In our experience we have seen many who have not presented health reform in a manner to make the best impression upon those whom they wish would receive their views. The Bible is full of wise counsel, and even the eating and drinking receive proper attention. The highest privilege that man can enjoy is to be a partaker of the divine nature, and faith that binds us in strong relationship to God will so fashion and mold mind and conduct that we become one with Christ. No one should through intemperate appetite so indulge his taste as to weaken any of the fine works of the human machinery and thus impair the mind or the body. Man is the Lord's purchased possession.

If we are partakers of the divine nature, we will live in communion with our Creator and value all of God's work which led David to exclaim, "I am fearfully and wonderfully made." We will not consider the organs of the body our own property, as if we had created them. All the faculties God has given to the human body are to be appreciated. . . . "For ye are bought with a price: therefore glorify God in your body, and in your spirit, which are God's" (1 Cor. 6:20).

We are not to treat unwisely one faculty of mind, soul, or body. We cannot abuse any of the delicate organs of the human body without having to pay the penalty because of transgression of nature's laws. Bible religion brought into practical life insures the highest culture of the intellect.

Temperance is exalted to a high level in the Word of God. Obeying His Word, we can rise higher and still higher. The danger of intemperance is specified. The advantage to be gained by temperance is laid open before us all through the Scriptures. The voice of God is addressing us, "Be ye therefore perfect, even as your Father which is in heaven is perfect" (Matt. 5:48). . . .

Health reform, wisely treated, will prove an entering wedge where the truth may follow with marked success.—*Review and Herald,* June 25, 1959.

POWER TO THINK AND TO DO

Acquaint now thyself with him, and be at peace: thereby good shall come unto thee. Job 22:21.

The law of love calls for the devotion of body, mind, and soul to the service of God and our fellow men. And this service, while making us a blessing to others, brings the greatest blessing to ourselves. Unselfishness underlies all true development. Through unselfish service we receive the highest culture of every faculty. More and more fully do we become partakers of the divine nature. We are fitted for heaven; for we receive heaven into our hearts.

Since God is the source of all true knowledge, it is . . . the first object of education to direct our minds to His own revelation of Himself. Adam and Eve received knowledge through direct communion with God; and they learned of Him through His works. All created things, in their original perfection, were an expression of the thought of God. To Adam and Eve nature was teeming with divine wisdom. But by transgression man was cut off from learning of God through direct communion and, to a great degree, through His works.

The earth, marred and defiled by sin, reflects but dimly the Creator's glory. It is true that His object lessons are not obliterated. Upon every page of the great volume of His created works may still be traced His handwriting. Nature still speaks of her Creator. Yet these revelations are partial and imperfect. And in our fallen state, with weakened powers and restricted vision, we are incapable of interpreting aright. We need the fuller revelation of Himself that God has given in His Written Word.

The Holy Scriptures are the perfect standard of truth. . . . Every human being, created in the image of God, is endowed with a power akin to that of the Creator—individuality, power to think and to do. The men in whom this power is developed are the men who bear responsibilities, who are leaders in enterprise, and who influence character. . . .

Let students be directed to the sources of truth, to the vast fields opened for research in nature and revelation. Let them contemplate the great facts of duty and destiny, and the mind will expand and strengthen. . . . Instead of some master passion becoming a power to destroy, every motive and desire are brought into conformity to the great principles of right. As the perfection of His character is dwelt upon, the mind is renewed, and the soul is re-created in the image of God. . . .

Higher than the highest human thought can reach is God's ideal for His children. Godliness—godlikeness—is the goal to be reached.—*Education,* pp. 16-18.

WE RECEIVE THE WISDOM OF ETERNITY

Give instruction to a wise man, and he will be yet wiser: teach a just man, and he will increase in learning. Prov. 9:9.

As we cherish and obey the promptings of the Spirit, our hearts are enlarged to receive more and more of His power, and to do more and better work. Dormant energies are aroused, and palsied faculties receive new life.

The humble worker who obediently responds to the call of God may be sure of receiving divine assistance. To accept so great and holy a responsibility is itself elevating to the character. It calls into action the highest mental and spiritual powers, and strengthens and purifies the mind and heart. Through faith in the power of God, it is wonderful how strong a weak man may become, how decided his efforts, how prolific of great results.

He who begins with a little knowledge, in a humble way, and tells what he knows, while seeking diligently for further knowledge, will find the whole heavenly treasure awaiting his demand. The more he seeks to impart light, the more light he will receive. The more one tries to explain the Word of God to others, with a love for souls, the plainer it becomes to himself. The more we use our knowledge and exercise our powers, the more knowledge and power we shall have.

Every effort made for Christ will react in blessing upon ourselves. If we use our means for His glory, He will give us more. As we seek to win others to Christ, bearing the burden of souls in our prayers, our own hearts will throb with the quickening influence of God's grace; our own affections will glow with more divine fervor; our whole Christian life will be more of a reality, more earnest, more prayerful.

The value of man is estimated in heaven according to the capacity of the heart to know God. This knowledge is the spring from which flows all power. God created man that every faculty might be the faculty of the divine mind; and He is ever seeking to bring the human mind into association with the divine. He offers us the privilege of cooperation with Christ in revealing His grace to the world, that we may receive increased knowledge of heavenly things.

Looking unto Jesus we obtain brighter and more distinct views of God, and by beholding we become changed. Goodness, love for our fellow men, becomes our natural instinct. We develop a character which is the counterpart of the divine character. Growing into His likeness, we enlarge our capacity for knowing God. More and more we enter into fellowship with the heavenly world, and we have continually increasing power to receive the riches of the knowledge and wisdom of eternity.
—*Christ's Object Lessons,* pp. 354-355.

TRUE STANDARDS OF CHRISTIAN EXCELLENCE

As he which hath called you is holy, so be ye holy in all manner of conversation; because it is written, Be ye holy; for I am holy. 1 Peter 1:15, 16.

It is the design of God that improvement shall be the lifework of all His people, and that in all their aims they should be guided and controlled by Christian principle and correct experience. But many fail to understand the true object of life; and under the influence of cherished errors, they sacrifice all there is of life that is really valuable. The true man is one who is willing to sacrifice his own interest for the good of others, and who forgets himself in ministering to their happiness.

Intellect is a mightier force than wealth or physical power. If sanctified and controlled by the Spirit of God, it can exert a powerful influence for good. Yet intellect alone does not make the man, according to the divine standard. When made a minister of vice, great intellect is a curse to the possessor and to all within its influence.

One's claim to a true manhood must be determined by the use of the powers which God has given him. Lord Byron had rare intellectual gifts; but he was not a man, according to God's standard. . . . This man was one of the world's distinguished men; still the Lord acknowledged him only as one who had abused his God-given talents. Many others whom God endowed with giant minds, and whom the world called great men, rallied under the banner of Satan, and used the gifts of God for the perversion of truth and of destruction of the souls of men. . . .

In contrast with the lives of such men is that of Martin Luther. He was not born a prince. He wore no royal crown. From a cloistered cell his voice was heard, and his influence felt. He had a noble, generous heart, as well as a vigorous intellect, and all his powers were exercised for the good of humanity. He stood bravely for truth and right, and breasted the world's opposition to benefit his fellow men.

That which will bless humanity is spiritual life. If the man is in harmony with God, he will depend continually upon Him for strength. "Be ye therefore perfect, even as your Father which is in heaven is perfect." It should be our lifework to press forward continually toward the perfection of Christian character, ever striving for conformity to the will of God, remembering that the efforts begun upon earth will continue throughout eternity. God has set before the human family an elevated standard, and he who is true to his God-given manhood will not only promote the happiness of his fellow creatures in this life, but will aid them to secure an eternal reward in the life to come.—*Signs of the Times,* June 17, 1886.

WISDOM THAT FULFILLS GOD'S PURPOSE

The fear of the Lord is the beginning of wisdom: and the knowledge of the holy is understanding. Prov. 9:10.

All the varied capabilities that men possess—of mind and soul and body—are given them by God, to be so employed as to reach the highest possible degree of excellence. But this cannot be a selfish and exclusive culture; for the character of God, whose likeness we are to receive, is benevolence and love. Every faculty, every attribute, with which the Creator has endowed us is to be employed for His glory and for the uplifting of our fellow men. And in this employment is found its purest, noblest, and happiest exercise.

Were this principle given the attention which its importance demands, there would be a radical change in some of the current methods of education. Instead of appealing to pride and selfish ambition, kindling a spirit of emulation, teachers would endeavor to awaken the love of goodness and truth and beauty—to arouse the desire for excellence. The student would seek the development of God's gifts in himself, not to excel others, but to fulfill the purpose of the Creator and to receive His likeness. Instead of being directed to merely earthly standards, or being actuated by the desire for self-exaltation, which in itself dwarfs and belittles, the mind would be directed to the Creator, to know Him and to become like Him. . . .

The great work of life is character building, and a knowledge of God is the foundation of all true education. . . . The law of God is a reflection of His character. Hence the psalmist says, "All thy commandments are righteousness"; and "through thy precepts I get understanding." God has revealed Himself to us in His Word and in the works of creation. Through the volume of inspiration and the book of nature we are to obtain a knowledge of God.

It is a law of the mind that it gradually adapts itself to the subjects upon which it is trained to dwell. If occupied with commonplace matters only, it will become dwarfed and enfeebled. If never required to grapple with difficult problems, it will after a time almost lose the power of growth. As an educating power the Bible is without a rival. In the Word of God the mind finds subject for the deepest thought, the loftiest aspiration. The Bible is the most instructive history that men possess. It came fresh from the fountain of eternal truth, and a divine hand has preserved its purity through all the ages.—*Patriarchs and Prophets,* pp. 595, 596.

ENLIGHTENED TO FULL RADIANCE

If we follow on to know the Lord: his going forth is prepared as the morning. Hosea 6:3.

We are living amid the perils of the last days, and we are to cleanse ourselves from all defilement, and put on the robe of Christ's righteousness. The work of God is to be steadily carried forward. We are to bring ourselves, body, soul, and spirit, into subjection to Christ. Unless we do this, the health of both body and soul will be endangered.

God desires His workers to gain daily an understanding of how to reason logically from cause to effect, arriving at wise, safe conclusions. He desires them to add to the strength of the memory. We cannot afford to make mistakes. As little children we are to sit at the feet of Christ, learning of Him how to work successfully. We are to ask God for sound judgment, and for light to impart to others. There is need of knowledge that is the fruit of experience. We should not allow a day to pass without gaining an increase of knowledge in temporal and spiritual things. We are to plant no stakes that we are not willing to take up and plant farther on, nearer the heights we hope to ascend.

The highest education is to be found in training the mind to advance day to day. The close of each day should find us a day's march nearer the overcomer's reward. Day by day our understanding is to ripen. Day by day we are to work out conclusions that will bring a rich reward in this life, and in the life to come. Looking daily to Jesus, instead of to what we ourselves have done, we shall make decided advancement in temporal as well as spiritual knowledge.

The end of all things is at hand. What we have done must not be allowed to place the period to our work. The Captain of our salvation says, ''Advance. The night cometh, in which no man can work.'' Constantly we are to increase in usefulness. Our lives are always to be under the power of Christ. Our lamps are to be kept burning brightly.

Prayer is a heaven-ordained means of success. Appeals, petitions, entreaties, between man and man, move men, and act as a part in controlling the affairs of nations. But prayer moves heaven. That power alone that comes in answer to prayer will make men wise in the wisdom of heaven, and enable them to work in the unity of the Spirit, joined together by the bonds of peace. Prayer, faith, confidence in God, bring a divine power that sets human calculations at their real worth—nothingness. . . .

He who places himself where God can enlighten him advances, as it were, from the partial obscurity of dawn to the full radiance of noonday.—*Australasian Union Conference Record,* Nov. 1, 1904.

ENJOYING LIFE'S REAL PLEASURES

I shall . . . praise him, who is the health of my countenance, and my God. Ps. 42:11.

The wise man says that wisdom's "ways are ways of pleasantness, and all her paths are peace." Many cherish the impression that devotion to God is detrimental to health and to cheerful happiness in the social relations of life. But those who walk in the path of wisdom and holiness find that "godliness is profitable unto all things, having promise of the life that now is, and of that which is to come." They are alive to the enjoyment of life's real pleasures, while they are not troubled with vain regrets over misspent hours, nor with gloom or horror of mind, as the worldling often is when not diverted by some exciting amusement.

It is true that there are many professing Christians who have diseased imaginations, and do not correctly represent the religion of the Bible. They are ever walking under a cloud. They seem to think it a virtue to complain of depression of spirits, great trials, and severe conflicts. This course is not in accordance with the words of the Saviour, "Let your light so shine before men, that they may see your good works, and glorify your Father which is in heaven." It is the duty of all to walk in the light, and to cultivate habitual cheerfulness of mind, that they may reflect light rather than gloom and darkness.

Godliness does not conflict with the laws of health, but is in harmony with them. Had men ever been obedient to the law of ten commandments, had they carried out in their lives the principles of these ten precepts, the curse of disease that now floods the world would not be. Men may teach that trifling amusements are necessary to keep the mind above despondency. The mind may indeed be thus diverted for the time being; but after the excitement is over, calm reflection comes. Conscience arouses, and makes her voice heard, saying, "This is not the way to obtain health or true happiness."

There are many amusements that excite the mind, but depression is sure to follow. Other modes of recreation are innocent and healthful; but useful labor that affords physical exercise will often have a more beneficial influence upon the mind, while at the same time it will strengthen the muscles, improve the circulation, and prove a powerful agent in the recovery of health.

"What man is he that desireth life, and loveth many days, that he may see good? . . . The righteous cry, and the Lord heareth, and delivereth them out of all their troubles."—*Signs of the Times,* Oct. 23, 1884.

THE HIGHWAY TO HEALTH

The eyes of the Lord are upon the righteous, and his ears are open unto their cry. Ps. 34:15.

The consciousness of rightdoing is the best medicine for diseased bodies and minds. The special blessing of God resting upon the receiver is health and strength. One whose mind is quiet and satisfied in God is on the highway to health. To have the consciousness that the eye of the Lord is upon us, and that His ear is open to our prayers, is a satisfaction indeed. To know that we have a never-failing Friend to whom we can confide all the secrets of the soul is a happiness which words can never express. Those whose moral faculties are clouded by disease are not the ones to rightly represent the Christian life or the beauties of holiness. They are too often in the fire of fanaticism, or the water of cold indifference or stolid gloom.

Those who do not feel that it is a religious duty to discipline the mind to dwell upon cheerful subjects will usually be found at one of two extremes: they will be elated by a continual round of exciting amusements, indulging in frivolous conversation, laughing, and joking, or they will be depressed, having great trials and mental conflicts, which they think but few have ever experienced or can understand. . . . Appropriate labor, the healthy exercise of all their powers, would withdraw their thoughts from themselves. . . .

If they would train their minds to dwell upon themes which have nothing to do with self, they might yet be useful. . . .

Despondent feelings are frequently the result of too much leisure. The hands and mind should be occupied in useful labor, lightening the burdens of others; and those who are thus employed will benefit themselves also. . . .

The mind should be drawn away from self; its powers should be exercised in devising means to make others happier and better. "Pure religion and undefiled before God and the Father is this, To visit the fatherless and widows in their affliction, and to keep himself unspotted from the world" (James 1:27).

True religion ennobles the mind, refines the taste, sanctifies the judgment, and makes its possessor a partaker of the purity and holiness of heaven. It brings angels near, and separates us more and more from the spirit and influence of the world. It enters into all the acts and relations of life, and gives us the "spirit of . . . a sound mind," and the result is happiness and peace.—*Signs of the Times,* Oct. 23, 1884.

MENTAL CULTURE GAINED BY BIBLE STUDY

By knowledge shall the chambers be filled with all precious and pleasant riches. Prov. 24:4.

For the mind and the soul, as well as for the body, it is God's law that strength is acquired by effort. It is exercise that develops. In harmony with this law, God has provided in His Word the means for mental and spiritual development.

The Bible contains all the principles that men need to understand in order to be fitted either for this life or the life to come. And these principles may be understood by all. No one with a spirit to appreciate its teaching can read a single passage from the Bible without gaining from it some helpful thought. But the most valuable teaching of the Bible is not to be gained by occasional or disconnected study. Its great system of truth is not so presented as to be discerned by the hasty or careless reader. . . . The truths that go to make up the great whole must be searched out and gathered up, "here a little, and there a little" (Isa. 28:10).

When thus searched out and brought together, they will be found to be perfectly fitted to one another. Each Gospel is a supplement to the others, every prophecy an explanation of another, every truth a development of some other truth. The types of the Jewish economy are made plain by the gospel. Every principle in the Word of God has its place, every fact its bearing. And the complete structure, in design and execution, bears testimony to its Author. Such a structure no mind but that of the Infinite could conceive or fashion.

In searching out the various parts and studying their relationship, the highest faculties of the human mind are called into intense activity. No one can engage in such study without developing mental power.

And not alone in searching out truth and bringing it together does the mental value of Bible study consist. It consists also in the effort required to grasp the themes presented. The mind occupied with commonplace matters only, becomes dwarfed and enfeebled. If never tasked to comprehend grand and far-reaching truths, it after a time loses the power of growth. As a safeguard against this degeneracy, and a stimulus to development, nothing else can equal the study of God's Word.

As a means of intellectual training, the Bible is more effective than any other book, or all other books combined. . . . No other study can impart such mental power as does the effort to grasp the stupendous truths of revelation. The mind thus brought in contact with the thoughts of the Infinite cannot but expand and strengthen.—*Education*, pp. 123, 124.

AIM FOR CONTINUAL ADVANCEMENT

Keep thy heart with all diligence; for out of it are the issues of life. Prov. 4:23.

Truly earnest men are few in our world, but they are greatly needed. The example of an energetic person is far-reaching; he has an electric power over others. He meets obstacles in his work; but he has the push in him, and instead of allowing his way to be hedged up, he breaks down every barrier. . . .

There are thorns in every path. All who follow the Lord's leading must expect to meet with disappointments, crosses, and losses. But a spirit of true heroism will help them to overcome these. Many greatly magnify seeming difficulties, and then begin to pity themselves and give way to despondency. Such need to make an entire change in themselves. They need to discipline themselves to put forth exertion, and to overcome all childish feelings. They should determine that life shall not be spent in working at trifles. Let them resolve to accomplish something, and then do it.

Many make good resolutions, but they are always going to do something and never get to it. About all their resolutions amount to is talk. In many cases, if they had more energy and accomplished something in spite of obstacles, they would have far better health.

Everyone should have an aim, an object, in life. The loins of the mind should be girded up, and the thoughts be trained to keep to the point as the compass to the pole. The mind should be directed in the right channel, according to well-formed plans. Then every step will be a step in advance. No time will be lost in following vague ideas and random plans. Worthy purposes should be kept constantly in view, and every thought and act should tend to their accomplishment. Let there ever be a fixedness of purpose to carry out that which is undertaken.

Success or failure in this life depends much upon the manner in which the thoughts are disciplined. If they are controlled as God directs that they shall be, they will be upon those subjects which will lead to greater devotion. If the thoughts are right, the words will be right. . . .

The afternoon sun of . . . life may be more mellow and productive of fruit than the morning sun. It may continue to increase in size and brightness until it drops behind the western hills. . . . Keep your heart and mind young by continuous exercise. . . .

The Bible is the best book in the world for intellectual culture. The grand themes presented in it, the dignified simplicity with which these themes are handled, the light which it sheds upon the mysteries of heaven, bring strength and vigor to the understanding.—*Review and Herald,* April 6, 1886.

CHRISTIANS TO MOVE ONWARD AND UPWARD

Be renewed in the spirit of your mind; and that ye put on the new man, which after God is created in righteousness and true holiness. Eph. 4:23, 24.

Wrong habits must be overcome. Right habits must be formed. Under the discipline of the greatest Teacher the world has ever known, Christians must move onward and upward toward perfection. This is God's command, and no one should say, I cannot do it. He should say instead, God requires me to be perfect, and He will give me strength to overcome all that stands in the way of perfection. He is the source of all wisdom, all power. . . .

Christians are to be light bearers, saying to all with whom they come in contact, ''Behold the Lamb of God, which taketh away the sin of the world.'' They are to be examples of piety, representing Christ in word, in spirit, in action. Their actions are to be a copy of the actions of the Saviour. Thus they are to show the superiority of Christ's principles over the principles of the world. They are to work upon a higher plane of action than do those who are not Christians. They are to bring the ennobling influence of the gospel into every phase of life. Their purity and usefulness are to be a source of illumination to others.

The world has set up a standard to suit the inclinations of unsanctified hearts, but this is not the standard of those who love Christ. The Redeemer has chosen them out of the world, and has left them His sinless life as a standard. He wants them to rise above all cheapness of word or action. . . . ''Gird up the loins of your mind, be sober, and hope to the end for the grace that is to be brought unto you at the revelation of Jesus Christ; . . . as he which hath called you is holy, so be ye holy in all manner of conversation; because it is written, Be ye holy; for I am holy.''

These words are to be believed and practiced. Christians are to be superior in wisdom, in knowledge, in skill, because they believe in God and His power. The Lord desires them to reach the highest round of the ladder, that they may glorify Him. He has a treasure-house of wisdom from which they may draw. . . .

The true Christian obtains an experience that brings holiness. The light of truth irradiates his understanding. A glow of love for the Redeemer clears away the cloud that has interposed between his soul and God. The will of God, pure, elevated, and sanctified, becomes his will. His countenance reveals the light of heaven. His body is a fit temple for the Holy Spirit. Holiness adorns his character. God can commune with him; for soul and body are in harmony with the principles of heaven.—*Signs of the Times,* July 17, 1901.

THE TEMPLE OF GOD

He died for all, that they which live should not henceforth live unto themselves, but unto him which died for them, and rose again. 2 Cor. 5:15.

Man is God's workmanship, His masterpiece, created for a high and holy purpose; and on every part of the human tabernacle God desires to write His law. Every nerve and muscle, every mental and physical endowment, is to be kept pure.

God designs that the body shall be a temple for His Spirit. How solemn then is the responsibility resting on every soul. If we defile our bodies, we are doing harm not only to ourselves, but to many others. . . .

Christ died that the moral image of God might be restored in humanity, that men and women might be partakers of the divine nature, having escaped the corruption that is in the world through lust. We are to use no power of our being for selfish gratification; for all our powers belong to Him, and are to be used to His glory. . . .

The human house, God's building, requires close, watchful guardianship. With David we can exclaim, "I am fearfully and wonderfully made." God's workmanship is to be preserved, that the heavenly universe and the apostate race may see that men and women are temples of the living God.

The perfection of character which God requires is the fitting up of the whole being as a temple for the indwelling of the Holy Spirit. The Lord requires the service of the entire being. He desires men and women to become all that He has made it possible for them to be. It is not enough for certain parts of the human machinery to be used. All parts must be brought into action, or the service is deficient. . . .

The physical life is to be carefully educated, cultivated, and developed, that through men and women the divine nature may be revealed in its fullness. God expects men to use the intellect He has given them. He expects them to use every reasoning power for Him. They are to give the conscience the place of supremacy that has been assigned to it. The mental and physical powers, with the affections, are to be so cultivated that they can reach the highest efficiency. Thus Christ is represented to the world. . . .

Is God pleased to see any of the organs or faculties He has given man neglected, misused, or deprived of the health and efficiency it is possible for them to have? Then cultivate the gift of faith. Be brave, and overcome every practice which mars the soul temple. We are wholly dependent on God, and our faith is strengthened by believing, though we cannot see God's purpose in His dealing with us, or the consequence of this dealing. Faith points forward and upward to things to come, laying hold of the only power that can make us complete in Him.—*Review and Herald,* Nov. 6, 1900.

EDEN, THE FIRST HOME

The Lord God . . . made . . . a woman, and brought her unto the man. . . . Therefore shall a man leave his father and his mother, and shall cleave unto his wife: and they shall be one flesh. Genesis 2:22-24.

God celebrated the first marriage. Thus the institution has for its originator the Creator of the universe. ''Marriage is honourable'' (Heb. 13:4); it was one of the first gifts of God to man, and it is one of the two institutions that, after the Fall, Adam brought with him beyond the gates of Paradise. When the divine principles are recognized and obeyed in this relation, marriage is a blessing; it guards the purity and happiness of the race, it provides for man's social needs, it elevates the physical, the intellectual, and the moral nature. . . .

The home of our first parents was to be a pattern for other homes as their children should go forth to occupy the earth. That home, beautified by the hand of God Himself, was not a gorgeous palace. . . . God placed Adam in a garden. This was his dwelling. . . . In the surroundings of the holy pair was a lesson for all time—that true happiness is found, not in the indulgence of pride and luxury, but in communion with God through His created works. If men would give less attention to the artificial, and would cultivate greater simplicity, they would come far nearer to answering the purpose of God in their creation. Pride and ambition are never satisfied, but those who are truly wise will find substantial and elevating pleasure in the sources of enjoyment that God has placed within the reach of all.

To the dwellers in Eden was committed the care of the garden, ''to dress it and to keep it.'' Their occupation was not wearisome, but pleasant and invigorating. God appointed labor as a blessing to man, to occupy his mind, to strengthen his body, and to develop his faculties. In mental and physical activity Adam found one of the highest pleasures of his holy existence. . . . The holy pair were not only children under the fatherly care of God but students receiving instruction from the all-wise Creator. . . . The order and harmony of creation spoke to them of infinite wisdom and power. They were ever discovering some attraction that filled their hearts with deeper love and called forth fresh expressions of gratitude.

So long as they remained loyal to the divine law, their capacity to know, to enjoy, and to love would continually increase. They would be constantly gaining new treasures of knowledge, discovering fresh springs of happiness, and obtaining clearer and yet clearer conceptions of the immeasurable, unfailing love of God.—*Patriarchs and Prophets,* pp. 46-51.

THE INFLUENCE OF A CHRISTIAN HOME

He that followeth me shall not walk in darkness, but shall have the light of life. John 8:12.

Our time, our strength, and our energies belong to God; and if they are consecrated to His service, our light will shine. It will affect first and most strongly those in our own homes, who are most intimately associated with us; but it will extend beyond the home, even to "the world." To many it will be a savor of life unto life; but there are some who will refuse to see the light, or to walk in it. They are of that class spoken of by our Saviour, when He said: "And this is the condemnation, that light is come into the world, and men loved darkness rather than light, because their deeds were evil." Such are in a very dangerous position; but their course does not excuse any of us from letting our light shine.

Suppose that because some ship had disregarded his warning beacon, and gone to pieces on the rocks, the lighthouse keeper should put out his lights, and say, "I will pay no more attention to the lighthouse"; what would be the consequence? But that is not the way he does. He keeps his lights burning all night, throwing their beams far out into the darkness, for the benefit of every mariner that comes within the dangerous reach of rocks and shoals. Were some ship to be wrecked because the lights went out, it would be telegraphed over the world that on such a night, at such a point, a ship went to pieces on the rocks because there was no light in the tower. But if some ships are wrecked because they pay no attention to the light, the lighthouse keeper is guiltless; they were warned, but they paid no heed.

What if the light in the household should go out? Then everyone in that house would be in darkness; and the result would be as disastrous as though the light were to go out in the lighthouse tower. Souls are looking at you, fellow Christians, to see whether you are drunken with the cares of this life, or are preparing for the future, immortal life. They will watch to see what the influence of your life is, and whether you are true missionaries at home, training your children for heaven.

The Christian's first duty is in the home. Fathers and mothers, yours is a great responsibility. You are preparing your children for life or for death; you are training them for an abiding place here in the earth, for self-gratification in this life, or for the immortal life, to praise God forever. And which shall it be? It should be the burden of your life to have every child that God has committed to your trust receive the divine mold.—*Signs of the Times,* Jan. 14, 1886.

AN ARGUMENT INFIDELS CANNOT RESIST

While ye have light, believe in the light, that ye may be the children of light. John 12:36.

A well-ordered Christian household is an argument that the infidel cannot resist. He finds no place for his cavils [trivial faultfinding]. And the children of such a household are prepared to meet the sophistries of infidelity. They have accepted the Bible as the basis of their faith, and they have a firm foundation that cannot be swept away by the incoming tide of skepticism.

Said Christ, "Ye are the light of the world." He has committed talents to our keeping. What are we doing with His entrusted gifts? Are we letting our light shine by using them for His glory and the benefit of our fellow men, or are we using them to advance our own selfish interests? Many are using them selfishly. They do not seem to realize that we are all judgment-bound, and must soon give an account for the use we have made of our God-given opportunities to do good. But what excuse will they give in that great day for not using in the cause of God their skill, their education, their tact, and their perseverance and zeal?

We need divine help if we would keep our lights burning. But Jesus died to provide that aid. He extends the invitation: "Let him take hold of my strength, that he may make peace with me; and he shall make peace with me." Cling to the arm of Infinite Power; then you will find Him precious to your soul, and all heaven will be at your command. "If we walk in the light, as he is in the light," we shall have the companionship of holy angels. To "Joshua" it was said, "Thus saith the Lord of hosts: If thou wilt walk in my ways, and if thou wilt keep my charge, . . . I will give thee places to walk among these that stand by." And who are "these that stand by"? They are the angels of God. Joshua must have a living confiding trust in God every day; and then angels would walk with him, and the power of God would rest upon him in all his labors.

Then, Christian friends, fathers and mothers, let your light grow dim—no, never! Let your heart grow faint, or your hands weary—no, never! And by and by the portals of the celestial city will be opened to you; and you may present yourselves and your children before the throne saying, "Here am I, and the children whom Thou hast given me." And what a reward for faithfulness that will be, to see your children crowned with immortal life in the beautiful city of God!—*Signs of the Times,* Jan. 14, 1886.

LAYING HOLD OF THE MIGHTY ONE OF HEAVEN

Let the beauty of the Lord our God be upon us: and establish thou the work of our hands upon us; yea, the work of our hands establish thou it. Ps. 90:17.

Your children should be taught to control their tempers and to cultivate a loving, Christlike spirit. So direct them that they will love the service of God, that they will take more pleasure in going to the house of worship than to places of amusement. Teach them that religion is a living principle. Had I been brought up with the idea that religion is a mere feeling, my life would have been a useless one. But I never let feeling come between Heaven and my soul. Whatever my feelings may be, I will seek God at the commencement of the day, at noon, and at night, that I may draw strength from the living Source of power.

[Mothers,] has . . . not [your time] been given you to be spent in beautifying the minds of your children, and cultivating loveliness of character? Should it not be spent in laying hold of the Mighty One of heaven, and seeking Him for power and wisdom to train your children for a place in His kingdom, to secure for them a life that will endure as long as the throne of Jehovah? . . .

Perhaps the mother sits at her work night after night, while her children go to bed without a prayer or a good-night kiss. She does not bind their tender hearts to her own by the cords of love; for she is "too busy." . . .

Some may wonder why it is that we say so much about home religion and the children. It is because of the terrible neglect of home duties on the part of so many. As the servants of God, parents, you are responsible for the children committed to your care. Many of them are growing up without reverence, growing up careless and irreligious, unthankful and unholy.

If these children had been properly trained and disciplined, if they had been brought up in the nurture and admonition of the Lord, heavenly angels would be in your homes. If you were true home missionaries, . . . you would be . . . fitting your children to stand by your side, as efficient workers in the cause of God.

What an impression it makes upon society to see a family united in the work and service of the Lord. Such a family is a powerful discourse in favor of the reality of Christianity. Others see that there is an influence at work in the family that affects the children, and that the God of Abraham is with them. And that which has such a powerful influence on the children is felt beyond the home, and affects other lives. If the homes of professed Christians had a right religious mold, they would exert a mighty influence for good. They would indeed be the "light of the world."—*Signs of the Times*, Jan. 14, 1886.

CHRIST BESTOWS THE GRACES NEEDED

That our sons may be as plants grown up in their youth; that our daughters may be as corner stones, polished after the similitude of a palace. Ps. 144:12.

The first and most urgent duty which the mother owes to her Creator is to train for Him the children that He has given her. . . . How careful, then, should be her language and behavior in the presence of these little learners. . . .

Mothers, awake to the fact that your influence and example are affecting the character and destiny of your children; and in view of your responsibility, develop a well-balanced mind, and a pure character, reflecting only the true, the good, and the beautiful.

Your compassionate Redeemer is watching you with love and sympathy, ready to hear your prayers, and to render you the assistance which you need. He knows the burdens of every mother's heart, and is her best friend in every emergency. His everlasting arms support the God-fearing, faithful mother. When upon earth, He had a mother that struggled with poverty, having many anxious cares and perplexities, and He sympathizes with every Christian mother in her cares and anxieties. That Saviour who took a long journey for the purpose of relieving the anxious heart of a woman whose daughter was possessed by an evil spirit will hear the mother's prayers, and will bless her children.

He who gave back to the widow her only son as he was carried to the burial is touched today by the woe of the bereaved mother. He who wept tears of sympathy at the grave of Lazarus, and gave back to Martha and Mary their buried brother; who pardoned Mary Magdalene; who remembered His mother when He was hanging in agony upon the cross; who appeared to the weeping women, and made them His messengers to spread the first glad tidings of a risen Saviour—He is woman's best friend today, and is ready to aid her in all the relations of life.

Our Saviour, who understands our heart struggles, and knows the weakness of our natures, pities our infirmities, forgives our errors, and bestows upon us the graces which we earnestly desire. Joy, peace, long-suffering, gentleness, faith, and charity are the elements of the Christian character. These precious graces are the fruit of the Spirit, and the Christian's crown and shield. Where these graces reign in the home, the sons are "as plants grown up in their youth," and the daughters "as corner stones, polished after the similitude of a palace." These heavenly attainments are not dependent upon circumstances, nor the will of imperfect judgment of man. Nothing can give more perfect contentment and satisfaction than the cultivation of a Christian character; the most exalted aspirations can aim at nothing higher.—*Signs of the Times,* Sept. 9, 1886.

CHRIST EASES THE BURDENS OF PARENTS

Come unto me, all ye that labour and are heavy laden, and I will give you rest. Take my yoke upon you, and learn of me; . . . and ye shall find rest unto your souls. Matt. 11:28, 29.

No work can equal that of the Christian mother. She takes up her work with a sense of what it is to bring up her children in the nurture and admonition of the Lord. How often will she feel her burden's weight heavier than she can bear; and then how precious the privilege of taking it all to her sympathizing Saviour in prayer. She may lay her burden at His feet, and find in His presence a strength that will sustain her, and give her cheerfulness, hope, courage, and wisdom in the most trying hours. How sweet to the care-worn mother is the consciousness of such a Friend in all her difficulties. If mothers would go to Christ more frequently, and trust Him more fully, their burdens would be easier, and they would find rest to their souls.

Jesus is a lover of children. The important responsibility of training her children should not rest alone upon the mother. . . . The father should encourage and sustain the mother in her work of care by his cheerful looks and kind words. . . . Her children must have her time and attention. . . . This training of children to meet the Bible standard will require time, perseverance, and prayer. This should be attended to if some things about the house are neglected.

Many times in the day is the cry of Mother, Mother, heard, first from one little troubled voice and then another. In answer to the cry, mother must turn here and there to attend to their demands. . . . A word of approval will bring sunshine to the heart for hours. Many precious beams of light and gladness can the mother shed here and there among her precious little ones. How closely can she bind those dear ones to her heart, that her presence will be to them the sunniest place in the world.

But frequently the patience of the mother is taxed with these numerous little trials, that seem scarcely worth attention. . . . She almost forgets herself time and again, but a silent prayer to her pitying Redeemer calms her nerves, and she is enabled to hold the reins of self-control with quiet dignity. She speaks with calm voice, but it has cost her an effort to restrain harsh words and subdue angry feelings, which, if expressed, would have destroyed her influence, which it would have taken time to regain. . . . As the parents wish God to deal with them, so should they deal with their children.

Our children are only the younger members of the Lord's family, entrusted to us to educate wisely, to patiently discipline, that they may form Christian characters, and be qualified to bless others in this life, and enjoy the life to come.—*Signs of the Times,* Sept. 13, 1877.

PARENTS TO TEACH OBEDIENCE

Children, obey your parents in the Lord: for this is right. Eph. 6:1.

The children are to be taught that their capabilities were given them for the honor and glory of God. To this end they must learn the lesson of obedience; for only by lives of willing obedience can they render to God the service He requires. Before the child is old enough to reason, he must be taught to obey. By gentle, persistent effort, the habit should be established. . . .

Let children be shown that true reverence is revealed by obedience. God has commanded nothing that is unessential, and there is no other way of manifesting reverence so pleasing to Him as by obedience to that which He has spoken.

The mother is the queen of the home, and the children are her subjects. She is to rule her household wisely, in the dignity of her motherhood. . . . Tell your children exactly what you require of them. Then let them understand that your word must be obeyed. Thus you are training them to respect the commandments of God, which plainly declare, ''Thou shalt,'' and ''Thou shalt not.''

Few parents begin early enough to teach their children to obey. The child is usually allowed to get two or three years the start of its parents, who forbear to discipline it, thinking it too young to learn to obey. But all this time self is growing strong in the little being, and every day makes harder the parent's task of gaining control. At a very early age children can comprehend what is plainly and simply told them, and by kind and judicious management can be taught to obey. Never should they be allowed to show their parents disrespect. Self-will should never be permitted to go unrebuked. The future well-being of the child requires kindly, loving, but firm discipline. . . .

Wise parents will not say to their children, ''Follow your own choice; go where you will, and do what you will''; but, ''Listen to the instruction of the Lord.'' Wise rules and regulations must be made and enforced, that the beauty of the homelife may not be spoiled. . . .

Children will be happier, far happier, under proper discipline than if left to do as their unrestrained impulses suggest. A child's truest graces consist in modesty and obedience—in attentive ears to hear the words of direction, in willing feet and hands to walk and work in the path of duty. . . .

Above all things, parents should surround their children with an atmosphere of cheerfulness, courtesy, and love. A home where love dwells and where it finds expression in looks, in words, in acts, is a place where angels delight to dwell.—*Counsels to Parents and Teachers,* pp. 111-115.

CHRIST, THE WIFE AND MOTHER'S STRENGTH

Her children arise up, and call her blessed; her husband also, and he praiseth her. Prov. 31:28.

It is true that the wheels of domestic machinery will not always run smoothly; there is much to try the patience and tax the strength. But while mothers are not responsible for circumstances over which they have no control, it is useless to deny that circumstances make a great difference with mothers in their lifework. But their condemnation is when circumstances are allowed to rule, and to subvert their principle, when they grow tired and unfaithful to their high trust, and neglect their known duty.

The wife and mother who nobly overcomes difficulties, under which others sink for want of patience and fortitude to persevere, not only becomes strong herself in doing her duty, but her experience in overcoming temptations and obstacles qualifies her to be an efficient help to others, both by words and example. Many who do well under favorable circumstances seem to undergo a transformation of character under adversity and trial; they deteriorate in proportion to their troubles. God never designed that we should be the sport of circumstances. . . .

[The true wife and mother] will perform her duties with dignity and cheerfulness, not considering that it is degrading to do with her own hands whatever is necessary for her to do in a well-ordered household. If she looks to God for her strength and comfort, and in His wisdom and fear seeks to do her daily duty, she will bind her husband to her heart, and see her children coming to maturity, honorable men and women, having moral stamina to follow the example of their mother.

There is no chance work in this life; the harvest will determine the character of the seed that has been sown. . . .

Mothers, you are developing character. Your compassionate Redeemer is watching you in love and sympathy, ready to hear your prayers, and render you the assistance which you need in your lifework. Love, joy, peace, long-suffering, gentleness, faith, and charity are the elements of the Christlike character. These precious graces are the fruits of the Spirit. They are the Christian's crown and shield. The highest daydreaming and most exalted aspirations can aim at nothing higher. Nothing can give more perfect content and satisfaction.

These heavenly attainments are not dependent upon circumstances, nor the will or imperfect judgment of man. The precious Saviour, who understands our heart struggles and the weaknesses of our natures, pities, and forgives us our errors, and bestows upon us the graces which we earnestly desire.—*Health Reformer,* Aug., 1877.

FATHERS TO SPEND TIME WITH CHILDREN

And, ye fathers, provoke not your children to wrath: but bring them up in the nurture and admonition of the Lord. Eph. 6:4.

While we have dwelt upon the importance of the mother's work and mission, we would not lightly pass over the duty and responsibility of the husband and father in the training of his children. His efforts should be in harmony with those of the God-fearing mother. He should manifest his love and respect for her as the woman he has chosen and the mother of his children. . . .

Fathers should . . . mingle with the children, sympathizing with them in their little troubles, binding them to their hearts by the strong bonds of love, and establishing such an influence over their expanding minds that their counsel will be regarded as sacred. . . .

Upon returning home from his business he should find it a pleasant change to spend some time with his children. He may take them into the garden, and show them the opening buds, and the varied tints of the blooming flowers. Through such mediums he may give them the most important lessons concerning the Creator, by opening before them the great book of nature, where the love of God is expressed in every tree, and flower, and blade of grass. He may impress upon their minds the fact that if God cares so much for the trees and flowers, He will care much more for the creatures formed in His image. He may lead them early to understand that God wants children to be lovely, not with artificial adornment, but with beauty of character, the charms of kindness and affection, which will make their hearts bound with joy and happiness.

Parents may do much to connect their children with God by encouraging them to love the things of nature which He has given them, and to recognize the hand of the Giver in all they receive. The soil of the heart may thus early be prepared for casting in the precious seeds of truth, which in due time will spring up and bear a rich harvest. Fathers, the golden hours which you might spend in getting a thorough knowledge of the temperament and character of your children, and the best methods of dealing with their young minds, are . . . precious.—*Signs of the Times,* Dec. 6, 1877.

The father's duty to his children should be one of his first interests. It should not be set aside for the sake of acquiring a fortune, or of gaining a high position in the world. In fact, those very conditions of affluence and honor frequently separate a man from his family, and cut off his influence from them more than anything else. If the father would have his children develop harmonious characters, and be an honor to him and a blessing to the world, he has a special work to do.—*Ibid.,* Dec. 20, 1877.

FATHERS TO LEAD CHILDREN TO RELIGIOUS LIGHT

Except the Lord build the house, they labour in vain that build it. Ps. 127:1.

What can we say to awaken the moral sensibilities of fathers, that they may understand and undertake their duty to their offspring? The subject is of intense interest and importance, having a bearing upon the future welfare of our country. We would solemnly impress upon fathers, as well as mothers, the grave responsibility they have assumed in bringing children into the world. It is a responsibility from which nothing but death can free them. True, the chief care and burden rests upon the mother during the first years of her children's lives, yet even then the father should be her stay and counsel, encouraging her to lean upon his large affections, and assisting her as much as possible. . . .

In that great day of reckoning it will be asked him: Where are the children that I entrusted to your care to educate for Me, that their lips might speak My praise, and their lives be as a diadem of beauty in the world, and they live to honor Me through all eternity?

In some children the moral powers strongly predominate. They have power of will to control their minds and actions. In others the animal passions are almost irresistible. To meet these diverse temperaments, which frequently appear in the same family, fathers, as well as mothers, need patience and wisdom from the divine Helper. . . .

The father should frequently gather his children around him, and lead their minds into channels of moral and religious light. He should study their different tendencies and susceptibilities, and reach them through the plainest avenues. Some may be best influenced through veneration and the fear of God; others through the manifestation of His benevolence and wise providence, calling forth their deep gratitude; others may be more deeply impressed by opening before them the wonders and mysteries of the natural world, with all its delicate harmony and beauty, which speak to their souls of Him who is the Creator of the heavens and the earth, and all the beautiful things therein.

Children who are gifted with the talent or love of music may receive impressions that will be lifelong, by the judicious use of those susceptibilities as the medium for religious instruction. . . . Many may be reached best through sacred pictures, illustrating scenes in the life and mission of Christ. . . .

While there should be a uniformity in the family discipline, it should be varied to meet the wants of different members of the family. It should be the parents' study . . . to . . . inspire them with a desire to attend to the highest intelligence and perfection of character.—*Signs of the Times,* Dec. 20, 1877.

THE WORK OF BOTH PARENTS IS IMPORTANT

[The Lord] blesses the home of the righteous. Prov. 3:33, N.I.V.

The Word of God should be judiciously brought to bear upon . . . youthful minds, and be their standard of rectitude, correcting their errors, enlightening and guiding their minds, which will be far more effectual in restraining and controlling the impulsive temperament than harsh words, which will provoke to wrath. . . .

A sunny countenance and cheerful, encouraging words will brighten the poorest home, and be as a talisman to guard the father and the children from the many temptations that allure them from the love of home. . . .

But the work of making home happy does not rest upon the mother alone. Fathers have an important part to act. The husband is the house-band of the home treasures, binding by his strong, earnest, devoted affection the members of the household, mother and children, together in the strongest bonds of union. It is for him to encourage, with cheerful words, the efforts of the mother in rearing her children.

The mother seldom appreciates her own work, and frequently sets so low an estimate upon her labor that she regards it as domestic drudgery. She goes through the same round day after day, week after week, with no special marked results. She cannot tell, at the close of the day, the many little things she has accomplished. Placed beside her husband's achievement, she feels that she has done nothing worth mentioning.

The father frequently comes in with a self-satisfied air, and proudly recounts what he has accomplished during the day. . . . She has not done much except take care of the children, cook the meals, and keep the house in order. She has not acted the merchant, bought nor sold; she has not acted the farmer, in tilling the soil; she has not acted the mechanic— therefore she has done nothing to make her weary. . . .

Could the veil be withdrawn, and father and mother see as God sees the work of the day, and see how His infinite eye compares the work of the one with that of the other, they would be astonished at the heavenly revelation. The father would view his labors in a more modest light, while the mother would have new courage and energy to pursue her labor with wisdom, perseverance, and patience.

Now she knows its value. While the father has been dealing with the things which must perish and pass away, the mother has been dealing with developing minds and character, working, not only for time, but for eternity. Her work, if done faithfully in God, will be immortalized.— *Signs of the Times*, Sept. 13, 1877.

CHILDREN TO DEVELOP WELL-BALANCED CHARACTERS

The Lord is exalted, for he dwells on high. . . . He will be the sure foundation for your times, a rich store of salvation and wisdom and knowledge; the fear of the Lord is the key to this treasure. Isa. 33:5, 6, N.I.V.

Guard your children from every objectionable influence possible; for in childhood they are more ready to receive impressions, either of moral dignity, purity, and loveliness of character, or of selfishness, impurity, and disobedience. Once let them become influenced by the spirit of murmuring, pride, vanity, and impurity, and the taint may be as indelible as life itself.

It is because the home training is defective that the youth are so unwilling to submit to proper authority. I am a mother; I know whereof I speak when I say that youth and children are not only safer but happier under wholesome restraint than when following their own inclination.—*The Adventist Home,* pp. 469, 470.

It should be the object of every parent to secure to his child a well-balanced, symmetrical character. This is a work of no small magnitude and importance—a work requiring earnest thought and prayer no less than patient, persevering effort. A right foundation must be laid, a framework, strong and firm, erected, and then day by day the work of building, polishing, perfecting must go forward.—*Counsels to Parents and Teachers,* pp. 107, 108.

The physical, mental, and spiritual capabilities should be developed in order to form a properly balanced character. Children should be watched, guarded, and disciplined in order to successfully accomplish this. It requires skill and patient effort to mold the young in the right manner. Certain evil tendencies are to be carefully restrained and tenderly rebuked; the mind is to be stimulated in favor of the right. The child should be encouraged in attempting to govern self, and all this is to be done judiciously, or the purpose desired is frustrated.

Parents may well inquire: "Who is sufficient for these things?" God alone is their sufficiency, and if they leave Him out of the question, seeking not His aid and counsel, hopeless indeed is their task. But by prayer, by study of the Bible, and by earnest zeal on their part they may succeed nobly in this important duty and be repaid a hundredfold for all their time and care. . . .

The Bible, a volume rich in instruction, should be their textbook. . . . Impressions made upon the minds of the young are hard to efface. How important, then, that these impressions should be of the right sort, bending the elastic faculties of youth in the right direction.—*Testimonies,* vol. 4, pp. 197, 198.

FATHER AS PRIEST; MOTHER AS TEACHER

Hear, my son, your father's instruction, and reject not your mother's teaching. Prov. 1:8, R.S.V.

The love that was in the heart of Christ is to be in our hearts, that we may reveal it to those around us. We need to be daily strengthened by the deep love of God, and to let this love shine forth to those around us. . . .

Parents, you have a church in your home, and God demands that you bring into this church the grace of heaven, which is beyond computation, and the power of heaven, which is without measure. You can have this grace and this power if you will. But you must educate yourselves in accordance with your baptismal vows. When you took these vows, you pledged yourself, in the name of the Father, the Son, and the Holy Spirit, that you would live unto God, and you have no right to break this pledge. The help of the three great powers is placed at your disposal.

When in the name of Christ you ask for grace to overcome, it will be given unto you; for the promise is "Ask, and it shall be given you" (Matt. 7:7). Yes, seek God for aid. If you are in perplexity, do not go to your neighbors. Learn to carry your troubles to God. If you seek you will find; if you knock, it shall be opened unto you. But this means faith, faith, faith. Exercise living faith in Christ. . . .

The father is the priest and house-band of the home. The mother is the teacher of the little ones from their babyhood, and the queen of the household. Never is she to be slighted. Never are careless, indifferent words to be spoken to her before the children. She is their teacher. In thought and word and deed the father is to reveal the religion of Christ, that his children may see plainly that he has a knowledge of what it means to be a Christian. . . .

In our work we are not to strive to make an appearance. We are to look upon Christ, beholding what manner of love the Father hath bestowed upon us, that we should be called the sons of God. And what a joy, what a power, will be with us as we do this! It will not be merely the excitement of feeling, but a deep abiding joy. We are to present the solid truths of the Word of God, that these truths may be impressed on the hearts of the people, and that men and women may be led to walk in the footsteps of the Redeemer. . . .

I pray that your eyes may be anointed with the heavenly eyesalve, that you may discern what is truth and what is error. We need to put on the white garments of Christ's righteousness. We need to walk and talk with God.—Manuscript 66, 1905.

MINISTERS TO BE FAITHFUL IN FAMILY LIFE

Train up a child in the way he should go: and when he is old, he will not depart from it. Prov. 22:6.

The father is the priest of the family. The souls of his wife and children, as God's property, should be to him of the highest value, and he should faithfully guide the formation of their characters. The care of his children from their infancy should be his first consideration; for it is for their present and eternal good that they develop right characters. He should carefully weigh his words and actions, considering their influence, and the results they may produce.

He who is engaged in the work of the gospel ministry must be faithful in his family life. It is as essential that as a father he should improve the talents God has given him for the purpose of making the home a symbol of the heavenly family, as that in the work of the ministry he should make use of his God-given powers to win souls for the church. As the priest in the home, and as the ambassador of Christ in the church, he should exemplify in his life the character of Christ. He must be faithful in watching for souls as one that must give an account.

In His service there must be seen no carelessness and inattentive work. God will not serve with the sins of men who have not a clear sense of the sacred responsibility involved in accepting a position as pastor of a church. He who fails to be a faithful, discerning shepherd in the home will surely fail of being a faithful shepherd to the flock of God in the church.—*Manuscript 42, 1903.*

Every family is a church, over which the parents preside. The first consideration of the parents should be to work for the salvation of their children. When the father and mother as priest and teacher of the family take their position fully on the side of Christ, a good influence will be exerted in the home. And this sanctified influence will be felt in the church and will be recognized by every believer. Because of the great lack of piety and sanctification in the home, the work of God is greatly hindered. No man can bring into the church an influence that he does not exert in his home life and in his business relations. . . .

The angels of God, who minister to those who shall be heirs of salvation, will help you to make your family a model of the heavenly family. Let there be peace in the home, and there will be peace in the church. This precious experience brought into the church will be the means of creating a kindly affection one for another. Quarrels will cease. True Christian courtesy will be seen among church members. The world will take knowledge of them that they have been with Jesus and have learned of Him. What an impression the church would make upon the world if all the members would live Christian lives!—*Child Guidance,* p. 549.

PARENTS TO COUNSEL THEIR CHILDREN

If sinners entice thee, consent thou not. Prov. 1:10.

Parents should encourage their children to confide in them and unburden to them their heart griefs, their daily little annoyances and trials. If they do this, the parents can learn to sympathize with their children, and pray for them and with them, that God would shield and guide them. They should point them to their never-failing Friend and Counselor, who will be touched with the feelings of their infirmities. He was tempted in all points like as we are, yet without sin.

Satan tempts children to be reserved to their parents, and choose their young and inexperienced companions as their confidants; such as cannot help them, or give them good advice. . . .

Children would be saved from many evils if they would be more familiar with their parents. Parents should encourage in their children a disposition to be open and frank with them, to come to them with their difficulties, and when they are perplexed as to what course is right, to lay the matter just as they view it before their parents, and ask advice of them.

Who are so well calculated to see and point out their dangers as godly parents? Who can understand the peculiar temperaments of their children as well as they? The mother who has watched every turn of the mind from infancy, and is acquainted with the natural disposition, is best prepared to counsel her children. Who can tell as well what traits of character to check and restrain as the mother, aided by the father?

Children who are Christians will prefer the love and approbation of their God-fearing parents above every earthly blessing. They will love and honor their parents. This should be one of the principal studies of their lives, How can I make my parents happy? Children who have not been disciplined and received right instruction have but little sense of their obligations to their parents. . . .

Active hands and minds do not find time to heed every temptation the enemy suggests; but idle hands and brains are all ready for Satan to control, and parents should teach their children that idleness is sin.—*Signs of the Time*s, June 6, 1878.

The Lord requires perfection from His redeemed family. He calls for perfection in character-building. Fathers and mothers especially need to understand the best methods of training children, that they may cooperate with God. Men and women, children and youth, are measured in the scales of heaven in accordance with that which they reveal in their home life. A Christian in the home is a Christian everywhere. Religion brought into the home exerts an influence that cannot be measured.—*The SDA Bible Commentary,* vol. 5, p. 1085.

STUDY THE DIVINE GUIDEBOOK IN WORSHIP

Study to shew thyself approved unto God, a workman that needeth not to be ashamed, rightly dividing the word of truth. 2 Tim. 2:15.

The Bible is a guide in the management of children. Here, if parents desire, they may find a course marked out for the education and training of their children, that they may make no blunders. . . . When this Guidebook is followed, parents, instead of giving unlimited indulgence to their children, will use more often the chastening rod; instead of being blind to their faults, their perverse tempers, and alive only to their virtues, they will have clear discernment and will look upon these things in the light of the Bible. They will know that they must command their children in the right way.—*Child Guidance,* p. 256.

The Word of God abounds in general principles for the formation of correct habits of living, and the testimonies, general and personal, have been calculated to call their attention more especially to these principles.—*Testimonies,* vol. 4, p. 323.

In arousing and strengthening a love for Bible study, much depends on the use of the hour of worship. The hours of morning and evening worship should be the sweetest and most helpful of the day. Let it be understood that into these hours no troubled, unkind thoughts are to intrude; that parents and children assemble to meet with Jesus, and to invite into the home the presence of holy angels. Let the services be brief and full of life, adapted to the occasion, and varied from time to time.

Let all join in the Bible reading and learn and often repeat God's law. It will add to the interest of the children if they are sometimes permitted to select the reading. Question them upon it, and let them ask questions. Mention anything that will serve to illustrate its meaning. When the service is not thus made too lengthy, let the little ones take part in prayer, and let them join in song, if it be but a single verse. . . .

Parents should take time daily for Bible study with their children. No doubt it will require effort and planning and some sacrifice to accomplish this; but the effort will be richly repaid. As a preparation for teaching His precepts, God commands that they be hidden in the hearts of the parents. "These words, which I command thee this day, shall be in thine heart," He says: "and thou shalt teach them diligently" (Deut. 6:6, 7). In order to interest our children in the Bible, we ourselves must be interested in it. To awaken in them a love for its study, we must love it. . . . All that God's Word commands, we are to obey. All that it promises, we may claim.—*Education,* pp. 186-189.

THE BIBLE IS THE VOICE OF GOD TO FAMILIES

Lo, children are an heritage of the Lord. Ps. 127:3.

Parents need to reform; ministers need to reform; they need God in their households. If they would see a different state of things, they must bring His Word into their families and must make it their counselor. They must teach their children that it is the voice of God addressed to them, and is to be implicitly obeyed. They should patiently instruct their children, kindly and untiringly teach them how to live in order to please God. The children of such a household are prepared to meet the sophistries of infidelity. They have accepted the Bible as the basis of their faith, and they have a foundation that cannot be swept away by the incoming tide of skepticism.

In too many households prayer is neglected. Parents feel that they have no time for morning and evening worship. They cannot spare a few moments to be spent in thanksgiving to God for His abundant mercies—for the blessed sunshine and the showers of rain, which cause vegetation to flourish, and for the guardianship of holy angels. They have no time to offer prayer for divine help and guidance and for the abiding presence of Jesus in the household. They go forth to labor . . . without one thought of God or heaven. They have souls so precious that rather than permit them to be hopelessly lost, the Son of God gave His life to ransom them. . . .

Like the patriarchs of old, those who profess to love God should erect an altar to the Lord wherever they pitch their tent. If ever there was a time when every house should be a house of prayer, it is now. Fathers and mothers should often lift up their hearts to God in humble supplication for themselves and their children. Let the father, as priest of the household, lay upon the altar of God the morning and evening sacrifice, while the wife and children unite in prayer and praise. In such a household Jesus will love to tarry.

From every Christian home a holy light should shine forth. Love should be revealed in action. It should flow out in all home intercourse, showing itself in thoughtful kindness, in gentle, unselfish courtesy. There are homes where this principle is carried out—homes where God is worshiped and truest love reigns. From these homes morning and evening prayer ascends to God as sweet incense, and His mercies and blessings descend upon the suppliants like the morning dew.—*Patriarchs and Prophets,* pp. 143, 144.

That which will make the character lovely in the home is that which will make it lovely in the heavenly mansions.—*Child Guidance,* p. 481.

FAMILY WORSHIP NOT TO BE NEGLECTED

Trust . . . in the living God, who giveth us richly all things to enjoy. Tim. 6:17.

We should be much happier and more useful, if our homelife and social intercourse were governed by the principles of the Christian religion, and illustrated the meekness and simplicity of Christ. . . . Let visitors see that we try to make all around us happy by our cheerfulness, sympathy, and love.

While we endeavor to secure the comfort and happiness of our guests, let us not overlook our obligation to God. The hour of prayer should not be neglected for any consideration. . . . At an early hour of the evening, when you can pray unhurriedly and understandingly, present your supplication, and raise your voices in happy, grateful praise. Let all who visit Christians see that the hour of prayer is the most sacred, the most precious, and the happiest hour of the day. Such an example will not be without effect.

These seasons of devotion exert a refining, elevating influence upon all who participate in them. Right thoughts and new and better desires will be awakened in the hearts of the most careless. The hour of prayer brings a peace and rest grateful to the weary spirit; for the very atmosphere of a Christian home is that of peace and restfulness.

In every act the Christian should seek to represent his Master, to make his service appear attractive. . . .

Nine tenths of the trials and perplexities that so many worry over are either imaginary, or brought upon themselves by their own wrong course. They should cease to talk of these trials, and [cease] to magnify them. The Christian may commit every worriment, every disturbing thing to God. Nothing is too small for our compassionate Saviour to notice; nothing is too great for Him to carry.

Then let us set our hearts and homes in order; let us teach our children that the fear of the Lord is the beginning of wisdom; and let us, by a cheerful, happy, well-ordered life, express our gratitude and love to Him "who giveth us richly all things to enjoy." But above all things, let us fix our thoughts and the affections of our hearts on the dear Saviour who suffered for guilty man, and thus opened heaven for us.

Love to Jesus cannot be hidden, but will make itself seen and felt. It exerts a wondrous power. It makes the timid bold, the slothful diligent, the ignorant wise. It makes the stammering tongue eloquent, and rouses the dormant intellect into new life and vigor. It makes the desponding hopeful, the gloomy joyous. Love to Christ will lead its possessor to accept responsibilities and cares for His sake, and to bear them in His strength.—*Signs of the Times*, Dec. 17, 1885.

EARLY TRAINING OF CHILDREN DETER- MINES THEIR FUTURE EXPERIENCE

Honour thy father and mother; which is the first commandmen with promise; that it may be well with thee, and thou mayest live lon on the earth. Eph. 6:2-3.

Few parents take time to think of how much depends on the instructio and training a child receives during the early years of its life. It is at thi time that the foundation of a child's character is laid. . . .

Mothers, do not forget that God requires you to give your childre constant, loving care. He does not want you to be a slave to your children but He does want you to teach them to live for Him. Day by day give then lessons that will prepare them for future usefulness. One lesson that yo will have to repeat over and over again is the lesson of obedience. Teacl your children that they are not to rule, that they are to respect your wishes and yield to your authority. Thus you are teaching them self-control. . .

When children lose their self-control, and speak passionate words, the parents should for a time keep silence, neither reproving no condemning. At such times silence is golden, and will do more to brin repentance than any words that can be uttered. Satan is well pleased whe parents irritate their children by speaking harsh, angry words. Paul ha given a caution on this point: "Fathers, provoke not your children t anger, lest they be discouraged." They may be very wrong, but yo cannot lead them to the right by losing patience with them. Let you calmness help to restore them to a proper frame of mind.

Jesus loves children and youth. He rejoices when He sees Sata repulsed in his efforts to overcome them. Many a youth is in imminen peril through manifold temptations, but the Saviour has the tendere sympathy for him, and sends His angels to guard and protect him. He i the good shepherd, ever ready to go into the wilderness to seek for th lost, straying sheep. . . .

Mothers, do you sigh for a missionary field? In your home you have missionary field in which you may labor with untiring energy an unflagging zeal, knowing that the results of your work will endur through all eternity. . . . The work of the mother who has a clos connection with Christ is of infinite worth. Her ministry of love makes th home a Bethel. Christ works with her, turning the common water of lif into the wine of heaven.

Christian parents, you are charged with the responsibility of showin the world the power and excellency of home religion. Be controlled b principle, not by impulse. Work with the consciousness that God is you helper. . . . Guided by Him, your children will grow up to bless and hono you in this life and in the life to come.—*Review and Herald,* Jan. 24 1907.

FAMILIES TO REFLECT THE GOODNESS OF GOD

As the father has compassion on his children, so the Lord has compassion on those that fear him. Ps. 103:13, N.I.V.

Bring the sunshine of heaven into your conversation. By speaking words that encourage and cheer, you will reveal that the sunshine of Christ's righteousness dwells in your soul. Children need pleasant words. It is essential to their happiness to feel approval resting upon them. Strive to overcome harshness of expression, and cultivate soft tones. Catch the beauty contained in the lessons of God's Word, and cherish this as essential to the happiness and success of your homelife. In a happy environment the children will develop dispositions that are sweet and sunshiny.

True beauty of character is not something that shines out only on special occasions; the grace of Christ dwelling in the soul is revealed under all circumstances. He who cherishes this grace as an abiding presence in the life will reveal beauty in character under trying as well as under easy circumstances. In the home, in the world, in the church, we are to live the life of Christ. There are souls all around in need of conversion. When the law of God is written upon the heart, and is witnessed to in a holy character, those who know not the power of the grace of Christ will be led to desire it, and will be converted.

A solemn review is now taking place in the courts above. The thought of the decisions now being made in heaven should urge parents to diligence in training their children in the fear and love of God. Not by severe words and punishment for wrongdoing will the most be accomplished, but by watchfulness and prayer, lest they be taken by the snares of the enemy. . . .

Every family that has a knowledge of the truth for this time, is to make it known to others. The Lord's people are to get ready for the doing of a special work. The children as well as the older members of the family are to act their part in seeking to save those who are perishing. From His youth Christ was, to all with whom He associated, an influence that drew them toward higher things. So the youth today may exert a power for good that will draw souls to God.

Parents need to appreciate more fully the responsibility and honor that God has placed upon them, in making them, to the child, the representative of Himself. The character revealed in the contact of daily life will interpret to the child, for good or for evil, those words of God:

"Like as a father pitieth his children, so the Lord pitieth them that fear him." "As one whom his mother comforteth, so will I comfort you."—*Signs of the Times,* Nov. 14, 1911.

GENTLENESS AND PATIENCE IN THE HOME

As a mother comforts her child, so will I comfort you. Isa. 66:13, N.I.V.

The home is a place where every heavenly grace may be developed. The Lord delights to dwell with those families who cultivate home religion, and with whom the spirit of praise and cheerfulness reigns. His people need to understand the principles that underlie the religion of Christ, and study how to make these principles the ruling element in the life. This will fill the home with sunshine. The fruit of faith will be seen in true service for Christ.

As those who profess to follow the meek and lowly Jesus, Christian parents should never permit temper to gain the mastery over them. Never should they strike their children in haste or anger. When they have done wrong, and you feel that they need correcting, take the matter to God in prayer. Kneeling before the Lord, tell your Father your grief because the Spirit of the Lord has been grieved. Seek for God's blessing and guidance in the training of your children. . . . When through the aid of the divine Spirit parents succeed in turning their young hearts to Him, God and angels rejoice.

Let parents remember that the example they set in the daily deportment, their children will follow. . . . Let them remember that scolding will accomplish nothing in the formation of Christian character. It will never bring about reformations, nor lead the youth to desire to become Christ's chosen ones.

By gentleness and patience, seek to win your children from wrong. Seek God for wisdom to train them so that they will love you and love God. When it is necessary to refuse them their desires, show them kindly that in doing this you are seeking their highest good. Love and cherish your children; but do not allow them to follow their own way, for this is the curse of the age in which we live. Show them where they make mistakes, and teach them that if they do not correct these wrongs, they can never be given a place in the mansions that Jesus is preparing for those who love Him. In this way you will retain their love and confidence. . . .

Children and youth need the influence of a cheerful example. They need pleasant instruction. . . . By an example of patience and forbearance, the Christian parent is to teach that evil temper and harshness have no place in the life of the believer in Christ, that these qualities are displeasing to God. As your children see you bringing into your lives the principles of truth, they too will be led to fight against wrong habits and practices, and with you will reflect the goodness and love of God.—*Signs of the Times*, Nov. 14, 1911.

USEFUL OCCUPATION BETTER THAN GAMES

It is God that girdeth me with strength, and maketh my way perfect. Ps. 18:32.

Educate men and women to bring up their children free from false, fashionable practices, to teach them to be useful. The daughters should be educated under the mothers to do useful labor, not merely indoor labor but out-of-door labor as well. Mothers could also train the sons, to a certain age, to do useful things indoors and out-of-doors.

There are plenty of necessary, useful things to do in our world that would make the pleasure-amusement exercise almost wholly unnecessary. Brain, bone, and muscle will acquire solidity and strength in using them to a purpose, doing good hard thinking, and in devising plans which shall train them [the youth] to develop powers of intellect and strength of the physical organs, which will be putting into practical use their God-given talents with which they may glorify God.

This was plainly laid out before our health institution and our college as the forcible reason why they should be established among us; but as it was in the days of Noah and Lot, so it is in our time. Men have sought out many inventions and have widely departed from God's purposes and His ways.

I do not condemn the simple exercise of playing ball; but this, even in its simplicity, may be overdone. I shrink always from the almost sure result which follows in the wake of these amusements. It leads to an outlay of means that should be expended in bringing the light of truth to souls that are perishing out of Christ. The amusements and expenditures of means for self-pleasing, which lead on step by step to self-glorifying, and the educating in these games for pleasure, produce a love and passion for such things that is not favorable to the perfection of Christian character. . . .

Suffering humanity needs help everywhere. The students may win their way to hearts by speaking words in season, by doing favors for those who need even physical labor. This will . . . bring a consciousness of the approval of God. It will be putting the talents, entrusted to you for wise improvement, to the exchangers. . . .

There are healthful methods of exercise that may be planned which will be beneficial to both soul and body. . . . It is our duty ever to seek to do good in the use of the muscles and brain God has given to youth, that they may be useful to others, making their labors lighter, . . . turning the minds of the students from fun and frolic which often carries them beyond the dignity of manhood and womanhood. . . . The Lord would have the mind elevated, seeking higher, nobler channels of usefulness.—*Selected Messages,* book 2, pp. 321-324.

TEACH CHILDREN TO BE WORKERS TOGETHER WITH GOD

The ways of the Lord are right, and the just shall walk in them. Hosea 14:9.

In the life of a Christian, the things of this world, the idols of pride, extravagance, and self-indulgence, are to have no place. God did not form the eye to be used for selfish purposes. He gave us the power of vision in order that we might behold and admire the Saviour in His works, which He has created for our pleasure.

As children prepare to attend one of our schools, wise parents will help them to understand that in school life they are to strive to form a character that will fit them to associate with the unfallen beings of the universe. And this they can do only through the overcoming power that Christ will give them. Without His grace, no one can form a Christlike character.

Parents, teach your children to become workers with you in the church. Educate them in such a way that they will delight to be workers together with God. Impress upon their minds the thought that as they grow older, their opportunities for service will enlarge, and their power and ability will increase proportionately. Let them understand that those who give themselves to God will become channels of blessing to others who know Him not. Teach them how to have power to prevail with God. If this were done faithfully by every parent, we should see consecrated workers everywhere.—Manuscript 67, 1903.   Church members, young and old, should be educated to go forth to proclaim this last message to the world. If they go in humility, angels of God will go with them, teaching them how to lift up the voice in prayer, how to raise the voice in song, and how to proclaim the gospel message for this time.—*Messages to Young People,* p. 217.

The idea of holding Bible readings is a heaven-born idea, and opens the way to put hundreds of young men and women into the field to do an important work, which otherwise could not have been done.

The Bible is unchained. It can be carried to every man's door, and its truths may be presented to every man's conscience. There are many who, like the noble Bereans, will search the Scriptures daily for themselves, when the truth is presented, to see whether or not these things are so. . . . Jesus, the world's Redeemer, bids men not only to read, but to ''search the scriptures.'' This is a great and important work, and it is committed to us, and in doing this we shall be greatly benefited; for obedience to Christ's command will not go unrewarded. He will crown with especial tokens of His favor this act of loyalty in following the light revealed in His Word.—*Ibid.,* p. 220.

FAMILY UNITED BY BONDS OF LOVE

She openeth her mouth with wisdom; and in her tongue is the law of kindness. Prov. 31:26.

Whenever the mother can speak a word of commendation for the good conduct of her children, she should do so. She should encourage them by words of approval and looks of love. These will be as sunshine to the heart of a child and will lead to the cultivation of self-respect and pride of character. . . .

Children have sensitive, loving natures. They are easily pleased and easily made unhappy. By gentle discipline in loving words and acts, mothers may bind their children to their hearts. To manifest severity and to be exacting with children are great mistakes. Uniform firmness and unimpassioned control are necessary to the discipline of every family. Say what you mean calmly, move with consideration, and carry out what you say without deviation.

It will pay to manifest affection in your association with your children. Do not repel them by lack of sympathy in their childish sports, joys, and griefs.—*Testimonies,* vol. 3, p. 532.

Infant children are a mirror for the mother, in which she may see reflected her own habits and deportment, and may trace even the tones of her own voice. How careful then should be her language and behavior in the presence of these little learners who take her for an example. If she wishes them to be gentle in manners and tractable, she must cultivate those traits in herself.

When children love and repose confidence in their mother, and have become obedient to her, they have been taught the first lessons in becoming Christians. . . .

In view of the individual responsibility of mothers, every woman should develop a well-balanced mind and pure character, reflecting only the true, the good, and the beautiful. The wife and mother may bind her husband and children to her heart by an unremitting love, shown in gentle words and courteous deportment, which, as a rule, will be copied by her children.

Politeness is cheap, but it has power to soften natures which would grow hard and rough without it. Christian politeness should reign in every household. The cultivation of a uniform courtesy, and a willingness to do by others as we would like them to do by us, would annihilate half the ills of life. The principle inculcated in the injunction, "Be kindly affectioned one to another," is the cornerstone of the Christian character. . . . Christian courtesy is the golden clasp which unites the members of the family in bonds of love, becoming closer and stronger every day.—*Health Reformer,* Aug., 1877.

COURTESY SHOULD REIGN IN THE HOME

Let love be without dissimulation. . . . Be kindly affectioned one to another . . . ; in honour preferring one another. Rom. 12:9, 10.

The principle inculcated by the injunction, ''Be kindly affectioned one to another,'' lies at the very foundation of domestic happiness. Christian courtesy should reign in every household. . . . The wife and mother may bind the hearts of her husband and children to her own by the strong cords of love, if in her intercourse with them she will manifest unvarying love in gentle words and courteous deportment.

Marked diversities of disposition and character frequently exist in the same family; for it is in the order of God that persons of varied temperaments should associate together. When this is the case, each member of the household should sacredly regard the feelings and respect the rights of the others. By this means mutual consideration and forbearance will be cultivated, prejudices will be softened, and rough points of character smoothed. Harmony may be secured, and the blending of the varied temperaments may be a benefit to each. . . .

[The true wife and mother] will perform her duties with dignity and cheerfulness, not considering it degrading to do with her own hands whatever it is necessary to do in a well-ordered household.

In order to be a good wife, it is not necessary that woman's nature should be utterly merged in that of her husband. Every individual has a life distinct from all others, an experience differing essentially from theirs. It is not the design of our Creator that our individuality should be lost in another's; He would have us possess our own characters, softened and sanctified by His sweet grace. He would hear our words fresh from our own hearts. He would have our yearning desires and earnest cries ascend to Him marked by our own individuality. All do not have the same exercises of mind, and God calls for no secondhand experience. Our compassionate Redeemer reaches His helping hand to us just where we are.

If woman looks to God for strength and comfort, and in His fear seeks to perform her daily duties, she will win the respect and confidence of her husband, and see her children coming to maturity honorable men and women, having moral stamina to do right. . . .

When the mother has gained the confidence of her children, and taught them to love and obey her, she has given them the first lesson in the Christian life. They must love and trust and obey their Saviour, as they love and trust and obey their parents. The love which in faithful care and right training the parents manifest for the child faintly mirrors the love of Jesus for His faithful people.—*Signs of the Times*, Sept. 9, 1886.

CHEERFULNESS IN THE HOME PROMOTES HAPPINESS

Pleasant words are as an honeycomb, sweet to the soul, and health to the bones. Prov. 16:24.

The mother should cultivate a cheerful, contented, happy disposition. Every effort in this direction will be abundantly repaid in both the physical well-being and the moral character of her children. A cheerful spirit will promote the happiness of her family and in a very great degree improve her own health.

Let the husband aid his wife by his sympathy and unfailing affection. If he wishes to keep her fresh and gladsome, so that she will be as sunshine in the home, let him help her bear her burdens. His kindness and loving courtesy will be to her a precious encouragement, and the happiness he imparts will bring joy and peace to his own heart. . . .

Great is the honor and the responsibility placed upon fathers and mothers, in that they are to stand in the place of God to their children. Their character, their daily life, their methods of training, will interpret His words to the little ones. Their influence will win or repel the child's confidence in the Lord's assurances.

Happy are the parents whose lives are a true reflection of the divine, so that the promises and commands of God awaken in the child gratitude and reverence; the parents whose tenderness and justice and long-suffering interpret to the child the love and justice and long-suffering of God; and who, by teaching the child to love and trust and obey them, are teaching him to love and trust and obey his Father in heaven. Parents who impart to a child such a gift have endowed him with a treasure more precious than the wealth of all the ages—a treasure as enduring as eternity.

In the children committed to her care, every mother has a sacred charge from God. "Take this son, this daughter," He says; "train it for Me; give it a character 'polished after the similitude of a palace,' that it may shine in the courts of the Lord forever." . . .

There is a God above, and the light and glory from His throne rests upon the faithful mother as she tries to educate her children to resist the influence of evil. No other work can equal hers in importance. . . .

The mother who appreciates this will regard her opportunities as priceless. Earnestly will she seek, in her own character and by her methods of training, to present before her children the highest ideal. . . . Diligently she will study His Word. She will keep her eyes fixed upon Christ, that her own daily experience, in the lowly round of care and duty, may be a true reflection of the one true Life.—*The Ministry of Healing,* pp. 374-378.

GREAT TRUTHS HANDED DOWN FROM FATHER TO SON

[The king] made him [Joseph] lord of his house, and ruler of all his possessions, to instruct his princes at his pleasure, and to teach his elders wisdom. Ps. 105:21, 22, R.S.V.

In his childhood, Joseph had been taught the love and fear of God. Often in his father's tent, under the Syrian stars, he had been told the story of the night vision at Bethel, of the ladder from heaven to earth, and the descending and ascending angels and of Him who from the throne above revealed Himself to Jacob. He had been told the story of the conflict beside the Jabbok, when, renouncing cherished sins, Jacob stood conqueror, and received the title of a prince with God.

A shepherd boy, tending his father's flocks, Joseph's pure and simple life had favored the development of both physical and mental power. By communion with God through nature and the study of the great truths handed down as a sacred trust from father to son, he had gained strength of mind and firmness of principle.

In the crisis of his life, when making that terrible journey from his childhood home in Canaan to the bondage which awaited him in Egypt, looking for the last time on the hills that hid the tents of his kindred, Joseph remembered his father's God. He remembered the lessons of his childhood, and his soul thrilled with the resolve to prove himself true—ever to act as became a subject of the King of heaven.

In the bitter life of a stranger and a slave, amidst the sights and sounds of vice and allurements of heathen worship, a worship surrounded with all the attractions of wealth and culture and the pomp of royalty, Joseph was steadfast. He had learned the lesson of obedience to duty. Faithfulness in every station, from the most lowly to the most exalted, trained every power for highest service.

At the time when he was called to the court of Pharaoh, Egypt was the greatest of nations. In civilization, art, learning, she was unequaled. Through a period of utmost difficulty and danger, Joseph administered the affairs of the kingdom; and this he did in a manner that won the confidence of the king and the people. Pharaoh "made him lord of his house, and ruler of all his substance: to bind his princes at his pleasure; and teach his senators wisdom" (K.J.V.). . . .

Loyalty to God, faith in the Unseen, was Joseph's anchor. In this lay the hiding of his power.

"The arms of his hands were made strong
By the hands of the mighty God of Jacob." . . .

Joseph and Daniel proved themselves true to the principles of their early training, true to Him whose representatives they were.—*Education,* pp. 52-57.

ABRAHAM'S EXAMPLE AS A FATHER

I know him, that he will command his children and his household after him, and they shall keep the way of the Lord, to do justice and judgment; that the Lord may bring upon Abraham that which he hath spoken of him. Gen. 18:19.

Of Abraham it is written that "he was called the Friend of God" (James 2:23), "the father of all them that believe" (Rom. 4:11). The testimony of God concerning this faithful patriarch is "Abraham obeyed my voice, and kept my charge, my commandments, my statutes, and my laws" (Gen. 26:5). . . . It was a high honor to which Abraham was called, that of being the father of the people who for centuries were the guardians and preservers of the truth of God for the world—of that people through whom all the nations of the earth should be blessed in the advent of the promised Messiah.

But He who called the patriarch judged him worthy. It is God that speaks. He who understands the thoughts afar off, and places the right estimate upon men, says, "I know him." There would be on the part of Abraham no betraying of the truth for selfish purposes. He would keep the law and deal justly and righteously. And he would not only fear the Lord himself, but would cultivate religion in his home. He would instruct his family in righteousness. The law of God would be the rule in his household.

Abraham's household comprised more than a thousand souls. Those who were led by his teachings to worship the one God found a home in his encampment; and here, as in a school, they received such instruction as would prepare them to be representatives of the true faith. Thus a great responsibility rested upon him. He was training heads of families, and his methods of government would be carried out in the households over which they should preside. . . .

Abraham sought, by every means in his power, to guard the inmates of his encampment against mingling with the heathen and witnessing their idolatrous practices, for he knew that familiarity with evil would insensibly corrupt the principles. The greatest care was exercised to shut out every form of false religion and to impress the mind with the majesty and glory of the living God as the true object of worship. . . .

Abraham's affection for his children and his household led him to guard their religious faith, to impart to them a knowledge of the divine statutes, as the most precious legacy he could transmit to them, and through them to the world. All were taught that they were under the rule of the God of heaven. There was to be no oppression on the part of parents, and no disobedience on the part of children. God's law had appointed to each his duties, and only in obedience to it could any secure happiness or prosperity.—*Patriarchs and Prophets,* pp. 140-142.

ABRAHAM OBEYED GOD'S VOICE

Abraham obeyed my voice, and kept my charge, my commandments, my statutes, and my laws. Gen. 26:5.

[Abraham's] own example, the silent influence of his daily life, was a constant lesson. The unswerving integrity, the benevolence and unselfish courtesy, which had won the admiration of kings, were displayed in the home. There was a fragrance about the life, a nobility and loveliness of character, which revealed to all that he was connected with Heaven. He did not neglect the soul of the humblest servant. In his household there was not one law for the master and another for the servant; a royal way for the rich and another for the poor. All were treated with justice and compassion, as inheritors with him of the grace of life.

"He will command his . . . household." There would be no sinful neglect to restrain the evil propensities of his children, no weak, unwise, indulgent favoritism; no yielding of his conviction of duty to the claims of mistaken affection. Abraham would not only give right instruction, but he would maintain the authority of just and righteous laws.

How few there are in our day who follow this example! On the part of too many parents there is a blind and selfish sentimentalism, miscalled love, which is manifested in leaving children, with their unformed judgment and undisciplined passions, to the control of their own will. This is the veriest cruelty to the youth, and a great wrong to the world. Parental indulgence causes disorder in families and in society. It confirms in the young the desire to follow inclination, instead of submitting to the divine requirements. Thus they grow up with a heart averse to doing God's will, and they transmit their irreligious, insubordinate spirit to their children and children's children. Like Abraham, parents should command their households after them. Let obedience to parental authority be taught and enforced as the first step in obedience to the authority of God. . . .

Those who seek to lessen the claims of God's holy law are striking directly at the foundation of the government of families and nations. Religious parents, failing to walk in His statutes, do not command their household to keep the way of the Lord. The law of God is not made the rule of life. The children, as they make homes of their own, feel under no obligation to teach their children what they themselves have never been taught. And this is why there are so many godless families. . . .

Not until parents themselves walk in the law of the Lord with perfect hearts will they be prepared to command their children after them. A reformation in this respect is needed—a reformation which shall be deep and broad.—*Patriarchs and Prophets,* pp. 142, 143.

HANNAH AND THE EARLY LIFE OF SAMUEL

And the child Samuel grew on, and was in favour both with the Lord, and also with men. 1 Sam. 2:26.

The fulfillment of Hannah's vow to dedicate her child to the Lord was not deferred until he could be presented at the tabernacle. From the earliest dawn of intellect she trained his infant mind to love and reverence God, and to regard himself as the Lord's. By every familiar object surrounding him she sought to lead his thoughts up to the Creator.

When separated from her child, the faithful mother's solicitude did not cease. He was the subject of her prayers. Every year she made him a little coat, and when she came with her husband to the yearly sacrifice, she presented it to the child as a token of her love. With every stitch of that coat she had breathed a prayer that he might be pure, noble, and true. She did not ask that he might be great, but earnestly pleaded that he might be good.

Her faith and devotion were rewarded. She saw her son, in the simplicity of childhood, walking in the love and fear of God. She saw him growing up to manhood in favor with God and man, humble, reverent, prompt in duty, and earnest in the service of his divine Master. . . .

Would that every mother could realize how great are her duties and her responsibilities, and how great will be the reward of faithfulness. The mother's daily influence upon her children is preparing them for everlasting life or eternal death. She exercises in her home a power more decisive than the minister in the desk, or even the king upon his throne. The day of God will reveal how much the world owes to godly mothers for men who have been unflinching advocates of truth and reform—men who have been bold to do and dare, who have stood unshaken amid trials and temptations; men who chose the high and holy interests of truth and the glory of God, before worldly honor or life itself.

When the Judgment shall sit, and the books shall be opened; when the "well done" of the great Judge is pronounced, and the crown of immortal glory is placed upon the brow of the victor, many will raise their crowns in sight of the assembled universe, and pointing to their mother say, "She made me all I am through the grace of God. Her instruction, her prayers, have been blessed to my eternal salvation."

Samuel became a great man in the fullest sense, as God estimates character. . . . Young men should be trained to stand firm for the right amid the prevailing iniquity, to do all in their power to arrest the progress of vice, and to promote virtue, purity, and true manliness. The impressions made upon the mind and character in early life are deep and abiding.—*Signs of the Times,* Nov. 3, 1881.

GOD'S CHURCH TO REFLECT HIS GLORY

Ye are a chosen generation, a royal priesthood, an holy nation, a peculiar people; that ye should shew forth the praises of him who hath called you out of darkness into his marvellous light. 1 Peter 2:9.

The church is God's appointed agency for the salvation of men. It was organized for service, and its mission is to carry the gospel to the world. From the beginning it has been God's plan that through His church shall be reflected to the world His fullness and His sufficiency. The members of the church, those whom He has called out of darkness into His marvelous light, are to show forth His glory. The church is the repository of the riches of the grace of Christ; and through the church will eventually be made manifest, even to "the principalities and powers in heavenly places" (Eph. 3:10), the final and full display of the love of God.

Many and wonderful are the promises recorded in the Scriptures regarding the church. "Mine house shall be called an house of prayer for all people" (Isa. 56:7). "I will make them and the places round about my hill a blessing" (Eze. 34:26). . . . "Behold, I have graven thee upon the palms of my hands; thy walls are continually before me" (Isa. 49:16).

The church is God's fortress, His city of refuge, which He holds in a revolted world. Any betrayal of the church is treachery to Him who has bought mankind with the blood of His only-begotten Son. From the beginning, faithful souls have constituted the church on earth. In every age the Lord has had His watchmen, who have borne a faithful testimony to the generation in which they lived. These sentinels gave the message of warning; and when they were called to lay off their armor, others took up the work. God brought these witnesses into covenant relation with Himself, uniting the church on earth with the church in heaven. He has sent forth His angels to minister to His church, and the gates of hell have not been able to prevail against His people.

Through centuries of persecution, conflict, and darkness, God has sustained His church. Not one cloud has fallen upon it that He has not prepared for; not one opposing force has risen to counterwork His work, that He has not foreseen. All has taken place as He predicted. He has not left His church forsaken, but has traced in prophetic declarations what would occur, and that which His Spirit inspired the prophets to foretell has been brought about. All His purposes will be fulfilled. His law is linked with His throne, and no power of evil can destroy it. Truth is inspired and guarded by God; and it will triumph over all opposition.— *The Acts of the Apostles,* pp. 9-12.

EVERY TRUE CHRISTIAN TO BE A LIGHT BEARER

I am the light of the world. John 9:5.

God desires us to shine as lights in the world. Darkness has covered the earth, and gross darkness the people; and Christ says to His followers, "Let your light so shine before men, that they may see your good works, and glorify your Father which is in heaven." We are to give the light of truth to others, ever asking, ever receiving, ever imparting, working in all simplicity through the sanctification of the Spirit.

Christ pointed out the position His people should occupy when He said, "Ye are the light of the world." From the members of the church there is to go forth an influence which shall enlighten others. The Light-giver arranges the lamps so that all in His house (the world) may be enlightened. He has an inexhaustible supply of light, and He places those who truly believe in Him where they will shine brighter and brighter. Constantly our light is to increase in brightness because we are constantly receiving light from the Source of all light. Beholding Christ, we are to become changed into His image, reflecting His light to the world.

Each soul united to Christ becomes a light in God's house. Each is to receive and impart, letting his light shine forth in clear, bright rays. We are held responsible by God if we do not let light shine to those who are in darkness. God has given each member of His church the work of giving light to the world, and those who faithfully act their part in this work will receive an increasing supply of light to impart. By His Spirit the Lord will mold and fashion the human agent, quickening his energies, and giving him light wherewith to enlighten others.

Life always shows itself in action. If the heart is living, it will send the lifeblood to every part of the body. Those whose hearts are filled with spiritual life will not need to be urged to reveal this life. The divine life will flow forth from them in rich currents of grace. As they pray, and as they speak, God is glorified.

There is no limit to the Lord's efficiency. He is prepared to advance and to add new territory to His kingdom; but His people must do their part in carrying forward this work. "Ask, and it shall be given you" is the promise. Our part is to rest on the word with unwavering faith, believing that God will do according to His promise. Let faith cut its way through the shadows of the enemy. When a questioning doubt arises, go to Christ, and let the soul be encouraged by communion with Him. The redemption He has purchased for us is complete. The offering He made was plenteous and without stint. Heaven has a never-failing supply of help for all who need help.—*Bible Echo,* June 11, 1900.

GOD GLORIFIED IN HUMAN LIFE

For we are labourers together with God; ye are God's husbandry, ye are God's building. 1 Cor. 3:9.

It is the Saviour's delight to see His followers colaborers with God, receiving bountifully all the means of fruit-bearing, and giving bountifully, as workers under Him. Christ glorified His Father by the fruit He bore, and the lives of His true followers will produce the same result. Receiving and imparting, His workers will produce much fruit. "Hitherto," Christ said to His disciples, "have ye asked nothing in my name: ask, and ye shall receive, that your joy may be full."

The God of providence still walks among us, though His footsteps are not seen, though His positive and direct workings are not recognized or understood. The world in its human wisdom knows not God. The Lord designs that through human beings His glory, not the glory of men, shall be manifested. It is His light that shines through His agencies. Providence and revelation work in divine harmony, revealing God as first, and last, and best in everything.

Christ is drawing sinners to Himself by the cords of love, seeking to unite them to Himself, that they may be laborers together with God, not in pride and self-sufficiency, but in meekness and lowliness. When sinners are converted, God is glorified before the principalities and powers of heaven and earth. These converted ones are a spectacle to the world, to angels, and to men. "Ye are my witnesses," God says. By looking to Me you are to become transformed in character. By the manifestation of Christlike forbearance and love you are to reveal this transformation.

By imparting to others the love and tenderness which God has so abundantly bestowed on us, we are to let our light shine. We should put every gift of God to the best possible use, making it a producer of good. To God we can give nothing which is not already His, but we can help the suffering ones around us. We can supply them with the necessities of this life, and at the same time speak to them of the wonderful love of God.

Christ has identified His interests with those of His people. He has plainly stated that we can minister to Him by ministering to His suffering ones. Words of encouragement and cheer, spoken when the soul is sick and the pulse of courage is low, these are regarded by the Saviour as if spoken to Himself. . . .

We are to be in the world as a corrective influence, as salt that retains its savor. Among an unholy, impure, idolatrous generation, we are to be pure and holy, showing that the grace of Christ has power to restore in man the divine likeness. We are to exert a saving influence upon those in the world.—*Bible Echo,* June 11, 1900.

BE ONE, AS CHRIST AND THE FATHER ARE ONE

Now I am no more in the world, but these are in the world, and I come to thee. Holy Father, keep through thine own name those whom thou hast given me, that they may be one, as we are. John 17:11.

Where shall we find the purity, goodness, and holiness where we shall be secure? Where is the fold where no wolves will enter? I tell you . . . the Lord has an organized body through whom He will work. There may be more than a score of Judases among them; there may be a rash Peter who will under circumstances of trial deny his Lord; there may be persons represented by John whom Jesus loved, but he may have a zeal that would destroy men's lives by calling down fire from heaven upon them to revenge an insult to Christ and to the truth. But the great Teacher seeks to give lessons of instruction to correct these existing evils. He is doing the same today with His church. He is pointing out their dangers. He is presenting before them the Laodicean message.

He shows them that all selfishness, all pride, all self-exaltation, all unbelief and prejudice, which lead to resistance of the truth and turn away from the true light, are dangerous, and unless repented of, those who cherish these things will be left in darkness as was the Jewish nation. Let every soul now seek to answer the prayer of Christ. Let every soul echo that prayer in mind, in petitions, in exhortations, that they all may be one even as Christ is one with the Father, and work to this end. In the place of turning the weapons of warfare within our own ranks, let them be turned against the enemies of God and the truth. Echo the prayer of Christ with your whole heart: "Holy Father, keep through thine own name those whom thou hast given me, that they may be one, as we are. . . . I pray not that thou shouldest take them out of the world, but that thou shouldest keep them from the evil" (John 17:11-15). . . .

The door of the heart must be opened to the Holy Spirit, for this is the sanctifier, and the truth is the medium. There must be an acceptance of the truth as it is in Jesus. This is the only genuine sanctification: "Thy word is truth." Oh, read the prayer of Christ for unity, "Keep through thine own name those whom thou hast given me, that they may be one as we are." The prayer of Christ is not only for those who are now His disciples, but for all those who shall believe on Christ through the words of His disciples, even to the end of the world. . . .

The Lord has had a church from that day, through all the changing scenes of time to the present period. . . . The Bible sets before us a model church. They are to be in unity with each other, and with God. When believers are united in Christ the living vine, the result is that they are one with Christ, full of sympathy and tenderness and love.—Manuscript 21, 1893.

PERFECT ONENESS WILL GIVE SUCCESS

That they all may be one; as thou, Father, art in me, and I in thee; that they also may be one in us: that the world may believe that thou hast sent me. John 17:21.

I urge our people to cease their criticism and evil-speaking, and go to God in earnest prayer, asking Him to help them to help the erring. Let them link up with one another and with Christ. Let them study the seventeenth of John, and learn how to pray and how to live the prayer of Christ. He is the Comforter. He will abide in their hearts, making their joy full. His words will be to them as the bread of life, and in the strength thus gained they will be enabled to develop characters that will be an honor to God. Perfect Christian fellowship will exist among them. There will be seen in their lives the fruit that always appears as the result of obedience to the truth.

Let us make Christ's prayer the rule of our life, that we may form characters that will reveal to the world the power of the grace of God. Let there be less talk about petty differences, and a more diligent study of what the prayer of Christ means to those who believe on His name. We are to pray for union, and then live in such a way that God can answer our prayers.

Perfect oneness—a union as close as the union existing between the Father and the Son—this is what will give success to the efforts of God' workers.—Manuscript 1, 1903.

Complete union with Christ and with one another is absolutely necessary to the perfection of believers. Christ's presence by faith in the hearts of believers is their power, their life. It brings union with God "Thou in me." Union with God through Christ makes the church perfect.—Undated manuscript 133.

He who seeks to serve others by self-denial and self-sacrifice will be given the attributes of character that commend themselves to God, and develop wisdom, true patience, forbearance, kindness, compassion. This gives him the chiefest place in the kingdom of God.—Manuscript 165, 1898.

Nothing can perfect a perfect unity in the church but the spirit of Christlike forbearance. Satan can sow discord; Christ alone can harmonize the disagreeing elements. . . . When you as individual workers of the church love God supremely and your neighbor as yourself, then there will be no labored efforts to be in unity, there will be a oneness in Christ, the ears to report will be closed, and no one will take up a reproach against his neighbor. The members of the church will cherish love and unity and be as one great family. Then we shall bear the credentials to the world that will testify that God has sent His Son into the world. Christ has said, "By this shall all men know that ye are my disciples, if ye have love one to another."—Letter 29, 1889.

PREPARE TO MEET THY GOD

The great day of the Lord is near, it is near, and hasteth greatly, even the voice of the day of the Lord. Zeph. 1:14.

I am bidden to call upon the churches to awake out of sleep. We must contend with invisible, supernatural foes. We are to put on the whole armor of God, that we may be prepared for the battles we have daily to fight.

I call upon those who have received light and knowledge to pray most earnestly, and to come up "to the help of the Lord, to the help of the Lord against the mighty." Who are these mighty foes? They are the powers who, in the days of Daniel, hindered the heavenly messengers from convincing the king of Persia of the work he was to do.

Our work of heralding the second coming of Christ is similar to that of John the Baptist, the forerunner of Christ at His first advent. We are to proclaim to the world the message, "The great day of the Lord is near." "Prepare to meet thy God." We are to do much more than we have yet done.

Among us, as among the children of Israel when they were being led to the Promised Land, are many who, unless they can see clearly every step in advance, will not move at the command of God to "go forward." They have but little faith, and but little of the spirit of self-denial. . . .

There is room in the work of God for all who are filled with the spirit of self-sacrifice. We have a solemn work before us. God is calling for men and women who are willing to experience travail of soul, men and women who are consecrated to His work. We need . . . men who have a solid experience in the things of God, who, when they encounter difficulties, will hold firmly to the work, saying, We will not fail nor be discouraged. We want men who will strengthen and build up the work, not tear down and seek to destroy that which others are trying to do. We need men and women whom God can work, the fallow ground of whose heart has been broken up.

We do not need workers who must be supported and carried by those who have long been in the faith. . . . We want workers who are not steeped in selfishness, those who are not self-sufficient. . . .

Satan will always cooperate with those who are willing to betray sacred trusts. There are traitors, . . . men who claim to be Sabbathkeepers, but who, instead of building up the work, hinder it by criticizing and falsely accusing their brethren.

Oh, how many might do a noble work in self-denial and self-sacrifice, who are absorbed in the little things of life! They are blind and cannot see afar off. They make a world of an atom and an atom of a world. They have become shallow streams, because they do not impart to others the Water of Life.—Manuscript 173, 1898.

EVERY MEMBER MAY RENDER SERVICE

As God's fellow workers we urge you not to receive God's grace in vain. 2 Cor. 6:1, N.I.V.

All our church members should feel a deep interest in home and foreign missions. Great spiritual blessing will come to them as they make self-sacrificing efforts to plant the standard of truth in new territory. The money invested in this work will bring rich returns. New converts, rejoicing in the light received from the Word, will in their turn give of their means to carry the light to others.

The Lord is calling upon His people to take up different lines of missionary work. Those in the highways and hedges are to hear the saving gospel message. Church members are to do evangelistic work in the homes of those of their friends and neighbors who have not yet received full evidence of the truth. . . .

Let those who take up this work make the life of Christ their constant study. Let them be intensely in earnest, using every capability in the Lord's service. Precious results will follow sincere, unselfish effort. From the great Teacher the workers will receive the highest of all education.

Many of God's people are to go forth with publications containing the light of present truth, into places where the third angel's message has never been proclaimed. The work of the canvasser-evangelist who is imbued with the Spirit of God is fraught with wonderful possibilities for good. The presentation of the truth, in love and simplicity, from house to house, is in harmony with the instruction that Christ gave His disciples when He sent them out on their first missionary tour. By songs of praise to God, humble, heartfelt prayers, and a simple presentation of Bible truth in the family circle, many will be reached. The Divine Worker will be present to send conviction to hearts. "I am with you alway" is His promise. With the assurance of the abiding presence of such a Helper, we may labor with faith and hope and courage.

The monotony of our service for God needs to be broken up. Every church member should be engaged in some line of work for God. Let those who are well established in the truth go into neighboring places, and hold meetings, giving a cordial invitation to all. Let there be in these meetings melodious songs, fervent prayers, and the reading of God's Word. . . .

There are others who can visit the homes of the people, reading to the members of the family on some simple impressive subject of Bible truth. . . .

There are those who, because of pressing home duties, may not be able to do house-to-house work. But let them not think that they can do nothing to help. They can encourage those who go out, and they can give of their means to help to sustain them.—Manuscript 150, 1903.

LET REPENTANT ONES BE FORGIVEN

Forgive, and ye shall be forgiven. Luke 6:37.

The Lord pardons all who repent of their sins. It is from those who do not repent, those who bolster themselves up in self-confidence, that He turns away. Never will He refuse to listen to the voice of tears and repentance. Never will He turn His face away from the humble soul who comes to Him in repentance and sorrow. . . .

The church member who believes the Word of God will never look indifferently upon a soul that humbles himself and confesses his sin. Let the repenting one be taken back with rejoicing. Christ came to the world to forgive everyone who says, "I repent. I am sorry for my sin." When a brother says, "God has forgiven me. Will you forgive?" clasp his hand, and say, "As I hope to be forgiven, I forgive."

"After this manner therefore pray ye: Our Father which art in heaven, hallowed be thy name. Thy kingdom come. Thy will be done in earth, as it is in heaven. Give us this day our daily bread. And forgive us our debts, as we forgive our debtors. And lead us not into temptation, but deliver us from evil: for thine is the kingdom, and the power, and the glory, for ever. Amen. For if ye forgive men their trespasses, your heavenly Father will also forgive you: but if ye forgive not men their trespasses, neither will your Father forgive your trespasses."

When the enemy is seeking in every way to destroy, shall church members unite with him to discourage a man who is repentant, and is asking for forgiveness? God has not placed any man as judge. "Judge not, that ye be not judged. For with what judgment ye judge, ye shall be judged: and with what measure ye mete, it shall be measured to you again. . . . Enter ye in at the strait gate, for wide is the gate, and broad is the way, that leadeth to destruction, and many there be which go in thereat: because strait is the gate, and narrow is the way, which leadeth unto life, and few there be that find it."

"And as Jesus passed forth from thence, he saw a man, named Matthew, sitting at the receipt of custom; and he saith unto him, Follow me. And he arose, and followed him.

"And it came to pass, as Jesus sat at meat in the house, behold, many publicans and sinners came and sat down with him and his disciples. And when the Pharisees saw it, they said unto his disciples, Why eateth your Master with publicans and sinners? But when Jesus heard that, he said unto them, They that be whole need not a physician, but they that are sick. But go ye and learn what that meaneth, I will have mercy, and not sacrifice: for I am not come to call the righteous, but sinners to repentance." Will you let this lesson sink deep into your hearts?— Letter 199, 1905.

AWAKE, AND WATCH FOR SOULS

I must work the works of him that sent me, while it is day: the night cometh, when no man can work. John 9:4.

Never have I felt more deeply than now the necessity of keeping the way of the Lord, and of doing His will at all times. Now is the time to do thorough work for eternity. We must be humble and trustful. We must make use of every talent that God gives us. We have been blessed with great and precious light from the Word of God, and we should study how to make the best use of this light. Individually we are on test and trial. God is watching to see how we will use His great blessings.

What can we say to arouse our people to use their entrusted talents to the honor and glory of God? The world's greatest need is consecrated effort for the conversion of souls. Thousands upon thousands are perishing without a knowledge of the truth. My soul is sometimes stirred to its very depths as I see the terrible picture. I would urge our people to seek to bring every thought into subjection to Christ, that all their powers may be employed in the work of saving souls. There should be no sleeping now. It is time for us to awake, and to watch for souls as they that must give account.

Will our churches now arise, and awake to the situation? The representatives of Christ are to carry a burden for souls. Every nation and kindred and tongue and people is to hear the last message of mercy to the world. When our church members have a better understanding of Bible truth, they will arouse from their drowsy slumber and will be ready to devote their money to the cause of God, and to give themselves in earnest labor under the guidance of the Holy Spirit. God's people are His agents, appointed to proclaim the truth in all parts of the world.

Christ has taught us to pray, "Thy kingdom come. Thy will be done in earth, as it is in heaven." This opens before us the height to which we are to attain by steady progress and continual advancement. As members of the church of Christ, we are to do His will on earth. If all would do unto others as they would have others do unto them, we would see indications of a converted world. Upon this principle the Christian is to build. We are to ascend a ladder whose top reaches to heaven.

Every church member is to engage in active service for the Master. "Why stand ye here all the day idle?" He asks. "Go work today in My vineyard. Work while it is day; for the night cometh, when no man can work."

"Ye are my witnesses, saith the Lord." Can we comprehend this? In Christ's stead we are to beseech men to become reconciled to God. . . . Acknowledge Him as your Redeemer, and you will become one with Him, even as He is one with the Father.—Letter 190, 1907.

CHURCH MEMBERS ARE BLESSED TO BLESS OTHERS

Ye are the salt of the earth. Matt. 5:13.

Christ's church is to be a blessing, and its members are to be blessed as they bless others. The object of God in choosing a people before all the world was not only that He might adopt them as His sons and daughters, but that through them He might confer on the world the benefits of divine illumination. When the Lord chose Abraham it was not simply to be the special friend of God, but to be a medium of the precious and peculiar privileges the Lord desired to bestow upon the nations. He was to be a light amid the moral darkness of his surroundings.

Whenever God blesses His children with light and truth, it is not only that they may have the gift of eternal life, but that those around them may also be spiritually enlightened. . . . "Ye are the salt of the earth." And when God makes His children salt, it is not only for their own preservation, but that they may be agents in preserving others.

The religion of Christ is not a selfish religion. It is not to be kept under lock and key, but it is to be an influence of power going forth from every genuine Christian to enlighten those that sit in darkness. Every soul connected with a true Christian will be made better thereby. We are to be God's light bearers, reflecting the steady beams of heaven upon others.

It is through the merits of Christ that all our spiritual and temporal blessings are given us to enjoy. The salvation of Christ was placed within our reach that we might lay hold upon it by faith, that we might weave the love of Christ into our characters, and practice it in our lives, that we might be a blessing to all our race. But not one of us can shed light upon others unless we ourselves have gathered rays of divine illumination from the Word of God. We must have the Christlike mold of character or we cannot be true representatives of our Lord.

We can do nothing without the help of God. The Spirit of God must work with our efforts, and if God's blessing attends us, we shall be channels of light. The Lord is willing to give us all an experience, which, if improved, will bring us from the lowlands of earth into close, heavenly relationship with God, and every fiber of selfishness will be uprooted from our natures.

Do you shine as living stones in God's building? . . . We have not the genuine religion, unless it exerts a controlling influence upon us in every business transaction. We should have practical godliness to weave into our lifework. We should have the transforming grace of Christ upon our hearts. We need a great deal less of self, and more of Jesus. . . .

We need plenteous grace to keep us humble, to make us prayerful, pitiful, tenderhearted, and courteous, that we may deal with others as the Lord designs we should.—*Signs of the Times*, Feb.3, 1890.

GOD DEALS WITH US AS WE DEAL WITH OTHERS

I will make them and the places round about my hill a blessing; and I will cause the shower to come down in his season; there shall be showers of blessing. Eze. 34:26.

Everyone who has to deal with others should make their case his own; for just as we deal with others will God deal with us. We are treating Christ as we treat His children; for He is represented in the person of His saints. The truth of God must sanctify the soul, refine and elevate the character, and we must obtain the heavenly mold, before we shall be fitted for the courts above.

Many are situated where they are brought in contact with believers in present truth, and with those who do not believe, and how important that all the lower lights should be trimmed and burning, that all may catch rays of light from the shining lamps of those who profess to be the followers of Christ. We need plenteous grace for this time of spiritual declension. . . .

Have you, who have hired help, let your light shine to your workmen, that they, too, may be laborers together with God? God has given you precious privileges and advantages in sending you the light of His truth, and you are to improve these blessings, and let others share your mercies. What large missionary fields there are right around your homes, what opportunities every day for you to speak of the value of God's promises. —*Signs of the Time*s, Feb. 3, 1890.

There is a work for every Christian to do right at his own door, in his own neighborhood. But how many lose sight of eternal interests and are completely swallowed up in their temporal affairs. There is no necessity for this, for Jesus says, "Seek ye first the kingdom of God, and his righteousness; and all these things shall be added unto you."

Make your own and your neighbor's eternal welfare the first and most important consideration. Your neighbors have souls to save or to lose, and God expects those to whom He has given the light to make decided, interested efforts for others. They must remember the holy claims of the truth in every transaction of life. Let believers and unbelievers see in the life of those who claim to have a knowledge of advanced truth a steady, clear, strong light shining forth in zeal, in devotion, in nobility of character, in their dealings with men. Then the Lord will deal bountifully with you, His servants. . . .

Suppose that you let your light shine, and through your devotion to the cause of God, a few others are led to consecrate their service to Him; then they will be a blessing to still others that you could not reach by your personal influence. The Lord says, "I will make . . . the places round about . . . a blessing." Your light is to be far-reaching.—*Ibid.*, Feb. 10, 1890.

GOD HONORS THEM THAT HONOR HIM

Them that honour me I will honour. 1 Sam. 2:30.

You are God's hired servant to give light, to give time, thought, tact, to His work; and if you do this, you will receive the approbation of your heavenly Father and the gift of eternal life. . . .

Be much in prayer. Let no person, or personal interest, separate you from God, who is the source of your strength. When you arise in the morning, gather all the members of your household together, as did Abraham, and invite them to seek God with you. If your business presses strongly, and urges you to your work, then there is still greater need to take time to pray, to present your petitions to the throne of grace, and secure the protecting care, the aid, the mercy and blessing of God. Do not grudge the time that God requires, and hurry through a faithless, formal prayer, that you may rush to your business.

God can do much for you, even in your labor, if you ask Him. He can send His angels to preserve you from accidents, from breakage, and losses of life and property. The reason why those who neglect the privileges that God has provided have no more comfort and peace and joy is that they do not pause to have communion with God, who is the source of their strength. Can God pour out His Spirit, can He bless us, where there is so much indifference to His service? He cannot give us His rich blessing without our cooperation in His plans. He says, "Them that honour me I will honour."

It is just as convenient, just as essential, for us to pray three times a day as it was for Daniel. Prayer is the life of the soul, the foundation of spiritual growth. In your home, before your family, and before your workmen, you should testify to this truth. And when you are privileged to meet with your brethren in the church, tell them of the necessity of keeping open the channel of communication between God and the soul. Tell them that if they will find heart and voice to pray, God will find answers to their prayers. Tell them not to neglect their religious duties. Exhort the brethren to pray. We must seek if we would find, we must ask if we would receive, we must knock if we would have the door opened unto us.

If there are only a few assembled, there are enough to claim the precious promises of God. The Father, the Son, and the holy angels will be present with you to behold your faith, your steadfast principle, and there you will have of the outpouring of God's Holy Spirit. God has rich blessings in store for those who will bring not only all the tithes into His storehouse, but also time and strength of bone and brain and muscle into His service.—*Signs of the Times*, Feb. 10, 1890.

THE ROUTE TO GREATER SPIRITUAL LIFE IN THE CHURCH

Marvel not that I said unto thee, Ye must be born again. John 3:7.

The question is often asked, Why is there not more power in the church? why not more vital godliness? The reason is, the requirements of God's Word are not complied with in verity and in truth; God is not loved supremely, and our neighbor as ourselves. This covers the entire ground. Upon these two commandments hang all the law and the prophets. Let these two requirements of God be obeyed explicitly, and there would be no discord in the church, no inharmonious notes in the family. With many the work is too superficial. Outward forms take the place of the inner work of grace. . . . The theory of the truth has converted the head, but the soul temple has not been cleansed from its idols. . . .

True conviction of sin, real heart sorrow because of wickedness, death to self, the daily overcoming of defects of character, and the new birth—these, represented as old things, Paul says had passed away, and all things had become new. Such a work many know nothing of. They grafted the truth into their natural hearts, and then went on as before, manifesting the same unhappy traits of character. What is now needed is the plain testimony borne in love from lips touched with living fire.

Church members do not show that living connection with God that they must have in order to win souls from darkness to light. Make the tree good, and good fruit will be the result. The work of the Spirit of God upon the heart is essential to godliness. It must be received into the hearts of those who accept the truth, and create in them clean hearts, before one of them can keep His commandments and be doers of the Word. "Marvel not," said the great Teacher unto the astonished Nicodemus, "Marvel not that I said unto thee, Ye must be born again."

The Bible is not studied as much as it should be; it is not made the rule of life. Were its precepts conscientiously followed, and made the basis of character, there would be steadfastness of purpose that no business speculations or worldly pursuits could seriously influence. A character thus formed, and supported by the Word of God, will abide the day of trial, of difficulties, and dangers. The conscience must be enlightened, and the life sanctified by the love of the truth received into the heart, before the influence will be saving upon the world.

What is needed is men of action for the time, prompt, determined, firm as a rock to principle, and prepared to meet any emergency. Why we are so weak, why there are so many irresponsible men among us, is because they do not connect with God; they have not an indwelling Saviour, and do not feel the love of Christ ever fresh and new. . . . No earthly relationship is as strong as this love. Nothing can compare with it.—*Review and Herald,* Aug. 28, 1879.

THE TEN VIRGINS REPRESENT
THE CHURCH

And at midnight there was a cry made, Behold, the bridegroom cometh; go ye out to meet him. Matt. 25:6.

Christ with His disciples is seated upon the Mount of Olives. The sun has set behind the mountains, and the heavens are curtained with the shades of evening. In full view is a dwelling house lighted up brilliantly as if for some festive scene. The light streams from the openings, and an expectant company wait around, indicating that a marriage procession is soon to appear.

In many parts of the East, wedding festivities are held in the evening. The bridegroom goes forth to meet his bride and bring her to his home. By torchlight the bridal party proceed from her father's house to his own, where a feast is provided for the invited guests. In the scene upon which Christ looks, a company are waiting the appearance of the bridal party, intending to join the procession.

Lingering near the bride's house are ten young women robed in white. Each carries a lighted lamp and a small flagon for oil. All are anxiously watching for the appearance of the bridegroom. But there is a delay. Hour after hour passes; the watchers become weary and fall asleep. At midnight the cry is heard, "Behold, the bridegroom cometh; go ye out to meet him." The sleepers, suddenly awaking, spring to their feet. They see the procession moving on, bright with torches and glad with music. They hear the voice of the bridegroom and the voice of the bride.

The ten maidens seize their lamps and begin to trim them, in haste to go forth. But five have neglected to fill their flasks with oil. They did not anticipate so long a delay, and they have not prepared for the emergency. In distress they appeal to their wiser companions, saying, "Give us of your oil; for our lamps are going out." But the waiting five, with their freshly trimmed lamps, have emptied their flagons. They have no oil to spare, and they answer, "Not so; lest there be not enough for us and you: but go ye rather to them that sell, and buy for yourselves."

While they went to buy, the procession moved on, and left them behind. The five with lighted lamps joined the throng and entered the house with the bridal train, and the door was shut. When the foolish virgins reached the banqueting hall, they received an unexpected denial.
. . .

As Christ sat looking upon the party that waited for the bridegroom, He told His disciples the story of the ten virgins, by their experience illustrating the experience of the church that shall live just before His second coming.—*Christ's Object Lessons,* pp. 405, 406.

TWO CLASSES OF WATCHERS

Thy word is a lamp unto my feet, and a light unto my path. Ps. 119:105.

The two classes of watchers represent the two classes who profess to be waiting for their Lord. They are called virgins because they profess a pure faith. By the lamps is represented the Word of God. The psalmist says, "Thy word is a lamp unto my feet, and a light unto my path." The oil is a symbol of the Holy Spirit. Thus the Spirit is represented in the prophecy of Zechariah. . . . "I have looked, and behold a candlestick all of gold, with a bowl upon the top of it, and his seven lamps thereon, and seven pipes to the seven lamps, . . . and two olive trees by it." . . .

From the two olive trees the golden oil was emptied through the golden pipes into the bowl of the candlestick, and thence into the golden lamps that gave light to the sanctuary. So from the holy ones that stand in God's presence His Spirit is imparted to the human instrumentalities who are consecrated to His service. The mission of the two anointed ones is to communicate to God's people that heavenly grace which alone can make His Word a lamp to the feet and a light to the path. "Not by might, nor by power, but by my spirit, saith the Lord of hosts."

In the parable, all the ten virgins went out to meet the bridegroom. All had lamps and vessels for oil. For a time there was seen no difference between them. So with the church that lives just before Christ's second coming. All have a knowledge of the Scriptures. All have heard the message of Christ's near approach, and confidently expect His appearing. But as in the parable, so it is now. A time of waiting intervenes, faith is tried; and when the cry is heard, "Behold, the bridegroom cometh," . . . many are unready. They have no oil in their vessels with their lamps. They are destitute of the Holy Spirit. . . .

The theory of truth, unaccompanied by the Holy Spirit, cannot quicken the soul or sanctify the heart. One may be familiar with the commands and promises of the Bible; but unless the Spirit of God sets the truth home, the character will not be transformed. Without the enlightenment of the Spirit, men will not be able to distinguish truth from error, and they will fall under the masterful temptations of Satan. . . .

Character is not transferable. No man can believe for another. No man can receive the Spirit for another. No man can impart to another the character which is the fruit of the Spirit's working.—*Christ's Object Lessons,* pp. 406-412.

THE WISE VIRGINS LET THEIR LIGHT SHINE

The wise took oil in their vessels with their lamps. Matt. 25:4.

In the parable the wise virgins had oil in their vessels with their lamps. Their light burned with undimmed flame through the night of watching. It helped to swell the illumination for the bridegroom's honor. Shining out in the darkness, it helped to illuminate the way to the home of the bridegroom, to the marriage feast.

So the followers of Christ are to shed light into the darkness of the world. Through the Holy Spirit, God's Word is a light as it becomes a transforming power in the life of the receiver. By implanting in their hearts the principles of His Word, the Holy Spirit develops in men the attributes of God. The light of His glory—His character—is to shine forth in His followers. Thus they are to glorify God, to lighten the path to the Bridegroom's home, to the city of God, to the marriage supper of the Lamb.

The coming of the bridegroom was at midnight—the darkest hour. So the coming of Christ will take place in the darkest period of this earth's history. The days of Noah and Lot picture the condition of the world just before the coming of the Son of man. The Scriptures pointing forward to this time declare that Satan will work with all power and ''with all deceivableness of unrighteousness'' (2 Thess. 2:9, 10). His working is plainly revealed by the rapidly increasing darkness, the multitudinous errors, heresies, and delusions of these last days. Not only is Satan leading the world captive, but his deceptions are leavening the professed churches of our Lord Jesus Christ. The great apostasy will develop into darkness deep as midnight, impenetrable as sackcloth of hair. To God's people it will be a night of trial, a night of weeping, a night of persecution for the truth's sake. But out of that night of darkness God's light will shine.

He causes ''the light to shine out of darkness'' (2 Cor. 4:6). When ''the earth was without form, and void; and darkness was upon the face of the deep,'' ''the Spirit of God moved upon the face of the waters. And God said, Let there be light: and there was light'' (Gen. 1:2, 3). So in the night of spiritual darkness, God's Word goes forth, ''Let there be light.'' To His people He says, ''Arise, shine; for thy light is come, and the glory of the Lord is risen upon thee'' (Isa. 60:1).

''Behold,'' says the Scripture, ''the darkness shall cover the earth, and gross darkness the people: but the Lord shall arise upon thee, and his glory shall be seen upon thee'' (verse 2).—*Christ's Object Lessons,* pp. 414, 415.

REVELATION OF GOD'S GLORY IN HUMANITY

If we walk in the light, as he is in the light, we have fellowship one with another, and the blood of Jesus Christ his Son cleanseth us from all sin. 1 John 1:7.

Christ does not bid His followers strive to shine. He says, *Let* your light shine. If you have received the grace of God, the light is in you. Remove the obstructions, and the Lord's glory will be revealed. The light will shine forth to penetrate and dispel the darkness. You cannot help shining within the range of your influence.

The revelation of His own glory in the form of humanity will bring heaven so near to men that the beauty adorning the inner temple will be seen in every soul in whom the Saviour dwells. Men will be captivated by the glory of an abiding Christ. And in currents of praise and thanksgiving from the many souls thus won to God, glory will flow back to the great Giver. . . .

Christ is coming with power and great glory. He is coming with His own glory and with the glory of the Father. He is coming with all the holy angels with Him. While all the world is plunged in darkness, there will be light in every dwelling of the saints. They will catch the first light of His second appearing. The unsullied light will shine from His splendor, and Christ the Redeemer will be admired by all who have served Him. While the wicked flee from His presence, Christ's followers will rejoice. The patriarch Job, looking down to the time of Christ's second advent, said, "Whom I shall see for myself, and mine eyes shall behold, and not a stranger" (Job 19:27, margin).

To His faithful followers Christ has been a daily companion and familiar friend. They have lived in close contact, in constant communion with God. Upon them the glory of the Lord has risen. In them the light of the knowledge of the glory of God in the face of Jesus Christ has been reflected. Now they rejoice in the undimmed rays of the brightness and glory of the King in His majesty. They are prepared for the communion of heaven; for they have heaven in their hearts. . . .

"And I heard as it were the voice of a great multitude, and as the voice of many waters, and as the voice of mighty thunderings, saying, Alleluia: for the Lord God omnipotent reigneth. Let us be glad and rejoice, and give honour to him: for the marriage of the Lamb is come, and his wife hath made herself ready. . . . And he saith unto me, Write, Blessed are they which are called unto the marriage supper of the Lamb" (Rev. 19:6-9). "He is Lord of lords, and King of kings; and they that are with him are called, and chosen, and faithful" (chap. 17:14).—*Christ's Object Lessons,* pp. 420, 421.

REFLECTING LIGHT FROM THE SUN OF RIGHTEOUSNESS

And we are his witnesses of these things; and so is also the Holy Ghost, whom God hath given to them that obey him. Acts 5:32.

God wants every member of the church to stand faithfully at his post of duty, to realize his responsibility, and create a heavenly atmosphere about his soul by continually gathering the bright rays of the Sun of Righteousness to shed upon the pathway of those about him. . . .

We are to be representatives of Christ, as Christ was a representative of the Father. We want to be able to attract souls to Jesus, to point them to the Lamb of Calvary, who taketh away the sin of the world. Christ does not clothe sin with His righteousness, but He removes the sin, and in its place He imputes His own righteousness. When your sin is cleansed, the righteousness of Christ goes before you, and the glory of the Lord is your rearward. Your influence will then be decidedly on the side of Christ; for instead of making self a center, you will make Christ a center, and will feel that you are a guardian of sacred trusts.

When you remember that Christ has paid the price of His own blood for your redemption and for the redemption of others, you will be moved to catch the bright rays of His righteousness, that you may shed them upon the pathway of those around you. You are not to look to the future, thinking that at some distant day you are to be made holy; it is now that you are to be sanctified through the truth. . . . Jesus says, "But ye shall receive power, after that the Holy Ghost is come upon you: and ye shall be witnesses unto me . . . unto the uttermost part of the earth" (Acts 1:8). We are to receive the Holy Ghost. . . . The Holy Spirit is the Comforter that Christ promised to His disciples to bring all things to their remembrance whatsoever He had said unto them.

Then let us cease to look to ourselves, but look to Him from whom all virtue comes. No one can make himself better, but we are to come to Jesus as we are, earnestly desiring to be cleansed from every spot and stain of sin, and receive the gift of the Holy Spirit. . . . By living faith we must lay hold of His promise, for He has said, "Though your sins be as scarlet, they shall be as white as snow; though they be red like crimson, they shall be as wool."

We are to be witnesses for Christ, reflecting upon others the light which the Lord permits to shine upon us. We are to be as faithful soldiers marching under the bloodstained banner of Prince Emmanuel. . . . The Captain of our salvation knows the plan of the battle, and we shall come off more than conquerors through Him.—*Signs of the Times*, April 4, 1892.

CHRIST'S PURPOSE TO SANCTIFY AND CLEANSE THE CHURCH

For this cause I bow my knees unto the Father of our Lord Jesus Christ, of whom the whole family in heaven and earth is named, that he would grant you, according to the riches of his glory, to be strengthened with might by his Spirit in the inner man. Eph. 3:14-16.

He [Christ] declares, *"All* power is given unto me in heaven and in earth.''* This unlimited power it is our privilege to claim.

The glory of God is His character. While Moses was in the mount, earnestly interceding with God, he prayed, ''I beseech thee, shew me thy glory.'' In answer God declared, ''I will make all my goodness pass before thee, and I will proclaim the name of the Lord before thee.'' . . .

The glory of God—His character—was then revealed: ''The Lord passed by before him, and proclaimed, The Lord, The Lord God, merciful and gracious, longsuffering, and abundant in goodness and truth, keeping mercy for thousands, forgiving iniquity and transgression and sin, and that will by no means clear the guilty.''

This character was revealed in the life of Christ. That He might by His own example condemn sin in the flesh, He took upon Himself the likeness of sinful flesh. Constantly He beheld the character of God; constantly He revealed this character to the world.

Christ desires His followers to reveal in their lives this same character.
. . .

Today it is still His purpose to sanctify and cleanse His church ''with the washing of water by the word, that he might present it to himself a glorious church, not having spot, or wrinkle, or any such thing.'' . . . No greater gift than the character that He revealed can Christ ask His Father to bestow upon those who believe on Him. What largeness there is in His request! What fullness of grace every follower of Christ has the privilege of receiving!

God works with those who properly represent His character. Through them His will is done on earth as it is done in heaven. Holiness leads its possessor to be fruitful, abounding in every good work. He who has the mind that was in Christ never becomes weary in well-doing. Instead of expecting promotion in this life, he looks forward to the time when the Majesty of heaven shall exalt the sanctified ones to His throne. . . .

O that we might more fully appreciate the honor Christ confers upon us! By wearing His yoke and learning of Him, we become like Him in aspiration, in meekness and lowliness, in fragrance of character, and unite with Him in ascribing praise and honor and glory to God as supreme.—*Signs of the Times*, Sept. 3, 1902.

"BE FILLED WITH ALL THE FULNESS OF GOD"

That Christ may dwell in your hearts by faith; that ye, being ooted and grounded in love, may be able to comprehend with all aints what is the breadth, and length, and depth, and height; and to now the love of Christ. Eph. 3:17-19.

Paul in his letter to the Colossians sets forth the rich blessings granted ɔ the children of God. He says: We "do not cease to pray for you, and to esire that ye might be filled with the knowledge of his will in all wisdom nd spiritual understanding; that ye might walk worthy of the Lord unto ll pleasing, being fruitful in every good work, and increasing in the nowledge of God; strengthened with all might, according to his glorious ower, unto all patience and longsuffering with joyfulness" (Col. :9-11).

Again he writes of his desire that the brethren at Ephesus might come to nderstand the height of the Christian's privilege. He opens before them, n the most comprehensive language, the marvelous power and nowledge that they might possess as sons and daughters of the Most ligh. It was theirs "to be strengthened with might by his Spirit in the nner man," to be "rooted and grounded in love," to "comprehend with ll saints what is the breadth, and length, and depth, and height; and to now the love of Christ, which passeth knowledge." But the prayer of the postle reaches the climax of privilege when he prays that "ye might be lled with all the fulness of God" (Eph. 3:16-19).

Here are revealed the heights of attainment that we may reach through aith in the promises of our heavenly Father, when we fulfill His equirements. Through the merits of Christ we have access to the throne f Infinite Power. "He that spared not his own Son, but delivered him up or us all, how shall he not with him also freely give us all things?" (Rom. :32). The Father gave His Spirit without measure to His Son, and we lso may partake of its fullness. . . .

Through Jesus the fallen sons of Adam become "sons of God." "Both e that sanctifieth and they who are sanctified are all of one: for which ause he is not ashamed to call them brethren" (Heb. 2:11). The hristian's life should be one of faith, of victory, and joy in God. . . . ʻruly spoke God's servant Nehemiah: "The *joy* of the Lord is your trength" (Neh. 8:10). And Paul says: "Rejoice in the Lord alway: and gain I say, Rejoice" (Phil. 4:4). "Rejoice evermore. Pray without easing. In every thing give thanks: for this is the will of God in Christ esus concerning you" (1 Thess. 5:16-18). . . .

It is only as the law of God is restored to its rightful position that there an be a revival of primitive faith and godliness among His professed eople.—*The Great Controversy,* pp. 476-478.

HOLY SPIRIT'S POWER NEEDED IN END-TIME

For the Holy Ghost shall teach you. Luke 12:12.

We are not to make less prominent the special truths that have separated us from the world, and made us what we are; for they are fraught with eternal interests. God has given us light in regard to the things that are now taking place, and with pen and voice we are to proclaim the truth to the world. But it is the life of Christ in the soul, it is the active principle of love imparted by the Holy Spirit, that alone will make our words fruitful. The love of Christ is the force and power of every message for God that ever fell from human lips.

Day after day is passing into eternity, bringing us nearer to the close of probation. As never before we must pray for the Holy Spirit to be more abundantly bestowed upon us, and we must look for its sanctifying influence to come upon the workers, that those for whom they labor may know that they have been with Jesus and have learned of Him.

We need spiritual eyesight, that we may see the designs of the enemy and as faithful watchmen proclaim the danger. We need power from above, that we may understand, as far as the human mind can, the great themes of Christianity and their far-reaching principles.

Those who are under the influence of the Spirit of God will not be fanatical, but calm and steadfast, free from extravagance in thought, word, or deed. Amid the confusion of delusive doctrines, the Spirit of God will be a guide and a shield to those who have not resisted the evidences of truth, silencing every other voice but that which comes from Him who is the truth.

We are living in the last days, when error of a most deceptive character is accepted and believed, while truth is discarded. The Lord will hold both ministers and people responsible for the light shining upon them. He calls upon us to work diligently in gathering up the jewels of truth, and placing them in the framework of the gospel. In all their divine beauty they are to shine forth in the moral darkness of the world. This cannot be accomplished without the aid of the Holy Spirit, but with this aid we can do all things. When we are endowed with the Spirit, we take hold by faith of infinite power.

There is nothing lost of that which comes from God. The Saviour of the world sends His messages to the soul, that the darkness of error may be dispelled. The work of the Spirit is immeasurably great. It is from this source that power and efficiency come to the worker for God.—*Gospel Workers,* pp. 288, 289.

THE TRANSFORMING POWER OF THE HOLY SPIRIT

[God] hath also given unto us his Holy Spirit. 1 Thess. 4:8.

When the power of the Holy Spirit is appreciated and felt in the heart, far less of self will be exhibited, and far more of the feeling of human brotherhood will be revealed. Our part is not to exhibit self, but to let the Holy Spirit work in us. Thus, self-deceived men and women may be rescued from delusion.

All, high or low, if they are unconverted, are on one common platform. Men may turn from one doctrine to another. This is being done, and will be done. . . . Yet they may know nothing of the meaning of the words, ''A new heart also will I give you.'' Accepting new theories, and uniting with a church, do not bring new life to anyone, even though the church with which he unites may be established on the true foundation. Connection with a church does not take the place of conversion. To subscribe the name to a church creed is not of the least value to anyone if the heart is not truly changed.

This question is a serious one, and its meaning should be fully realized. Men may be church members, and may apparently work earnestly, performing a round of duties from year to year, and yet be unconverted. . . . But when the truth is received as truth by the heart, it has passed through the conscience, and has captivated the soul with its pure principles. It is placed in the heart by the Holy Spirit, who reveals its beauty to the mind, that its transforming power may be seen in the character. . . .

With the great truth we have been privileged to receive, we should, and under the Holy Spirit's power we could, become living channels of light. We could then approach the mercy seat; and seeing the bow of promise, kneel with contrite hearts, and seek the kingdom of heaven with a spiritual violence that would bring its own reward. We would take it by force, as did Jacob. Then our message would be the power of God unto salvation. Our supplications would be full of earnestness, full of a sense of our great need; and we would not be denied. The truth would be expressed by life and character, and by lips touched with the living coal from off God's altar.

When this experience is ours, we shall be lifted out of our poor, cheap selves that we have cherished so tenderly. We shall empty our hearts of the corroding power of selfishness, and shall be filled with praise and gratitude to God. We shall magnify the Lord, the God of all grace, who has magnified Christ. And He will reveal His power through us, making us as sharp sickles in the harvest field. God calls upon His people to reveal Him.—*Review and Herald,* Feb. 14, 1899.

TRUE RELIGION NEEDED IN THE CHURCH TODAY

These men are the servants of the most high God, which shew unto us the way of salvation. Acts 16:17.

We need true religion in the church. It is God's purpose that we shall show that we are born again, and that we are working out in our lives the great, heaven-born principles of truth. Thus only can we gain eternal life in the kingdom of glory. . . .

There might be a thousand more laborers than there are now if God's people would deny themselves, and take up the cross, and follow Jesus. What we need is the sanctification of the Holy Spirit, and we need it every day. What we need is men of prayer, men who in quietness and humility, without any display or excitement, are overcoming self.

What we need . . . is to settle in to the living principles of present truth. Satan is creeping in with his sophistry to undermine the principles of our faith. You remember how when Paul and Silas were teaching in a certain place, a woman met them, and cried saying, "These men are the servants of the most high God, which shew unto us the way of salvation." This woman was possessed with a spirit of divination, and by soothsaying brought her masters much gain. Her influence had helped to strengthen idolatry.

"But Paul, being grieved, turned and said to the spirit, I command thee in the name of Jesus Christ to come out of her. And he came out the same hour."

But, you say, she spoke good words, and why should Paul rebuke her? It was Satan speaking through her, hoping to mingle his sophistry with the truths taught by those who were proclaiming the Word of God.

The same danger exists today. The enemy is trying to bring in his sophistry through those who ought to be on their knees before God, praying for an understanding of what saith the Scriptures, that they may stand against the evil influences that fill the world. God desires scientific sophistry to be purged from every heart. He desires us to rebuke every evil devising, every evil work. If we allow such devising to go unrebuked, we shall have to suffer the consequences. . . . God wants us to go to Him for light, and to carry His presence with us wherever we go. . . .

The enemy will present his sophistries, with little fibers that would take hold of your experience and undermine your faith. I pray that your eyes may be anointed with the heavenly eyesalve, that you may discern what is truth and what is error. We need to put on the white garments of Christ's righteousness. We need to walk and talk with God.—Manuscript 66, 1905.

CHRIST'S FOLLOWERS TO STAND FIRMLY FOR THE RIGHT

For Zion's sake will I not hold my peace, . . . until the righteousness thereof go forth as brightness, and the salvation thereof as a lamp that burneth. Isa. 62:1.

God calls upon His workers, in this age of diseased piety and perverted principle, to reveal a healthy, influential spirituality. . . . This God requires of you. Every jot of your influence is to be used on the side of Christ. You are now to call things by the right name, and stand firm in defense of the truth as it is in Jesus.

It behooves every soul whose life is hid with Christ in God to come to the front now, and to contend for the faith once delivered to the saints. Truth must be defended and the kingdom of God advanced as they would be were Christ in person on this earth. . . .

When the Holy Spirit controls the minds of our church members, there will be seen in our churches a much higher standard in speech, in ministry, in spirituality, than is now seen. The church members will be refreshed by the water of life, and the laborers, working under one Head, even Christ, will reveal their Master in spirit, in word, in deed, and will encourage one another to press forward in the grand, closing work in which we are engaged. There will be a healthy increase of unity and love, which will bear testimony to the world that God sent His Son to die for the redemption of sinners. Divine truth will be exalted; and as it shines forth as a lamp that burneth, we shall understand it more and still more clearly.

The testing truth for this time is not the fabrication of any human. It is from God. . . .

In every movement Christ's followers are to reveal their regard for Christian principles—loving God supremely, and their neighbor as themselves; reflecting light and blessing on the pathway of those who are in darkness; comforting those who are cast down; sweetening the bitter waters in the place of giving their fellow pilgrims gall to drink.

Let us increase in a knowledge of the truth, giving all praise and glory to Him who is one with the Father. Let us seek most earnestly for the heavenly anointing, the Holy Spirit. Let us have a pure, growing Christianity, that in the heavenly courts we may at last be pronounced complete in Christ.

"Behold, the bridegroom cometh; go ye out to meet him." Lose no time now in rising and trimming your lamps. Lose no time in seeking perfect unity with one another. We must expect difficulties. Trials will come. Christ, the captain of our salvation, was made perfect through suffering. His followers will encounter the enemy many times, and will be severely tried; but they need not despair. Christ says to them, "Be of good cheer; I have overcome the world."—*Pacific Union Recorder,* Dec. 17, 1903.

PRAISE TO GOD HAS IRRESISTIBLE POWER

They that feared the Lord spake often one to another: and the Lord hearkened, and heard it, and a book of remembrance was written before him for them that feared the Lord, and that thought upon his name. Mal. 3:16.

To the Christian is granted the joy of gathering rays of eternal light from the throne of glory, and of reflecting these rays not only on his own path, but on the paths of those with whom he associates. By speaking words of hope and encouragement, of grateful praise and kindly cheer, he may strive to make those around him better, to elevate them, to point them to heaven and glory, and to lead them to seek, above all earthly things, the eternal substance, the immortal inheritance, the riches that are imperishable.

"Rejoice in the Lord alway," says the apostle, "and again I say, Rejoice." Wherever we go, we should carry an atmosphere of Christian hopefulness and cheer; then those who are out of Christ will see attractiveness in the religion we profess; unbelievers will see the consistency of our faith. We need to have more distinct glimpses of heaven, the land where all is brightness and joy. We need to know more of the fullness of the blessed hope. If we are constantly "rejoicing in hope," we shall be able to speak words of encouragement to those whom we meet. . . .

Not alone in daily association with believers and unbelievers are we to glorify God by speaking often one to another in words of gratitude and rejoicing. As Christians, we are exhorted not to forsake the assembling of ourselves together, for our own refreshing, and to impart the consolation we have received. In these meetings, held from week to week, we should dwell upon God's goodness and manifold mercies, upon His power to save from sin. In features, in temper, in words, in character, we are to witness that the service of God is good. Thus we proclaim that "the law of the Lord is perfect, converting the soul."

Our prayer and social meetings should be seasons of special help and encouragement. . . . This can best be done by having a fresh experience daily in the things of God, and by not hesitating to speak of His love in the assemblies of His people. . . .

If we thought and talked more of Jesus, and less of ourselves, we should have much more of His presence. If we abide in Him, we shall be so filled with peace, faith, and courage, and shall have so victorious an experience to relate when we come to meeting, that others will be refreshed by our clear, strong testimony for God. These precious acknowledgments to the praise of the glory of His grace, when supported by a Christlike life, have an irresistible power, which works for the salvation of souls.—*Southern Watchman,* March 7, 1905.

WE HAVE A "MORE SURE WORD OF PROPHECY"

For we have not followed cunningly devised fables, when we made known unto you the power and coming of our Lord Jesus Christ. 2 Peter 1:16.

The apostle was well qualified to speak of the purposes of God concerning the human race; for during the earthly ministry of Christ he had seen and heard much that pertained to the kingdom of God. "We have not followed cunningly devised fables," he reminded the believers, "when we made known unto you the power and coming of our Lord Jesus Christ, but were eyewitnesses of his majesty. For He received from God the Father honour and glory, when there came such a voice to him from the excellent glory, This is my beloved Son, in whom I am well pleased. And this voice which came from heaven we heard, when we were with him in the holy mount."

Yet convincing as was this evidence of the certainty of the believers' hope, there was another still more convincing in the witness of prophecy, through which the faith of all must be confirmed and securely anchored. "We have also," Peter declared, "a more sure word of prophecy; whereunto ye do well that ye take heed, as unto a light that shineth in a dark place, until the day dawn, and the day star arise in your hearts: knowing this first, that no prophecy of the scripture is of any private interpretation. For the prophecy came not in old time by the will of man: but holy men of God spake as they were moved by the Holy Ghost."

While exalting the "sure word of prophecy" as a safe guide in times of peril, the apostle solemnly warned the church against the torch of false prophecy, which would be uplifted by "false teachers," who would privily bring in "damnable heresies, even denying the Lord" (2 Peter 2:1). These false teachers, arising in the church and accounted true by many of their brethren in the faith, the apostle compared to "wells without water, clouds that are carried with a tempest; to whom the mist of darkness is reserved for ever." "The latter end is worse with them," he declared, "than the beginning. For it had been better for them not to have known the way of righteousness, than, after they have known it, to turn from the holy commandment delivered unto them." . . .

Not all, however, would be ensnared by the enemy's devices. As the end of all things earthly should approach, there would be faithful ones able to discern the signs of the times. While a large number of professing believers would deny their faith by their works, there would be a remnant who would endure to the end. . . . "Wherefore, beloved, seeing that ye look for such things, be diligent that ye may be found of him in peace, without spot, and blameless."—*The Acts of the Apostles,* pp. 534-536.

CHERISHED EVIL MUST BE REPLACED BY CHRIST'S LOVE

Whoever loves his brother lives in the light, and there is nothing in him to make him stumble. 1 John 2:10, N.I.V.

They [the disciples] rejoiced in the sweetness of communion with saints. . . . But gradually a change came. The believers began to look for defects in others. Dwelling upon mistakes, giving place to unkind criticism, they lost sight of the Saviour and His love. They became more strict in regard to outward ceremonies, more particular about the theory than the practice of the faith. In their zeal to condemn others, they overlooked their own errors. They lost the brotherly love that Christ had enjoined, and, saddest of all, they were unconscious of their loss. They did not realize that happiness and joy were going out of their lives and that, having shut the love of God out of their hearts, they would soon walk in darkness.

John, realizing that brotherly love was waning in the church, urged upon believers the constant need of this love. His letters to the church are full of this thought. "Beloved, let us love one another," he writes; "for love is of God; and every one that loveth is born of God, and knoweth God." . . .

It is not the opposition of the world that most endangers the church of Christ. It is the evil cherished in the hearts of believers that works their most grievous disaster and most surely retards the progress of God's cause. There is no surer way of weakening spirituality than by cherishing envy, suspicion, faultfinding, and evil surmising. On the other hand, the strongest witness that God has sent His Son into the world is the existence of harmony and union among men of varied dispositions who form His church. This witness it is the privilege of the followers of Christ to bear. But in order to do this, they must place themselves under Christ's command. Their characters must be conformed to His character and their wills to His will.

"A new commandment I give unto you," Christ said, "That ye love one another; as I have loved you, that ye also love one another" (John 13:34). What a wonderful statement; but, oh, how poorly practiced! In the church of God today brotherly love is sadly lacking. Many who profess to love the Saviour do not love one another. Unbelievers are watching to see if the faith of professed Christians is exerting a sanctifying influence upon their lives; and they are quick to discern the defects in character, the inconsistencies in action.

Let Christians not make it possible for the enemy to point to them and say, Behold how these people, standing under the banner of Christ, hate one another. Christians are all members of one family, all children of the same heavenly Father, with the same blessed hope of immortality. Very close and tender should be the tie that binds them together.—*The Acts of the Apostles,* pp. 547-550.

JESUS, THE CHIEF CORNERSTONE OF THE CHURCH

Behold, I lay in Sion a chief corner stone, elect, precious: and he that believeth on him shall not be confounded. 1 Peter 2:6.

Upon the foundation that Christ Himself had laid, the apostles built the church of God. In the Scriptures the figure of the erection of a temple is frequently used to illustrate the building of the church. Zechariah refers to Christ as the Branch that should build the temple of the Lord. . . .

In the quarry of the Jewish and the Gentile world the apostles labored, bringing out stones to lay upon the foundation. In his letter to the believers at Ephesus, Paul said, "Now therefore ye are no more strangers and foreigners, but fellow-citizens with the saints, and of the household of God; and are built upon the foundation of the apostles and prophets, Jesus Christ himself being the chief corner stone; in whom all the building fitly framed together groweth unto an holy temple in the Lord: in whom ye also are builded together for an habitation of God through the Spirit" (Eph. 2:19-22). . . .

The apostles built upon a sure foundation, even the Rock of Ages. To this foundation they brought the stones that they quarried from the world. Not without hindrance did the builders labor. Their work was made exceedingly difficult by the opposition of the enemies of Christ. They had to contend against the bigotry, prejudice, and hatred of those who were building upon a false foundation. Many who wrought as builders of the church could be likened to the builders of the wall in Nehemiah's day, of whom it is written: "They which builded on the wall, and they that bare burdens, with those that laded, every one with one of his hands wrought in the work, and with the other hand held a weapon" (Neh. 4:17).

Kings and governors, priests and rulers, sought to destroy the temple of God. But in the face of imprisonment, torture, and death, faithful men carried the work forward; and the structure grew, beautiful and symmetrical. At times the workmen were almost blinded by the mists of superstition that settled around them. At times they were almost overpowered by the violence of their opponents. But with unfaltering faith and unfailing courage they pressed on with the work.

One after another the foremost of the builders fell by the hand of the enemy. Stephen was stoned; James was slain by the sword; Paul was beheaded; Peter was crucified; John was exiled. Yet the church grew. New workers took the place of those who fell, and stone after stone was added to the building. Thus slowly ascended the temple of the church of God.—*The Acts of the Apostles*, pp. 595-597.

BUILDING OF GOD'S TEMPLE GOES FORWARD

Now therefore ye are no more strangers and foreigners, but fellow-citizens with the saints, and of the household of God; and are built upon the foundation of the apostles and prophets, Jesus Christ himself being the chief corner stone. Eph. 2:19, 20.

The enemy of righteousness left nothing undone in his effort to stop the work committed to the Lord's builders. But God "left not himself without witness" (Acts 14:17). Workers were raised up who ably defended the faith once delivered to the saints. History bears record to the fortitude and heroism of these men. Like the apostles, many of them fell at their post, but the building of the temple went steadily forward. The workmen were slain, but the work advanced.

The Waldenses, John Wycliffe, Huss and Jerome, Martin Luther and Zwingli, Cranmer, Latimer, and Knox, the Huguenots, John and Charles Wesley, and a host of others brought to the foundation material that will endure throughout eternity. And in later years those who have so nobly endeavored to promote the circulation of God's Word, and those who by their service in heathen lands have prepared the way for the proclamation of the last great message—these also have helped to rear the structure.

Through the ages that have passed since the days of the apostles, the building of God's temple has never ceased. We may look back through the centuries and see the living stones of which it is composed gleaming like jets of light through the darkness of error and superstition. Throughout eternity these precious jewels will shine with increasing luster, testifying to the power of the truth of God. The flashing light of these polished stones reveals the strong contrast between light and darkness, between the gold of truth and the dross of error.

Paul and the other apostles, and all the righteous who have lived since then, have acted their part in the building of the temple. But the structure is not yet complete. We who are living in this age have a work to do, a part to act. We are to bring to the foundation material that will stand the test of fire—gold, silver, and precious stones, "polished after the similitude of a palace" (Ps. 144:12). To those who thus build for God, Paul speaks words of encouragement . . . : "If any man's work abide which he hath built thereupon, he shall receive a reward." . . . The Christian who faithfully presents the word of life, leading men and women into the way of holiness and peace, is bringing to the foundation material that will endure, and in the kingdom of God He will be honored as a wise builder.—*The Acts of the Apostles*, pp. 598, 599.

THE CHURCH WILL TRIUMPH OVER EVERY OBSTACLE

They went forth, and preached everywhere, the Lord working with them, and confirming the word with signs following. Mark 16:20.

As Christ sent forth His disciples, so today He sends forth the members of His church. The same power that the apostles had is for them. If they will make God their strength, He will work with them, and they shall not labor in vain. Let them realize that the work in which they are engaged is one upon which the Lord has placed His signet.

God said to Jeremiah, "Say not, I am a child: for thou shalt go to all that I shall send thee, and whatsoever I command thee thou shalt speak. Be not afraid of their faces: for I am with thee to deliver thee" (Jer. 1:7, 8). Then the Lord put forth His hand and touched His servant's mouth, saying, "Behold, I have put my words in thy mouth" (verse 9). And He bids us go forth to speak the words He gives us, feeling His holy touch upon our lips.

Christ has given to the church a sacred charge. Every member should be a channel through which God can communicate to the world the treasures of His grace, the unsearchable riches of Christ. There is nothing that the Saviour desires so much as agents who will represent to the world His Spirit and His character. There is nothing that the world needs so much as the manifestation through humanity of the Saviour's love. All heaven is waiting for men and women through whom God can reveal the power of Christianity.

The church is God's agency for the proclamation of truth, empowered by Him to do a special work; and if she is loyal to Him, obedient to all His commandments, there will dwell within her the excellency of divine grace. If she will be true to her allegiance, if she will honor the Lord God of Israel, there is no power that can stand against her.

Zeal for God and His cause moved the disciples to bear witness to the gospel with mighty power. Should not a like zeal fire our hearts with a determination to tell the story of redeeming love, of Christ and Him crucified? It is the privilege of every Christian, not only to look for, but to hasten, the coming of the Saviour.

If the church will put on the robe of Christ's righteousness, withdrawing from all allegiance with the world, there is before her the dawn of a bright and glorious day. God's promise to her will stand fast forever. He will make her an eternal excellency, a joy of many generations. . . . When the message of God meets with opposition, He gives it additional force, that it may exert greater influence. Endowed with divine energy, it will cut its way through the strongest barriers and triumph over every obstacle.—*The Acts of the Apostles,* pp. 599-601.

THE CHURCH DOES NOT FALL

In that day the remnant of Israel and the survivors of the house of Jacob will no more lean upon him that smote them, but will lean upon the Lord, the Holy One of Israel, in truth. A remnant will return, the remnant of Jacob, to the mighty God. Isa. 10:20, 21, R.S.V.

In vision I saw two armies in terrible conflict. One army was led by banners bearing the world's insignia; the other was led by the bloodstained banner of Prince Immanuel. Standard after standard was left to trail in the dust as company after company from the Lord's army joined the foe and tribe after tribe from the ranks of the enemy united with the commandment-keeping people of God. An angel flying in the midst of heaven put the standard of Immanuel into many hands, while a mighty general cried out with a loud voice: "Come into line. Let those who are loyal to the commandments of God and the testimony of Christ now take their position. Come out from among them, and be ye separate." . . .

The battle raged. Victory alternated from side to side. Now the soldiers of the cross gave way, "as when a standardbearer fainteth" (Isa. 10:18). But their apparent retreat was but to gain a more advantageous position. Shouts of joy were heard. A song of praise to God went up, and angel voices united in the song, as Christ's soldiers planted His banner on the walls of fortresses till then held by the enemy. The Captain of our salvation was ordering the battle and sending support to His soldiers. His power was mightily displayed, encouraging them to press the battle to the gates. He taught them terrible things in righteousness as He led them on step by step, conquering and to conquer.

At last the victory was gained. The army following the banner with the inscription, "The commandments of God, and the faith of Jesus," was gloriously triumphant.—*Testimonies,* vol. 8, p. 41.

There are many doctrines current in our world. There is many a religion current that numbers its thousands and tens of thousands, but there is but one that bears the superscription and the stamp of God. There is a religion of man and a religion of God. We must have our souls riveted to the eternal Rock. . . .

Satan will work his miracles to deceive; he will set up his power as supreme. The church may appear as about to fall, but it does not fall. It remains, while the sinners in Zion will be sifted out—the chaff separated from the precious wheat. This is a terrible ordeal, but nevertheless it must take place. None but those who have been overcoming by the blood of the Lamb and the word of their testimony will be found with the loyal and true, without spot or stain of sin, without guile in their mouths. We must be divested of our self-righteousness and arrayed in the righteousness of Christ.—*Selected Messages,* book 2, pp. 379, 380.

CHRIST'S COMMENDATION TO THE MERCIFUL

Blessed are the merciful: for they shall obtain mercy. Matt. 5:7.

The Lord Jesus said, ''Blessed are the merciful: for they shall obtain mercy.'' There never was a time when there was greater need for the exercise of mercy than today. The poor are all around us, the distressed, the afflicted, the sorrowing, and those who are ready to perish.

Those who have acquired riches have acquired them through the exercise of the talents that were given them of God; but these talents for the acquiring of property were given to them that they might relieve those who are in poverty. These gifts were bestowed upon men by Him who maketh His sun to shine and His rain to fall upon the just and the unjust, that by the fruitfulness of the earth men might have abundant supplies for all their need. The fields have been blessed of God, and of His goodness He hath prepared for the poor.

In the providence of God events have been so ordered that the poor are always with us, in order that there may be a constant exercise in the human heart of the attributes of mercy and love. Man is to cultivate the tenderness and compassion of Christ; he is not to separate himself from the sorrowing, the afflicted, the needy, and the distressed.—*Signs of the Times*, June 13, 1892.

There are many who complain of God because the world is so full of want and suffering, but God never meant that this misery should exist. He never meant that one man should have an abundance of the luxuries of life while the children of others cry for bread. The Lord is a God of benevolence.—*Testimonies,* vol. 6, p. 273.

If men would do their duty as faithful stewards of their Lord's goods, there would be no cry for bread, none suffering in destitution, none naked and in want. It is the unfaithfulness of men that brings about the state of suffering in which humanity is plunged. If those whom God has made stewards would but appropriate their Lord's goods to the object for which He gave to them, this state of suffering would not exist. The Lord tests men by giving them an abundance of good things, just as He tested the rich man of the parable. If we prove ourselves unfaithful in the righteous mammon, who shall entrust us the true riches? It will be those who have stood the test on the earth, who have been found faithful, who have obeyed the words of the Lord in being merciful, in using their means for the advancement of His kingdom, that will hear from the lips of the Master, ''Well done, good and faithful servant; thou hast been faithful over a few things, I will make thee ruler over many things.''—*Review and Herald,* June 26, 1894.

JESUS WAS A FRIEND TO EVERY HUMAN BEING

Then said he, Lo, I come to do thy will, O God. Heb. 10:9.

Christ's dignity as a divine teacher was of an order higher than the dignity of priests and rulers. It was distinct from all worldly pomp; for it was divine. He dispensed with all worldly display, and showed that He regarded the gradations of society, fixed by opulence and rank, as of no value. He had . . . stepped down from His high command to bring to human beings power to become the sons of God; and earthly rank was not of the least value with Him. He could have brought with Him ten thousand angels if they would have helped Him in His work of redeeming the race.

Christ passed by the homes of the wealthy, the courts of royalty, the renowned seats of learning, and made His home in obscure and despised Nazareth. His life, from its beginning to its close, was a life of lowliness and humility. Poverty was made sacred by His life of poverty. He would not put on a dignity of attitude that would debar men and women, however lowly, from coming into His presence and listening to His teaching. . . .

No teacher ever placed such signal honor upon man as did our Lord Jesus Christ. He was known as the friend of publicans and sinners. He mingled with all classes, and sowed the world with truth. In the marketplace and the synagogue He proclaimed His message. He relieved every species of suffering, both physical and spiritual. Beside all waters He sowed the seeds of truth. His one desire was that all might have spiritual and physical soundness. He was the friend of every human being. Was He not pledged to bring life and light to all who would receive Him? Was He not pledged to give them power to become the sons of God? He gave Himself wholly and entirely to the work of soul-saving. . . .

As He "went about doing good," every day's experience was an outpouring of His life. In one way only could such a life be sustained. Jesus lived in dependence upon God and communion with Him. To the secret place of the Most High, under the shadow of the Almighty, men now and then repair; they abide for a season, and the result is manifest in noble deeds; then their faith fails, the communion is interrupted, and the lifework marred. But the life of Jesus was a life of constant trust, sustained by continual communion; and His service for heaven and earth was without failure or faltering. As a man He supplicated the throne of God, until His humanity was charged with a heavenly current that connected humanity with divinity. Receiving life from God, He imparted life to men.—*Signs of the Times*, June 7, 1905.

WHO IS MY NEIGHBOR?

Which now of these three, thinkest thou, was neighbour unto him that fell among the thieves? And he [the lawyer] said, He that shewed mercy on him. Then said Jesus unto him, Go, and do thou likewise. Luke 10:36, 37.

Any human being who needs our sympathy and our kind offices is our neighbor. The suffering and destitute of all classes are our neighbors; and when their wants are brought to our knowledge, it is our duty to relieve them as far as possible.— *Testimonies,* vol. 4, pp. 226, 227.

He who loves God will not only love his fellow men, but will regard with tender compassion the creatures which God has made. When the Spirit of God is in man, it leads him to relieve rather than to create suffering.

After the Lord had laid bare the indifference and disregard to the priest and Levite toward their fellow man, He introduced the good Samaritan. He journeyed along the way, and when he saw the sufferer, he had compassion on him; for he was a doer of the law. This had been an actual occurrence, and was known to be exactly as represented. Christ . . . inquired which one of the travelers had been a neighbor to him that fell among thieves. . . . The Samaritan, who was one of a despised people, cared for his suffering brother, and did not pass by on the other side. He treated his neighbor as he would desire to be treated were he in a similar condition.

By this parable the duty of man to his fellow man is forever settled. We are to care for every case of suffering, and to look upon ourselves as God's agents to relieve the needy to the very uttermost of our ability. We are to be laborers together with God. There are some who manifest great affection for their relatives, for their friends and favorites, who yet fail to be kind and considerate to those who need tender sympathy, who need kindness and love.

With earnest hearts, let us inquire, Who is my neighbor? Our neighbors are not merely our associates and special friends, they are not simply those who belong to our church, or who think as we do. Our neighbors are the whole human family. We are to do good to all men, and especially to those who are of the household of faith. We are to give to the world an exhibition of what it means to carry out the law of God.—*Review and Herald,* Jan. 1, 1895.

Go to your neighbors one by one, and come close to them till their hearts are warmed by your unselfish interest and love. Sympathize with them, pray for them, watch for opportunities to do them good, and as you can, gather a few together and open the Word of God to their darkened minds. Keep watching, as he who must render an account for the souls of men, and make the most of the privileges that God gives you of laboring with Him in His moral vineyard.—*Ibid.,* March 13, 1888.

FOLLOW THE TRUE MEDICAL MISSIONARY WORKER

Then said Jesus unto his disciples, If any man will come after me let him deny himself, and take up his cross, and follow me. Matt. 16:24.

Those who labor as Christ, the great Medical Missionary, labored, must be spiritual-minded. But not all who are doing medical missionary work are exalting God and His truth. Not all are submitting to the guidance of the Holy Spirit. . . .

I pray that I may have wisdom and power from God to present to you that which constitutes gospel medical missionary work. This is a great and important branch of our denominational work. But many have lost sight of the pure, ennobling principles underlying acceptable medical missionary work. . . .

What language could so forcibly express God's love for the human family as it is expressed by the gift of His only-begotten Son for our redemption. The Innocent bore the chastisement of the guilty. ''God so loved the world, that he gave his only begotten Son, that whosoever believeth in him should not perish, but have everlasting life.'' . . .

Study Christ's definition of a true missionary: ''Whosoever will come after me, let him deny himself, and take up his cross, and follow me.''

Following Christ, as spoken of in these words, is not a pretense. . . . Jesus expects His disciples to follow closely in His footsteps, enduring what He endured, suffering what He suffered, overcoming as He overcame. He is anxiously waiting to see His professed followers revealing the spirit of self-sacrifice.

Those who receive Christ as a personal Saviour, choosing to be partakers of His suffering, to live His life of self-denial, to endure shame for His sake, will understand what it means to be a genuine medical missionary.

When all our medical missionaries live the new life in Christ, when they take His Word as their guide, they will have a much clearer understanding of what constitutes genuine medical missionary work. This work will have a deeper meaning to them when they obey the law engraven on the tables of stone by the finger of God, including the Sabbath commandment, concerning which Christ Himself spoke through Moses to the children of Israel. . . .

I am instructed to say, Follow your Leader. He is the Way, the Truth, and the Life. He is your example. Upon all medical missionary workers rests the responsibility of keeping in view Christ's life of unselfish service. They are to keep their eyes fixed on Jesus.—*Pacific Union Recorder,* Dec. 17, 1903.

THE WORLD NEEDS A REVELATION OF CHRIST

That ye may be blameless and harmless, the sons of God, without rebuke, in the midst of a crooked and perverse nation, among whom ye shine as lights in the world. Phil. 2:15.

We are living in the midst of an "epidemic of crime," at which thoughtful, God-fearing men everywhere stand aghast. The corruption that prevails, it is beyond the power of the human pen to describe. Every day brings fresh revelations of political strife, bribery, and fraud. Every day brings its heart-sickening record of violence and lawlessness, of indifference to human suffering, of brutal, fiendish destruction of human life. Every day testifies to the increase of insanity, murder, and suicide. Who can doubt that satanic agencies are at work among men with increasing activity to distract and corrupt the mind, and defile and destroy the body?

And while the world is filled with these evils, the gospel is too often presented in so indifferent a manner as to make but little impression upon the consciences or the lives of men. Everywhere there are hearts crying out for something which they have not. They long for a power that will give them mastery over sin, a power that will deliver them from the bondage of evil, a power that will give health and life and peace. Many who once knew the power of God's Word have dwelt where there is no recognition of God, and they long for the divine presence.

The world needs today what it needed nineteen hundred years ago—a revelation of Christ. A great work of reform is demanded, and it is only through the grace of Christ that the work of restoration, physical, mental, and spiritual, can be accomplished.—*The Ministry of Healing,* pp. 142, 143.

To everyone who becomes a partaker of His grace the Lord appoints a work for others. Individually we are to stand in our lot and place, saying, "Here am I; send me" (Isa. 6:8). Upon the minister of the Word, the missionary nurse, the Christian physician, the individual Christian, whether he be merchant or farmer, professional man or mechanic—the responsibility rests upon all. It is our work to reveal to men the gospel of their salvation. Every enterprise in which we engage should be a means to this end. . . .

Let all cultivate their physical and mental powers to the utmost of their ability, that they may work for God where His providence shall call them. The same grace that came from Christ to Paul and Apollos, that distinguished them for their spiritual excellencies, will today be imparted to devoted Christian missionaries. God desires His children to have intelligence and knowledge, that with unmistakable clearness and power His glory may be revealed in our world.—*Ibid.,* pp. 148, 149.

FOLLOW CHRIST IN SERVICE AND SELF-DENIAL

Christ made himself of no reputation, and took upon him the form of a servant, and was made in the likeness of men. Phil. 2:7.

How many there are who accept Christ, and apparently live a Christian life, until their circumstances change! Perhaps they come into the possession of property. Thus God tests them, to see if they will be wise stewards. But they fail to endure the proving. They use for self-gratification that which they should devote to feeding the hungry and clothing the naked. In want and distress, God's children are calling to Him. Many are dying for want of the necessaries of life. . . .

There is a world to be warned. To us has been entrusted this work. At any cost we must practice the truth. We are to stand as self-sacrificing minutemen, willing to suffer the loss of life itself, if need be, in the service of God. There is a great work to be done in a short time. . . . Everyone who is finally crowned victor will, by noble, determined effort to serve God, have earned the right to be clothed with Christ's righteousness. To enter the crusade against Satan, bearing aloft the bloodstained banner of the cross of Christ—this is the duty of every Christian. . . .

The most difficult sermon to preach and the hardest to practice is self-denial. The greedy sinner, self, closes the door to the good which might be done, but which is not done because money is invested for selfish purposes. But it is impossible for anyone to retain the favor of God and enjoy communion with the Saviour, and at the same time be indifferent to the interests of his fellow beings who have no life in Christ, who are perishing in their sins.

Christ has left us a wonderful example of self-sacrifice. He pleased not Himself, but spent His life in the service of others. He made sacrifices at every step, sacrifices which none of His followers can ever make, because they have never occupied the position He occupied before He came to this earth. He was commander of the heavenly host, but He came here to suffer for sinners. He was rich, yet for our sakes He became poor, that through His poverty we might be made rich. Because He loved us, He laid aside His glory and took upon Him the form of a servant. He gave His life for us. What are we giving for Him? . . .

As we follow Him in the path of self-denial, lifting the cross and bearing it after Him to His Father's home, we shall reveal in our lives the beauty of the Christ-life. At the altar of self-sacrifice—the appointed place of meeting between God and the soul—we receive from the hand of God the celestial torch which searches the heart, revealing the need of an abiding Christ.—*Review and Herald,* Jan. 31, 1907.

GOD'S LOVE ENABLES US TO IMPART LIGHT

If thou draw out thy soul to the hungry, and satisfy the afflicted soul; then shall thy light rise in obscurity, and thy darkness be as the noon day. Isa. 58:10.

All around us are heard the wails of a world's sorrow. On every hand are the needy and distressed. It is ours to aid in relieving and softening life's hardships and misery.

Practical work will have far more effect than mere sermonizing. We are to give food to the hungry, clothing to the naked, and shelter to the homeless. And we are called to do more than this. The wants of the soul, only the love of Christ can satisfy. If Christ is abiding in us, our hearts will be full of divine sympathy. The sealed fountains of earnest, Christlike love will be unsealed.

God calls not only for our gifts for the needy, but for our cheerful countenance, our hopeful words, our kindly handclasp. When Christ healed the sick, He laid His hands upon them. So should we come in close touch with those whom we seek to benefit.

There are many from whom hope has departed. Bring back the sunshine to them. Many have lost their courage. Speak to them words of cheer. Pray for them. There are those who need the bread of life. Read to them from the Word of God. Upon many is a soul sickness which no earthly balm can reach nor physician heal. Pray for these souls, bring them to Jesus. Tell them that there is a balm in Gilead and a Physician there.

Light is a blessing, a universal blessing, pouring forth its treasures on a world unthankful, unholy, demoralized. So it is with the light of the Sun of Righteousness. The whole earth, wrapped as it is in the darkness of sin and sorrow, and pain, is to be lighted with the knowledge of God's love. From no sect, rank, or class of people is the light shining from heaven's throne to be excluded.

The message of hope and mercy is to be carried to the ends of the earth. Whosoever will, may reach forth and take hold of God's strength and make peace with Him, and he shall make peace. No longer are the heathen to be wrapped in midnight darkness. The gloom is to disappear before the bright beams of the Sun of Righteousness. . . .

It was the golden oil emptied by the heavenly messengers into the golden tubes, to be conducted from the golden bowl into the lamps of the sanctuary, that produced a continuous bright and shining light. It is the love of God continually transferred to man that enables him to impart light. Into the hearts of all who are united to God by faith the golden oil of love flows freely, to shine out again in good works, in real, heartfelt service for God.—*Christ's Object Lessons,* pp. 417-419.

LOVE, THE RULING PRINCIPLE OF ACTION

Let us not love in word . . . ; but in deed and in truth. 1 John 3:18.

Divine love makes its most touching appeals to the heart when it calls upon us to manifest the same tender compassion that Christ manifested. That man only who has unselfish love for his brother has true love for God. The true Christian will not willingly permit the soul in peril and need to go unwarned, uncared for. He will not hold himself aloof from the erring, leaving them to plunge farther into unhappiness and discouragement or to fall on Satan's battleground.

Those who have never experienced the tender, winning love of Christ cannot lead others to the fountain of life. His love in the heart is a constraining power, which leads men to reveal Him in the conversation, in the tender, pitiful spirit, in the uplifting of the lives of those with whom they associate. Christian workers who succeed in their efforts must know Christ; and in order to know Him, they must know His love. In heaven their fitness as workers is measured by their ability to love as Christ loved and to work as He worked.

"Let us not love in word," the apostle writes, "but in deed and in truth." The completeness of Christian character is attained when the impulse to help and bless others springs constantly from within. It is the atmosphere of this love surrounding the soul of the believer that makes him a savor of life unto life, and enables God to bless his work.

Supreme love for God and unselfish love for one another—this is the best gift that our heavenly Father can bestow. This love is not an impulse, but a divine principle, a permanent power. The unconsecrated heart cannot originate or produce it. Only in the heart where Jesus reigns is it found. "We love him, because he first loved us." In the heart renewed by divine grace, love is the ruling principle of action. It modifies the character, governs the impulses, controls the passions, and ennobles the affections. This love, cherished in the soul, sweetens the life and sheds a refining influence on all around.

John strove to lead the believers to understand the exalted privileges that would come to them through the exercise of the spirit of love. This redeeming power, filling the heart, would control every other motive and raise its possessors above the corrupting influences of the world. And as this love was allowed full sway and became the motive power in the life, their trust and confidence in God and His dealing with them would be complete.—*The Acts of the Apostles,* pp. 550-552.

REFLECT RAYS OF LIGHT TO OTHERS

Let us consider one another to provoke unto love and to good works. Heb. 10:24.

The Christian pilgrim is not left to walk in darkness. Jesus leads the way. Those who follow Him walk in the sunshine of His presence. The path the pilgrim treads is clear and well defined. Christ's righteousness goes before him—the righteousness that makes possible the good works characterizing the life of every true Christian. God is his rearward. He walks in the light as Christ is in the light. As he travels onward in the Christian journey, he combines faith with earnest endeavor to win others to accompany him. Constantly receiving the light of Christ's presence, constantly he reflects this light to others in words of encouragement and deeds of self-denial. He bears the sign of obedience to God's law, which distinguishes him from those who are not following the pathway that leads to life eternal. . . .

He who walks in the light . . . heeds the apostle's admonition to provoke his fellow pilgrims to love and good works. Those who have a careful regard for one another's needs, those who speak words of kindly sympathy, those who give thoughtful assistance to others, to help them in their work, encourage not only their fellow men, but themselves as well, because they thus become laborers together with God. . . .

Let us make straight paths, lest the lame be turned out of the way. Let no one follow a crooked path that someone else has made; for thus he would not only go astray himself, but would make this crooked path plainer for someone else to follow. . . . Determine that as for yourself, you will walk in the path of obedience. Know for a certainty that you are standing under the broad shield of Omnipotence. Realize that the characteristics of Jehovah must be revealed in your life, and that in you must be accomplished a work that will mold your character after the divine similitude. Yield yourself to the guidance of Him who is head over all. . . .

Talk light; walk in the light. "God is light, and in him is no darkness at all." Study not how to please self. Lose sight of self, and behold the multitudes perishing in their sins. Gather to your souls the courage that can come only from the Light of the world. Forgetting self, help the many who are within reach around you. Talk faith, and your faith will increase. . . . Walk so that your life will reflect rays of light to others. Confide in the love of Jesus, and you will have grace to save perishing souls. Your path will be as the path of the just—a "shining light, that shineth more and more unto the perfect day."—*Signs of the Times*, June 3, 1903.

WE MAY CONNECT A SOUL TO HEAVEN

For so hath the Lord commanded us, saying, I have set thee to be a light of the Gentiles, that thou shouldest be for salvation unto the ends of the earth. Acts 13:47.

Many professed Christians are laying upon the foundation-stone wood, hay, and stubble, which the fires of the last day will consume. They engage in work that wearies, work that occupies golden hours; but it is not work that need be done. Their time is occupied, their energies exhausted, in that which will bring no precious returns either in this life or in the future, immortal life. What a difference will be seen when spiritual work engages the mind, when the talents are employed in the service of Jesus! The light that He has given us will then shine forth in direct, concentrated rays to others. All that we do for Jesus will enable us to enjoy this life better.

Oh, that all could see, as I have seen, the joy of those who have labored to the best of their ability, in humility and meekness, to help souls to come to Jesus! Oh, the joy that will be realized by the workers when the souls saved through their instrumentality express their gratitude in the mansions above!

While Christ will be glorified as the only Redeemer, there will be an overflow of gratitude from the saved for the human instrumentalities employed in their salvation. Their gratitude to those who rescued them will find expression in words like these: "I was pursuing a course that was a dishonor and an offense to my Redeemer; you manifested a love for my soul; you opened to me the Word of God. I was on the brink of ruin; your prayers, your tearful entreaties, your earnest interest, arrested my attention. I thought that you must have the truth or you would not be so earnest for the salvation of others. I read the Word of God for myself, and found that what you told me was the truth. I am saved, and I will praise my Redeemer for His matchless mercy and pardoning love."

Those who think they can do but little should improve every opportunity to do that little. It may be the smallest link in the longest chain. Separated from other influences, it may appear of little worth; but in God's great chain of circumstances it may be the link which connects a soul to Heaven. All can do something if they will; but too often selfishness prevents them from doing what they might, until the souls whom they might have saved are beyond the reach of human effort.

Dear brethren and sisters, you need divine enlightenment. When you have such a close connection with the world's Redeemer as you should have, you will be led to make prompt, determined, personal efforts to save your fellow men. The future of God's people lies in the present. —*Signs of the Times*, Jan. 28, 1886.

FISHERS OF MEN NEED THE DIVINE PRESENCE

Now when he had left speaking, he said unto Simon, Launch out into the deep, and let down your nets for a draught. . . . And when they had this done, they inclosed a great multitude of fishes: and their net brake. Luke 5:4-6.

Everyone who in living faith follows Jesus, with an eye single to His glory, will see the salvation of God just as surely as these discouraged, despondent fishermen saw their boats filled by the miraculous draught. It was because Christ was in the ship that they were successful in their efforts to catch fish. The indwelling presence of the Saviour is equally necessary in the work of winning souls.

In order to save humanity, Christ, the Majesty of heaven, the King of glory, laid aside His kingly crown and royal robe, clothed His divinity with humanity, and came to this earth as our Redeemer. For thirty-three years He lived the life of a man among men, meeting the temptations that we must meet, and overcoming through the strength imparted from above. His divinity was not manifested in any display of pomp and royal power. He could have surrounded Himself with legions of heavenly angels, thereby inducing everyone to believe on Him; but this would not have been in accordance with God's purpose.

Christ came to stand at the head of humanity, and to demonstrate that through the power of the Holy Spirit it is possible for man to withstand Satan's temptations. With his long human arm the Saviour encircled humanity, while with His divine arm He grasped the throne of the Infinite. . . .

We may endeavor to meet the enemy's temptations in our own strength, doing the best we can to overcome; but we shall meet with disappointment after disappointment. This was the condition in which Christ found the disciples, after their night of unrewarded toil. They were annoyed and perplexed. Directing them to "launch out into the deep," Christ said, "Let down your nets for a draught."

Long had the fishermen toiled that night; often had they been disappointed in their expectations, as time and again the net was drawn up empty. When the Divine Presence was with them, and they, at His bidding, once more cast their net into the sea, what an abundance they gathered in! They were unprepared to handle so large a draught. . . . The sight of the miraculous draught of fish swept away the unbelief of the Galilean fishermen, and they were ready to respond to Christ's invitation to follow Him, and to learn to be fishers of men. . . . However long and faithfully we may toil in our human strength, we can hope for no real results; but as soon as we welcome Christ into the heart, He will work with and through us, to the salvation of souls.—Manuscript 67, 1903.

THE WORLD NEEDS HEALTH PRINCIPLES

They shall lay hands on the sick, and they shall recover. Mark 16: 18.

In teaching health principles, keep before the mind the great object of reform—that its purpose is to secure the highest development of body and mind and soul. Show that the laws of nature, being the laws of God, are designed for our good; that obedience to them promotes happiness in this life, and aids in the preparation for the life to come.

Lead the people to study the manifestation of God's love and wisdom in the works of nature. Lead them to study that marvelous organism, the human system, and the laws by which it is governed. Those who perceive the evidences of God's love, who understand something of the wisdom and beneficence of His laws, and the results of obedience, will come to regard their duties and obligations from an altogether different point of view. Instead of looking upon an observance of the laws of health as a matter of sacrifice or self-denial, they will regard it, as it really is, as an inestimable blessing.

Every gospel worker should feel that the giving of instruction in the principles of healthful living is a part of his appointed work. Of this work there is great need, and the world is open for it.

Everywhere there is a tendency to substitute the work of organizations for individual effort. Human wisdom tends to consolidation, to centralization, to the building up of great churches and institutions. Multitudes leave to institutions and organizations the work of benevolence; they excuse themselves from contact with the world, and their hearts grow cold. They become self-absorbed and unimpressible. Love for God and man dies out of the soul.

Christ commits to His followers an individual work—a work that cannot be done by proxy. Ministry to the sick and the poor, the giving of the gospel to the lost, is not to be left to committees or organized charities. Individual responsibility, individual effort, personal sacrifice, is the requirement of the gospel.

"Go out into the highways and hedges, and compel them to come in," is Christ's command, "that my house may be filled" (Luke 14:23). He brings men into touch with those whom they seek to benefit. "Bring the poor that are cast out to thy house," He says. "When thou seest the naked, that thou cover him" (Isa. 58:7). "They shall lay hands on the sick, and they shall recover" (Mark 16:18). Through direct contact, through personal ministry, the blessings of the gospel are to be communicated.—*The Ministry of Healing,* pp. 146-148.

REVEAL THE PRECIOUSNESS OF JESUS

And it came to pass, that, while they communed together and reasoned, Jesus himself drew near, and went with them. . . . And they said one to another, Did not our heart burn within us, while he talked with us by the way, and while he opened to us the scriptures? Luke 24:15-32.

We should speak of Christ to those who know Him not. We should do as Christ did. Wherever He was, in the synagogue, by the wayside, in the boat thrust out a little from the land, at the Pharisee's feast or the table of the publican, He spoke to men of the things pertaining to the higher life. The things of nature, the events of daily life, were bound up by Him with the words of truth. The hearts of His hearers were drawn to Him; for He had healed their sick, had comforted their sorrowing ones, and had taken their children in His arms and blessed them. When He opened His lips to speak, their attention was riveted upon Him, and every word was to some soul a savor of life unto life.

So it should be with us. Wherever we are, we should watch for opportunities of speaking to others of the Saviour. If we follow Christ's example in doing good, hearts will open to us as they did to Him. Not abruptly, but with tact born of divine love, we can tell them of Him who is the "chiefest among ten thousand" and the One "altogether lovely" (S. of Sol. 5:10, 16). This is the very highest work in which we can employ the talent of speech.—*Christ's Object Lessons,* pp. 338, 339.

The example of Christ in linking Himself with the interests of humanity should be followed by all who preach His Word, and by all who have received the gospel of His grace. We are not to renounce social communion. We should not seclude ourselves from others. In order to reach all classes, we must meet them where they are. They will seldom seek us of their own accord. Not alone from the pulpit are the hearts of men touched by divine truth. There is another field of labor, humbler, it may be, but fully as promising. It is found in the home of the lowly, and in the mansion of the great; at the hospitable board, and in gatherings of innocent social enjoyment. . . .

Wherever we go, we are to carry Jesus with us, and to reveal to others the preciousness of our Saviour. . . . Through the social relations, Christianity comes in contact with the world. Everyone who has received the divine illumination is to brighten the pathway of those who know not the Light of life. . . . Christ is pleased with His followers when they show that, though human, they are partakers of the divine nature. . . . The light that shines upon them they reflect upon others in works that are luminous with the love of Christ.—*The Desire of Ages,* pp. 152, 153.

PRESENT TRUTH IN LOVE

The Lord God, merciful and gracious, longsuffering, and abundant in goodness and truth. Ex. 34:6.

The Lord is soon to come. The angels are holding the four winds, in order that God's people may do their long-neglected work. We are not half awake to what might be done in our world. . . .

House-to-house work is one very successful way of reaching souls. But it is not the only way that God has provided for the advancement of His work. Decided proclamations of truth are to be made. But in regard to this line of work I am instructed to say to our people: Be guarded. In bearing the message make no personal thrusts at other churches. . . . Let us be careful of our words. Let not our ministers follow their own impulses in denouncing and exposing the mysteries of iniquity. Upon these themes often silence is eloquence.

Many are deceived. Speak the truth in tones and words of love. Let Christ be exalted. Keep to the affirmative of truth. Never leave the straight path God has marked out, for the purpose of giving someone a thrust. That thrust may do much harm and no good. It may quench conviction in many minds. Let the truth tell the story of the inconsistency of those in error.

People cannot be expected to see at once the advantage of truth over the error they have cherished. The best way to expose the fallacy of error is to present the evidences of truth. This is the greatest rebuke that can be given to error. Dispel the cloud of darkness resting on minds by reflecting the bright light of the Sun of Righteousness.

You may have opportunity to speak to other churches. In improving these opportunities, remember the words of the Saviour, "Be ye therefore wise as serpents, and harmless as doves." Do not arouse the malignity of the enemy by making denunciatory speeches. Thus you would close doors against the entrance of truth. Clear-cut messages are to be borne. But guard against arousing antagonism. Restrain all harsh expressions.

There are many souls to be saved. In words and deed be wise unto salvation, representing Christ to all with whom you come in contact. Let all see that your feet are shod with the preparation of the gospel of peace and goodwill to men. Wonderful are the results we shall see if we enter the work imbued with the Spirit of Christ. If we carry the Word forward, in righteousness, mercy, and love, help will come in our necessity. Truth will triumph and bear away the victory.—*Pacific Union Recorder,* Oct. 23, 1902.

THOUSANDS TO BE WARNED IN THE CITIES

And when they had prayed, the place was shaken where they were assembled together; and they were all filled with the Holy Ghost, and they spake the word of God with boldness. Acts 4:31.

When I think of the cities in which so little work has been done, in which there are so many thousands to be warned of the soon coming of the Saviour, I feel an intensity of desire to see men and women going forth to the work in the power of the Spirit, filled with Christ's love for perishing souls.

The heathen in the cities at our doors have been strangely neglected. Organized effort should be made to save them. We are now to work to convert . . . those who are living within the shadow of our doors. A new song is to be put in their mouths, and they are to go forth to impart to others now in darkness the light of the third angel's message.

We all need to be wide awake, that, as the way opens, we may advance the work in the large cities. We are far behind in following the light given us to enter the cities and erect memorials for God. Step by step we are to lead souls into the full light of truth. Many are longing for spiritual food. We are to continue working until a church is organized and a humble house of worship built. I am greatly encouraged to believe that many persons not of our faith will help considerably by their means. The light given me is that in many places, especially in the great cities . . . , help will be given by such persons. . . .

Those who undertake to work for God in our cities must go forward in faith, doing their very best. As they watch and work and pray, God will hear and answer their petitions. They will obtain an experience that will be invaluable to them in their afterwork. "Faith is the substance of things hoped for, the evidence of things not seen."

My mind is deeply stirred. In every city there is work to be done. Laborers are to go into our large cities. . . .

We need to feel the vivifying influence of the Holy Spirit as the disciples felt it on the day of Pentecost. Of their experience at that time we read: "And when they had prayed, the place was shaken where they were assembled together; and they were all filled with the Holy Ghost, and they spake the Word of God with boldness. And the multitude of them that believed were of one heart and of one soul: neither said any of them that ought of the things which he possessed was his own." Selfishness was expelled from the heart. "And with great power gave the apostles witness of the resurrection of the Lord Jesus: and great grace was upon them all."—*Pacific Union Recorder,* Oct. 23, 1902.

THE FIELDS ARE READY TO HARVEST

Say not ye, There are yet four months, and then cometh harvest? behold, I say unto you, Lift up your eyes, and look on the fields; for they are white already to harvest. John 4:35.

God's servants are not to exhaust their time and strength in working especially for those whose whole lifetime has been devoted to the service of Satan, till the entire being is corrupted. As the outcasts come—and they will come, as they came to Christ—we are to forbid them not. We are to reach out to them a helping hand. But God calls for workers to reach those of the higher classes, who, if converted, could in turn work for those of their own standing. He desires to see converted talent and converted influence in the ministry enlisted in His service. The Lord is working upon men and women of talent and influence, leading them to connect with those who are giving the last message of mercy to the world.

A mistake has been made in setting young men and young women at work in the slums of our great cities. Few will be saved as a result of this work. . . . The Lord has shown me that our work is to bring into the truth those who will be producers as well as consumers. There are men of talent and influence who are longing for something they have not yet received. Let the truth in its simplicity be presented to them. If converted, they would exert a powerful influence for the truth.

God has men whom He will call into His service, men who will not carry forward the work in the lifeless way in which it has been carried forward in the past. Many who have not yet heard the message to be given to the world have learned the meaning of self-denial and self-sacrifice. Men will come into the truth who will work with earnestness and zeal, tact and understanding. Let none discourage these zealous workers. In some things they will make some mistakes, and will need to be corrected and instructed. But have not men who have been longer in the truth made mistakes, and needed correction and instruction? When they made mistakes, the Lord did not cast them off, but healed them and strengthened them, presenting them with His banner to hold aloft.

God selects His messengers, and gives them His message; and He says, "Forbid them not." New methods must be introduced. God's people must awaken to the necessity of the time in which they are living.

[Christ] knew that when the Holy Spirit should be poured out on the disciples, the harvest of His seed-sowing would be reaped. Thousands would be converted in a day. . . .

Time is passing, and the Lord calls upon the workers in all lines of His work to lift up their eyes and behold the fields all ripe for the harvest.—*Pacific Union Recorder,* Oct. 23, 1902.

242

DOING GOD'S WILL IN WARNING THE LOST

As the servants of Christ, doing the will of God from the heart; with good will doing service, as to the Lord, and not to men. Eph. 6:6, 7.

Last night a scene was presented before me. I may never feel free to reveal all of it, but I will reveal a little.

It seemed that an immense ball of fire came down upon the world, and crushed large houses. From place to place rose the cry, "The Lord has come! The Lord has come!" Many were unprepared to meet Him, but a few were saying, "Praise the Lord!"

"Why are you praising the Lord?" inquired those upon whom was coming sudden destruction.

"Because we now see what we have been looking for."

"If you believed that these things were coming, why did you not tell us?" was the terrible response. "We did not know about these things. Why did you leave us in ignorance? Again and again you have seen us; why did you not become acquainted with us, and tell us of the judgment to come, and that we must serve God, lest we perish? Now we are lost!"

Every church member is to train the intellect, in order that he may gain a clear understanding of the will of God concerning him; everyone is to educate the voice, that he may communicate a knowledge of the Scriptures to those who are in ignorance. May God help us to stand, like Daniel, in our lot and place during the days of probation that remain.

Parents, teach your children regarding the things that are coming upon the earth, and lead them to prepare to meet their Lord in peace. Gain a knowledge of the Scriptures. Do not fill the head with the nonsense of novels. Brain nerve power is required by those who desire to comprehend the truth so clearly that they can teach it intelligently to others. We have none too much brainpower. Never can we afford to use tobacco, or alcoholic liquors, or any other injurious substance; for we must strive to keep our minds clear for the work of saving souls. The Lord is pleased with those who manifest fervid earnestness in His service. It is the privilege of everyone to cultivate faithfully every God-given power.

In that glad day . . . the ransomed ones will exclaim: "Worthy, worthy, is the Lamb that was slain, and lives again, a triumphant Conqueror." What joy the worker will then feel in going to those to whom he has spoken with trembling and in fearfulness—those to whom he has opened the Scriptures and with whom he has prayed, thus balancing their souls on the right side. . . . All His providences will then be made plain.—Manuscript 102, 1904.

HEART MISSIONARIES ARE NEEDED

He died for all, that those who live might live no longer for themselves but for him who for their sake died and was raised. 2 Cor. 5:15, R.S.V.

Those who take up their appointed work will not only be a blessing to others, but they will themselves be blessed. The consciousness of duty well done will have a reflex influence upon their own souls. The despondent will forget their despondency, the weak will become strong, the ignorant intelligent, and all will find an unfailing helper in Him who has called them.

The church of Christ is organized for service. Its watchword is ministry. Its members are soldiers, to be trained for conflict under the Captain of their salvation. Christian ministers, physicians, teachers, have a broader work than many have recognized. They are not only to minister to the people, but to teach them to minister. They should not only give instruction in right principles, but educate their hearers to impart these principles. Truth that is not lived, that is not imparted, loses its life-giving power, its healing virtue. Its blessing can be retained only as it is shared.

The monotony of our service for God needs to be broken up. Every church member should be engaged in some line of service for the Master. Some cannot do so much as others, but everyone should do his utmost to roll back the tide of disease and distress that is sweeping over our world. . . .

Educated workers who are consecrated to God can do service in a greater variety of ways and can accomplish more extensive work than can those who are uneducated. Their discipline of mind places them on vantage ground. But those who have neither great talents nor extensive education may minister acceptably to others. God will use men who are willing to be used. It is not the most brilliant or the most talented persons whose work produces the greatest and most lasting results. Men and women are needed who have heard a message from heaven. The most effective workers are those who respond to the invitation, ''Take my yoke upon you, and learn of me'' (Matt. 11:29).

It is heart missionaries that are needed. He whose heart God touches is filled with a great longing for those who have never known His love. Their condition impresses him with a sense of personal woe. Taking his life in his hand, he goes forth, a heaven-sent, heaven-inspired messenger, to do a work in which angels can cooperate.—*The Ministry of Healing,* pp. 148-150.

SUCCESS THROUGH HOUSE-TO-HOUSE MINISTRY

I kept back nothing that was profitable unto you, but have shewed you, and have taught you publickly, and from house to house, testifying both to the Jews, and also to the Greeks, repentance toward God, and faith toward our Lord Jesus Christ. Acts 20:20, 21.

The work . . . has had to commence small; but . . . it can be managed so as to become self-sustaining. One great means by which this can be accomplished will be by the well-directed efforts of those already in the truth to bring in others who will be a strength and support to the work. This was the way the Christian church was established. Christ first selected a few persons, and bade them follow Him. Then they went in search of their relatives and acquaintances and brought them to Christ. This is the way we are to labor. A few souls brought out and fully established on the truth will, like the first disciples, be laborers for others. . . . The burden now is to convince souls of the truth. This can best be done by personal efforts, by bringing the truth into their houses, praying with them, and opening to them the Scriptures.—*Review and Herald,* Dec. 8, 1885.

Our Saviour went from house to house, healing the sick, comforting the mourners, soothing the afflicted, speaking peace to the disconsolate. He took the little children in His arms and blessed them and spoke words of hope and comfort to the weary mothers. With unfailing tenderness and gentleness, He met every form of human woe and affliction.

Not for Himself, but for others did He labor. He was the servant of all. It was His meat and drink to bring hope and strength to all with whom He came in contact. And as men and women listened to the truths that fell from His lips . . . hope sprang up in their hearts. In His teaching there was an earnestness that sent His words home with convicting power.—*Gospel Workers,* p. 188.

Paul, as well as laboring publicly, went from house to house preaching repentance toward God and faith toward our Lord Jesus Christ. He met with men at their homes, and besought them with tears, declaring unto them the whole counsel of God. Jesus came in personal contact with men. He did not stand aloof and apart from those who needed His help. . . . We must come close to the hearts of those who need our ministry. We must open the Bible to the understanding, present the claims of God's law, read the promises to the hesitating, urge the backward, arouse the careless, strengthen the weak.—*Review and Herald,* April 24, 1888.

Do not neglect speaking to your neighbors, and doing them all the kindness in your power. . . . We need to seek for the spirit that constrained the apostle Paul to go from house to house, pleading with tears, and teaching "repentance toward God, and faith toward our Lord Jesus Christ."—*Ibid.,* March 13, 1888.

ACTS OF SYMPATHY OPEN DOORS

The Son of man came not to be ministered unto, but to minister, and to give his life a ransom for many. Matt. 20:28.

Many have no faith in God and have lost confidence in man. But they appreciate acts of sympathy and helpfulness. As they see one with no inducement of earthly praise or compensation coming to their homes to minister to the sick, to feed the hungry, to clothe the naked, and comfort the sad, and ever tenderly pointing all to Him of whose love and pity the human worker is but the messenger—as they see this, their hearts are touched. Gratitude springs up; faith is kindled. They see that God cares for them, and they are prepared to listen to the teaching of His Word.

Whether in foreign missions or in the home field, all missionaries, both men and women, will gain much more ready access to the people, and will find their usefulness greatly increased, if they are able to minister to the sick. Women who go as missionaries to heathen lands may thus find opportunity for giving the gospel to the women of those lands, when every other door of access is closed. All gospel workers should know how to give the simple treatments that do so much to relieve pain and remove disease.

Gospel workers should be able also to give instruction in the principles of healthful living. There is sickness everywhere, and much of it might be prevented by attention to the laws of health. The people need to see the bearing of health principles upon their well-being, both for this life and for the life to come. They need to be awakened to their responsibility for the human habitation fitted up by their Creator as His dwelling place, and over which He desires them to be faithful stewards.

Thousands need and would gladly receive instruction concerning the simple methods of treating the sick—methods that are taking the place of the use of poisonous drugs. There is great need of instruction in regard to dietetic reform. Wrong habits of eating and use of unhealthful food are in no small degree responsible for the intemperance and crime and wretchedness that curse the world.

In teaching health principles, keep before the mind the great object of reform—that its purpose is to secure the highest development of body and mind and soul. Show that the laws of nature, being the laws of God, are designed for our good; that obedience to them promotes happiness in this life, and aids in the preparation for the life to come.—*Review and Herald,* Dec. 24, 1914.

INVITE THE YOUTH TO YOUR HOMES

Inasmuch as ye have done it unto one of the least of these my brethren, ye have done it unto me. Matt. 25:40.

We are in a world of sin and temptation, and youth are perishing out of Christ all around us, and He wants you to labor for the youth in every conceivable way that you can. If you have a house, and a pleasant home, then invite the youth that have no homes, invite the youth that are in need of help, that are in need of sympathy and kind words, courtesy, and respect. They want all this. If you want to bring them to Christ, you must show your love and respect for the purchase of His blood, the souls whom He has ransomed by the infinite cost of His own precious life, and is not that enough to lead us, as soon as we are a branch in the vine, to bear fruit? . . .

In heaven we shall see those youth that we helped, those youth that we invited to our house, those youth that we led from temptation, those youth that we tried to win away from being drunkards and tobacco users and wine drinkers and all these habits which are taking the underpinning out of the house, befogging the brain, and taking away the reason, and leaving men without a sound mind, and a sound body. . . . What do we want? A face that will reflect the sunshine of the glory of God, we want a face that reflects the likeness of the divine. We want a character reshaped. We want that the image of Christ should be restored to us. May God help us that we may . . . do our best in our lifetime.

You have no time to devote to the theater or the dance hall. You have no time to grumble. It is lost, lost. You have no time to play cards. You have no time to attend horse races. You have no time to attend shows. How is it with my soul? . . . Have I a living connection with God? If I have, I must seek to win these souls that are attracted with these outward pleasures. Satan has managed it. Satan has devised it that one pleasure should crowd on the heels of another, a feverish excitement. No time to contemplate God, no time to think of heaven or heavenly things, no time to study the Bible, no time to put forth interested efforts for those that are out of Christ.

But those that . . . are giving themselves to Jesus . . . can hear that voice that shall pronounce the benediction, "Come, ye blessed of my Father, inherit the kingdom prepared for you from the foundation of the world." There, you see, that is election. . . . It was prepared for every soul that would be obedient to God and that would work in Christ's lines, because that when they obtain the treasure of heavenly reward, they enter into the joy of their Lord, because their joy was full of Christ's joy which was to win souls to the Saviour.—Manuscript 43, 1894.

YOUTH TO HELP YOUTH

Let us therefore follow after the things which make for peace, and things wherewith one may edify another. Rom. 14:19.

I addressed the students earnestly, urging upon them the instruction of the Word, and bidding them keep in mind the higher school, to which, if faithful, they will soon be transferred. . . .

I desire that these students shall do their best, and not lay any stumbling block in their own path or in the path of others; but that individually they shall strive to be Christians, seeking by diligent study and earnest prayer to gain the training essential for acceptable service in the cause of God.

I long to see the youth helping one another to a higher Christian experience. We are preparing for the grand review of that day when every case shall be forever decided. In view of this solemn event, not only the youth, but all who are striving for eternal life, need to put every power of heart and mind into the work of learning Christ's way. We have severe conflicts to meet, and important victories to gain. . . .

Humble your heart before the Lord. Keep heart and mind pure and clean, and free from worldly entanglements. Every power of the sanctified life will be brought into the service of God.

"At a certain battle, when one of the regiments of the attacking force was being beaten back by the enemy, the ensign in front stood his ground as the troops retreated. The captain shouted to him to bring back the colors; but the reply of the ensign was, 'Bring the men up to the colors.' " This is the spirit we are to manifest. It devolves upon every faithful standard bearer to bring the men up to the colors. The Lord calls for wholeheartedness. Many professing Christians lack the courage and the energy to bring themselves and those connected with them up to the true standard. Will not the standard bearers, as brave, true men, bring the men up to the colors, remembering that Christ, the Captain of our salvation, is on the field?

From all countries the Macedonian call is sounding, Come over and help us. God has opened fields before us. If human instrumentalities will cooperate with divine agencies, many souls will be won to the truth. The Spirit of the Lord will be graciously manifested. . . .

Let every sanctified heart now respond, by seeking to proclaim the life-giving message. . . . If men and women in humility and faithfulness will take up their God-appointed work, divine power will be revealed in the conversion of souls to the truth. Wonderful will be the results of their efforts.—Letter 44, 1911.

THE POWER OF INFLUENCE

Make straight paths for your feet, lest that which is lame be turned out of the way. Heb. 12:13.

We cannot realize how powerful for good or for evil is our influence upon those with whom we associate. . . .

My dear young friends, you may maintain the simplicity of true Godliness. You may follow on to know the Lord, that His going forth is prepared as the morning. You may know that He is your helper. You will have an increase of light and joy and hope and consolation in Jesus Christ, as you commit the keeping of your souls to the heavenly Powers, and become separated from corrupt worldly influences.

To make straight paths for our feet—this is our work. "Let us run with patience the race that is set before us, looking unto Jesus the author and finisher of our faith." He will be with us every day as we advance in the narrow path, and through the strait gate that leads to life everlasting. He will be your helper and your strength. Let us praise Him more. We all have received very much for which to praise Him. Then let us talk much of Him, and let us love Him.

Here are younger children. Christ loves you. When the mothers brought the little children to Jesus that He might place His hands on them in blessing, the disciples were going to send them away. The Master was giving important lessons to the people, and the disciples thought He should not be disturbed. Jesus heard their words. Said He, "Forbid them not . . . : for of such is the kingdom of heaven."

I feel a deep interest in every one of these little children, and we hope that you will all treat them very tenderly. In the family let those who are older be patient and kind to their younger brothers and sisters. They may help to educate the little ones in a knowledge of the Bible. Do not put the vim into your voice when you speak to them. Put in the blessedness that comes from doing right, from pleasing the Lord. . . .

If you will continually seek help of the Lord, you will not, when you come to the evening season of prayer, feel that you must repent of harsh or discouraging words, and unkind actions during the day. Take right hold of Christ by a living faith, and then encourage the younger children. They will do wrong sometimes, and they may get into mischief, but do not become discouraged. Shield them so far as possible from temptation, and encourage them to obey the Lord. . . .

Let us plead with the Lord in the home and in the church, that we may be of good courage, and may go forward step by step, onward and upward toward heaven.—Manuscript 61, 1907.

PRESS CLOSE TO THOSE WHO NEED HELP

For the Son of man is come to seek and to save that which was lost. Luke 19:10.

The whole heavenly universe are intensely interested in every penitent soul that comes to Jesus; and they are interested, too, in the impenitent—in those whom they hope to see saved by repentance and reformation. Angels are watching our every act. They are familiar with every word uttered. They are intensely desirous of seeing us value above all else the instruction of God's Word. They desire us to learn Christ's meekness and lowliness—the highest of all sciences, the science of gladness and humility and love through Christ Jesus.

The angels desire that we shall learn that the Son of man came "to save that which was lost." Christ came not to save that which is good and righteous, but "that which was lost." Brethren and sisters, when you see a soul slipping away from the truth, and endangering his hope of eternal salvation, press close to his side, and seek to help him in every way you can. Inquire into his needs; pray with him; labor kindly, patiently, with him; never despair of helping him.

Church members have a work to do along the line of taking an interest in the youth. They should shake hands with them, and manifest a kindly interest in their welfare. Let us shield the youth, so far as possible, from worldly temptations and allurements. If possible, let us find some employment for them, whereby their minds may be occupied with that which is ennobling. This is genuine ministry—a ministry that God approves, and that lifts up before the one who ministers, as well as before the one ministered unto, a standard against the enemy. Satan cannot overcome by his wiles those who in word and deed are ministers of righteousness. . . .

To everyone is given the privilege of helping his fellow men to place their feet on the Rock of Ages. . . .

Christ never ceases to seek us when we wander from the fold. With unwearying steps He searches until He finds us, and brings us back to His fold. Again and again we would have perished, had it not been for His loving care. . . . Little do we realize the strength of the forces that are now at work in this world. The whole heavenly host are seeking to save that which was lost; the fallen angels are working with a power from beneath to counteract the efforts of Christ and His colaborers. . . .

May God help us to fight the good fight of faith, and to clothe ourselves with the whole armor, and, having done all, to stand. . . . Let us watch for souls as do those that must give an account.—Manuscript 102, 1904.

GOD CALLS YOUNG PEOPLE

O God, thou hast taught me from my youth: and hitherto have I declared thy wondrous works. Ps. 71:17.

There is a great work to be done in the Master's vineyard. To accomplish this work, God calls for men to whom He has given ability for service. He does nothing without man's cooperation.

Whenever the Lord has a work to be done, He calls not only the commanding officers, but all the workers. He calls young men and women who are strong and active in mind. He desires them to bring into the work their fresh, healthy powers of brain, bone, and muscle. They are to take part in the conflict against principalities and powers, and spiritual wickedness in high places.

Men have nothing but that which God has given them in trust. They are not to indulge pride or to boast of their talents. They owe to God all that makes it possible for them to labor for Him. Yet every man has a part to act in preparing himself for service. By earnest study, taxing effort, he is to cultivate all his powers. Then divine power will surely combine with his efforts.

Some young men are urging their way into the work who have no real fitness for it. They do not understand that they need to be taught before they can teach. They point to men who with little preparation have labored with a measure of success. But if these men have been successful, it is because they put their heart and soul into the work. . . . The cause of God needs efficient men. . . .

Redemption, what is it? It is the training process for heaven. This training means more than a knowledge of books. It means a knowledge of Christ, emancipation from ideas, habits, and practices that have been gained in the school of the prince of darkness. The soul must be delivered from all that is opposed to loyalty to God. Resistance of evil must be encouraged. . . .

God gives all an opportunity in this life to develop character. All may fill their appointed place in His great plan. The Lord accepted Samuel from his very childhood, because his heart was pure, and he had reverence for God. He was given to God, a consecrated offering, and the Lord made him, even in his childhood, a channel of light.

A life consecrated as was Samuel's is of great value in God's sight. If the youth of today will consecrate themselves as did Samuel, the Lord will accept them and use them in His work. Of their life they may be able to say with the psalmist, "O Lord, thou hast taught me from my youth: and hitherto have I declared thy wondrous works."—Manuscript 51, 1900.

"PURE RELIGION" AND "MY NEIGHBOR" DEFINED

Pure religion and undefiled before God and the Father is this, To visit the fatherless and widows in their affliction, and to keep himself unspotted from the world. James 1:27.

What is pure religion? Christ has told us that pure religion is the exercise of pity, sympathy, and love in the home, in the church, and in the world. This is the kind of religion to teach to the children, and is the genuine article. Teach them that they are not to center their thoughts upon themselves, but that wherever there is human need and suffering, there is a field for missionary work. . . .

There are many who ask, as did the lawyer, "Who is my neighbor?" The answer comes down to us in the circumstances that happened near Jericho, when the priest and the Levite passed by on the other side, and left the poor, bruised, and wounded stranger to be taken care of by the good Samaritan. Everyone who is in suffering need is our neighbor. Every straying son and daughter of Adam, who has been ensnared by the enemy of souls, and bound in the slavery of wrong habits that blight the God-given manhood or womanhood, is my neighbor. . . .

Would that children might be educated from their babyhood, through their childhood and youth, to understand what is the missionary work to be done right around them. Let the home be made a place for religious instruction. Let parents become mouthpieces of the Lord God of Israel, to teach the precepts of true Christianity, and let them be examples of what the principles of love can make men and women.

We are to think and care for others who need our love, our tenderness, and care. We should ever remember that we are representatives of Christ, and that we are to share the blessings that He gives, not with those who can recompense us again, but with those who will appreciate the gifts that will supply their temporal and spiritual necessities. Those who give feasts for the purpose of helping those who have but little pleasure, for the purpose of bringing brightness into their dreary lives, for the purpose of relieving their poverty and distress, are acting unselfishly and in harmony with the instruction of Christ.—*Review and Herald,* Nov. 12, 1895.

Good deeds are the fruit that Christ requires us to bear: kind words, deeds of benevolence, of tender regard for the poor, the needy, the afflicted. When hearts sympathize with hearts burdened with discouragement and grief, when the hand dispenses to the needy, when the naked are clothed, the stranger made welcome to a seat in your parlor and a place in your heart, angels are coming very near, and an answering strain is responded to in heaven.—*Testimonies,* vol. 2, p. 25.

REACHING OUT THROUGH LITERATURE EVANGELISM

I am among you as he that serveth. Luke 22:27.

Canvassing for our publications is an important and most profitable line of evangelistic work. Our publications can go to places where meetings cannot be held. In such places the faithful evangelistic canvasser takes the place of the living preacher. . . .

May the Lord move upon many of our young men and women to enter the canvassing field as canvassing evangelists. By the canvassing work the truth is presented to thousands that otherwise would not hear it. Our time for work is short. Many, very many, need the promptitude of the "quickly" in them, to lead them to arouse and go to work. The Lord calls for workers just now. . . .

Why is there not now more diligent seeking of the Lord, that hundreds may be filled with the Holy Spirit, and may go forth quickly to proclaim the truth, "the Lord working with them and confirming the Word with signs following"? Our commission is to let the light shine forth everywhere from the press. By the printed page the light reaches the isolated ones, who have no opportunity to hear the living preachers. This is most blessed missionary work. Canvassers can be the Lord's helping hand, opening doors for the entrance of the truth.

Let Christian youth be selected to handle the books containing present truth. . . . This is a sacred work, and those who enter it should be able to bear witness for Christ.

Those youth who go into this work should be connected with those older in experience, who, if they are devoted to God, can be a great blessing to them, teaching them in the things of God, and showing them how best to work for Him. If the youth will work out their own salvation with fear and trembling, they will know by experience that God is working with them, to will and to do of His good pleasure.

Not only men, but women, can enter the canvassing field. And canvassers are to go out two by two. This is the Lord's plan.

I am instructed to encourage decided efforts to secure helping hands to do missionary work, to give Bible instruction and to sell books containing present truth. Thus skillful work may be done in hunting for souls. Young men, your help is called for. Make a covenant with God by sacrifice. Take hold of His work. He is your sufficiency. "Be strong, yea, be strong."—*Pacific Union Recorder,* Oct. 23, 1902.

THE RELIEF OF PHYSICAL NEEDS

The people which sat in darkness saw great light; and to them which sat in the region and shadow of death light is sprung up. Matt. 4:16.

There are many now in the shadow of death who need to be instructed in the truths of the gospel. Nearly the whole world is lying in wickedness. To every believer in Christ words of hope have been given for those who sit in darkness. . . .

Earnest, devoted young people are needed to enter the work as nurses. . . . The Lord wants wise men and women, who can act in the capacity of nurses, to comfort and help the sick and suffering. O that all who are afflicted might be ministered to by Christian physicians and nurses who could help them to place their weary, pain-racked bodies in the care of the Great Healer, in faith looking to him for restoration! If through judicious ministration the patient is led to give his soul to Christ and to bring his thoughts into obedience to the will of God, a great victory is gained.

In our daily ministrations we see many careworn, sorrowful faces. What does the sorrow on these faces show? It shows the need of the soul for the peace of Christ. Men and women, longing for something they have not, have sought to supply their want at earth's broken cisterns. Let these hear a voice saying, "Ho, every one that thirsteth, come ye to the waters." Weary souls, seeking you know not what, come to the water of life. All heaven is yearning over you. "Come to me, that ye might have life."

There are many lines of work to be carried forward by the missionary nurse. There are opportunities for well-trained nurses to go into homes and there endeavor to awaken an interest in the truth. In almost every community there are large numbers who will not listen to the teaching of God's Word or attend any religious service. If these are reached by the gospel, it must be carried to their homes. Often the relief of their physical needs is the only avenue by which they can be approached.

Missionary nurses who care for the sick and relieve the distress of the poor will find many opportunities to pray with them, to read to them from God's Word, and to speak of the Saviour. They can pray with and for the helpless ones who have not strength of will to control the appetites that passion has degraded. They can bring a ray of hope into the lives of the defeated and disheartened. The revelation of unselfish love, manifested in acts of disinterested kindness, will make it easier for these suffering ones to believe in the love of Christ.—*Review and Herald*, Dec. 24, 1914.

THE MINISTRY OF MUSIC

My tongue will sing of your righteousness. Ps. 51:14, N.I.V.

Instruction in singing is greatly needed in every school. Much more interest should be manifested. . . . Students who have learned to sing, with melodious voices, sweet gospel songs in such a way that the words are easily understood can do much good as singing evangelists. They will find many opportunities to use the talent that God has given them, carrying melody and sunshine into many lonely places darkened by sin and sorrow and affliction, by singing to those who seldom have the privileges of any kind of gospel ministry.

Go out into the highways and the hedges. Endeavor to reach the higher as well as the lower classes. Enter the homes of the rich and the poor. As you go from house to house to sing, ask, "Would you be pleased to have us sing? We should be glad to hold a song service with you, and to offer a few words of prayer to ask God to keep us." Not many will refuse you entrance.—Manscript 67, 1903.

A spirit of devotion was cherished in the schools of the prophets. . . . Students . . . were taught how to pray, how to approach their Creator, how to exercise faith in Him, and how to understand and obey the teachings of His Spirit. Sanctified intellects brought forth from the treasure house of God things new and old, and the Spirit of God was manifested in prophecy and sacred song.

Music was made to serve a holy purpose, to lift the thoughts to that which is pure, noble, and elevating, and to awaken in the soul devotion and gratitude to God. What a contrast between the ancient custom and the uses to which music is now too often devoted! How many employ this gift to exalt self, instead of using it to glorify God! A love for music leads the unwary to unite with world lovers in pleasure gatherings where God has forbidden His children to go. Thus that which is a great blessing when rightly used, becomes one of the most successful agencies by which Satan allures the mind from duty and from the contemplation of eternal things.

Music forms a part of God's worship in the courts above, and we should endeavor, in our songs of praise, to approach as nearly as possible to the harmony of the heavenly choirs. The proper training of the voice is an important feature in education, and should not be neglected. Singing, as a part of religious service, is as much an act of worship as is prayer.—*Patriarchs and Prophets,* p. 594.

THE JOY OF SERVICE FOR CHRIST

He which soweth bountifully shall reap also bountifully. 2 Cor. 9:6.

Ministry means service, and to this ministry we are all called. It is a dishonor to God for anyone to choose a life of self-pleasing. My brethren and sisters, do you realize that every year thousands and thousands of souls are perishing, dying in their sins because the light of truth has not been flashed upon their pathway? . . .

There is a great work to be done in our world. Men and women are to be converted, not by the gift of tongues nor by the working of miracles, but by the preaching of Christ crucified. Why delay the effort to make the world better? Why wait for some wonderful thing to be done, some costly apparatus to be provided? However humble your sphere, however lowly your work, if you labor in harmony with the teachings of the Saviour, He will reveal Himself through you, and your influence will draw souls to Him. He will honor the meek and lowly ones, who seek earnestly to do service for Him. Into all that we do, whether our work be in the shop, on the farm, or in the office, we are to bring the endeavor to save souls.

We are to sow beside all waters, keeping our souls in the love of God, working while it is day, using the means entrusted to us in the Master's service. Whatever our hands find to do, we are to do it with cheerfulness; whatever sacrifice we are called upon to make, we are to make it cheerfully. As we sow beside all waters, we shall realize the truth of the words, ''He which soweth bountifully shall reap also bountifully.''

We owe everything to grace, sovereign grace. Grace ordained our redemption, our regeneration, and our adoption to heirship with Jesus Christ. Let this grace be revealed to others.

The Saviour takes those whom He finds will be molded, and uses them for His own name's glory. He uses material that others would pass by, and works in all who will give themselves to Him. He delights to take apparently hopeless material, those whom Satan has debased, and through whom he has worked, and make them the subjects of His grace. He rejoices to deliver them from suffering, and from the wrath that is to fall upon the disobedient. He makes His children His agents in the accomplishment of this work, and in its success, even in this life, they find a precious reward.

But what is this compared with the joy that will be theirs in the great day of final revealing?—*Review and Herald,* Jan. 5, 1905.

THE ETERNAL REWARD OF REACHING OUT

When thou makest a feast, call the poor, the maimed, the lame, the blind: and thou shalt be blessed; for they cannot recompense thee: for thou shalt be recompensed at the resurrection of the just. Luke 14:13, 14.

It is the reward of Christ's workers to enter into His joy. That joy, to which Christ Himself looks forward with eager desire, is presented in His request to His Father, "I will that they also, whom thou hast given me, be with me where I am."

The angels were waiting to welcome Jesus, as He ascended after His resurrection. The heavenly host longed to greet again their loved Commander, returned to them from the prison house of death. Eagerly they pressed about Him as He entered the gates of heaven. But He waved them back. His heart was with the lonely, sorrowing band of disciples whom He had left upon Olivet. It is still with His struggling children on earth, who have the battle with the destroyer yet to wage. "Father," He says, "I will that they also, whom thou hast given me, be with me where I am."

Christ's redeemed ones are His jewels, His precious and peculiar treasure. "They shall be as the stones of a crown"—"the riches of the glory of his inheritance in the saints." In them "he shall see the travail of his soul, and shall be satisfied."

And will not His workers rejoice when they, too, behold the fruit of their labors? . . .

Every impulse of the Holy Spirit leading men to goodness and to God is noted in the books of heaven, and in the day of God everyone who has given himself as an instrument for the Holy Spirit's working will be permitted to behold what his life has wrought.

Wonderful will be the revealing as the lines of holy influence, with their precious results, are brought to view. What will be the gratitude of souls that will meet us in the heavenly courts, as they understand the sympathetic, loving interest which has been taken in their salvation! All praise, honor, and glory will be given to God and to the Lamb for our redemption; but it will not detract from the glory of God to express gratitude to the instrumentality He has employed in the salvation of souls ready to perish.

The redeemed will meet and recognize those whose attention they have directed to the uplifted Saviour. What blessed converse they have with these souls! "I was a sinner," it will be said, . . . "and you came to me, and drew my attention to the precious Saviour as my only hope. And I believed in Him." . . . What rejoicing there will be as these redeemed ones meet and greet those who have had a burden in their behalf!—*Review and Herald,* Jan. 5, 1905.

BE READY FOR THE COMING OF CHRIST

Looking for that blessed hope, and the glorious appearing of the great God and our Saviour Jesus Christ; who gave himself for us, that he might redeem us from all iniquity, and purify unto himself a peculiar people, zealous of good works. Titus 2:13, 14.

This scripture teaches a very different lesson from that which is presented in the words of many who profess to believe the gospel. We are exhorted to live soberly, righteously, and godly in this present world, and to look for the glorious appearing of the great God and our Saviour Jesus Christ. Some have made an objection to my work, because I teach that it is our duty to be looking for Christ's personal appearing in the clouds of heaven. They have said, "You would think that the day of the Lord was right upon us to hear Mrs. White speak in reference to the coming of Christ; and she has been preaching on that same subject for the last forty years, and the Lord has not yet come."

This very objection might have been brought against the words of Christ Himself. He said by the mouth of the beloved disciple, "Behold, I come quickly," and John responds, "Even so, come, Lord Jesus." Jesus spoke these words as words of warning and encouragement to His people; and why should we not heed them? The Lord has said that it is the faithful who will be found watching and waiting for Him. It was the unfaithful servant who said, "My Lord delayeth his coming," and began to smite his fellow servants, and eat and drink with the drunken.

The exact time of Christ's second coming is not revealed. Jesus said, No man knoweth the day nor the hour. But He also gave signs of His coming, and said, "When ye shall see all these things, know that it is near, even at the doors." He bade them, as the signs of His coming should appear, "Look up, and lift up your heads; for your redemption draweth nigh." And in view of these things the apostle wrote: "Ye, brethren, are not in darkness, that that day should overtake you as a thief. Ye are all the children of light, and the children of the day." Since we know not the hour of Christ's coming, we must live soberly and godly in this present world, "Looking for that blessed hope, and the glorious appearing of the great God and our Saviour Jesus Christ." . . .

His people are to preserve their peculiar character as His representatives. There is work for every one of them to do. The rich should bring their means, the honored their influence, the learned their wisdom, the poor their virtue, if they would be effective workers with God. They are to bring themselves into right relation with God, that they may reflect the light of the glory of God that shines in the face of Jesus Christ. . . . They are to warn men of the coming judgments. They are to represent Christ to the people.—*Signs of the Times,* June 24, 1889.

GROWING UP INTO CHRIST

I have set the Lord always before me: because he is at my right hand, I shall not be moved. Ps. 16:8.

Many have an idea that they must do some part of the work alone. They have trusted in Christ for the forgiveness of sin, but now they seek by their own efforts to live aright. But every such effort must fail. Jesus says, "Without me ye can do nothing." Our growth in grace, our joy, our usefulness—all depend upon our union with Christ. It is by communion with Him, daily, hourly—by abiding in Him—that we are to grow in grace. . . .

You gave yourself to God, to be His wholly, to serve and obey Him, and you took Christ as your Saviour. You could not yourself atone for your sins or change your heart; but having given yourself to God, you believe that He for Christ's sake did all this for you. By *faith* you became Christ's and by faith you are to grow up in Him—by giving and taking. You are to *give* all—your heart, your will, your service—give yourself to Him to obey all His requirements; and you must *take* all—Christ, the fullness of all blessing, to abide in your heart, to be your strength, your righteousness, your everlasting helper—to give you power to obey.

Consecrate yourself to God in the morning; make this your very first work. Let your prayer be, "Take me, O Lord, as wholly Thine. I lay all my plans at Thy feet. Use me today in Thy service. Abide with me, and let all my work be wrought in Thee." This is a daily matter. Each morning consecrate yourself to God for that day. Surrender all your plans to Him, to be carried out or given up as His providence shall indicate. Thus day by day you may be giving your life into the hands of God, and thus your life will be molded more and more after the life of Christ.

A life in Christ is a life of restfulness. There may be no ecstasy of feeling, but there should be an abiding, peaceful trust. Your hope is not in yourself; it is in Christ. Your weakness is united to His strength, your ignorance to His wisdom, your frailty to His enduring might. So you are not to look to yourself, not to let the mind dwell upon self, but look to Christ. Let the mind dwell upon His love, upon the beauty, the perfection, of His character. Christ in His self-denial, Christ in His humiliation, Christ in His purity and holiness, Christ in His matchless love—this is the subject for the soul's contemplation. It is by loving Him, copying Him, depending wholly upon Him, that you are to be transformed into His likeness.—*Steps to Christ,* pp. 69-71.

OUR SUFFICIENCY IS IN CHRIST ALONE

God forbid that I should glory, save in the cross of our Lord Jesus Christ, by whom the world is crucified unto me, and I unto the world. Gal. 6:14.

By faith—faith that renounces all self-trust—the needy suppliant is to lay hold upon infinite power.

No outward observances can take the place of simple faith and entire renunciation of self. . . . We can only consent for Christ to accomplish the work. Then the language of the soul will be, Lord, take my heart; for I cannot give it. It is Thy property. Keep it pure, for I cannot keep it for Thee. Save me in spite of myself, my weak, unchristlike self. Mold me, fashion me, raise me into a pure and holy atmosphere, where the rich current of Thy love can flow through my soul.

It is not only at the beginning of the Christian life that this renunciation of self is to be made. At every advance step heavenward it is to be renewed. All our good works are dependent on a power outside of ourselves. Therefore there needs to be a continual reaching out of the heart after God, a continual, earnest, heartbreaking confession of sin and humbling of the soul before Him. Only by constant renunciation of self and dependence on Christ can we walk safely.

The nearer we come to Jesus and the more clearly we discern the purity of His character, the more clearly we shall discern the exceeding sinfulness of sin and the less we shall feel like exalting ourselves. Those whom heaven recognizes as holy ones are the last to parade their own goodness. The apostle Peter became a faithful minister of Christ, and he was greatly honored by divine light and power; he had an active part in the upbuilding of Christ's church; but Peter never forgot the fearful experience of his humiliation; his sin was forgiven; yet well he knew that for the weakness of character which had caused his fall only the grace of Christ could avail. He found in himself nothing in which to glory.

None of the apostles or prophets ever claimed to be without sin. Men who have lived nearest to God, men who would sacrifice life itself rather than knowingly commit a wrong act, men whom God had honored with divine light and power, have confessed the sinfulness of their own nature. They have put no confidence in the flesh, have claimed no righteousness of their own, but have trusted wholly in the righteousness of Christ. So will it be with all who behold Christ.

At every advance step in Christian experience our repentance will deepen. . . . Then our lips will not be opened in self-glorification. We shall know that our sufficiency is in Christ alone.—*Christ's Object Lessons,* pp. 159-161.

THE GREATEST IN THE KINGDOM

Whosoever therefore shall humble himself as this little child, the same is greatest in the kingdom of heaven. Matt. 18:4.

The disciples had just been disputing as to who should be the greatest in the kingdom of heaven. They could not agree. One would claim the honor for himself; another for himself. None of the disciples were in a proper frame of mind to comprehend the significance of coming events, or to appreciate the solemnity of the present occasion. They were not prepared to participate in the Passover Supper.

Christ looked upon them sadly. Trials, He knew, were before them, and His great heart of love went out to them in tender pity and sympathy. As a manifestation of His love for them, He "took a towel, and girded himself. After that he poureth water into a bason, and began to wash the disciples' feet, and to wipe them with the towel wherewith he was girded." This was a great rebuke to them all. . . .

"So after he had washed their feet, and had taken his garments, and was set down again, he said unto them, Know ye what I have done to you? Ye call me Master and Lord: and ye say well; for so I am. If I then, your Lord and Master, have washed your feet; ye also ought to wash one another's feet. For I have given you an example, that ye should do as I have done to you." . . .

By the ordinance of humility we are taught an impressive lesson. Christ had shown to us the necessity of walking humbly before God, and of realizing what He has done for us by the gift of His Son. Christ knew that His disciples would never forget the lesson on humility given them at the Last Supper. In taking upon Himself the humblest form of service, He administered to the twelve the sternest rebuke that could have been given them.

In the eighteenth of Matthew there is recorded another lesson on humility. These lessons in the Word are given for our admonition. Those who neglect to profit by them are inexcusable.

The disciples came "unto Jesus, saying, Who is the greatest in the kingdom of heaven? And Jesus called a little child unto him, and set him in the midst of them, and said, Verily I say unto you, Except ye be converted, and become as little children, ye shall not enter into the kingdom of heaven. Whosoever therefore shall humble himself as this little child, the same is greatest in the kingdom of heaven."

Many do not realize that by walking humbly with God, we place ourselves in a position where the enemy cannot take advantage of us. . . . Only when we submit, as willing children, to be trained and disciplined, can God use us to His glory.—Manuscript 102, 1904.

INFLUENCE MAY BLESS THOUSANDS

Your faith in God has gone forth everywhere, so that we need not say anything. 1 Thess. 1:8, R.S.V.

The life of Christ was an ever-widening, shoreless influence, an influence that bound Him to God and to the whole human family. Through Christ, God has invested man with an influence that makes it impossible for him to live to himself. Individually we are connected with our fellow men, a part of God's great whole, and we stand under mutual obligations. No man can be independent of his fellow men; for the well-being of each affects others. It is God's purpose that each shall feel himself necessary to others' welfare, and seek to promote their happiness.

Every soul is surrounded by an atmosphere of its own—an atmosphere, it may be, charged with the life-giving power of faith, courage, and hope, and sweet with the fragrance of love. Or it may be heavy and chill with the gloom of discontent and selfishness, or poisonous with the deadly taint of cherished sin. By the atmosphere surrounding us, every person with whom we come in contact is consciously or unconsciously affected.

This is a responsibility from which we cannot free ourselves. Our words, our acts, our dress, our deportment, even the expression of the countenance, has an influence. Upon the impression thus made there hang results for good or evil which no man can measure. Every impulse thus imparted is seed sown which will produce its harvest. It is a link in the long chain of human events, extending, we know not whither. If by our example we aid others in the development of good principles, we give them power to do good. In their turn they exert the same influence upon others, and they upon still others. Thus by our unconscious influence thousands may be blessed.

Throw a pebble into the lake, and a wave is formed, and another and another; and as they increase, the circle widens, until it reaches the very shore. So with our influence. Beyond our knowledge or control it tells upon others in blessing. . . .

The silent witness of a true, unselfish, godly life carries an almost irresistible influence. By revealing in our own life the character of Christ we cooperate with Him in the work of saving souls. It is only by revealing in our life His character that we can cooperate with Him. And the wider the sphere of our influence, the more good we may do.—*Christ's Object Lessons,* pp. 339, 340.

ACQUIRING THE DIVINE BEAUTY OF MEEKNESS

Seek ye the Lord, all ye meek of the earth, which have wrought his judgment; seek righteousness, seek meekness: it may be ye shall be hid in the day of the Lord's anger. Zeph. 2:3.

Those who have felt their need of Christ, those who have mourned because of sin and have sat with Christ in the school of affliction, will learn meekness from the divine Teacher. . . .

The statement made by Moses under the inspiration of the Holy Spirit, that he was the meekest man upon the earth, would not have been regarded by the people of his time as a commendation; it would rather have excited pity or contempt. But Jesus places meekness among the first qualifications for His kingdom. In His own life and character the divine beauty of this precious grace is revealed. . . .

Through all the lowly experiences of life He consented to pass, walking among the children of men, not as a king, to demand homage, but as one whose mission it was to serve others. There was in His manner no taint of bigotry, no cold austerity. The world's Redeemer had a greater than angelic nature, yet united with His divine majesty were meekness and humility that attracted all to Himself.

Jesus emptied Himself, and in all that He did, self did not appear. He subordinated all things to the will of His Father. When His mission on earth was about to close, He could say, "I have glorified thee on the earth: I have finished the work which thou gavest me to do" (John 17:4). . . .

It is the love of self that destroys our peace. While self is all alive, we stand ready continually to guard it from mortification and insult; but when we are dead, and our life is hid with Christ in God, we shall not take neglects or slights to heart. We shall be deaf to reproach and blind to scorn and insult. "Love suffereth long and is kind" (1 Cor. 13:4, R.V.). . . .

Happiness drawn from earthly sources is as changeable as varying circumstances can make it; but the peace of Christ is a constant and abiding peace. It does not depend upon any circumstances in life, on the amount of worldly goods or the number of earthly friends. Christ is the fountain of living water, and happiness drawn from Him can never fail.

The meekness of Christ, manifested in the home, will make the inmates happy; it provokes no quarrel, gives back no angry answer, but soothes the irritated temper and diffuses a gentleness that is felt by all within its charmed circle. Wherever cherished, it makes the families of earth a part of the one great family above.—*Thoughts From the Mount of Blessing,* pp. 13-17.

MEEKNESS, AN ADORNING OF THE SOUL

The Lord taketh pleasure in his people: he will beautify the meek with salvation. Ps. 149:4.

The most precious fruit of sanctification is the grace of meekness. When this grace presides in the soul, the disposition is molded by its influence. There is a continual waiting upon God and a submission of the will to His. The understanding grasps every divine truth, and the will bows to every divine precept, without doubting or murmuring. True meekness softens and subdues the heart and gives the mind a fitness for the engrafted Word. It brings the thoughts into obedience to Jesus Christ. It opens the heart to the Word of God, as Lydia's was opened. It places us with Mary, as learners at the feet of Jesus. "The meek will he guide in judgment: and the meek will he teach his way" (Ps. 25:9).

The language of the meek is never that of boasting. Like the child Samuel, they pray, "Speak, Lord; for thy servant heareth" (1 Sam. 3:9). . . .

Meekness in the school of Christ is one of the marked fruits of the Spirit. It is a grace wrought by the Holy Spirit as a sanctifier, and enables its possessor at all times to control a rash and impetuous temper. When the grace of meekness is cherished by those who are naturally sour or hasty in disposition, they will put forth the most earnest efforts to subdue their unhappy temper. Every day they will gain self-control, until that which is unlovely and unlike Jesus is conquered. They become assimilated to the Divine Pattern, until they can obey the inspired injunction, "Be swift to hear, slow to speak, slow to wrath" (James 1:19). . . .

Meekness is the inward adorning, which God estimates as of great price. The apostle speaks of this as more excellent and valuable than gold or pearls or costly array. While the outward adorning beautifies only the mortal body, the ornament of meekness adorns the soul and connects finite man with the infinite God. This is the ornament of God's own choice. He who garnished the heavens with the orbs of light has by the same Spirit promised that "he will beautify the meek with salvation." Angels of heaven will register as best adorned those who put on the Lord Jesus and walk with Him in meekness and lowliness of mind.

There are high attainments for the Christian. He may ever be rising to higher attainments.—*The Sanctified Life,* pp. 14-16.

AN IMPERISHABLE JEWEL

Let not yours be the outward adorning with . . . decoration of gold, and wearing of fine clothing, but let it be the hidden person of the heart with the imperishable jewel of a gentle and quiet spirit, which in God's sight is very precious. 1 Peter 3:3, 4, R.S.V.

While at Brother Harris's I had an interview with a sister who wore gold, and yet professed to be looking for Christ's coming. We spoke of the express declaration of Scripture against the wearing of gold. But she referred to where Solomon was commanded to beautify the Temple, and to the statement that the streets of the City of God were pure gold. She said that if we could improve our appearance by wearing gold, so as to have influence in the world, it was right.

I replied that we were poor fallen mortals, and instead of decorating these bodies because Solomon's Temple was gloriously adorned, we should remember our fallen condition, and that it cost the suffering and death of the Son of God to redeem us. This thought should cause us self-abasement.

Jesus is our pattern. If He would lay aside His humiliation and sufferings, and cry, "If any man will come after Me, let him please himself, and enjoy the world, and he shall be My disciple," the multitude would believe and follow Him. But Jesus will come to us in no other character than that of the meek, crucified One. If we would be with Him in heaven, we must be like Him on earth. The world will claim its own; and whoever will overcome must leave what belongs to it.—*Life Sketches,* pp. 113, 114.

In the day when the accounts of all are balanced, will you feel . . . that the beauty of the outward man was sought, while the inward beauty of the soul was almost entirely neglected?

Have not our sisters sufficient zeal and moral courage to place themselves without excuse upon the Bible platform? The apostle has given most explicit direction on this point: "I will therefore . . . that women adorn themselves in modest apparel, with shamefacedness and sobriety; not with broided hair, or gold, or pearls, or costly array; but . . . with good works."—*Testimonies,* vol. 4, p. 630.

Love of dress and pleasure is wrecking the happiness of thousands. . . . To dress plainly, abstaining from display of jewelry and ornaments of every kind, is in keeping with our faith.—*Ibid.,* vol. 3, p. 366.

The inward adorning of a meek and quiet spirit is priceless. In the life of the true Christian the outward adorning is always in harmony with the inward peace and holiness. . . . It is right to love beauty and desire it; but God desires us to love and seek first the highest beauty, that which is imperishable.—*The Acts of the Apostles,* p. 523.

RELIEVING THE WORLD'S MISERY

Lay up for yourselves treasures in heaven . . . : for where your treasure is, there will your heart be also. Matt. 6:20, 21.

Where their treasure is, there will their heart be also. Those who have the Lord's talents of means are placed under a heavy responsibility. They are not to invest money merely for the gratification of selfish desires, for whatever is spent in this way is just that much kept from the Lord's treasury. Through the sovereign goodness of God, the Holy Spirit works through the human agent, and causes him to make smaller or larger investments in the cause of God, to make them redound to the glory of God.

Whenever you think of using the Lord's money for your own selfish gratification, remember that there are many who are in deep poverty who cannot purchase either food or clothing, and they are God's heritage. We are to do good to all men, and especially to those who are of the household of faith. If those who have abundant means are God's agents in dealing in truth, they will use their treasures wisely, so that none of the household of faith need to go hungry or naked.

The reason there is such accumulated misery in our world is because those who have been entrusted with money expend it to gratify unsanctified desires, in purchasing needless ornaments of gold and precious stones, and in procuring fancy articles for adornment's sake. But at the same time those who have been purchased by the blood of Christ are starving for food, and their cry entereth into the ears of the God of Sabaoth. . . . In every place where the truth is to go, those who are to be colaborers with God have a work to to do. . . .

Earnest work must be done, not only by a few ministers, but by the whole membership of the church. The Lord God of heaven calls upon men to put away their idols, to cut off every extravagant desire, to indulge in nothing that is simply for display and parade, and to study economy in purchasing garments and furniture. Do not expend one dollar of God's money in purchasing needless articles. Your money means the salvation of souls. Then let it not be spent for gems, for gold, or precious stones.

Souls for whom Christ died are perishing in their sins, and we are continually bound about because of want of means wherewith to advance the cause of God. Would you not rather have gems in the crown which Jesus shall place upon your head than expend your money for precious stones to please the fancy here in this world? . . . Every pound is needed, every shilling can be put to use, and invested in such a way as to bring you imperishable treasure.—Letter 90, 1895.

CHOOSE THE ROBE WOVEN IN HEAVEN'S LOOM

They shall walk with me in white: for they are worthy. Rev. 3:4.

Lead the youth to see that in dress, as in diet, plain living is indispensable to high thinking. Lead them to see how much there is to learn and to do; how precious are the days of youth as a preparation for the lifework. Help them to see what treasures there are in the Word of God, in the book of nature, and in the records of noble lives.

Let their minds be directed to the suffering which they might relieve. Help them to see that by every dollar squandered in display, the spender is deprived of means for feeding the hungry, clothing the naked, and comforting the sorrowful.

They cannot afford to miss life's glorious opportunities, to dwarf their minds, to ruin their health, and to wreck their happiness, for the sake of obedience to mandates that have no foundation in reason, in comfort, or in comeliness.

At the same time the young should be taught to recognize the lesson of nature, "He hath made every thing beautiful in its time" (Eccl. 3:11, R.V.). In dress, as in all things else, it is our privilege to honor our Creator. He desires our clothing to be not only neat and healthful, but appropriate and becoming.

A person's character is judged by his style of dress. A refined taste, a cultivated mind, will be revealed in the choice of simple and appropriate attire. Chaste simplicity in dress, when united with modesty of demeanor, will go far toward surrounding a young woman with that atmosphere of sacred reserve which will be to her a shield from a thousand perils.

Let girls be taught that the art of dressing well includes the ability to make their own clothing. . . . It will be a means of usefulness and independence that she cannot afford to miss. . . .

Let the youth and little children be taught to choose for themselves that royal robe woven in heaven's loom—the "fine linen, clean and white" (Rev. 19:8), which all the holy ones of earth will wear. This robe, Christ's own spotless character, is freely offered to every human being. But all who receive it will receive and wear it here.

Let the children be taught that as they open their minds to pure, loving thoughts and do loving and helpful deeds, they are clothing themselves with His beautiful garment of character. This apparel will make them beautiful and beloved here, and will hereafter be their title of admission to the palace of the King. His promise is: "They shall walk with me in white: for they are worthy."—*Education*, pp. 248, 249.

THE WIDOW'S MITE MEASURED BY MOTIVE

And he said, Of a truth I say unto you, that this poor widow hath cast in more than they all. Luke 21:3.

The poor widow who cast two mites into the treasury of the Lord showed love, faith, and benevolence. She gave all that she had, trusting to God's care for the uncertain future. Her little gift was pronounced by our Saviour the greatest that day cast into the treasury. Its value was measured, not by the worth of the coin, but by the purity of the motive which prompted her.

God's blessing upon that sincere offering has made it the source of great results. The widow's mite has been like a tiny stream flowing down through the ages, widening and deepening in its course, and contributing in a thousand directions to the extension of the truth and the relief of the needy.

The influence of that small gift has acted and reacted upon thousands of hearts in every age and in every country. As the result, unnumbered gifts have flowed into the treasury of the Lord from the liberal, self-denying poor. And again, her example has stimulated to good works thousands of ease-loving, selfish, and doubting ones, and their gifts also have gone to swell the value of her offering.

Liberality is a duty on no account to be neglected; but let not rich or poor for a moment entertain the thought that their offerings to God can atone for their defects of Christian character. Says the great apostle: "Though I bestow all my goods to feed the poor, and though I give my body to be burned, and have not charity, it profiteth me nothing."

Again, he sets forth the fruits of true charity: "Charity suffereth long, and is kind; charity envieth not; charity vaunteth not itself, is not puffed up, doth not behave itself unseemly, seeketh not her own, is not easily provoked, thinketh no evil; rejoiceth not in iniquity, but rejoiceth in the truth; beareth all things, believeth all things, hopeth all things, endureth all things. Charity never faileth." If we would be accepted as the followers of Christ, we must bring forth the fruits of His Spirit; for our Saviour Himself declares: "Ye shall know them by their fruits."

It is to cultivate a spirit of benevolence in us that the Lord calls for our gifts and offerings. He is not dependent upon men for means to sustain His cause. He declares, by the prophet: "Every beast of the forest is mine, and the cattle upon a thousand hills. I know all the fowls of the mountains; and the wild beasts of the field are mine. . . . The world is mine and the fulness thereof."—*Signs of the Times,* Jan. 21, 1886.

USING RICHES FOR THE LORD

If riches increase, set not your heart upon them. Ps. 62:10.

Listen to the words of your Redeemer: " . . . Riches are mine. I have placed them in your hands to be wisely employed in My service, to aid the suffering, to invest in opening the gospel to those who are in darkness. Riches must not be your trust, your god, or your saviour."

The channels for doing good are many, and they stand wide open. Your barns are large, too large already. If they overflow, instead of building larger, send your treasure before you into heaven. There are widows to feed, orphans to be taken under the guardianship of your home, and share your ample stores; there are souls perishing for the bread of life; missions are to be supported, meetinghouses to be built. If God's cause demands a part, not only of your interest, but of your principal, you are to give back to Him His own. He calls upon you to sow now, that you may reap your harvest with eternal joy.

God's gifts increase as they are imparted. We see this illustrated in the case of the poor widow whom the prophet Elisha, by a miracle, relieved from debt. She had only one jar of oil; but the prophet told her to borrow vessels of her neighbors, and the oil poured from that one jar continued to flow till all the vessels were filled. The supply ceased only when no more vessels were brought to receive it. So it will be now. So long as we let the gifts of God flow into channels of good, the Lord will supply the flow.

Christ says to His sons and daughters, "Ye are the light of the world." But who gave you light? You did not have it in you naturally. God is the source of light; the truth has shone into our hearts, to be reflected to others. True love to God will produce love to man. This is what we need—love that is patient, self-sacrificing, persevering, intelligent, practical.

The Lord has given you means, that in putting it to a right use you may develop good and noble traits of character. . . .

The Lord is coming. You have no time to lose. You are not to do as did the inhabitants of the antediluvian world—plant and build, eat and drink, marry and give in marriage, the same as the careless worldling. Let the books of heaven present a different record from that which now appears. Make haste to redeem the time; provide yourselves bags which wax not old, a treasure in the heavens that faileth not.—*Signs of the Times,* Jan. 14, 1886.

WHAT THE SPIRIT OF LIBERALITY WILL DO

There is that scattereth, and yet increaseth. . . . The liberal soul shall be made fat: and he that watereth shall be watered also himself. Prov. 11:24, 25.

Many have pitied the lot of the Israel of God in being compelled to give systematically, besides making liberal offerings yearly. An all-wise God knew best what system of benevolence would be in accordance with His providence, and has given His people directions in regard to it. It has ever proved that nine tenths are worth more to them than ten tenths. Those who have thought to increase their gains by withholding from God, or by bringing Him an inferior offering—the lame, the blind, or the diseased—have been sure to suffer loss.

Providence, though unseen, is ever at work in the affairs of men. God's hand can prosper or withhold, and He frequently withholds from one while He seems to prosper another. All this is to test and prove man to reveal the heart. He lets misfortune overtake one brother while He prospers others to see if those whom He favors have His fear before their eyes and will perform the duty enjoined upon them in His Word to love their neighbor as themselves and to help their poorer brother from a love to do good. Acts of generosity and benevolence were designed by God to keep the hearts of the children of men tender and sympathetic and to encourage in them an interest and affection for one another in imitation of the Master, who for our sakes became poor, that we through His poverty might be made rich. The law of tithing was founded upon an enduring principle and was designed to be a blessing to man.

The system of benevolence was arranged to prevent the great evil, covetousness.—*Testimonies,* vol. 3, pp. 546, 547.

The small streams of beneficence must be ever kept flowing into the treasury. God's providence is far ahead, moving onward much faster than our liberalities.—*Welfare Ministry,* p. 268.

When the grace of Christ is expressed in the words and works of the believers, light will shine forth to those who are in darkness; for while the lips are speaking to the praise of God, the hand will be stretched out in beneficence for the help of the perishing.

We read that on the day of Pentecost, when the Holy Spirit descended upon the disciples, no man said that aught that he possessed was his own. All they owned was held for the advance of the wonderful reformation. And thousands were converted in a day. When the same spirit actuates believers today, and they give back to God of His own with the same liberality, a wide and far-reaching work will be accomplished.—*Ibid.,* p. 271.

LIKE DANIEL, BE HONEST AND UPRIGHT

The integrity of the upright shall guide them. Prov. 11:3.

The case of Daniel, portrayed in a very limited manner by the prophetic pencil, has a lesson for us. It reveals the fact that a businessman is not necessarily a sharp policy man. He can be a man instructed of God at every step. Daniel while the prime minister of the kingdom of Babylon, was a prophet of God, receiving the light of heavenly inspiration. . . .

Especially are businessmen needed, not irreligious businessmen, but those who will weave the great, grand principles of truth into all their business transactions. Men who have qualifications for the work need to have their talents exercised and perfected by most thorough study and training. Not one businessman that has any appointment in the work need to be a novice. If men in any line of work need to improve their opportunities to become wise, efficient businessmen, it is those who are using their ability in the work of building up the kingdom of God in our world.

The lessons for the present time are for all to understand, but they are very feebly appreciated. There should be greater thoroughness in labor; and more vigilant waiting, more vigilant watching and praying, and more vigilant working, in prospect of the events now taking place, and which are swelling to large importance as we near the close of this earth's history. The human agent is to reach for perfection, to be an ideal Christian, complete in Jesus Christ.

Those who labor in business lines should exercise every precaution against error through wrong principles or methods. Their record may be like that of Daniel in the courts of Babylon. In all his business transactions, when subjected to the closest scrutiny, there was not found one item that was faulty. He was a sample of what every business man may be. But the heart must be converted and consecrated. The motives must be right with God. The inner lamp must be supplied with the oil that flows from the true messengers of heaven through the golden tubes into the golden bowl. Then the Lord's communication never comes to man in vain.

God will not accept the most splendid services unless self is laid upon the altar, a living, consuming sacrifice. The root must be holy, else there can be no sound, healthful fruit, which alone is acceptable to God. . . . While worldly ambition and worldly projects and the greatest plans and purposes of men shall fade like the grass, "they that be wise shall shine as the brightness of the firmament; and they that turn many to righteousness as the stars for ever and ever."—*Special Testimonies,* Series A, No. 9, pp. 65, 66.

STRICT INTEGRITY TO MARK THE CHRISTIAN

Thou shalt have a perfect and just weight, a perfect and just measure shalt thou have: that thy days may be lengthened in the land which the Lord thy God giveth thee. Deut. 25:15.

In all the details of life, Christians are to follow the principles of strict integrity. These are not the principles that govern the world; for there Satan is master, and his principles of deception and oppression bear sway. But Christians serve under a different Master, and their actions must be wrought in God. They must put aside all desire for selfish gain.

To some, deviation from perfect fairness in business deal[s] may look like a small thing, but our Saviour does not thus regard it. His words on this point are plain and explicit: "He that is faithful in that which is least is faithful also in much; and he that is unjust in the least is unjust also in much." A man who will overreach in a small matter will overreach in a larger matter if the temptation comes to him.

Christ's followers are obliged to be more or less connected with the world in business matters. In His prayer for them the Saviour says, "I pray not that thou shouldest take them out of the world, but that thou shouldest keep them from the evil." Christians are to buy and sell with the realization that the eye of God is upon them. Never are they to use false balances or deceitful weights. . . .

In every action of life the true Christian is just what he desires those around him to think he is. He is guided by truth and uprightness. He does not scheme; therefore he has nothing to gloss over. He may be criticized, he may be tested; but through all, his unbending integrity shines out like pure gold. He is a friend and benefactor to all connected with him; and his fellow men place confidence in him; for he is trustworthy.

Does he employ laborers to gather in his harvest? He does not keep back their hard-earned money. Has he means for which he has no immediate use? He relieves the necessities of his less fortunate brother. He does not seek to enlarge his possessions by taking advantage of the untoward circumstances of his neighbor. He accepts only a fair price for that which he sells. If there are defects in the articles sold, he frankly tells the buyer, even though by so doing he may seem to work against his own pecuniary interests.

A man may not have a pleasant exterior; but if he has a reputation for straightforward, honest dealing, he is respected. . . . A man who steadfastly adheres to the truth wins the confidence of all. Not only do Christians trust him; worldlings are constrained to acknowledge the worth of his character.—*Signs of the Times,* Feb. 19, 1902.

LIVING STONES, AGLOW WITH WONDROUS LIGHT

To whom coming, as unto a living stone, disallowed indeed of men, but chosen of God, and precious, ye also, as lively stones, are built up a spiritual house . . . acceptable to God by Jesus Christ. 1 Peter 2:4, 5.

When the sacred work of God shall be purified from all the rubbish which has been accumulating for years, the name of God will be glorified in your midst. When the Holy Spirit controls human agents, there will be none of the underhand business which has been practiced. Honesty, truthfulness, and a willingness that all should understand the methods of working will be seen. The characters of the workers will be built up with pure, solid timbers. Straightforwardness in deal will be seen in all God's commandment-keeping people. Every thread of the web will be originated by the Lord, and each worker will draw his thread into the web to help compose the pattern. The pattern will come from the great loom perfect in its design.

Three thousand years ago, David asked the question, "Wherewithal shall a young man cleanse his way? by taking heed thereto according to thy word." Souls already impure need to be cleansed, purified, and sanctified. Then the testimony can be borne, "God, who commanded the light to shine out of darkness, hath shined in our hearts, to give the light of the knowledge of the glory of God in the face of Jesus Christ."

In this world we are to shine in good works. The Lord requires His people who handle sacred things to be alone with God, to reflect the principles of heaven in every business transaction, to reflect the light of God's character, God's love, as Christ reflected it. [As we look] unto Jesus, all our lives will be aglow with that wondrous light. Every part of us is to be light; then whichever way we turn, light will be reflected from us to others. . . .

The fruit of the Spirit—what is it? Gloom, and sadness, and mourning, and tears? No, no; the fruit of the Spirit is love, joy, peace, long-suffering, gentleness, goodness, faith, meekness, temperance. These graces will be seen in every stone that helps to compose the temple of God. All the stones are not of the same dimension or shape, but every stone has its place in the temple.

In the temple there is not one misshapen stone. Each is perfect, and in the diversity there is unity, making a complete whole. One thing is sure, every stone is a living stone, a stone that emits light. Now is the time for the stones taken from the quarry of the world to be brought into the workshop of God, and hewed, squared, and polished, that they may shine.—*Special Instruction Regarding Royalties,* pp. 20, 21.

OBEDIENCE, THE FRUIT OF FAITH

If ye will obey my voice indeed, and keep my covenant, then ye shall be a peculiar treasure unto me above all people: for all the earth is mine. Ex. 19:5.

Obedience—the service and allegiance of love—is the true sign of discipleship. Thus the Scripture says, ''This is the love of God, that we keep His commandments'' (1 John 5:3). ''He that saith, I know him, and keepeth not his commandments, is a liar, and the truth is not in him'' (chap. 2:4). Instead of releasing man from obedience, it is faith, and faith only, that makes us partakers of the grace of Christ, which enables us to render obedience.

We do not earn salvation by our obedience, for salvation is the free gift of God, to be received by faith. But obedience is the fruit of faith. ''Ye know that he was manifested to take away our sins; and in him is no sin. Whosoever abideth in him sinneth not'' (chap. 3:5, 6). Here is the true test. If we abide in Christ, if the love of God dwells in us, our feelings, our thoughts, our purposes, our actions, will be in harmony with the will of God as expressed in the precepts of His holy law. ''Little children, let no man deceive you; he that doeth righteousness is righteous, even as he is righteous'' (verse 7). Righteousness is defined by the standard of God's holy law, as expressed in the ten precepts given on Sinai.

The so-called faith in Christ which professes to release men from the obligation of obedience to God is not faith, but presumption. ''By grace are ye saved through faith'' (Eph. 2:8). But ''faith, if it hath not works, is dead'' (James 2:17). Jesus said of Himself before He came to earth, ''I delight to do thy will, O my God: yea, thy law is within my heart'' (Ps. 40:8). And just before He ascended again to heaven, He declared, ''I have kept my Father's commandments, and abide in his love'' (John 15:10). The Scripture says, ''Hereby we do know that we know him, if we keep his commandments'' (1 John 2:3). . . .

The condition of eternal life is now just what it always has been—just what it was in Paradise before the fall of our first parents—perfect obedience to the law of God, perfect righteousness. If eternal life were granted on any condition short of this, then the happiness of the whole universe would be imperiled. The way would be open for sin, with all its train of woe and misery, to be immortalized. . . .

The more our sense of need drives us to Him and to the Word of God, the more exalted views we shall have of His character, and the more fully we shall reflect His image.—*Steps to Christ,* pp. 60-65.

THE GROUND OF FORGIVENESS

The Lord is far from the wicked: but he heareth the prayer of the righteous. Prov. 15:29.

We ourselves owe everything to God's free grace. Grace in the covenant ordained our adoption. Grace in the Saviour effected our redemption, our regeneration, and our exaltation to heirship with Christ. Let this grace be revealed to others.

Give the erring one no occasion for discouragement. Suffer not a Pharisaical hardness to come in and hurt your brother. Let no bitter sneer rise in mind or heart. Let no tinge of scorn be manifest in the voice. If you speak a word of your own, if you take an attitude of indifference, or show suspicion or distrust, it may prove the ruin of a soul. He needs a brother with the Elder Brother's heart of sympathy to touch his heart of humanity. Let him feel the strong clasp of a sympathizing hand, and hear the whisper, Let us pray. God will give a rich experience to you both.

Prayer unites us with one another and with God. Prayer brings Jesus to our side, and gives to the fainting, perplexed soul new strength to overcome the world, the flesh, and the devil. Prayer turns aside the attacks of Satan.

When one turns away from human imperfections to behold Jesus, a divine transformation takes place in the character. The Spirit of Christ working upon the heart conforms it to His image. Then let it be your effort to lift up Jesus. Let the mind's eye be directed to "the Lamb of God, which taketh away the sin of the world" (John 1:29). And as you engage in this work, remember that "he which converteth the sinner from the error of his way, shall save a soul from death, and shall hide a multitude of sins" (James 5:20).

"But if ye forgive not men their trespasses, neither will your Father forgive your trespasses" (Matt. 6:15). Nothing can justify an unforgiving spirit. He who is unmerciful toward others shows that he himself is not a partaker of God's pardoning grace. In God's forgiveness the heart of the erring one is drawn close to the great heart of Infinite Love. The tide of divine compassion flows into the sinner's soul, and from him to the souls of others. The tenderness and mercy that Christ has revealed in His own precious life will be seen in those who become sharers of His grace. . . .

We are not forgiven *because* we forgive, but *as* we forgive. The ground of all forgiveness is found in the unmerited love of God; but by our attitude toward others we show whether we have made that love our own.—*Christ's Object Lessons,* pp. 250, 251.

ENCOURAGE A SPIRIT OF KINDLINESS

To speak evil of no one, to avoid quarreling, to be gentle, and to show perfect courtesy toward all men. Titus 3:2, R.S.V.

How many useful and honored workers in God's cause have received a training amid the humble duties of the most lowly positions in life! Moses was the prospective ruler of Egypt, but God could not take him from the king's court to do the work appointed him. Only when he had been for forty years a faithful shepherd was he sent to be the deliverer of his people. Gideon was taken from the threshing-floor to be the instrument in the hands of God for delivering the armies of Israel. Elisha was called to leave the plow and do the bidding of God. Amos was a husbandman, a tiller of the soil, when God gave him a message to proclaim.

All who become coworkers with Christ will have a great deal of hard, uncongenial labor to perform, and their lessons of instruction should be wisely chosen, and adapted to their peculiarities of character, and the work which they are to pursue.

The Lord has presented to me, in many ways and at various times, how carefully we should deal with the young—that it requires the finest discrimination to deal with minds. Everyone who has to do with the education and training of youth needs to live very close to the great Teacher, to catch His spirit and manner of work. Lessons are to be given which will affect their character and lifework.

They should be taught that the gospel of Christ tolerates no spirit of caste, that it gives no place to unkind judgment of others, which tends directly to self-exaltation. The religion of Jesus never degrades the receiver, nor makes him coarse and rough; nor does it make him unkind in thought and feeling toward those for whom Christ died. . . .

Some are in danger of making the externals all-important, of overestimating the value of mere conventionalities. . . .

Anything that would encourage ungenerous criticism, a disposition to notice and expose every defect or error, is wrong. It fosters distrust and suspicion, which are contrary to the character of Christ, and detrimental to the mind thus exercised. Those who are engaged in this work gradually depart from the true spirit of Christianity.

The most essential, enduring education is that which will develop the nobler qualities, which will encourage a spirit of universal kindliness, leading the youth to think no evil of anyone, lest they misjudge motives and misinterpret words and actions. The time devoted to this kind of instruction will yield fruit to everlasting life.—*Gospel Workers*, pp. 332-334.

KEEP CHRIST IN VIEW

Looking unto Jesus the author and finisher of our faith; who for the joy that was set before him endured the cross, despising the shame, and is set down at the right hand of the throne of God. Heb. 12:2.

If suspicions and envy and jealousies and evil surmisings are cherished, these will exclude the blessing of God, for Jesus cannot dwell in a heart where these things are cherished. The soul temple must be cleansed of every defilement. . . .

Christ foresaw the danger of all these things, and just prior to giving His life for the world He prayed to His Father that His disciples might be one with Christ as He was one with the Father. . . . Nothing can grieve the Spirit of God more than variance among those who are engaged as laborers in His vineyard, because the same spirit they entertain is diffused among the churches. Such seed, once sown, is difficult to eradicate. It requires time and labor and distress of soul to adjust things, and bring in a state of harmony and peace. All heaven is laboring for the unity of the church, and the professed followers of Christ are working at cross-purposes with God, because they will not heed His instruction, but will bring in dissension. . . .

The one running in a race will surely lose his victory if he keeps looking behind him or from side to side to see if his fellows are coming out ahead of him. He must run to win the crown of immortal glory, looking unto Jesus, who is the author and finisher of his faith.

This work in which we are engaged is a grand, a holy, a sacred work. We cannot for a moment be off our guard. The crown, the crown, the imperishable crown to be won, is to be kept before the one running the race. So run that ye may obtain. . . . Look not to man. Your responsibility is to God, and He will render to every man according as his work shall be. . . . We behold, and catch the bright beams in the face of Jesus Christ. We receive as much as we can bear. Let us not stop to quarrel over circumstances, but keep Christ in view. Through the transforming power of the Holy Ghost we become assimilated to the image of the blessed Object we behold.

Do not murmur nor find fault. . . . The image of Christ is engraven upon the soul [that looks upon Jesus] and reflected back in spirit, in words, in true service for our fellow beings. Christ's joy is in our hearts, and our joy is full. This is true religion. Let us make sure to obtain it, and to be kind, to be courteous, to have love in the soul—that kind of love which flows forth and is expressed in good works, which is a light to shine to the world, and which makes our joy full.—Manuscript 26, 1889.

JESUS WILLED US PEACE

Peace I leave with you, my peace I give unto you: not as the world giveth, give I unto you. Let not your heart be troubled, neither let it be afraid. John 14:27.

Before our Lord went to His agony on the cross, He made His will. He had no silver or gold or houses to leave to His disciples. He was a poor man, as far as earthly possessions were concerned. Few in Jerusalem were so poor as He. But He left His disciples a richer gift than any earthly monarch could bestow on his subjects. "Peace I leave with you, my peace I give unto you," He said; "not as the world giveth, give I unto you. Let not your heart be troubled, neither let it be afraid."

He left them the peace which had been His during His life on the earth, which had been with Him amidst poverty, buffeting, and persecution, and which was to be with Him during His agony in Gethsemane and on the cruel cross.

The Saviour's life on this earth, though lived in the midst of conflict, was a life of peace. While angry enemies were constantly pursuing Him, He said, "He that sent me is with me: the Father hath not left me alone; for I do always those things that please him." No storm of satanic wrath could disturb the calm of that perfect communion with God. And He says to us, "My peace I give unto you."

Those who take Christ at His word, and surrender their souls to His keeping, their lives to His ordering, will find peace and quietude. Nothing of the world can make them sad when Jesus makes them glad by His presence. In perfect acquiescence there is perfect rest. The Lord says, "Thou wilt keep him in perfect peace, whose mind is stayed on thee: because he trusteth in thee.". . .

Every man's experience testifies to the truth of the words of Scripture: "The wicked are like the troubled sea, when it cannot rest.". . . Sin has destroyed our peace. . . . The masterful passions of the heart no human power can control. We are as helpless here as were the disciples to quiet the raging storm. But He who spoke peace to the billows of Galilee, has spoken the word of peace for every soul. However fierce the tempest, those who turn to Jesus with the cry, "Lord, save us," will find deliverance. His grace, which reconciles the soul to God, quiets the strife of human passion, and in His love the heart is at rest. "He maketh the storm a calm, so that the waves thereof are still. . . . So he bringeth them unto their desired haven.". . .

The heart that is in harmony with God is a partaker of the peace of heaven, and will diffuse its blessed influence all around. The spirit of peace will rest like dew upon hearts weary and troubled with worldly strife.—*Signs of the Times,* Dec. 27, 1905.

DISCIPLINE PREPARES YOUTH FOR HIGH DESTINY

When wisdom entereth into thine heart, and knowledge is pleasant unto thy soul; discretion shall preserve thee, understanding shall keep thee. Proverbs 2:10, 11.

Now, as in the days of Israel, every youth should be instructed in the duties of practical life. Each should acquire a knowledge of some branch of manual labor by which, if need be, he may obtain a livelihood. This is essential, not only as a safeguard against the vicissitudes of life, but from its bearing upon physical, mental, and moral development. Even if it were certain that one would never need to resort to manual labor for his support, still he should be taught to work. Without physical exercise, no one can have a sound constitution and vigorous health; and the discipline of well-regulated labor is no less essential to the securing of a strong and active mind and a noble character. . . .

Let the youth be led to understand the object of their creation, to honor God and bless their fellow men; let them see the tender love which the Father in heaven has manifested toward them, and the high destiny for which the discipline of this life is to prepare them, the dignity and honor to which they are called, even to become the sons of God, and thousands would turn with contempt and loathing from the low and selfish aims and the frivolous pleasures that have hitherto engrossed them. They would learn to hate sin and to shun it, not merely from hope of reward or fear of punishment, but from a sense of its inherent baseness, because it would be a degrading of their God-given powers, a stain upon their Godlike manhood. . . .

The elements of character that make a man successful and honored among men—the irrepressible desire for some greater good, the indomitable will, the strenuous exertion, the untiring perseverance—are not to be crushed out. By the grace of God they are to be directed to objects as much higher than mere selfish and temporal interests as the heavens are higher than the earth.

And the education begun in this life will be continued in the life to come. Day by day the wonderful works of God, the evidences of His wisdom and power in creating and sustaining the universe, the infinite mystery of love and wisdom in the plan of redemption, will open to the mind in new beauty. . . . Even in this life we may catch glimpses of His presence and may taste the joy of communion with heaven, but the fullness of its joy and blessing will be reached in the hereafter. Eternity alone can reveal the glorious destiny to which man, restored to God's image, can attain.—*Patriarchs and Prophets,* pp. 601, 602.

TENDER REGARD FOR ELDERLY WORKERS

" 'Rise up in the presence of the aged, show respect for the elderly and revere your God. I am the Lord.' " Lev. 19:32, N.I.V.

The history of John affords a striking illustration of the way in which God can use aged workers. When John was exiled to the Isle of Patmos, there were many who thought him to be past service, an old and broken reed, ready to fall at any time. But the Lord saw fit to use him still. Though banished from the scenes of his former labor, he did not cease to bear witness to the truth. Even in Patmos he made friends and converts. His was a message of joy, proclaiming a risen Saviour who on high was interceding for His people until He should return to take them to Himself. And it was after John had grown old in the service of his Lord that he received more communications from heaven than he had received during all the former years of his life.

The most tender regard should be cherished for those whose life interest has been bound up with the work of God. These aged workers have stood faithful amid storm and trial. They may have infirmities, but they still possess talents that qualify them to stand in their place in God's cause. Though worn, and unable to bear the heavier burdens that younger men can and should carry, the counsel they can give is of the highest value.

They may have made mistakes, but from their failures they have learned to avoid errors and dangers. . . . They have borne test and trial, and though they have lost some of their vigor, the Lord does not lay them aside. He gives them special grace and wisdom.

Those who have served their Master when the work went hard, who endured poverty and remained faithful when there were few to stand for truth, are to be honored and respected. . . . Let the younger men realize that in having such workers among them they are highly favored. Let them give them an honored place in their councils.

As those who have spent their lives in the service of Christ draw near to the close of their earthly ministry, they will be impressed by the Holy Spirit to recount the experiences they have had in connection with the work of God. The record of His wonderful dealings with His people, of His great goodness in delivering them from trial, should be repeated to those newly come to the faith. God desires the old and tried laborers to stand in their place, doing their part to save men and women from being swept downward by the mighty current of evil. He desires them to keep the armor on till He bids them lay it down.—*The Acts of the Apostles,* pp. 572-574.

WHEN INFIRMITIES COME, TRUST IN GOD

The Lord Jehovah is my strength and my song; he also is become my salvation. Therefore with joy shall ye draw water out of the wells of salvation. Isaiah 12:2, 3.

Now when you can no longer be active, and infirmities press upon you, all that God requires of you is to trust Him. Commit the keeping of your soul to Him as unto a faithful Creator. His mercies are sure, His covenant is everlasting. Happy is the man whose hope is in the Lord his God, who keepeth truth forever. Let your mind grasp the promises and hold to them. If you cannot call to mind readily the rich assurance contained in the precious promises, listen to them from the lips of another. What fullness, what love and assurance are found in these words from the lips of God Himself, proclaiming His love, His pity and interest in the children of His care:

"The Lord, The Lord God, merciful and gracious, longsuffering, and abundant in goodness and truth, keeping mercy for thousands, forgiving iniquity and transgression and sin" (Ex. 34:6, 7).

The Lord is full of compassion for His suffering ones. What sins are too great for His pardon? He is merciful, and as such is infinitely more ready and more pleased to pardon than to condemn. He is gracious, not looking for wrong in us; He knoweth our frame; He remembereth that we are but dust. In His boundless compassion and mercy He heals all our backslidings, loving us freely while we are yet sinners, withdrawing not His light, but shining on us for Christ's sake.

Will you . . . always trust in Jesus, who is your righteousness? The love of God is shed abroad in your heart by the Holy Ghost, which is graciously given unto you. You are one with Christ. He will give you grace to be patient, He will give you grace to be trustful, He will give you grace to overcome restlessness, He will warm your heart with His own sweet Spirit, He will revive your soul in its weakness. Only a few days more to be as pilgrims and strangers in this world, seeking for a better country, even an heavenly. Our home is in heaven. Then stay your soul in confidence upon God. Roll all your burdens upon Him.

Oh, how many times has your heart been touched with the beauty of the Saviour's countenance, charmed with the loveliness of His character, and subdued with the thought of His suffering. Now He wants you to lean your whole weight upon Him. . . . "And in that day thou shalt say, O Lord, I will praise thee: though thou wast angry with me, thine anger is turned away, and thou comfortedst me. Behold, God is my salvation; I will trust, and not be afraid" (Isa. 12:1, 2).—*Selected Messages,* book 2, pp. 231, 232.

CULTIVATE THE TALENT OF SPEECH

Let your speech be alway with grace, seasoned with salt, that ye may know how ye ought to answer every man. Col. 4:6.

It is the work of parents to train their children to proper habits of speech. The very best school for this culture is the homelife. From the earliest years the children should be taught to speak respectfully and lovingly to their parents and to one another. They should be taught that only words of gentleness, truth, and purity must pass their lips. Let the parents themselves be daily learners in the school of Christ. Then by precept and example they can teach their children the use of "sound speech, that cannot be condemned" (Titus 2:8). This is one of the greatest and most responsible of their duties.—*Christ's Object Lessons,* pp. 337, 338.

The power of speech is a talent that should be diligently cultivated. Of all the gifts we have received from God, none is capable of being a greater blessing than this. With the voice we convince and persuade, with it we offer prayer and praise to God, and with it we tell others of the Redeemer's love. How important, then, that it be so trained as to be most effective for good. . . .

By diligent effort all may acquire the power to read intelligibly, and to speak in a full, clear, round tone, in a distinct and impressive manner. By doing this we may greatly increase our efficiency as workers for Christ.

Every Christian is called to make known to others the unsearchable riches of Christ. . . .

The right culture and use of the power of speech has to do with every line of Christian work; it enters into the homelife, and into all our intercourse with one another. We should accustom ourselves to speak in pleasant tones, to use pure and correct language, and words that are kind and courteous. Sweet, kind words are as dew and gentle showers to the soul. The Scripture says of Christ that grace was poured into His lips that He might "know how to speak a word in season to him that is weary" (Ps. 45:2; Isa. 50:4). And the Lord bids us, "Let your speech be alway with grace" (Col. 4:6), "that it may minister grace unto the hearers" (Eph. 4:29).

In seeking to correct or reform others we should be careful of our words. . . . All who would advocate the principles of truth need to receive the heavenly oil of love. Under all circumstances reproof should be spoken in love. Then our words will reform but not exasperate. Christ by His Holy Spirit will supply the force and the power. This is His work.—*Ibid.,* pp. 335-337.

SPEAK EVIL OF NO MAN

Woe unto the world because of offences! for it must needs be that offences come; but woe to that man by whom the offence cometh! Matt. 18:7.

Words of reproach react on one's own soul. The training of the tongue should begin with ourselves personally. Let us speak evil of no man.

"Wherefore if thy hand or thy foot offend thee, cut them off, and cast them from thee: it is better for thee to enter into life halt or maimed, rather than having two hands or two feet to be cast into everlasting fire."

There may be cherished by us certain wrong things that are seemingly as dear as a hand or a foot. These things are to be put away from us forever. Never are our peculiar, unsanctified ideas to be pressed upon others. . . .

There is a great work to be done among church members. Many who are not called upon to enter the public ministry may do much good in their home church by speaking advisedly with their lips. The talent of speech should be used to glorify God. Too often it is used to convey evil reports. This grieves away the Holy Spirit. Let us remember that we have a Saviour who has bidden us [to] come unto Him with all our burdens. He will give us peace of mind, and He, too, will adjust that which to us seems so full of entangling difficulties. "Come unto me," He pleads, "all ye that labour and are heavy laden, and I will give you rest." . . .

Those who have indulged in words of complaint and criticism shall . . . pledge that henceforth, by the Lord's help, they will not speak evil of their brethren and sisters, but will take everything to God in prayer, and follow out the instruction He has given regarding the pointing out of wrongs in our fellow men. Every church member may in his daily conduct be so exemplary, so prudent and careful in speech, so kind and compassionate, that he will be esteemed by all as one who fears and loves God. Such a man will have an influence for good over all his associates.

We are fallible, and have erred many times. Let us return to the Lord with repentance and confession. As we assemble to participate in the ordinances of the Lord's house, let us make every wrong right, so far as lies in our power. When bowing before a brother, washing his feet, ask yourself, "Have I aught in my heart that separates me from this brother? Have I said or done anything that estranges us?" If so, take it away by heartily confessing your sin. Thus heart will be cemented to heart, and the blessing of God will be manifest.—Manuscript 102, 1904.

THE JOY OF WELL-CHOSEN WORDS

To make an apt answer is a joy to a man, and a word in season, how good it is! Prov. 15:23, R.S.V.

"A word spoken in due season, how good is it!" (K.J.V.). Souls are perishing for the lack of personal labor. . . .

The bright and cheerful side of religion will be represented by all who are daily consecrated to God. We should not dishonor our Lord by a mournful relation of trials that appear grievous. All trials that are received as educators will produce joy. The whole religious life will be uplifting, elevating, ennobling, fragrant with good words and works. . . . [God] desires every soul to triumph in the keeping power of the Redeemer.

The psalmist says: . . . "Give unto the Lord the glory due unto his name. . . . Worship the Lord in the beauty of holiness." . . . "Sing unto the Lord, . . . and give thanks at the remembrance of his holiness."

In the gracious blessings which our heavenly Father has bestowed upon us, we may discern innumerable evidences of a love that is infinite, and a tender pity surpassing a mother's yearning sympathy for her wayward child. When we study the divine character in the light of the cross, we see mercy, tenderness, and forgiveness blended with equity and justice. In the language of John we exclaim, "Behold, what manner of love the Father hath bestowed upon us, that we should be called the sons of God."

We see in the midst of the throne One bearing in hands, and feet, and side the marks of suffering endured to reconcile man to God, and God to man. Matchless mercy reveals to us a Father, infinite, dwelling in light unapproachable, yet receiving us to Himself through the merits of His Son. The cloud of vengeance which threatened only misery and despair, in the reflected light from the cross reveals the writing of God: "Live, sinner, live! ye penitent and believing souls, live! I have paid a ransom."

We must gather about the cross. Christ and Him crucified must be the theme of contemplation, of conversation, and of our most joyful emotion. We should have special praise services for the purpose of keeping fresh in our thoughts everything that we receive from God, and of expressing our gratitude for His great love, and our willingness to trust everything to the Hand that was nailed to the cross for us. . . . We should learn to talk the language of Canaan, to sing the songs of Zion. By the mystery and glory of the cross we can estimate the value of man, and then we shall see and feel the importance of working for our fellow men, that they may be exalted to the throne of God.—*Southern Watchman,* March 7, 1905.

POUR OUT PRAISE AND THANKSGIVING

I will praise the name of God with a song, and will magnify him with thanksgiving. Ps. 69:30.

The voice is a wonderful organ. It is a wonderful blessing, and let us use it wholly on Christ's side, and not praise the devil by complaining of the hardness of the way to heaven. Suppose we give to the world a living example of the beauty there is in religion and Jesus Christ by the offerings we present to God, talking of His goodness, and telling of His power.

If you feel disposed to murmur, let it die before you give it breath, and let your voice and tongue be educated, and then when you open your eyes in the morning the very first thing will be, ''I thank the Lord; He has kept me through the night. I thank Thee, Jesus Christ, for the peace that is in my heart,'' and morning, noon, and night you have a gratitude offering. It comes up before God as sweet perfume.

And Jesus said He would give us the Comforter. What is the Comforter? It is the Holy Spirit of God. What is the Holy Spirit? It is the representative of Jesus Christ, it is our Advocate that stands by our side and places our petitions before the Father all fragrant with His merits. There He accepts the petition of the humblest saint. He doesn't ask you how much money you have, or how heavy you are loaded with property, but the very humblest saint that brings his petition to God, and [his] thank offering is made fragrant with the riches of His grace, and the Father accepts it as your offering, and the blessing comes to you, grace for grace.

As you pour out your thank offering, God is glorified, and He gives you more. As you pour out thanksgiving He gives you more joy. We learn to praise God from whom all blessings flow. Shall we not begin right here to turn over the page and forget our murmurings and complainings and faultfinding, and educate the tongue to courteous words, and loving words, and sympathetic words, and tender kindness for one another of His children?

Let us show Christ formed within, the hope of glory, by the fruit that we bear, and thus we can evidence to the world a living Saviour. . . . He arose. He broke the fetters of the tomb. In triumph He rejoices over the rent sepulchre of Joseph. ''I am the resurrection and the life.'' Glory to God. I praise Him, the resurrection and the life. You have . . . a living Saviour.

Then hang your helpless souls on Jesus Christ. Abide in the vine, and bear fruit to His glory, and His joy shall be in you, and your joy shall be full. . . . May the Holy Spirit of God impress the heart, and may the character reveal the loveliness of Jesus Christ, because you are His representatives.—Manuscript 43, 1894.

WE ARE TO USE OUR TIME WISELY

Be . . . not slothful in business; fervent in spirit; serving the Lord. Rom. 12:10, 11.

The talent of time is precious. Every day it is given to us in trust, and we shall be called upon to give an account of it to God. It is to be used to God's glory, and if we would prolong our lives, if we would gain the life that measures with the life of God, we must give the mind pure food. No time should be wasted that might have been used to good account.

Jesus Christ is our spiritual touchstone. He reveals the Father. Nothing should be given as food to the brain that will bring before the mind any mist or cloud in regard to the Word of God. No careless inattention should be shown in regard to the cultivation of the soil of the heart.—Manuscript 15, 1898.

Upon the right improvement of our time depends our success in acquiring knowledge and mental culture. The cultivation of the intellect need not be prevented by poverty, humble origin, or unfavorable surroundings. Only let the moments be treasured. A few moments here and a few there, that might be frittered away in aimless talk; the morning hours so often wasted in bed; the time spent in traveling on the trams or railway cars, or waiting at the station; the moments of waiting for meals, waiting for those who are tardy in keeping an appointment—if a book were kept at hand, and these fragments of time were improved in study, reading, or careful thought, what might not be accomplished. A resolute purpose, persistent industry, and careful economy of time will enable men to acquire knowledge and mental discipline which will qualify them for almost any position of influence and usefulness.

It is the duty of every Christian to acquire habits of order, thoroughness, and dispatch. . . . Decide how long a time is required for a given task, and then bend every effort toward accomplishing the work in the given time. The exercise of the willpower will make the hands move deftly.—*Christ's Object Lessons,* pp. 343, 344.

It is wrong to waste our time, wrong to waste our thoughts. We lose every moment that we devote to self-seeking. If every moment were valued and rightly employed, we should have time for everything that we need to do for ourselves or for the world. In the expenditure of money, in the use of time, strength, opportunities, let every Christian look to God for guidance.—*The Ministry of Healing,* p. 208.

God grants men the gift of time for the purpose of promoting His glory.—*Counsels to Parents and Teachers,* p. 354.

WITNESSING BY OUR ACTIONS

Let us not be weary in well doing: for in due season we shall reap, if we faint not. Gal. 6:9.

Again and again I am instructed to charge our people with their individual responsibility to work, and believe, and pray. The reception of Bible truth will lead to continual self-denial; for self-indulgence can never be found in a Christlike experience. Truly converted men and women will reveal the cross of Calvary in their daily actions. There are many Seventh-day Adventists who do not understand that to accept the cause of Christ means to accept His cross. The only evidence they give in their lives of their discipleship is in the name they bear. But the true Christian regards his stewardship as a sacred thing. He perseveringly studies the Word, and yields up his life to the service of Christ.

The word of encouragement is given, "Be not weary in well doing," "always abounding in the work of the Lord." There is a world to be saved, a work to be done that can be accomplished only by the proclamation of the gospel message. "God so loved the world, that he gave his only begotten Son, that whosoever believeth in him should not perish, but have everlasting life." Should we not thank the Lord with heart and soul for His unspeakable gift? Should we not be willing to devote every capability and talent to the work of representing Christ before the world? . . .

"Good works" will begin to appear when the experience of repentance and conversion is brought into the life. . . . It is . . . by showing that we are changed in character, through a belief of the truth, that we make known to others the transforming power of the grace of God.—*Review and Herald,* Feb. 25, 1909.

"Let him that is taught in the word communicate unto him that teacheth in all good things. Be not deceived; God is not mocked: for whatsoever a man soweth, that shall he also reap" (Gal. 6:6-7). Wonderful truth! This is a two-edged sword which cuts both ways. This life and death question is before the whole human race. The choice we make in this life will be our choice through all eternity. We shall receive either eternal life or eternal death. There is no middle ground, no second probation.

We are called upon to overcome in this life as Christ overcame. Heaven has provided us with abundant opportunities and privileges, so that we may overcome as Christ overcame, and sit down with Him on His throne. But in order to be overcomers, there must be in our lives no petting of fleshly inclinations. All selfishness must be cut out by the roots. . . .

The more the heart is wrapped up in Christ, the more secure is the treasure in the eternal world.—*The SDA Bible Commentary,* vol. 6, p. 1112.

TRUE CHARACTER RADIATES FROM WITHIN

Ye are the light of the world. Matt. 5:14.

"Ye are the light of the world." The Jews thought to confine the benefits of salvation to their own nation; but Christ showed them that salvation is like the sunshine. It belongs to the whole world. The religion of the Bible is not to be confined between the covers of a book, nor within the walls of a church. It is not to be brought out occasionally for our own benefit, and then to be carefully laid aside again. It is to sanctify the daily life, to manifest itself in every business transaction and in all our social relations.

True character is not shaped from without, and put on; it radiates from within. If we wish to direct others in the path of righteousness, the principles of righteousness must be enshrined in our own hearts. Our profession of faith may proclaim the theory of religion, but it is our practical piety that holds forth the word of truth. The consistent life, the holy conversation, the unswerving integrity, the active, benevolent spirit, the godly example—these are the mediums through which light is conveyed to the world.—*The Desire of Ages,* pp. 306, 307.

As the sun goes forth on its errand of love, dispelling the shades of night and awakening the world to life, so the followers of Christ are to go forth on their mission, diffusing the light of heaven upon those who are in the darkness of error and sin.

In the brilliant light of the morning, the towns and villages upon the surrounding hills stood forth clearly, making an attractive feature of the scene. Pointing to them, Jesus said, "A city set on a hill cannot be hid." And He added, "Neither do men light a lamp, and put it under the bushel, but on the stand; and it shineth unto all that are in the house" (Matt. 5:14, 15, R.V.).

Most of those who listened to the words of Jesus were peasants and fishermen whose lowly dwellings contained but one room, in which the single lamp on its stand shone to all in the house. Even so, said Jesus, "Let your light so shine before men, that they may see your good works, and glorify your Father which is in heaven" (verse 16).

No other light ever has shone or ever will shine upon fallen man save that which emanates from Christ. Jesus, the Saviour, is the only light that can illuminate the darkness of a world lying in sin. Of Christ it is written, "In him was life; and the life was the light of men" (John 1:4). It was by receiving of His life that His disciples could become light bearers. The life of Christ in the soul, His love revealed in the character, would make them the light of the world.—*Thoughts From the Mount of Blessing,* pp. 39, 40.

THE WORLD NEEDS PEOPLE OF NOBLE CHARACTER

And whatsoever ye do, do it heartily, as to the Lord, and not unto men; knowing that of the Lord ye shall receive the reward of the inheritance; for ye serve the Lord Christ. Col. 3:23, 24.

True education does not ignore the value of scientific knowledge or literary acquirements; but above information it values power; above power, goodness; above intellectual acquirements, character. The world does not so much need men of great intellect as of a noble character. It needs men in whom ability is controlled by steadfast principle.

"Wisdom is the principal thing; therefore get wisdom" (Prov. 4:7). "The tongue of the wise useth knowledge aright" (chap. 15:2). True education imparts this wisdom. It teaches the best use not only of one but of all our powers and acquirements. Thus it covers the whole circle of obligation—to ourselves, to the world, and to God.

Character building is the most important work ever entrusted to human beings; and never before was its diligent study so important as now. Never was any previous generation called to meet issues so momentous; never before were young men and young women confronted by perils so great as confront them today. . . .

In true education the selfish ambition, the greed for power, the disregard for the rights and needs of humanity, that are the curse of our world, find a counterinfluence. God's plan of life has a place for every human being. Each is to improve his talents to the utmost; and faithfulness in doing this, be the gifts few or many, entitles one to honor. In God's plan there is no place for selfish rivalry. Those who measure themselves by themselves, and compare themselves among themselves, are not wise (2 Cor. 10:12). Whatever we do is to be done "as of the ability which God giveth" (1 Peter 4:11). . . .

In every generation and in every land the true foundation and pattern for character building have been the same. The divine law, "Thou shalt love the Lord thy God with all thy heart . . . ; and thy neighbour as thyself" (Luke 10:27), the great principle made manifest in the character and life of our Saviour, is the only secure foundation and the only sure guide. . . .

It is as true now as when the words were spoken to Israel of obedience to His commandments: "This is your wisdom and your understanding in the sight of the nations" (Deut. 4:6).

Here is the only safeguard for individual integrity, for the purity of the home, the well-being of society, or the stability of the nation. Amidst all life's perplexities and dangers and conflicting claims the one safe and sure rule is to do what God says.—*Education*, pp. 225-229.

WE ARE TO REFLECT CHRIST'S LOVE

Then said Jesus to them again, Peace be unto you: as my Father hath sent me, even so send I you. John 20:21.

We should earnestly seek to know and appreciate the truth, that we may present it to others as it is in Jesus. We need to have a correct estimate of the value of our own souls; then we would not be as reckless in regard to our course of action as at present. We would seek most earnestly to know God's way; we would work an opposite direction from selfishness, and our constant prayer would be that we might have the mind of Christ, that we might be molded and fashioned after His likeness. It is in looking to Jesus and beholding His loveliness, having our eyes steadfastly fixed upon Him, that we become changed into His image. He will give grace to all that keep His way, and do His will, and walk in truth. . . .

I beseech you whose names are registered on the church book as worthy members, to be indeed worthy, through the virtue of Christ. Mercy and truth and the love of God are promised to the humble and contrite soul. . . .

All heaven is filled with amazement, that when this love, so broad, so deep, so rich and full, is presented to men who have known the grace of our Lord Jesus Christ, they are so indifferent, so cold and unmoved. . . .

The infinite treasures of truth have been accumulating from age to age. No representation could adequately impress us with the extent, the richness, of these vast resources. They are awaiting the demand of those who appreciate them. These gems of truth are to be gathered up by God's remnant people, to be given by them to the world; but self-confidence and obduracy of soul refuse the blessed treasure. ''God so loved the world, that he gave his only begotten Son, that whosoever believeth in him should not perish, but have everlasting life.'' Such love cannot be measured, neither can it be expressed. John calls upon the world to behold ''what manner of love the Father hath bestowed upon us, that we should be called the sons of God.'' It is a love that passeth knowledge.

In the fullness of the sacrifice, nothing was withheld. Jesus gave Himself. God designs that His people shall love one another as Christ loved us. They are to educate and train the soul for this love. They are to reflect this love in their own character, to reflect it to the world. Each should look upon this as his work. . . . Christ's fullness is to be presented to the world by those who have become partakers of His grace. They are to do that for Christ which Christ did for the Father—represent His character.—*Review and Herald,* Dec. 23, 1890.

GOD ALONE CAN RENEW THE HEART

For it is God which worketh in you both to will and to do of his good pleasure. Phil. 2:13.

Far more than we do, we need to understand the issues at stake in the conflict in which we are engaged. We need to understand more fully the value of the truths that God has given for this time and the danger of allowing our minds to be diverted from them by the great deceiver.

The infinite value of the sacrifice required for our redemption reveals the fact that sin is a tremendous evil. Through sin the whole human organism is deranged, the mind is perverted, the imagination corrupted. Sin has degraded the faculties of the soul. Temptations from without find an answering chord within the heart, and the feet turn imperceptibly toward evil.

As the sacrifice in our behalf was complete, so our restoration from the defilement of sin is to be complete. There is no act of wickedness that the law will excuse; there is no unrighteousness that will escape its condemnation. The life of Christ was a perfect fulfillment of every precept of the law. He said, "I have kept my Father's commandments" (John 15:10). His life is our standard of obedience and service.

God alone can renew the heart. "It is God who worketh in you both to will and to work, for His good pleasure" (Phil. 2:13, A.R.V.). But we are bidden: "Work out your own salvation" (verse 12, A.R.V.).

Wrongs cannot be righted, nor can reformations in character be made, by a few feeble, intermittent efforts. . . . The struggle for conquest over self, for holiness and heaven, is a lifelong struggle. Without continual effort and constant activity there can be no advancement in the divine life, no attainment of the victor's crown.

The strongest evidence of man's fall from a higher state is the fact that it costs so much to return. The way of return can be gained only by hard fighting, inch by inch, every hour. By a momentary act of the will, one may place himself in the power of evil; but it requires more than a momentary act of will to break these fetters and attain to a higher, holier life. The purpose may be formed, the work begun; but its accomplishment will require toil, time, and perseverance, patience and sacrifice.

Beset with temptations without number, we must resist firmly or be conquered. . . . Paul's sanctification was the result of a constant conflict with self. He said: "I die daily" (1 Cor. 15:31). His will and his desires every day conflicted with duty and the will of God. Instead of following inclination, he did God's will, however crucifying to his own nature. God leads His people on step by step.—*Testimonies,* vol. 8, pp. 312, 313.

THE HIGHEST EVIDENCE OF NOBILITY

He that is slow to anger is better than the mighty; and he that ruleth his spirit than he that taketh a city. Prov. 16:32.

He [who is slow to anger] has conquered self—the strongest foe man has to meet.

The highest evidence of nobility in a Christian is self-control. He who can stand unmoved amid a storm of abuse is one of God's heroes.

To rule the spirit is to keep self under discipline; to resist evil; to regulate every word and deed by God's great standard of righteousness. He who has learned to rule his spirit will rise above the slights, the rebuffs, the annoyances, to which we are daily exposed, and these will cease to cast a gloom over his spirit.

It is God's purpose that the kingly power of sanctified reason, controlled by divine grace, shall bear sway in the lives of human beings. He who rules his spirit is in possession of this power.

In childhood and youth the character is most impressible. The power of self-control should then be acquired. By the fireside and at the family board influences are exerted the results of which are as enduring as eternity. More than any natural endowment, the habits established in early years will decide whether a man shall be victorious or vanquished in the battle of life.

In the use of language, there is, perhaps, no error that old and young are more ready to pass over lightly in themselves than hasty, impatient speech. They think it is a sufficient excuse to plead, ''I was off my guard, and did not really mean what I said.'' But God's Word does not treat it lightly. . . .

The largest share of life's annoyances, its heartaches, its irritations, is due to uncontrolled temper. In one moment, by hasty, passionate, careless words, may be wrought evil that a whole lifetime's repentance cannot undo. Oh, the hearts that are broken, the friends estranged, the lives wrecked, by the harsh, hasty words of those who might have brought help and healing!

Overwork sometimes causes a loss of self-control. But the Lord never compels hurried, complicated movements. Many gather to themselves burdens that the merciful heavenly Father did not place on them. Duties He never designed them to perform chase one another wildly. God desires us to realize that we do not glorify His name when we take so many burdens that we are overtaxed and, becoming heart-weary and brain-weary, chafe and fret and scold. We are to bear only the responsibilities that the Lord gives us, trusting in Him, and thus keeping our hearts pure and sweet and sympathetic.—*Review and Herald,* Oct. 31, 1907.

SELF-CONTROL THROUGH CHRIST

Good sense makes a man slow to anger, and it is his glory to overlook an offense. Prov. 19:11, R.S.V.

There is a wonderful power in silence. When impatient words are spoken to you, do not retaliate. Words spoken in reply to one who is angry usually act as a whip, lashing the temper into greater fury. But anger met by silence quickly dies away. Let the Christian bridle his tongue, firmly resolving not to speak harsh, impatient words. With the tongue bridled, he may be victorious in every trial of patience through which he is called to pass.

In his own strength man cannot rule his spirit. But through Christ he may gain self-control. In his strength he may bring his thoughts and words into subjection to the will of God. The religion of Christ brings the emotions under the control of reason and disciplines the tongue. Under its influence the hasty temper is subdued, and the heart is filled with patience and gentleness.

Hold firmly to the One who has all power in heaven and in earth. Though you so often fail to reveal patience and calmness, do not give up the struggle. Resolve again, this time more firmly, to be patient under every provocation. And never take your eyes off your divine Example.

God's ideal for His children is higher than the highest human thought can reach. ''Be ye therefore perfect, even as your Father which is in heaven is perfect.'' This command is a promise. The plan of redemption contemplates our complete recovery from the power of Satan. Christ always separates the contrite soul from sin. He came to destroy the works of the devil. And He has made provision that the Holy Spirit shall be imparted to every repentant soul to keep him from sinning.

The tempter's agency is not to be accounted an excuse for one wrong act. Satan is jubilant when he hears the professed followers of Christ making excuses for their deformity of character. It is these excuses that lead to sin. A holy temper, a Christlike life, is attainable by every repenting, believing child of God.—*Review and Herald,* Oct. 31, 1907.

Christ gave Himself for the saving of the sinner. Those whose sins are forgiven, who love Jesus, will be united with Him. They will bear the yoke of Christ. This yoke is not to hamper them, not to make their religious life one of unsatisfying toil. No; the yoke of Christ is to be the very means by which the Christian life is to become one of pleasure and joy. The Christian is to be joyful in contemplation of that which the Lord has done in giving His only-begotten Son to die for the world, ''that whosoever believeth in him should not perish, but have everlasting life.''—*Messages to Young People,* p. 138.

KEEP YOUR WILL ON THE LORD'S SIDE

The world passeth away, and the lust thereof: but he that doeth the will of God abideth for ever. 1 John 2:17.

Pure religion has to do with the will. The will is the governing power in the nature of man, bringing all the other faculties under its sway. The will is not the taste or the inclination, but it is the deciding power, which works in the children of men unto obedience to God, or unto disobedience. . . .

You cannot control your impulses, your emotions, as you may desire, but you can control the will, and you can make an entire change in your life. By yielding up your will to Christ, [you] will be hid with Christ in God, and allied to the power which is above all principalities and powers. You will have strength from God that will hold you fast to His strength; and a new light, even the light of living faith, will be possible to you. But your will must cooperate with God's will, not with the will of associates through whom Satan is constantly working to ensnare and destroy you. . . .

By steadfastly keeping the will on the Lord's side, [you will bring] every emotion . . . into captivity to the will of Jesus. You will then find your feet on solid rock. It will take, at times, every particle of willpower that you possess, but it is God that is working for you, and you will come forth from the molding process a vessel unto honor.

Talk faith. Keep on God's side of the line. Set not your foot on the enemy's side, and the Lord will be your helper. He will do for you that which it is not possible for you to do for yourself. The result will be that you will become like a "cedar of Lebanon." Your life will be noble, and your works will be wrought in God. There will be in you a power, an earnestness, and a simplicity that will make you a polished instrument in the hands of God.

You need to drink daily at the fountain of truth, that you may understand the secret of pleasure and joy in the Lord. But you must remember that your will is the spring of all your actions. This will, that forms so important a factor in the character of man, was at the Fall given into the control of Satan. . . .

But the infinite sacrifice of God in giving Jesus, His beloved Son, to become a sacrifice for sin, enables Him to say, without violating one principle of His government, "Yield yourself up to Me; give Me that will; take it from the control of Satan, and I will take possession of it; then I can work in you to will and to do of My good pleasure." When He gives you the mind of Christ, your will becomes as His will, and your character is transformed to be like Christ's character.—*Messages to Young People,* pp. 151-154.

DAILY PRAYER, ESSENTIAL TO GROWTH IN GRACE

The end of all things is at hand: be ye therefore sober, and watch unto prayer. 1 Peter 4:7.

If we would develop a character which God can accept, we must form correct habits in our religious life. Daily prayer is as essential to growth in grace, and even to spiritual life itself, as is temporal food to physical well-being. We should accustom ourselves to often lift the thoughts to God in prayer. If the mind wanders, we must bring it back; by persevering effort, habit will finally make it easy. We cannot for one moment separate ourselves from Christ with safety. We may have His presence to attend us at every step, but only by observing the conditions which He has Himself laid down.

Religion must be made the great business of life. Everything else should be held subordinate to this. All our powers of soul, body, and spirit must be engaged in Christian warfare. We must look to Christ for strength and grace, and we shall gain the victory as surely as Jesus died for us.

We must come nearer to the cross of Christ. Penitence at the foot of the cross is the first lesson of peace we have to learn. The love of Jesus—who can comprehend it? Infinitely more tender and self-denying than a mother's love! If we would know the value of a human soul, we must look in living faith upon the cross, and thus begin the study which shall be the science and the song of the redeemed through all eternity. The value of our time and our talents can be estimated only by the greatness of the ransom paid for our redemption. What ingratitude we manifest toward God when we rob Him of His own by withholding from Him our affections and our service! Is it too much to give ourselves to Him who has sacrificed all for us? Can we choose the friendship of the world before the immortal honors which Christ proffers—"to sit with me in my throne, even as I also overcame, and am set down with my Father in his throne"?
. . .

Those who are . . . working upon the plan of addition in obtaining the Christian graces, have the assurance that God will work upon the plan of multiplication in granting them the gifts of His Spirit.

Peter addresses those who have obtained like precious faith: "Grace and peace be multiplied unto you through the knowledge of God, and of Jesus our Lord." By divine grace, all who will may climb the shining steps from earth to heaven, and at last, "with songs and everlasting joy," enter through the gates into the city.—*Review and Herald*, Nov. 15, 1887.

DIVINE POWER AND HUMAN EFFORT

For the grace of God that bringeth salvation hath appeared to all men, Teaching us that, denying ungodliness and worldly lusts, we should live soberly, righteously, and godly, in this present world. Titus 2:11, 12.

While Christ is cleansing the sanctuary, the worshipers on earth should carefully review their life, and compare their character with the standard of righteousness. As they see their defects, they should seek the aid of the Spirit of God to enable them to have moral strength to resist the temptations of Satan, and to reach the perfection of the standard. They may be victors over the very temptations which seemed too strong for humanity to bear; for the divine power will be combined with their human effort, and Satan cannot overcome them.

All heaven has been looking on with interest, and ready to do whatever God might appoint, to help fallen men and women to become what God would have them. God will work for His children, but not without their cooperation. They must have indomitable energy, and a constant desire to become all that it is possible for them to be.

They should seek to cultivate their powers and develop characters that will be meet for a holy heaven. Then and then only will the servants of God be bright and shining lights in the world. Then they will bring energy into their Christian life, for they will put all their powers to the task, and respond to the efforts that have been made to uplift, refine, and purify them, that they may shine in the courts above. They will bring all their powers under the control of the Spirit of God; they will study His Word, and listen for His voice, to direct, encourage, strengthen, and advance them in their religious experience.

They will not be childish and be turned aside by the temptations of Satan. They will deny themselves, not appealing to their own sympathies, for they will be of a heroic spirit. They will hoard up the great and precious truths of God's Word; they will feed upon them, and grow into strong, well-developed men and women in Christ, sons and daughters of God.

The greatness of the truth which they contemplate will expand the mind and elevate the character. They will not be novices in the understanding of God's Word, nor dwarfs in religious experience. Conflict with the enemies of truth will not shatter them nor weaken their energies; it will only serve to drive them nearer to Him who is mighty to save. They will receive the discipline that will give efficiency to all their faculties. Heaven will be brought near to them in sympathy and cooperation, and they will be indeed a spectacle to the world, to angels and to men; for they will be marked characters on account of their purity, their strength of purpose, their firmness, their usefulness in the world.—*Review and Herald,* April 8, 1890.

CHRIST PUTS ON US HIS PERFECTION OF CHARACTER

Yield yourselves unto God, . . . and your members as instruments of righteousness unto God. Rom. 6:13.

Those who are called of God to labor in word and doctrine should ever be learners in the school of Christ. . . . Those who do not feel the importance of going on from strength to strength will not grow in grace and in the knowledge of our Lord and Saviour Jesus Christ.

All heaven is interested in the work that is going on in the earth today. The angels look with interest upon those who are honored in having a part to act as colaborers with God. When the servants of Christ have a realizing sense of the presence of One who is mighty to save, they will be filled with gratitude to God for the power of His grace. . . . Those who dedicate their all to Christ will learn how to win souls; for they will have a close connection with the Redeemer of the world. . . .

Jesus is the light of the world, and you are to fashion your life after His. You will find help in Christ to form a strong, symmetrical, beautiful character. Satan cannot make of none effect the light shining forth from such character. The Lord has a work for each of us to do. He does not provide that we shall be sustained by the influence of human praise and petting; He means that every soul shall stand in the strength of the Lord. God has given us His best gift, even His only-begotten Son, to uplift, ennoble, and fit us, by putting on us His own perfection of character, for a home in His kingdom. Jesus came to our world and lived as He expects His followers to live. If we are self-indulgent, and too lazy to put forth earnest effort to cooperate with the wonderful work of God, we shall meet with loss in this life, and loss in the future, immortal life.

God designs that we shall work, not in a despairing manner, but with strong faith and hope. As we search the Scriptures, and are enlightened to behold the wonderful condescension of the Father in giving Jesus to the world, that all who believe on Him should not perish but have everlasting life, we should rejoice with joy unspeakable and full of glory.

Everything that can be gained by education, God means we shall use for the advancement of the truth. True, vital godliness must be reflected from the life and character, that the cross of Christ may be lifted up before the world, and the value of the soul be revealed in the light of the cross. Our minds must be opened to understand the Scriptures, that we may gain spiritual power by feeding upon the bread of heaven.—*Review and Herald,* April 8, 1890.

CHARACTER IS POWER

We have peace with God through our Lord Jesus Christ: by whom also we have access by faith into this grace wherein we stand, and rejoice in hope of the glory of God. Rom. 5:1, 2.

Christ has given us no assurance that to attain perfection of character is an easy matter. A noble, all-round character is not inherited. It does not come to us by accident. A noble character is earned by individual effort through the merits and grace of Christ. God gives the talents, the powers of the mind; we form the character. It is formed by hard, stern battles with self. Conflict after conflict must be waged against hereditary tendencies. We shall have to criticize ourselves closely, and allow not one unfavorable trait to remain uncorrected. . . .

A character formed according to the divine likeness is the only treasure that we can take from this world to the next. Those who are under the instruction of Christ in this world will take every divine attainment with them to the heavenly mansions. . . .

The heavenly intelligences will work with the human agent who seeks with determined faith that perfection of character which will reach out to perfection in action. To everyone engaged in this work Christ says, I am at your right hand to help you.

As the will of man cooperates with the will of God, it becomes omnipotent. Whatever is to be done at His command may be accomplished in His strength. All His biddings are enablings.—*Christ's Object Lessons,* pp. 331-333.

Character is power. The silent witness of a true, unselfish, godly life carries an almost irresistible influence. By revealing in our own life the character of Christ we cooperate with Him in the work of saving souls. It is only by revealing in our life His character that we can cooperate with Him. And the wider the sphere of our influence, the more good we may do. When those who profess to serve God follow Christ's example, practicing the principles of the law in their daily life; when every act bears witness that they love God supremely and their neighbor as themselves, then will the church have power to move the world. . . .

We know not what results a day, an hour, or a moment may determine, and never should we begin the day without committing our ways to our heavenly Father. . . . When unconsciously we are in danger of exerting a wrong influence, the angels will be by our side, prompting us to a better course, choosing our words for us, and influencing our actions. Thus our influence may be a silent, unconscious, but mighty power in drawing others to Christ and the heavenly world.—*Ibid.,* pp. 340-342.

SET YOUR MARK HIGH

I press toward the mark for the prize of the high calling of God in Christ Jesus. Phil. 3:14.

Let no one say, I cannot remedy my defects of character. If you come to this decision, you will certainly fail of obtaining everlasting life. The impossibility lies in your own will. If you will not, then you cannot overcome. The real difficulty arises from the corruption of an unsanctified heart, and an unwillingness to submit to the control of God.

Many whom God has qualified to do excellent work accomplish very little, because they attempt little. Thousands pass through life as if they had no definite object for which to live, no standard to reach. Such will obtain a reward proportionate to their works.

Remember that you will never reach a higher standard than you yourself set. Then set your mark high, and step by step, even though it be by painful effort, by self-denial and sacrifice, ascend the whole length of the ladder of progress. Let nothing hinder you. Fate has not woven its meshes about any human being so firmly that he need remain helpless and in uncertainty. Opposing circumstances should create a firm determination to overcome them. The breaking down of one barrier will give greater ability and courage to go forward. Press with determination in the right direction, and circumstances will be your helpers, not your hindrances.

Be ambitious, for the Master's glory, to cultivate every grace of character. In every phase of your character building you are to please God. This you may do; for Enoch pleased Him though living in a degenerate age. And there are Enochs in this our day.

Stand like Daniel, that faithful statesman, a man whom no temptation could corrupt. Do not disappoint Him who so loved you that He gave His own life to cancel your sins. He says, "Without Me ye can do nothing" (John 15:5). Remember this. If you have made mistakes, you certainly gain a victory if you see these mistakes and regard them as beacons of warning. Thus you turn defeat into victory, disappointing the enemy and honoring your Redeemer.—*Christ's Object Lessons,* pp. 331, 332.

Your time, your influence, your capabilities, your skill—all must be accounted for to Him who gives all. . . . Persevere in the work that you have begun, until you gain victory after victory. Educate yourselves for a purpose. Keep in view the highest standard, that you may accomplish greater and still greater good, thus reflecting the glory of God.—*The Youth's Instructor,* Jan. 25, 1910.

WE SHALL REAP WHAT WE HAVE SOWN

The servant of the Lord must not strive; but be gentle unto all men, apt to teach, patient. 2 Tim. 2:24.

Those who are truly connected with God will not be at variance with one another. The spirit of harmony, peace, and love, His Spirit ruling in their hearts, will create harmony, love, and unity. The opposite of this works in the children of Satan; there is with them a continual contradiction. Strife and envy and jealousy are the ruling elements. The characteristic of the Christian is the meekness of Christ. Benevolence, kindness, mercy, and love originate from Infinite Wisdom, while the opposite is the unholy fruit of a heart that is not in harmony with Jesus Christ. . . .

What a work is this—the education of children! . . . If the parents had studied more of Christ and less of the world, if they had cared less to imitate the customs and fashions of the present age, and devoted time and painstaking effort to mold the minds and characters of their children after the divine Model, then they could send them forth with moral integrity to be carried forward in the branches of education to qualify them for any position of trust. . . .

The harvest is ours, to reap that which we have sown. If you sow distrust, envy, jealousy, self-love, bitterness of thought and feelings, this harvest you will be sure to reap. This will be a sowing of dragon's teeth to reap the same.

If you manifest kindness, love, tender thoughtfulness to your students, you will reap the same in return. If teachers are severe, critical, overbearing, not sensitive of others' feelings, they will receive the same in return. A man who wishes to preserve his self- respect and dignity must be careful not to sacrifice the respect and dignity of others. This rule should be sacredly observed toward the dullest, the youngest, and most blundering scholars.

What God will do with these apparently uninteresting youth, you do not know. God has accepted and chosen, in the past, just such specimens to do a great work for Him. His Spirit, operating upon the heart, has acted like an electric battery, arousing the apparently benumbed faculties to vigorous and persevering action. The Lord saw in these rough, uninteresting, unhewn stones precious metal that will endure the test of storm and tempest and the fiery ordeal of heat. God seeth not as man seeth; God judgeth not as man judgeth—He searcheth the heart. . . .

The younger members of the Lord's family shall be impressed that they are created in the image of their Maker, and that their spirit must represent the spirit of Christ.—Manuscript 2, 1881.

THE LORD KNOWS ALL THE THOUGHTS

And thou, Solomon my son, know thou the God of thy father, and serve him with a perfect heart and with a willing mind: for the Lord searcheth all hearts and understandeth all the imaginations of the thoughts: if thou seek him, he will be found of thee. 1 Chron. 28:9.

You should keep off from Satan's enchanted ground and not allow your minds to be swayed from allegiance to God. Through Christ you may and should be happy and should acquire habits of self-control. Even your thoughts must be brought into subjection to the will of God and your feelings under the control of reason and religion. Your imagination was not given you to be allowed to run riot and have its own way without any effort at restraint or discipline. If the thoughts are wrong the feelings will be wrong; and the thoughts and feelings combined make up the moral character.

When you decide that as Christians you are not required to restrain your thoughts and feelings, you are brought under the influence of evil angels and invite their presence and their control. If you yield to your impressions and allow your thoughts to run in a channel of suspicion, doubt, and repining you will be among the most unhappy of mortals. . . .

Man has been placed in a world of sorrow, care, and perplexity. He is placed here to be tested and proved, as were Adam and Eve, that he may develop a right character and bring harmony out of discord and confusion. There is much for us to do that is essential to our own happiness and that of others. And there is much for us to enjoy. Through Christ we are brought into connection with God. His mercies place us under continual obligation; feeling unworthy of His favors, we are to appreciate even the least of them.

For all that you have and are, . . . you are indebted to God. He has given you powers that, to a certain extent, are similar to those which He Himself possesses; and you should labor earnestly to develop these powers, not to please and exalt self, but to glorify Him. . . .

This earth is the Lord's. Here it may be seen that nature, animate and inanimate, obeys His will. God created man a superior being; he alone is formed in the image of God and is capable of partaking of the divine nature, of cooperating with his Creator and executing His plans. . . . How wonderfully, with what marvelous beauty, has everything in nature been fashioned. Everywhere we see the perfect works of the great Master Artist. The heavens declare His glory; and the earth, which is formed for the happiness of man, speaks to us of His matchless love. . . . I call your attention to these blessings from the bounteous hand of God. Let the fresh glories of each new morning awaken praise in your hearts for these tokens of His loving care.—*Testimonies,* vol. 5, pp. 310-312.

A DAILY REVEALING OF CHRIST'S PRESENCE

The path of the just is as the shining light, that shineth more and more unto the perfect day. Prov. 4:18.

We must turn away from a thousand topics that invite attention. There are matters that consume time and arouse inquiry, but end in nothing. The highest interests demand the close attention and energy that are too often given to comparatively insignificant things.

Accepting new theories does not bring new life to the soul. Even an acquaintance with facts and theories important in themselves is of little value unless put to a practical use. We need to feel our responsibility to give our souls food that will nourish and stimulate spiritual life. . . .

We are not doing the will of God when we speculate upon things that He has seen fit to withhold from us. The question for us to study is: "What is truth, the truth for this time, which is to be cherished, loved, honored, and obeyed?" The devotees of science have been defeated and disheartened in their efforts to find out God. What they need to inquire at this time is: "What is the truth that will enable us to win the salvation of our souls?"

Christ revealed God to His disciples in a way that performed in their hearts a special work, such as He has long been urging us to allow Him to do in our hearts. There are many who, in dwelling too largely upon theory, have lost sight of the living power of the Saviour's example. They have lost sight of Him as the humble, self-denying worker. What they need is to behold Jesus. Daily we need the fresh revealing of His presence. We need to follow more closely His example of self-renunciation and sacrifice.

We need the experience that Paul had when he wrote: "I am crucified with Christ: nevertheless I live; yet not I, but Christ liveth in me" (Gal. 2:20).

The knowledge of God and of Jesus Christ expressed in character is an exaltation above everything else that is esteemed on earth or in heaven. It is the very highest education. It is the key that opens the portals of the heavenly city. This knowledge it is God's purpose that all who put on Christ shall possess. . . .

Treasure every ray of light. Cherish every desire of the soul after God. Give yourselves the culture of spiritual thoughts and holy communings. . . . Having repented of our sins, confessed them, and found pardon, we are to continue to learn of Christ until we come into the full noontide of a perfect gospel faith.—*Testimonies,* vol. 8, pp. 316-318.

JESUS DESIRES THAT WE BECOME ONE WITH HIM

Let this mind be in you, which was also in Christ Jesus. Phil. 2:5.

Jesus desires to efface the image of the earthly from the minds of His followers, and to impress upon them the image of the heavenly, that they may become one with Himself, reflecting His character, and showing forth the praises of Him who hath called them out of darkness into His marvelous light. If you have been permitted to stand in the presence of the Sun of Righteousness, it is not that you may absorb and conceal the bright beams of Christ's righteousness, but that you may become a light to others. . . . There are persons who have received the precious light of the righteousness of Christ, but they do not act upon it. . . . They prefer the sophistry of the enemy rather than the plain, "Thus saith the Lord." . . .

The character we cultivate, the attitude we assume today, is fixing our future destiny. We are all making a choice, either to be with the blessed, inside the City of Light, or to be with the wicked, outside the city. The principles which govern our actions on earth are known in heaven, and our deeds are faithfully chronicled in the books of record. It is there known whether our characters are after the order of Christ. . . . Are we wise virgins? . . . This is the question which we are deciding today by our character and attitude. . . .

To be pardoned in the way that Christ pardons is not only to be forgiven, but to be renewed in the spirit of our mind. The Lord says, "A new heart will I give unto thee." The image of Christ is to be stamped upon the very mind, and heart, and soul. The apostle says, "And we have the mind of Christ." Without the transforming process which can come alone through divine power, the original propensities to sin are left in the heart in all their strength, to forge new chains, to impose a slavery that can never be broken by human power. . . .

When Christ comes, the balances of heaven will weigh the character, and decide whether it is pure, sanctified, and holy. . . .

Happiness is the result of holiness, and conformity to the will of God. Those who would be saints in heaven, must first be saints upon the earth; for when we leave this earth, we shall take our character with us, and this will be simply taking with us some of the elements of heaven imparted to us through the righteousness of Christ. . . .

The experience that follows complete surrender to God, is righteousness, peace, and joy in the Holy Ghost.—*Review and Herald,* Aug. 19, 1890.

TREASURES OF DIVINE GRACE AT OUR DISPOSAL

Every man that hath this hope in him purifieth himself, even as he is pure. 1 John 3:3.

It is the privilege of every earnest seeker for truth and righteousness, to rely upon the sure promises of God. The Lord Jesus makes manifest the fact that the treasures of divine grace are placed entirely at our disposal, in order that we may become channels of light. We cannot receive the riches of the grace of Christ without desiring to impart them to others. When we have the love of Christ in our hearts, we shall feel that it is our duty and privilege to communicate it.

The sun shining in the heavens, pours its bright beams into all the highways and byways of life. It has sufficient light for thousands of worlds like ours. And so it is with the Sun of Righteousness; His bright beams of healing and gladness are amply sufficient to save our little world, and are efficacious in establishing security in every world that has been created. Christ declares that our heavenly Father is more willing to give the Holy Spirit to them that ask Him, than earthly parents are to give gifts to their children.

The day of Pentecost furnished a wonderful occasion. In the outpouring of the Holy Spirit, what a testimony was given to the abundance of the grace of Christ! Why is it that those who claim to believe advanced truth live so far beneath their privileges? Why do they mingle self with all they do? If they will cast out self, Jesus will pour into the thirsty soul a constant supply from the river of life. . . .

It is growth in knowledge of the character of Christ that sanctifies the soul. To discern and appreciate the wonderful work of the atonement, transforms him who contemplates the plan of salvation. By beholding Christ, he becomes changed into the same image, from glory to glory, as by the Spirit of the Lord. The beholding of Jesus becomes an ennobling, refining process to the actual Christian. He sees the Pattern, and grows into its likeness, and then how easily are dissensions, emulations, and strife adjusted. The perfection of Christ's character is the Christian's inspiration. When we see Him as He is, desire awakes to be like Him, and this elevates the whole man; for "every man that hath this hope in him purifieth himself, even as He is pure." . . .

The power of Christ is to be the comfort, the hope, the crown of rejoicing, of everyone that follows Jesus in his conflict, in his struggles in life.—*Review and Herald,* Aug. 26, 1890.

THE TRUTH OF GOD REFINES THE TASTE

Love is patient and kind; love is not jealous or boastful; it is not arrogant or rude. 1 Cor. 13:4, 5, R.S.V.

The truth of God is designed to elevate the receiver, to refine his taste, and to sanctify his judgment. The character of the Christian should be holy, his manners comely, his words without guile. There should be a continual effort to imitate the society he hopes soon to join, that of angels who have never fallen by sin.

No man can be a Christian without having the Spirit of Christ; and if he has the Spirit of Christ, it will be manifested in kind words and a refined, courteous deportment. . . . External change will testify to an internal change. The truth is the sanctifier, the refiner. Received into the heart, it works with hidden power, transforming the character. But those who profess to be followers of Christ, and are at the same time rough, unkind, and uncourteous in words and deportment, have not learned of Jesus. A blustering, overbearing, faultfinding man is not a Christian; for to be a Christian is to be Christlike. . . .

Very many who are seeking for happiness will be disappointed in their hopes, because they seek it amiss, and are indulging in sinful tempers and selfish feelings. By neglecting to discharge the little duties and observe the little courtesies of life, they violate the principles on which happiness depends. True happiness is not to be found in self-gratification, but in the path of duty. God desires man to be happy, and for this reason He gave him the precepts of His law, that in obeying these he might have joy at home and abroad. While he stands in his moral integrity, true to principle, and having the control of all his powers, he cannot be miserable. With its tendrils twined about God, the heart will be full of peace and joy, and the soul will flourish amid unbelief and depravity.

Kind words, pleasant looks, a cheerful countenance, throw a charm around the Christian that makes his influence almost irresistible. It is the religion of Christ in the heart that causes the words to be gentle, and the demeanor winning, even to those in the humblest walks of life. In forgetfulness of self, in the light and peace and happiness he is constantly bestowing on others, is seen the true dignity of the man. This is a way to gain respect, and extend the sphere of usefulness, which costs but little; and the one who pursues this course will not complain that he does not receive the honor that is his due. But Bible rules must be written on the heart; Bible rules must be carried into the everyday life.—*Signs of the Times,* Nov. 11, 1886.

THE BUILDING BLOCKS OF NOBLE CHARACTERS

Love does not insist on its own way; it is not irritable or resentful; it does not rejoice at wrong, but rejoices in the right. Love bears all things, believes all things, hopes all things, endures all things. 1 Cor. 13:5-7, R.S.V.

Pleasant, kind, and well-bred Christians will have an influence for God and His truth; it cannot be otherwise. The light borrowed from Heaven will shed its brightening rays through them to the pathway of others, leading them to exclaim, "O Lord of hosts, blessed is the man whose strength is in thee."

The words we speak, our daily deportment, are the fruit growing upon the tree. If the fruit is sour and unpalatable, the rootlets of that tree are not drawing nourishment from a pure source. If our characters are meek and lowly, if our affections are in harmony with our Saviour, we will show that our life is hid with Christ in God, and we leave behind us a bright track. Our life will be in such marked contrast to that of unbelievers, that our associates will discern that we have been with Jesus and learned of Him.

The Christian need not become a recluse; but while necessarily associating with the world, he will not be of the world. Christian politeness should be cultivated, and daily put in practice. That unkind word should be left unspoken; that selfish disregard of the happiness of others should give place to thoughtful sympathy. True courtesy, blended with truth and justice, will make the life not only useful, but beautiful and fragrant with love and good works. . . .

Virtue, honesty, kindness, and faithful integrity make noble characters; those who possess these characteristics will win esteem, even of unbelievers, and their influence in the church will be very precious. We are required to be right in important matters; but faithfulness in little things will fit us for higher positions of trust.

On the part of many, there is a great lack of true courtesy. Much is said of the improvements that have been made since the days of the patriarchs; but those living in that age could boast of a higher state of refinement, and of more true courtesy of manners, than are possessed by the people in this age of boasted enlightenment. Integrity, justice, and Christian kindness, blended, make a beautiful combination. Courtesy is one of the graces of the Spirit. It is an attribute of heaven.

The angels never fly into a passion, never are envious, selfish, and jealous. No harsh or unkind words escape their lips. And if we are to be the companions of angels, we too must be refined and courteous. . . . A Christian will cultivate that charity that is not easily provoked, that suffereth long and is kind, that hopeth all things, endureth all things.—*Signs of the Times,* Nov. 11, 1886.

TRANSFORMATION OF CHARACTER TAKES PLACE HERE

Blessed is the man whose strength is in thee. Ps. 84:5.

We are none of us what we may be, what God would have us be, and what His Word requires us to be. And it is our unbelief that shuts us away from God; for we may at any time lift up our souls to Him, and find grace and strength. When Christ shall come, our vile bodies are to be changed, and made like His glorious body; but the vile character will not be made holy then. The transformation of character must take place before His coming. Our natures must be pure and holy; we must have the mind of Christ, that He may behold with pleasure His image reflected upon our souls.

Enoch was a marked character, and many look upon his life as something far above what the generality of mortals can ever reach. But Enoch's life and character, which were so holy that he was translated to heaven without seeing death, represent the lives and characters of all who will be translated when Christ comes. His life was what the life of every individual may be if he will live near to God. We should remember that Enoch was surrounded by unholy influences. The society around him was so depraved that God brought a flood of waters on the world to destroy its inhabitants for their corruption.

Were Enoch upon the earth today, his heart would be in harmony with all of God's requirements; he would walk with God, although surrounded by influences the most wicked and debasing. The palm tree well represents the life of a Christian. It stands upright amid the burning desert sands, and dies not; for it draws sustenance from springs beneath the surface.

Joseph preserved his integrity when surrounded by idolaters in Egypt, in the midst of sin and blasphemy and corrupting influences. When [he was] tempted to turn aside from the path of virtue, his answer was, "How shall I do this great wickedness, and sin against God?" Enoch, Joseph, and Daniel depended upon a strength that was infinite; and this is the only course of safety for Christians to pursue in our day.

The lives of these marked men were hid with Christ in God. They were loyal to God, pure amid depravity, devout and fervent when brought in contact with atheism and idolatry. Through divine grace they cultivated only such qualities as were favorable to the development of pure and holy characters.

Thus it may be with us. The spirit which Enoch, Joseph and Daniel possessed, we may have; we may draw from the same source of strength, possess the same power of self-control, and the same graces may shine out in our lives.—*Signs of the Times,* Nov. 11, 1886.

WHAT YOU THINK, YOU ARE

Casting down imaginations, and every high thing that exalteth itself against the knowledge of God, and bringing into captivity every thought to the obedience of Christ. 2 Cor. 10:5.

More precious than the golden wedge of Ophir is the power of right thought. We need to place a high value upon the right control of our thoughts; for such control prepares us to labor for the Master. It is necessary for our peace and happiness in this life that our thoughts center in Christ. As a man thinketh, so is he.

The merciful shall find mercy, and the pure in heart shall see God. Every impure thought defiles the soul, impairs the moral sense, and tends to obliterate the impressions of the Holy Spirit. It dims the spiritual vision, so that men cannot behold God. The Lord may and does forgive the repenting sinner; but though forgiven, the soul is marred. All impurity of speech and thought must be shunned by him who would have clear discernment of spiritual truth.

Evil thoughts destroy the soul. The converting power of God changes the heart, refining and purifying the thoughts. Unless a determined effort is made to keep the thoughts centered on Christ, grace cannot reveal itself in the life. The mind must engage in the spiritual warfare. Every thought must be brought into captivity to the obedience of Christ. All the habits must be brought under God's control.

We need a constant sense of the ennobling power of pure thoughts and the damaging influence of evil thoughts. Let us place our thoughts upon holy things. Let them be pure and true; for the only security for any soul is right thinking. We are to use every means that God has placed within our reach for the government and cultivation of our thoughts. We are to bring our minds into harmony with Christ's mind. His truth will sanctify us, body, soul, and spirit, and we shall be enabled to rise above temptation.

"The prince of this world cometh," said Jesus, "and hath nothing in me." There was in Him nothing that responded to Satan's sophistry. He did not consent to sin. Not even by a thought did He yield to temptation. So may it be with us. Christ's humanity was united with divinity; He was fitted for the conflict by the indwelling of the Holy Spirit. . . . So long as we are united to Him by faith, sin has no more dominion over us. God reaches for the hand of faith in us to direct it to lay fast hold upon the divinity of Christ, that we may attain to perfection of character. . . . Every promise in God's Word is ours.

"By every word that proceedeth out of the mouth of God" are we to live. . . . Look not to circumstances or to the weakness of self, but to the power of the Word. All its strength is yours.—*Signs of the Times,* Aug. 23, 1905.

CHARACTER THE RESULT OF SINGLE ACTS

He that is faithful in that which is least is faithful also in much. Luke 16:10.

It is conscientious attention to what the world terms "little things" that makes life a success. Little deeds of charity, little acts of self-denial, speaking simple words of helpfulness, watching against little sins—this is Christianity. A grateful acknowledgment of daily blessings, a wise improvement of daily opportunities, a diligent cultivation of entrusted talents—this is what the Master calls for.

He who faithfully performs small duties will be prepared to answer the demands of larger responsibilities. The man who is kind and courteous in the daily life, who is generous and forbearing in his family, whose constant aim it is to make home happy, will be the first to deny self and make sacrifices when the Master calls.

We may be willing to give our property to the cause of God, but this will not count unless we give Him also a heart of love and gratitude. Those who would be true missionaries in foreign fields must first be true missionaries in the home. Those who desire to work in the Master's vineyard must prepare themselves for this by a careful cultivation of the little piece of vineyard He has entrusted to their care.

As a man "thinketh in his heart, so is he." Many thoughts make up the unwritten history of a single day; and these thoughts have much to do with the formation of character. Our thoughts are to be strictly guarded; for one impure thought makes a deep impression on the soul. An evil thought leaves an evil impress on the mind. If the thoughts are pure and holy, the man is better for having cherished them. By them the spiritual pulse is quickened, and the power for doing good is increased. And as one drop of rain prepares the way for another in moistening the earth, so one good thought prepares the way for another. . . .

The longest chain is composed of separate links. If one of these links is faulty, the chain is worthless. Thus it is with character. A well-balanced character is formed by single acts well performed. One defect, cultivated instead of being overcome, makes the man imperfect, and closes against him the gate of the Holy City. He who enters heaven must have a character that is without spot or wrinkle or any such thing. Naught that defileth can ever enter there. In all the redeemed host not one defect will be seen.

God's work is perfect as a whole because it is perfect in every part, however minute. He fashions the tiny spear of grass with as much care as He would exercise in making a world. If we desire to be perfect, even as our Father in heaven is perfect, we must be faithful in doing little things.—*Messages to Young People,* pp. 143-145.

WE ABIDE IN CHRIST BY A LIVING FAITH

And what agreement hath the temple of God with idols? for ye are the temple of the living God; as God hath said, I will dwell in them, and walk in them; and I will be their God, and they shall be my people. 2 Cor. 6:16.

We are abiding in Christ by a living faith. He is abiding in our hearts by our individual appropriating of faith. We have the companionship of the divine presence, and as we realize this presence our thoughts are brought into captivity to Jesus Christ. Our spiritual exercises are in accordance with the vividness of our sense of this companionship. Enoch walked with God in this way; and Christ is dwelling in our hearts by faith when we will consider what He is to us, and what a work He has wrought out for us in the plan of redemption. We shall be most happy in cultivating a sense of this great gift of God to our world and to us personally.

These thoughts have a controlling power upon the whole character. I want to impress upon your mind that you may have a divine companion with you, if you will, always. . . .

As the mind dwells upon Christ, the character is molded after the divine similitude. The thoughts are pervaded with a sense of His goodness, His love. We contemplate His character, and thus He is in all our thoughts. His love encloses us. If we gaze even a moment upon the sun in its meridian glory, when we turn away our eyes the image of the sun will appear in everything upon which we look.

Thus it is when we behold Jesus; everything we look upon reflects His image, the Sun of Righteousness. We cannot see anything else, or talk of anything else. His image is imprinted upon the eye of the soul, and affects every portion of our daily life, softening and subduing our whole nature. By beholding, we are conformed to the divine similitude, even the likeness of Christ. To all with whom we associate we reflect the bright and cheerful beams of His righteousness. We have become transformed in character; for heart, soul, mind, are irradiated by the reflection of Him who loved us and gave Himself for us. Here again there is the realization of a personal, living influence dwelling in our hearts by faith.

When His words of instruction have been received, and have taken possession of us, Jesus is to us an abiding presence, controlling our thoughts and ideas and actions. . . .

Jesus Christ is everything to us—the first, the last, the best in everything. Jesus Christ, His Spirit, His character, colors everything; it is the warp and woof, the very texture of our entire being. . . . Continuing to look unto Jesus, we reflect His image to all around us. —*Messages to Young People,* pp. 159-161.

THE THOUGHTS MUST BE CENTERED UPON GOD

Wherefore gird up the loins of your mind, be sober, and hope to the end for the grace that is to be brought unto you at the revelation of Jesus Christ. 1 Peter 1:13.

A storm is coming, relentless in its fury. Are we prepared to meet it?

We need not say: The perils of the last days are soon to come upon us. Already they have come. We need now the sword of the Lord to cut to the very soul and marrow of fleshly lusts, appetites, and passions.

Minds that have been given up to loose thought need to change. "Girding up the loins of your mind, be sober and set your hope perfectly on the grace that is to be brought unto you at the revelation of Jesus Christ; as children of obedience, not fashioning yourselves according to your former lusts in the time of your ignorance: but like as he who called you is holy, be ye yourselves also holy in all manner of living; because it is written, Ye shall be holy; for I am holy" (1 Peter 1:13-16, A.R.V.). The thoughts must be centered upon God. Now is the time to put forth earnest effort to overcome the natural tendencies of the carnal heart.

Our efforts, our self-denial, our perseverance, must be proportionate to the infinite value of the object of which we are in pursuit. Only by overcoming as Christ overcame shall we win the crown of life.

Man's great danger is in being self-deceived, indulging self-sufficiency, and thus separating from God, the source of his strength. Our natural tendencies, unless corrected by the Holy Spirit of God, have in them the seeds of moral death. . . .

In order to receive help from Christ, we must realize our need. We must have a true knowledge of ourselves. It is only he who knows himself to be a sinner that Christ can save. Only as we see our utter helplessness and renounce all self-trust, shall we lay hold on divine power.

It is not only at the beginning of the Christian life that this renunciation of self is to be made. At every advance step heavenward it is to be renewed. All our good works are dependent on a power outside of ourselves; therefore there needs to be a continual reaching out of the heart after God, a constant, earnest confession of sin and humbling of the soul before Him. Perils surround us; and we are safe only as we feel our weakness and cling with the grasp of faith to our mighty Deliverer. . . .

"Every word of God is pure: He is a shield unto them that put their trust in Him" (Prov. 30:5).—*Testimonies,* vol. 8, pp. 315, 316.

THE SCIENCE OF CHRISTIANITY

I keep under my body, and bring it into subjection: lest that by any means, when I have preached to others, I myself should be a castaway. 1 Cor. 9:27.

The Christian life is a battle and a march. In this warfare there is no release; the effort must be continuous and persevering. It is by unceasing endeavor that we maintain the victory over the temptations of Satan. Christian integrity must be sought with resistless energy and maintained with a resolute fixedness of purpose.

No one will be borne upward without stern, persevering effort in his own behalf. All must engage in this warfare for themselves. Individually we are responsible for the issue of the struggle; though Noah, Job, and Daniel were in the land, they could deliver neither son nor daughter by their righteousness.

There is a science of Christianity to be mastered—a science as much deeper, broader, higher than any human science as the heavens are higher than the earth. The mind is to be disciplined, educated, trained; for we are to do service for God in ways that are not in harmony with inborn inclination. There are hereditary and cultivated tendencies to evil that must be overcome. Often the training and education of a lifetime must be discarded, that one may become a learner in the school of Christ.

Our hearts must be educated to become steadfast in God. We are to form habits of thought that will enable us to resist temptation. We must learn to look upward. The principles of the Word of God—principles that are as high as heaven, and that compass eternity—we are to understand in their bearing upon our daily life. Every act, every word, every thought, is to be in accord with these principles.

The precious graces of the Holy Spirit are not developed in a moment. Courage, fortitude, meekness, faith, unwavering trust in God's power to save, are acquired by the experience of years. By a life of holy endeavor and firm adherence to the right the children of God are to seal their destiny.

We have no time to lose. We know not how soon our probation may close. Eternity stretches before us. The curtain is about to be lifted. Christ is soon to come. The angels of God are seeking to attract us from ourselves and from earthly things. Let them not labor in vain.

When Jesus rises up in the most holy place, lays off His mediatorial robes, and clothes Himself with the garments of vengeance, the mandate will go forth: "He that is unjust, let him be unjust still: . . . and he that is righteous, let him be righteous still: and he that is holy, let him be holy still. And, behold, I come quickly; and My reward is with me" (Rev. 22:11, 12).—*Testimonies*, vol. 8, pp. 313-315.

LIVING THE CHARACTER OF CHRIST

Be diligent that ye may be found of Him in peace, without spot, and blameless. 2 Peter 3:14.

The greatest work that can be done in our world is to glorify God by living the character of Christ.—*Testimonies,* vol. 6, p. 439.

In the second letter addressed by Peter to those who had obtained "like precious faith" with himself, the apostle sets forth the divine plan for the development of Christian character. He writes:

"Grace and peace be multiplied unto you through the knowledge of God, and of Jesus our Lord, according as his divine power hath given unto us all things that pertain unto life and godliness, through the knowledge of him that hath called us to glory and virtue: whereby are given unto us exceeding great and precious promises: that by these ye might be partakers of the divine nature, having escaped the corruption that is in the world through lust.

"And beside this, giving all diligence, add to your faith virtue; and to virtue knowledge; and to knowledge temperance; and to temperance patience; and to patience godliness; and to godliness brotherly kindness; and to brotherly kindness charity. For if these things be in you, and abound, they make you that ye shall neither be barren nor unfruitful in the knowledge of our Lord Jesus Christ" (2 Peter 1:2-8).

These words are full of instruction, and strike the keynote of victory. The apostle presents before the believers the ladder of Christian progress, every step of which represents advancement in the knowledge of God, and in the climbing of which there is to be no standstill. Faith, virtue, knowledge, temperance, patience, godliness, brotherly kindness, and charity are the rounds of the ladder. We are saved by climbing round after round, mounting step after step, to the height of Christ's ideal for us. Thus He is made unto us wisdom, and righteousness, and sanctification, and redemption.

God has called His people to glory and virtue, and these will be manifest in the lives of all who are truly connected with Him. Having become partakers of the heavenly gift, they are to go on unto perfection, being "kept by the power of God through faith" (1 Peter 1:5).

It is the glory of God to give His virtue to His children. He desires to see men and women reaching the highest standard; and when by faith they lay hold of the power of Christ, when they plead His unfailing promises, and claim them as their own, when with an importunity that will not be denied they seek for the power of the Holy Spirit, they will be made complete in Him.—*The Acts of the Apostles,* pp. 529, 530.

THE KNOWLEDGE OF GOD IS VITAL

Let not the wise man glory in his wisdom, neither let the mighty man glory in his might, let not the rich man glory in his riches: but let him that glorieth glory in this, that he understandeth and knoweth me. Jer. 9:23, 24.

Having received the faith of the gospel, . . . the believer is to add to his character virtue, and thus cleanse the heart and prepare the mind for the reception of the knowledge of God. This knowledge is the foundation of all true education and of all true service. It is the only real safeguard against temptation; and it is this alone that can make one like God in character. Through the knowledge of God and of His Son, Jesus Christ, are given to the believer "all things that pertain unto life and godliness." No good gift is withheld from him who sincerely desires to obtain the righteousness of God.

"This is life eternal," Christ said, "that they might know thee the only true God, and Jesus Christ, whom Thou hast sent" (John 17:3). And the prophet Jeremiah declared: . . . "I am the Lord which exercise lovingkindness, judgment, and righteousness, in the earth: for in these things I delight, saith the Lord" (Jer. 9:24). Scarcely can the human mind comprehend the breadth and depth and height of the spiritual attainments of him who gains this knowledge.

None need fail of attaining, in his sphere, to perfection of Christian character. By the sacrifice of Christ, provision has been made for the believer to receive all things that pertain to life and godliness. God calls upon us to reach the standard of perfection and places before us the example of Christ's character. In His humanity, perfected by a life of constant resistance of evil, the Saviour showed that through cooperation with Divinity, human beings may in this life attain to perfection of character. This is God's assurance to us that we, too, may obtain complete victory.

Before the believer is held out the wonderful possibility of being like Christ, obedient to all the principles of the law. . . . The holiness that God's Word declares he must have before he can be saved is the result of the working of divine grace as he bows in submission to the discipline and restraining influences of the Spirit of truth. Man's obedience can be made perfect only by the incense of Christ's righteousness, which fills with divine fragrance every act of obedience.

The part of the Christian is to persevere in overcoming every fault. Constantly he is to pray to the Saviour to heal the disorders of his sin-sick soul. He has not the wisdom or the strength to overcome; these belong to the Lord, and He bestows them on those who in humiliation and contrition seek Him for help.—*The Acts of the Apostles,* pp. 530-532.

THE NECESSITY OF CONSTANT GROWTH IN GRACE

Give diligence to make your calling and election sure: for if ye do these things, ye shall never fall. 2 Peter 1:10.

The work of transformation from unholiness to holiness is a continuous one. Day by day God labors for man's sanctification, and man is to cooperate with Him, putting forth persevering efforts in the cultivation of right habits. He is to add grace to grace; and as he thus works on the plan of addition, God works for him on the plan of multiplication. Our Saviour is always ready to hear and answer the prayer of the contrite heart, and grace and peace are multiplied to His faithful ones. Gladly He grants them the blessings they need in their struggle against the evils that beset them.

There are those who attempt to ascend the ladder of Christian progress; but as they advance they begin to put their trust in the power of man, and soon lose sight of Jesus, the Author and Finisher of their faith. The result is failure—the loss of all that has been gained. Sad indeed is the condition of those who, becoming weary of the way, allow the enemy of souls to rob them of the Christian graces that have been developing in their hearts and lives. "He that lacketh these things," declares the apostle, "is blind, and cannot see afar off, and hath forgotten that he was purged from his old sins."

The apostle Peter had had a long experience in the things of God. His faith in God's power to save had strengthened with the years, until he had proved beyond question that there is no possibility of failure before the one who, advancing by faith, ascends round by round, ever upward and onward, to the topmost round of the ladder that reaches even to the portals of heaven.

For many years Peter had been urging upon the believers the necessity of a constant growth in grace and in a knowledge of the truth; and now, knowing that soon he would be called to suffer martyrdom for his faith, he once more drew attention to the precious privileges within the reach of every believer. In the full assurance of his faith the aged disciple exhorted his brethren to steadfastness of purpose in the Christian life. "Give diligence," he pleaded, "to make your calling and election sure: for if ye do these things, ye shall never fall: for so an entrance shall be ministered unto you abundantly into the everlasting kingdom of our Lord and Saviour Jesus Christ."

Precious assurance! Glorious is the hope before the believer as he advances by faith toward the heights of Christian perfection!—*The Acts of the Apostles,* pp. 532, 533.

JOHN'S CHARACTER REFLECTED CHRIST

Herein is love, not that we loved God, but that he loved us, and sent his Son to be the propitiation for our sins. Beloved, if God so loved us, we ought also to love one another. 1 John 4:10, 11.

The confiding love and unselfish devotion manifested in the life and character of John present lessons of untold value to the Christian church. John did not naturally possess the loveliness of character that his later experience revealed. By nature he had serious defects. He was not only proud, self-assertive, and ambitious for honor, but impetuous, and resentful under injury. He and his brother were called ''sons of thunder.'' Evil temper, the desire for revenge, the spirit of criticism, were all in the beloved disciple. But beneath all this the divine Teacher discerned the ardent, sincere, loving heart. Jesus rebuked his self-seeking, disappointed his ambitions, tested his faith. But He revealed to him that for which his soul longed—the beauty of holiness, the transforming power of love. . . .

The lessons of Christ, setting forth meekness and humility and love as essential to growth in grace and a fitness for His work, were of the highest value to John. He treasured every lesson and constantly sought to bring his life into harmony with the divine pattern. . . . His Master's lessons were graven on his soul. When he testified of the Saviour's grace, his simple language was eloquent with the love that pervaded his whole being.

It was John's deep love for Christ which led him always to desire to be close by His side. The Saviour loved all the Twelve, but John's was the most receptive spirit. He was younger than the others, and with more of the child's confiding trust he opened his heart to Jesus. Thus he came more into sympathy with Christ, and through him the Saviour's deepest spiritual teaching was communicated to the people.

Jesus loves those who represent the Father, and John could talk of the Father's love as no other of the disciples could. He revealed to his fellow men that which he felt in his own soul, representing in his character the attributes of God. The glory of the Lord was expressed in his face. The beauty of holiness which had transformed him shone with a Christlike radiance from his countenance. In adoration and love he beheld the Saviour until likeness to Christ and fellowship with Him became his one desire, and in his character was reflected the character of his Master.—*The Acts of the Apostles,* pp. 539-545.

THE DISCIPLES REVEALED THE LOVE OF CHRIST

Hereby perceive we the love of God, because he laid down his life for us: and we ought to lay down our lives for the brethren. 1 John 3:16.

After the ascension of Christ, John stands forth as a faithful, earnest laborer for the Master. . . . He enjoyed the outpouring of the Spirit . . . and with fresh zeal and power he continued to speak to the people the words of life, seeking to lead their thoughts to the Unseen. He was a powerful preacher, fervent, and deeply in earnest. In beautiful language and with a musical voice he told of the words and works of Christ, speaking in a way that impressed the hearts of those who heard him. The simplicity of his words, the sublime power of the truths he uttered, and the fervor that characterized his teachings, gave him access to all classes.

The apostle's life was in harmony with his teachings. The love of Christ which glowed in his heart led him to put forth earnest, untiring labor for his fellow men, especially for his brethren in the Christian church.

Christ had bidden the first disciples love one another as He had loved them. Thus they were to bear testimony to the world that Christ was formed within, the hope of glory. "A new commandment I give unto you," He had said, "That ye love one another; as I have loved you, that ye also love one another" (John 13:34). At the time when these words were spoken, the disciples could not understand them; but after they had witnessed the sufferings of Christ, after His crucifixion and resurrection, and ascension to heaven, and after the Holy Spirit had rested on them at Pentecost, they had a clearer conception of the love of God and of the nature of that love which they must have for one another. . . .

After the descent of the Holy Spirit, when the disciples went forth to proclaim a living Saviour, their one desire was the salvation of souls. They rejoiced in the sweetness of communion with saints. They were tender, thoughtful, self-denying, willing to make any sacrifice for the truth's sake. In their daily association with one another, they revealed the love that Christ had enjoined upon them. By unselfish words and deeds they strove to kindle this love in other hearts.

Such a love the believers were ever to cherish. They were to go forward in willing obedience to the new commandment. So closely were they to be united with Christ that they would be enabled to fulfill all His requirements. Their lives were to magnify the power of a Saviour who could justify them by His righteousness.—*The Acts of the Apostles,* pp. 546-548.

CONTEMPLATING HEAVENLY THINGS

God . . . hath raised us up together, and made us sit together in heavenly places in Christ Jesus. Eph. 2:4-6.

If we would bear in mind the momentous events which are soon to take place, we would not be so weak in character. We would feel that we were living in the presence of God, and awed and amazed we should heed the injunction, "Be still, and know that I am God." Oh, when shall we ever realize the full value of our Saviour's work and intercession? When shall we rely upon Him with full confidence, and live a noble, pure, and devoted life? To what heights may the imagination reach when sanctified and inspired by the virtue of Christ! We may take in the glories of the future, eternal world. We may live as seeing Him who is invisible. Walk by faith and not by sight. . . .

Through searching the Scriptures we may come to understand what we are to Christ, and what He is to us. By beholding Him we are to become changed into His image, becoming colaborers with Him, representatives of Him in life and character. We must learn to realize that we are to live as the sons and daughters of God, loving God supremely, and our neighbors as ourselves. We are to live a pure, perfect life for Christ's sake. We are to love perfection because Jesus is the embodiment of perfection, the great center of attraction. The life we now live we must live by faith in the Son of God.

If we follow Christ we shall not have a spasmodical experience, and be moved by circumstances and influenced by our surroundings. We shall not let feeling control us, and indulge in fretting, envying, faultfinding, jealousy, and vanity.

It is indulgence in these things that puts us out of harmony with the harmonious life of Christ, and prevents us from becoming overcomers. We should be actuated by the noble purpose of winning daily victories, and by watchfulness and sincere prayer attain to complete control of self. When petty trials come upon us, and words are spoken that cut and bruise the soul, speak to yourself and say, "I am a child of God, heir with Jesus Christ, a colaborer with heaven, and I cannot afford to easily take offense, to be always thinking of self; for this will produce a distorted character, and is unworthy of my high calling. My heavenly Father has given me a work to do, and let me do it worthily for His name's sake."

We should consider earnestly and continually the excellence of the character of Jesus Christ, that we may impart His blessings and lead men to follow in His footsteps.—*Signs of the Times,* July 10, 1893.

GOD'S CHILDREN TO BE LIGHT BEARERS

Let your light so shine before men, that they may see your good works, and glorify your Father which is in heaven. Matt. 5:16.

God never designed that one man's mind or judgment should be a controlling power. Whenever He has had a special work to be done, He has always had men ready to meet the demand. In every age, when the divine voice has asked, Who will go for us? the response has come, "Here am I, send me." In ancient times the Lord had connected with His work men of varied talents. Abraham, Isaac, Jacob, Moses with his meekness and wisdom, and Joshua with his varied capabilities were all enlisted in God's service. The music of Miriam, the courage and piety of Deborah, the filial affection of Ruth, the obedience and faithfulness of Samuel—all were needed. Elijah with his stern traits of character, God used at His appointed time to execute judgment upon Jezebel.

God will not give His Spirit to those who make no use of the heavenly gift. But those who are drawn out of and away from themselves, seeking to enlighten, encourage, and bless others, will have increased ability and energy to expend. The more light they give, the more they receive.— *Southern Watchman,* Oct. 31, 1905.

In all ages the "Spirit of Christ which was in them" (1 Peter 1:11) has made God's true children the light of the people of their generation. Joseph was a light bearer in Egypt. In his purity and benevolence and filial love he represented Christ in the midst of a nation of idolaters. While the Israelites were on their way from Egypt to the Promised Land, the truehearted among them were a light to the surrounding nations. Through them God was revealed to the world. From Daniel and his companions in Babylon, and from Mordecai in Persia, bright beams of light shone out amid the darkness of the kingly courts.

In like manner the disciples of Christ are set as light bearers on the way to heaven; through them the Father's mercy and goodness are made manifest to a world enshrouded in the darkness of misapprehension of God. By seeing their good works, others are led to glorify the Father who is above; for it is made manifest that there is a God on the throne of the universe whose character is worthy of praise and imitation. The divine love glowing in the heart, the Christlike harmony manifested in the life, are as a glimpse of heaven granted to men of the world, that they may appreciate its excellence.

It is thus that men are led to believe "the love that God hath to us" (1 John 4:16). Thus hearts once sinful and corrupt are purified and transformed, to be presented "faultless before the presence of His glory with exceeding joy" (Jude 24).—*Thoughts From the Mount of Blessing,* pp. 41, 42.

ENOCH WALKED WITH GOD

By faith Enoch was translated that he should not see death; . . . for before his translation he had this testimony, that he pleased God. Heb. 11:5.

The knowledge of God that works transformation of character is our great need. If we fulfill His purpose, there must be in our lives a revelation of God that shall correspond to the teaching of His Word.

The experience of Enoch and of John the Baptist represents what ours should be. Far more than we do, we need to study the lives of these men—he who was translated to heaven without seeing death, and he who, before Christ's first advent, was called to prepare the way of the Lord, to make His paths straight.

Of Enoch it is written that he lived sixty-five years and begat a son; after that he walked with God three hundred years. During those earlier years, Enoch had loved and feared God, and had kept His commandments. But after the birth of his first son he reached a higher experience; he was drawn into closer relationship with God. As he saw the child's love for its father, its simple trust in his protection; as he felt the deep, yearning tenderness of his own heart for that firstborn son, he learned a precious lesson of the wonderful love of God to man in the gift of His Son, and the confidence which the children of God may repose in their heavenly Father. The infinite, unfathomable love of God through Christ became the subject of his meditations day and night. With all the fervor of his soul he sought to reveal that love to the people among whom he dwelt. . . .

His faith waxed stronger, his love became more ardent, with the lapse of centuries. To him prayer was as the breath of the soul. He lived in the atmosphere of heaven. . . .

The power of God that wrought with His servant was felt by those who heard. Some gave heed to the warning and renounced their sins; but the multitudes mocked at the solemn message. . . .

For three hundred years Enoch had been seeking purity of heart, that he might be in harmony with heaven. For three centuries he had walked with God. Day by day he had longed for a closer union; nearer and nearer had grown the communion, until God took him to Himself. He had stood at the threshold of the eternal world, only a step between him and the land of the blest; and now the portals opened, the walk with God, so long pursued on earth, continued, and he passed through the gates of the Holy City, the first from among men to enter there. . . .

To such communion God is calling us. As was Enoch's must be their holiness of character who shall be redeemed from among men at the Lord's second coming.—*Testimonies*, vol. 8, pp. 329-331.

A PREACHER OF RIGHTEOUSNESS

As it was in the days of Noah, so will it be in the days of the Son of man. They ate, they drank, they married, they were given in marriage, until the day when Noah entered the ark, and the flood came, and destroyed them all. Luke 17:26, 27, R.S.V.

It is the nature of sin to spread and increase. Since the first sin of Adam, from generation to generation it has spread like a contagious disease. While the world was yet in its infancy, sin became fearful in its proportions. Hatred of God's law, and, as the sure result, hatred of all goodness, became universal. God, who had created man and given him with an unsparing hand the bounties of His providence, was dishonored by the beings He had created, slighted and despised by the recipients of His gifts. But though sinful man forgot His benevolent Benefactor, God did not forget the creature He had formed. Not only did He send "rain from heaven, and fruitful seasons," filling man's heart with "food and gladness," but He sent him also messages of warning and entreaty. Man's wickedness was fully set before him, and the result of transgressing the divine law.

In the days of Noah, the wickedness of the world became so great that God could no longer bear with it. . . . But He pitied the race, and in His love provided a refuge for all who would accept it. He gave the message to Noah to be given to the people: "My spirit shall not always strive with man." . . . The Spirit of God continued to strive with rebellious man until the time specified had nearly expired, when Noah and his family entered the ark, and the hand of God closed its door. Mercy had stepped from the golden throne, no longer to intercede for the guilty sinner.

All the men of that generation were not in the fullest sense of the term heathen idolaters. Many had a knowledge of God and His law; but they not only rejected the message of the faithful preacher of righteousness themselves, but used all their influence to prevent others from being obedient to God. To everyone comes a day of trial and trust. That generation had their day of opportunity and privilege while Noah was sounding the note of warning of the coming destruction; but they yielded their minds to the control of Satan rather than of God, and he deceived them, as he did our first parents. He set before them darkness and falsehood in the place of light and truth; and they accepted his sophistry and lies, because they were acceptable to them, and in harmony with their corrupt lives, while truth that would have saved them was rejected as a delusion. Numbers were not on the side of right.—*Signs of the Times,* April 1, 1886.

NOAH STOOD LIKE A ROCK

And it repented the Lord that he had made man on the earth, and it grieved him at his heart. . . . But Noah found grace in the eyes of the Lord. Gen. 6:6-8.

The world was arrayed against God's justice and His laws, and Noah was regarded as fanatic. Satan, when tempting Eve to disobey God, said to her, "Ye shall not surely die." Great men, worldly, honored, and wise men, repeated the same story, "Ye shall not surely die." "The threatenings of God," they said, "are for the purpose of intimidating, and will never be verified. You need not be alarmed. Such an event as the destruction of the world by the God who made it, and the punishment of the beings He has created, will never take place." . . . So the people did not humble their hearts before God, but continued their disobedience and wickedness, the same as though God had not spoken to them through His servant.

But Noah stood like a rock amid the tempest. He was surrounded by every species of wickedness and moral corruption; but amid popular contempt and ridicule, amid universal wickedness and disobedience, he distinguished himself by His holy integrity and unwavering faithfulness. While the world around him were disregarding God, and were indulging in all manner of extravagant dissipation which led to violence and crimes of every kind, the faithful preacher of righteousness declared to that generation that a flood of water was to deluge the world because of the unsurpassed wickedness of its inhabitants. He warned them to repent and believe, and find refuge in the ark.

The message of Noah was to him a reality. Amid the scoffs and jeers of the world, he was an unbending witness for God. His meekness and righteousness were in bright contrast to the revolting crimes, intrigue, and violence continually practiced around him. A power attended his words; for it was the voice of God to man through His servant. Connection with God made him strong in the strength of infinite power, while for one hundred and twenty years his solemn warning voice fell upon the ears of the men of that generation in regard to events, which, so far as human wisdom could judge, seemed impossible. Some were deeply convicted, and would have heeded the words of warning; but there were so many to jest and ridicule that they partook of the same spirit, resisted the invitations of mercy, refused to reform, and were soon among the boldest and most defiant scoffers; for none are so reckless, and go to such lengths in sin, as those who have once had light, but have resisted the convicting Spirit of God. . . . How simple and childlike, amid the unbelief of a scoffing world, was the faith of Noah. . . . He gave to the world an example of believing just what God said.—*Signs of the Times,* April 1, 1886.

NOAH PROCLAIMED GOD'S WORD WITH FORCE

Thus did Noah; according to all that God commanded him, so did he. Gen. 6:22.

The words that had been spoken to Adam were rehearsed [by Noah]— that sin and Satan should not always triumph. There was to be victory for those who feared God. When his voice was lifted in warning of what God was about to bring upon the world in judgment because of the wickedness of men, great opposition was manifested against the words of the messenger. The opposition, however, was not entirely worldwide; for some believed the message of Noah, and zealously repeated the warning.

But the men who were accounted wise were sought, and were urged to present arguments by which the message of Noah might be counteracted. And as the world was at peace and not at war with the prince of evil, they were glad of any excuse to set aside the "Thus saith the Lord" and to listen to the philosophers of the age, who presented the impossibility of such a change taking place in the forces of nature as Noah predicted. There is no enmity between fallen man and fallen angels; both are evil through apostasy, and evil, wherever it exists, is in league against God. Fallen men and fallen angels were united for the dethronement of God.

Thus it was that the wise men of this world talked of science and the fixed laws of nature, and declared that there could be no variation in these laws, and that this message of Noah could not possibly be true. The talented men of Noah's time set themselves in league against God's will and purpose and scorned the message and the messenger that He had sent. . . . Noah could not controvert their philosophies, or refute the claims of science so called; but he could proclaim the word of God; for he knew it contained the infinite wisdom of the Creator, and, as he sounded it everywhere, it lost none of its force and reality because men of the world treated him with ridicule and contempt.

Noah did not mix the soft, pleasing deceptions of Satan with his message. He did not utter the sentiment of many of his day who declared that God was too merciful to do such a terrible work. Many asserted that God would grant the wicked another season of probation; but Noah did not indulge them in the faintest hope that those who neglected the present opportunity, who rejected the present message, would be favored with another opportunity of salvation. . . . He knew the power of God, and realized that God would fulfill His word. His fear of God did not separate him from God, but served to draw him closer to Him, and to lead him to pour out his soul in earnest supplication.—*Signs of the Times*, April 18, 1895.

ABRAHAM'S UNQUESTIONING OBEDIENCE

The Lord said unto Abram, Get thee out of thy country, and from thy kindred and from thy father's house, unto a land that I will shew thee: And I will make of thee a great nation, and I will bless thee, and make thy name great; and thou shalt be a blessing. Gen. 12:1, 2.

God selected Abraham as His messenger through whom to communicate light to the world. The word of God came to him, not with the presentation of flattering prospects in this life of large salary, of great appreciation and worldly honor. "Get thee out of thy country . . . unto a land that I will shew thee" was the divine message to Abraham. The patriarch obeyed, and "went out, not knowing whither he went," as God's light bearer, to keep His name alive in the earth. He forsook his country, his home, his relatives, and all pleasant associations connected with his early life, to become a pilgrim and a stranger. . . . Before God can use him, Abraham must be separated from his former associations, that he may not be controlled by human influence or rely upon human aid. Now that he has become connected with God, this man must henceforth dwell among strangers. His character must be peculiar, differing from all the world. He could not even explain his course of action so as to be understood by his friends, for they were idolaters. Spiritual things must be spiritually discerned; therefore his motives and his actions were beyond the comprehension of his kindred and friends.

Abraham's unquestioning obedience was one of the most striking instances of faith and reliance upon God to be found in the Sacred Record. With only the naked promise that his descendants should possess Canaan, without the least outward evidence, he followed on where God should lead, fully and sincerely complying with the conditions on his part, and confident that the Lord would faithfully perform His word. The patriarch went wherever God indicated his duty; he passed through wildernesses without terror; he went among idolatrous nations, with the one thought: "God has spoken; I am obeying His voice; He will guide, He will protect me."

Just such faith and confidence as Abraham had the messengers of God need today. But many whom the Lord could use will not move onward, hearing and obeying the one Voice above all others. . . . The Lord would do much more for His servants if they were wholly consecrated to Him, esteeming His service above the ties of kindred and all other earthly associations.—*Testimonies,* vol. 4, pp. 523, 524.

ABRAHAM'S UNFALTERING FAITH

Take now thy son, thine only son Isaac, whom thou lovest, and . . . offer him . . . for a burnt offering. Gen. 22:2.

The Lord saw fit to test the faith of Abraham by a most fearful trial. If he had endured the first test and had patiently waited for the promise to be fulfilled in Sarah, and had not taken Hagar as his wife, he would not have been subjected to the closest test that was ever required of man. The Lord bade Abraham, "Take now thy son, . . . whom thou lovest, and get thee into the land of Moriah; and offer him there for a burnt offering." . . .

Abraham did not disbelieve God and hesitate, but early in the morning he took two of his servants and Isaac, his son, and the wood for the burnt offering, and went unto the place of which God had told him. . . . Abraham did not suffer paternal feelings to control him and lead him to rebel against God. The command of God was calculated to stir the depths of his soul. "Take now thy son." Then, as though to probe the heart a little deeper, He added, "Thine only son Isaac, whom thou lovest"; that is, the only son of promise, "and offer him." . . .

Three days this father traveled with his son, having sufficient time to reason and doubt God if he was disposed to doubt. But he did not distrust God. . . .

Abraham believed that Isaac was the son of promise. He also believed that God meant just what He said when He bade him to go offer him as a burnt offering. He . . . believed that God who had in His providence given Sarah a son in her old age, and who had required him to take that son's life, could also . . . bring up Isaac from the dead.

Abraham left the servants by the way and proposed to go alone with his son to worship some distance from them. . . . Firmly walked on that stern, loving, suffering father by the side of his son. As they came to the place which God had pointed out to Abraham, he built there an altar and laid the wood in order, ready for the sacrifice, and then informed Isaac of the command of God to offer him as a burnt offering. He repeated to him the promise that God several times had made to him, that through Isaac he should become a great nation, and that in performing the command of God in slaying him, God would fulfill His promise. . . .

Isaac believed in God. . . . After affectionately embracing his father, he submitted to be bound and laid upon the wood. And as his father's hand was raised to slay his son, an angel of God, who had marked all the faithfulness of Abraham . . . , called to him out of heaven, and said, "Abraham. . . . Lay not thine hand upon the lad . . . : for now I know that thou fearest God, seeing thou hast not withheld thy son, thine only son from me."—*The Story of Redemption,* pp. 80-82.

JOSEPH RESOLVES TO BE TRUE TO GOD

And Joseph said unto [his brethren], Fear not: . . . As for you, ye thought evil against me: but God meant it unto good . . . to save much people alive. Gen. 50:19, 20.

Joseph with his captors was on the way to Egypt. . . . The boy could discern in the distance the hills among which lay his father's tents. Bitterly he wept at the thought of that loving father in his loneliness and affliction. Again the scene at Dothan came up before him. He saw his angry brothers and felt their fierce glances bent upon him. The stinging, insulting words that had met his agonized entreaties were ringing in his ears. With a trembling heart he looked forward to the future. What a change in situation—from the tenderly cherished son to the despised and helpless slave! Alone and friendless, what would be his lot in the strange land to which he was going? For a time, Joseph gave himself up to uncontrolled grief and terror.

But, in the providence of God, even this experience was to be a blessing to him. He had learned in a few hours that which years might not otherwise have taught him. His father, strong and tender as his love had been, had done him wrong by his partiality and indulgence. This unwise preference had angered his brothers and provoked them to the cruel deed that had separated him from his home. Its effects were manifest also in his own character. Faults had been encouraged that were now to be corrected. He was becoming self-sufficient and exacting. Accustomed to the tenderness of his father's care, he felt that he was unprepared to cope with the difficulties before him. . . .

Then his thoughts turned to his father's God. In his childhood he had been taught to love and fear Him. Often in his father's tent he had listened to the story of the vision that Jacob saw as he fled from his home an exile and a fugitive. He had been told of the Lord's promises to Jacob, and how they had been fulfilled—how, in the hour of need, the angels of God had come to instruct, comfort, and protect him. And he had learned of the love of God in providing for men a Redeemer. Now all these precious lessons came vividly before him. Joseph believed that the God of his fathers would be his God. He then and there gave himself fully to the Lord, and he prayed that the Keeper of Israel would be with him in the land of his exile.

His soul thrilled with the high resolve to prove himself true to God—under all circumstances to act as became a subject of the King of heaven. He would serve the Lord with undivided heart. . . . One day's experience had been the turning point in Joseph's life. Its terrible calamity had transformed him from a petted child to a man, thoughtful, courageous, and self-possessed.—*Patriarchs and Prophets,* pp. 213, 214.

JOCHEBED'S INFLUENCE ON MOSES

By faith Moses, when he was come to years, refused to be called the son of Pharaoh's daughter; choosing rather to suffer affliction with the people of God, than to enjoy the pleasures of sin for a season. Heb. 11:24, 25.

Younger than Joseph or Daniel was Moses when removed from the sheltering care of his childhood home; yet already the same agencies that shaped their lives had molded his. Only twelve years did he spend with his Hebrew kindred; but during these years was laid the foundation of his greatness; it was laid by the hand of one little known to fame.

Jochebed was a woman and a slave. Her lot in life was humble, her burden heavy. But through no other woman, save Mary of Nazareth, has the world received greater blessing. Knowing that her child must soon pass beyond her care, to the guardianship of those who knew not God, she the more earnestly endeavored to link his soul with heaven. She sought to implant in his heart love and loyalty to God. And faithfully was the work accomplished. Those principles of truth that were the burden of his mother's teaching and the lesson of her life, no after influence could induce Moses to renounce.

From the humble home in Goshen the son of Jochebed passed to the palace of the Pharaohs, to the Egyptian princess, by her to be welcomed as a loved and cherished son. In the schools of Egypt, Moses received the highest civil and military training. Of great personal attractions, noble in form and stature, of cultivated mind and princely bearing, and renowned as military leader, he became the nation's pride. The king of Egypt was also a member of the priesthood; and Moses, though refusing to participate in the heathen worship, was initiated into all the mysteries of the Egyptian religion.

Egypt at this time being still the most powerful and most highly civilized of nations, Moses, as its prospective sovereign, was heir to the highest honors this world could bestow. But his was a nobler choice. For the honor of God and the deliverance of His downtrodden people, Moses sacrificed the honors of Egypt. Then, in a special sense, God undertook his training. . . .

He had yet to learn the lesson of dependence upon divine power. . . . In the wilds of Midian, Moses spent forty years as a keeper of sheep. . . . In the care of the sheep and the tender lambs he must obtain the experience that would make him a faithful, long-suffering shepherd to Israel. . . .

Amidst the solemn majesty of the mountain solitudes, Moses was alone with God. . . . Here his self-sufficiency was swept away.—*Education,* pp. 61-63.

The greatness of Egypt is in the dust. . . . But the work of Moses can never perish. The great principles of righteousness which he lived to establish are eternal.—*Ibid.,* p. 69.

MOSES' LEADERSHIP INSPIRED CONFIDENCE

Og the king of Bashan came out against us, he and all his people, to battle at Edrei. And the Lord said unto me; Fear him not: for I will deliver him, and all his people, and his land, into thy hand. . . . And we smote him until none was left to him remaining. Deut. 3:1-3.

Before them [Israel] lay the powerful and populous kingdom of Bashan, crowded with great stone cities that to this day excite the wonder of the world. . . . The houses were constructed of huge black stones, of such stupendous size as to make the buildings absolutely impregnable to any force that in those times could have been brought against them. It was a country filled with wild caverns, lofty precipices, yawning gulfs, and rocky strongholds. The inhabitants of this land, descendants from a giant race, were themselves of marvelous size and strength, and so distinguished for violence and cruelty as to be the terror of all surrounding nations; while Og, the king of the country, was remarkable for size and prowess, even in a nation of giants.

But the cloudy pillar moved forward, and following its guidance the Hebrew hosts advanced to Edrei, where the giant king, with his forces, awaited their approach. Og had skillfully chosen the place of battle. The city of Edrei was situated upon the border of a tableland rising abruptly from the plain, and covered with jagged, volcanic rocks. It could be approached only by narrow pathways. . . .

When the Hebrews looked upon the lofty form of that giant of giants towering above the soldiers of his army; when they saw the hosts that surrounded him, and beheld the seemingly impregnable fortress, behind which unseen thousands were entrenched, the hearts of many in Israel quaked with fear. But Moses was calm and firm; the Lord had said concerning the king of Bashan, ''Fear him not: for I will deliver him, and all his people, and his land, into thy hand; and thou shalt do unto him as thou didst unto Sihon king of the Amorites, which dwelt at Heshbon.''

The calm faith of their leader inspired the people with confidence in God. They trusted all to His omnipotent arm, and He did not fail them. Not mighty giants nor walled cities, armed hosts nor rocky fortresses, could stand before the Captain of the Lord's host. The Lord led the army; the Lord discomfited [overthrew] the enemy. The Lord conquered in behalf of Israel. The giant king and his army were destroyed, and the Israelites soon took possession of the whole country. . . .

The hosts of Bashan had yielded before the mysterious power enshrouded in the cloudy pillar.—*Patriarchs and Prophets,* pp. 435-438.

The difficulties that seem so formidable, that fill your soul with dread, will vanish as you move forward in the path of obedience, humbly trusting in God.—*Ibid.,*p. 437.

DEBORAH'S SUPPORT FOR BARAK

Village life . . . ceased until I, Deborah, arose . . . as a mother in Israel. When they chose new gods, war came to the city gates, and not a shield or spear was seen among forty thousand in Israel. Judges 5:7, 8, N.I.V.

For twenty years, the Israelites groaned under the yoke of the oppressor; then they turned from their idolatry, and with humiliation and repentance cried unto the Lord for deliverance. They did not cry in vain. There was dwelling in Israel a woman illustrious for her piety, and through her the Lord chose to deliver His people. Her name was Deborah. She was known as a prophetess, and in the absence of the usual magistrates, the people had sought to her for counsel and justice.

The Lord communicated to Deborah His purpose to destroy the enemies of Israel, and bade her send for a man named Barak. . . . and make known to him the instructions which she had received. She accordingly sent for Barak, and directed him to assemble ten thousand men of the tribes of Naphtali and Zebulun, and make war upon the armies of King Jabin.

Barak knew the scattered, disheartened, and unarmed condition of the Hebrews, and the strength and skill of their enemies. Although he had been designated by the Lord Himself as the one chosen to deliver Israel, and had received the assurance that God would go with him and subdue their enemies, yet he was timid and distrustful. He accepted the message from Deborah as the word of God, but he had little confidence in Israel, and feared that they would not obey his call. He refused to engage in such a doubtful undertaking unless Deborah would accompany him, and thus support his efforts by her influence and counsel. . . .

Barak now marshaled an army of ten thousand men, and marched to Mount Tabor, as the Lord had directed. Sisera immediately assembled an immense and well-equipped force, expecting to surround the Hebrews and make them an easy prey. The Israelites . . . looked with terror upon the vast armies spread out in the plain beneath them equipped with all the implements of warfare. . . . Large, scythelike knives were fastened to the axles, so that the chariots, being driven through ranks of the enemy, would cut them down like wheat before the sickle.

The Israelites had established themselves in a strong position in the mountains to await a favorable opportunity for an attack. Encouraged by Deborah's assurance that the very day had come for signal victory, Barak led his army down into the open plain, and boldly made a charge upon the enemy. The God of battle fought for Israel and neither skill in warfare, nor superiority of numbers and equipment, could withstand them. The hosts of Sisera were panic-stricken. . . . God alone could have discomfited the enemy, and the victory could be ascribed to Him alone.—*Signs of the Times,* June 16, 1881.

329

GIDEON LEADS THREE HUNDRED MEN TO VICTORY

And the Lord looked upon him, and said, Go in this thy might, and thou shalt save Israel from the hand of the Midianites: have not I sent thee? Judges 6:14.

Gideon was the son of Joash, of the tribe of Manasseh. The division to which this family belonged held no leading position, but the household of Joash was distinguished for courage and integrity. . . . To Gideon came the divine call to deliver his people. . . .

Suddenly the ''angel of the Lord'' appeared and addressed him with the words, ''Jehovah is with thee, thou mighty man of valor.''

''Oh my Lord,'' was his answer, ''if the Lord be with us, why then is all this befallen us?'' . . .

The Messenger of heaven replied, ''Go in this thy might and thou shalt save Israel from the hand of the Midianites; have not I sent thee?'' . . .

The entire force under Gideon's command numbered only thirty-two thousand men; but with the vast host of the enemy spread out before him, the word of the Lord came to him: ''The people that are with thee are too many for me to give the Midianites into their hands, lest Israel vaunt themselves against Me, saying, Mine own hand hath saved me. Now therefore go to, proclaim in the ears of the people, saying, Whosoever is fearful and afraid, let him return and depart early from mount Gilead.'' . . .

Gideon obeyed the Lord's direction, and with a heavy heart he saw twenty-two thousand, or more than two thirds of his entire force, depart for their homes. Again the word of the Lord came to him: ''The people are yet too many; bring them down unto the water, and I will try them for thee.'' . . . A few hastily took a little water in the hand and sucked it up as they went on; but nearly all bowed upon their knees, and leisurely drank from the surface of the stream. Those who took the water in their hands were but three hundred out of ten thousand; yet these were selected; all the rest were permitted to return to their homes. By the simplest means character is often tested. . . .

The three hundred chosen men not only possessed courage and self-control, but they were men of faith. . . . God could direct them. . . .

In the dead of the night, at a signal from Gideon's war horn, the three companies sounded their trumpets; then, breaking their pitchers and displaying the blazing torches, they rushed upon the enemy with the terrible war cry, ''The sword of the Lord, and of Gideon!'' . . . One hundred and twenty thousand of the invaders perished. . . . No words can describe the terror of the surrounding nations when they learned what simple means had prevailed against the power of a bold, warlike people.—*Patriarchs and Prophets,* pp. 546-553.

GIDEON SHOWS COURTESY TO THE EPHRAIMITES

God hath delivered into your hands the princes of Midian, Oreb and Zeeb: and what was I able to do in comparison of you? Then their anger was abated toward him, when he had said that. Judges 8:3.

Gideon returned from pursuing the enemies of the nation, to meet censure and accusation from his own countrymen. When at his call the men of Israel had rallied against the Midianites, the tribe of Ephraim had remained behind. They looked upon the effort as a perilous undertaking; and as Gideon sent them no special summons, they availed themselves of this excuse not to join their brethren. But when the news of Israel's triumph reached them, the Ephraimites were envious because they had not shared it.

After the rout of the Midianites, the men of Ephraim had, by Gideon's direction, seized the fords of the Jordan, thus preventing the escape of the fugitives. By this means a large number of the enemy were slain, among whom were two princes, Oreb and Zeeb. Thus the men of Ephraim followed up the battle, and helped complete the victory. Nevertheless, they were jealous and angry, as though Gideon had been led by his own will and judgment. They did not discern God's hand in the triumph of Israel, they did not appreciate His power and mercy in their deliverance. . . .

Returning with the trophies of victory, they angrily reproached Gideon: "Why hast thou served us thus, that thou calledst us not, when thou wentest to fight with the Midianites?"

"What have I done now, in comparison of you?" said Gideon. "Is not the *gleaning* of the grapes of Ephraim better than the *vintage* of Abiezer? *God* hath delivered into your hands the princes of Midian, Oreb and Zeeb: and what was I able to do in comparison of you?"

The spirit of jealousy might easily have been fanned into a quarrel that would have caused strife and bloodshed; but Gideon's modest answer soothed the anger of the men of Ephraim, and they returned in peace to their homes. Firm and uncompromising where principle was concerned, and in war a "mighty man of valour," Gideon displayed also a spirit of courtesy that is rarely witnessed.

The people of Israel, in their gratitude at deliverance from the Midianites, proposed to Gideon that he should become their king, and that the throne should be confirmed to his descendants. This proposition was in direct violation of the principles of the theocracy. God was the king of Israel, and for them to place a man upon the throne would be a rejection of their Divine Sovereign. Gideon recognized this fact; his answer shows how true and noble were his motives. "I will not rule over you," he declared; "neither shall my son rule over you: the Lord shall rule over you."—*Patriarchs and Prophets,* pp. 554, 555.

ABIGAIL REVEALS UNSELFISHNESS AND WISDOM

When Abigail saw David, she hasted, and . . . fell before David on her face, and bowed herself to the ground, and fell at his feet, and said, Upon me, my lord, upon me let this iniquity be. 1 Sam. 25:23, 24.

David and his men . . . protected from the . . . marauders the flocks and herds of a very wealthy man named Nabal, who had vast possessions in Carmel. Nabal was a decendant of Caleb, but his character was churlish and niggardly.

David and his men were in sore need of provisions while at this place, and when the son of Jesse heard that Nabal was shearing his sheep he sent out ten young men, "and David said unto the young men, Get you up to Carmel, and go to Nabal, and greet him in my name." . . .

David and his men had been like a wall of protection to the shepherds and flocks of Nabal as they pastured in the mountains. And he courteously petitioned that supplies be given them in their great need from the abundance of this rich man. . . . "And Nabal answered David's servants, and said, Who is David? and who is the son of Jesse? . . . Shall I then take my bread, and my water, and my flesh that I have killed for my shearers, and give it unto men, whom I know not whence they be?"

When the young men returned empty-handed, disappointed, and disgusted, and related the affair to David, he was filled with indignation. . . . David commanded his men to gird on their swords, and equip themselves for an encounter. . . .

One of the servants of Nabal hastened to Abigail, the wife of Nabal, . . . and told her what had happened. . . .

Without consulting her husband, or telling him of her intention, Abigail made up an ample supply of provisions, and started out to meet the army of David. She met them in a covert of a hill. "And when Abigail saw David, she hasted, and . . . fell before David on her face, and bowed herself to the ground, and fell at his feet, and said, Upon me, my lord, upon me let this iniquity be: and let thine handmaid, I pray thee, speak in thine audience." Abigail addressed David with as much reverence as though speaking to a crowned monarch. . . . With kind words she sought to soothe his irritated feelings. . . . With utter unselfishness of spirit, she desired him to impute the whole blame of the matter to her, and not to charge it to her poor, deluded husband. . . .

What a spirit is this! With nothing of ostentation or pride, but full of the wisdom and love of God, Abigail revealed the strength of her devotion to her household. Whatever was her husband's disposition, he was her husband still, and she made it plain to the indignant captain that the unkind course of her husband was in nowise premeditated against him as a personal affront.—*Signs of the Times,* Oct. 26, 1888.

ABIGAIL'S INFLUENCE PREVENTS TRAGEDY

And David said to Abigail, Blessed be the Lord God of Israel, which sent thee this day to meet me: and blessed be thy advice, and blessed be thou, which hast kept me this day from coming to shed blood. 1 Sam. 25:32, 33.

The piety of Abigail, like the fragrance of a flower, breathed out all unconsciously in face and word and action. The Spirit of the Son of God was abiding in her soul. Her heart was full of purity, and gentleness, and sanctified love. Her speech, seasoned with grace, and full of kindness and peace, shed a heavenly influence. Better impulses came to David, and he trembled as he thought what might have been the consequences of his rash purpose. An entire household would have been slain, containing more than one precious, God-fearing person like Abigail, who had engaged in the blessed ministry of good. Her words healed the sore and bruised heart of David.

Would that there were more women who would soothe the irritated feelings, prevent rash impulses, and quell great evils by words of calm and well-directed wisdom. "Blessed are the peacemakers: for they shall be called the children of God."

A consecrated Christian life is ever shedding light and comfort and peace. It is purity, tact, simplicity, and usefulness. It is controlled by that unselfish love that sanctifies the influence. It is full of Christ, and leaves a track of light wherever its possessor may go. Abigail was a wise reprover and counselor. David's passion died away under the power of her influence and reasoning. He was convinced that he had taken an unwise course, and had lost control of his own spirit. He received the rebuke with humility of heart. . . . He gave thanks and blessing because she advised him righteously.

There are many who, when they are reproved or advised, think it praiseworthy if they receive the rebuke without becoming impatient. But how few take reproof with gratitude of heart, and bless those who seek to save them from pursuing an evil course.

Abigail rejoiced that her mission had been successful, and that she had been instrumental in saving her household from death. David rejoiced that through her timely advice he had been prevented from committing deeds of violence and revenge. Upon reflection, he realized that it would have been a matter of disgrace to him before Israel, and a remembrance that would always have caused him the keenest remorse. He felt that he and his men had the greatest cause for gratitude. . . .

When David heard the tidings of the death of Nabal, he gave thanks that God had taken vengeance into His own hands.—*Signs of the Times,* Oct. 26, 1888.

DAVID LEARNS THROUGH HARDSHIP

And David reigned over all Israel; and David executed judgment and justice unto all his people. 2 Sam. 8:15.

A few miles south of Jerusalem, "the city of the great King," is Bethlehem, where David, the son of Jesse, was born more than a thousand years before the infant Jesus was cradled in the manger and worshiped by the Wise Men from the East. Centuries before the advent of the Saviour, David, in the freshness of boyhood, kept watch of his flocks as they grazed on the hills surrounding Bethlehem. The simple shepherd boy sang the songs of his own composing, and the music of his harp made a sweet accompaniment to the melody of his fresh young voice. The Lord had chosen David, and was preparing him, in his solitary life with his flocks, for the work He designed to commit to his trust in afteryears. —*Patriarchs and Prophets,* p. 637.

David in his youth was intimately associated with Saul, and his stay at court and his connection with the king's household gave him an insight into the cares and sorrows and perplexities concealed by the glitter and pomp of royalty. He saw of how little worth is human glory to bring peace to the soul. And it was with relief and gladness that he returned from the king's court to the sheepfolds and the flocks.

When by the jealousy of Saul driven a fugitive into the wilderness, David, cut off from human support, leaned more heavily upon God. The uncertainty and unrest of the wilderness life, its unceasing peril, its necessity for frequent flight, the character of the men who gathered to him there—"every one that was in distress, and every one that was in debt, and everyone that was discontented" (1 Sam. 22:2)—all rendered the more essential a stern self-discipline.

These experiences aroused and developed power to deal with men, sympathy for the oppressed, and hatred of injustice. Through years of waiting and peril, David learned to find in God his comfort, his support, his life. He learned that only by God's power could he come to the throne; only in His wisdom could he rule wisely. It was through the training in the school of hardship and sorrow that David was able to make the record—though afterward marred with his great sin—that he "executed judgment and justice unto all his people."—*Education,* p. 152.

The love that moved him, the sorrows that beset him, the triumphs that attended him, were all themes for his active thought; and as he beheld the love of God in all the providences of his life, his heart throbbed with more fervent adoration and gratitude, his voice rang out in a richer melody, his harp was swept with more exultant joy; and the shepherd boy proceeded from strength to strength, from knowledge to knowledge; for the Spirit of the Lord was upon him.—*Patriarchs and Prophets,* p. 642.

SOLOMON LEARNS FROM SUFFERING

O Lord my God, thou hast made thy servant king instead of David my father: and I am but a little child: I know not how to go out or come in. . . . Give therefore thy servant an understanding heart to judge thy people, that I may discern between good and bad. 1 Kings 3:7-9.

The discipline of David's early experience was lacking in that of Solomon. In circumstances, in character, and in life, he seemed favored above all others. Noble in youth, noble in manhood, the beloved of his God, Solomon entered on a reign that gave high promise of prosperity and honor. Nations marveled at the knowledge and insight of the man to whom God had given wisdom. But the pride of prosperity brought separation from God. From the joy of divine communion Solomon turned to find satisfaction in the pleasures of sense. Of this experience he says:

"I made me great works; I builded me houses; I planted me vineyards: I made me gardens and orchards . . . : I got me servants and maidens . . . : I gathered me also silver and gold, and the peculiar treasures of kings and of the provinces: I gat me men singers and women singers, and the delights of the sons of men, as musical instruments, and that of all sorts. So I was great, and increased more than all that were before me in Jerusalem. . . . And whatsoever mine eyes desired I kept not from them, I withheld not my heart from any joy; for my heart rejoiced in all my labour. . . .

"Then I looked on all the works that my hands had wrought, and on the labour that I had laboured to do: and, behold, all was vanity and vexation of spirit, and there was no profit under the sun. And I turned myself to behold wisdom, and madness, and folly: for what can the man do that cometh after the king? even that which hath been already done" (Eccl. 2:4-12).

"I hated life. . . . Yea, I hated all my labour which I had taken under the sun" (verses 17, 18).

By his own bitter experience, Solomon learned the emptiness of a life that seeks in earthly things its highest good. . . .

In his later years, turning wearied and thirsting from earth's broken cisterns, Solomon returned to drink at the fountain of life. The history of his wasted years, with their lessons of warning, he by the Spirit of inspiration recorded for after generations. And thus, although the seed of his sowing was repeated by his people in harvests of evil, the lifework of Solomon was not wholly lost. For him at last the discipline of suffering accomplished its work.

But with such a dawning, how glorious might have been his life's day, had Solomon in his youth learned the lesson that suffering had taught in other lives!—*Education,* pp. 152-154.

ELISHA DEMONSTRATES STEADFASTNESS

And Elijah said unto him [Elisha], Tarry, I pray thee, here; for the Lord hath sent me to Jordan. And he said, As the Lord liveth, and as thy soul liveth, I will not leave thee. 2 Kings 2:6.

The early years of the prophet Elisha were passed in the quietude of country life, under the teaching of God and nature and the discipline of useful work. In a time of almost universal apostasy his father's household were among the number who had not bowed the knee to Baal. Theirs was a home where God was honored and where faithfulness to duty was the rule of daily life.

The son of a wealthy farmer, Elisha had taken up the work that lay nearest. While possessing the capabilities of a leader among men, he received a training in life's common duties. In order to direct wisely, he must learn to obey. By faithfulness in little things, he was prepared for weightier trusts. Of a meek and gentle spirit, Elisha possessed also energy and steadfastness. He cherished the love and fear of God, and in the humble round of daily toil he gained strength of purpose and nobleness of character, growing in divine grace and knowledge. While cooperating with his father in the home duties, he was learning to cooperate with God.

The prophetic call came to Elisha while with his father's servants he was plowing in the field. As Elijah, divinely directed in seeking a successor, cast his mantle upon the young man's shoulders, Elisha recognized and obeyed the summons. He "went after Elijah, and ministered unto him" (1 Kings 19:21). It was no great work that was at first required of Elisha; commonplace duties still constituted his discipline. He is spoken of as pouring water on the hands of Elijah, his master. As the prophet's personal attendant, he continued to prove faithful in little things, while with daily strengthening purpose he devoted himself to the mission appointed him by God. . . .

As he turned to follow Elijah he was bidden by the prophet to return home. He must count the cost—decide for himself to accept or reject the call. But Elisha understood the value of his opportunity. Not for any worldly advantage would he forgo the possibility of becoming God's messenger, or sacrifice the privilege of association with His servant.

As time passed, and Elijah prepared for translation, so Elisha was prepared to become his successor. And again his faith and resolution were tested. Accompanying Elijah in his round of service, . . . he was at each place invited by the prophet to turn back. . . . As often as the invitation to turn back was given, his answer was, "As the Lord liveth, and as thy soul liveth, I will not leave thee" (2 Kings 2:2). . . . For this work Elisha's early training under God's direction had prepared him.—*Education,* pp. 58-61.

CAPTIVE MAID SHOWS CONCERN FOR NAAMAN

The Syrians . . . had brought away captive out of the land of Israel a little maid; and she waited on Naaman's wife. And she said unto her mistress, Would God my lord were with the prophet that is in Samaria! for he would recover him of his leprosy. 2 Kings 5:2, 3.

"Naaman, captain of the host of the king of Syria, was . . . a mighty man in valour, but he was a leper."

Ben-hadad, king of Syria, had defeated the armies of Israel. . . . Since that time the Syrians had maintained against Israel a constant border warfare, and in one of their raids they had carried away a little maid who, in the land of her captivity, "waited on Naaman's wife." A slave, far from her home, this little maid was nevertheless one of God's witnesses, unconsciously fulfilling the purpose for which God had chosen Israel as His people.

As she ministered in that heathen home, her sympathies were aroused in behalf of her master; and, remembering the wonderful miracles of healing wrought through Elisha, she said to her mistress, "Would God my lord were with the prophet that is in Samaria! for he would recover him of his leprosy." She knew that the power of Heaven was with Elisha, and she believed that by this power Naaman could be healed.

The conduct of the captive maid, the way that she bore herself in that heathen home, is a strong witness to the power of early home training. There is no higher trust than that committed to fathers and mothers in the care and training of their children. Parents have to do with the very foundations of habit and character. By their example and teaching the future of their children is largely decided.

Happy are the parents whose lives are a true reflection of the divine, so that the promises and commands of God awaken in the child gratitude and reverence; the parents whose tenderness and justice and long-suffering interpret to the child the love and justice and long-suffering of God, and who by teaching the child to love and trust and obey them, are teaching him to love and trust and obey his Father in heaven. Parents who impart to the child such a gift have endowed him with a treasure more precious than the wealth of all the ages, a treasure as enduring as eternity. . . .

The parents of that Hebrew maid, as they taught her of God, did not know the destiny that would be hers. But they were faithful to their trust; and in the home of the captain of the Syrian host, their child bore witness to the God whom she had learned to honor.

Naaman heard of the words that the maid had spoken to her mistress; and, obtaining permission from the king, he went forth to seek healing. —*Prophets and Kings,* pp. 244-246.

ISAIAH RESPONDS TO GOD'S CALL

I heard the voice of the Lord, saying, Whom shall I send, and who will go for us? Then said I, Here am I; send me. Isa. 6:8.

In the year that King Uzziah died, Isaiah was permitted in vision to look into the holy place, and into the holy of holies in the heavenly sanctuary. The curtains of the innermost sanctuary were drawn aside, and a throne high and lifted up, towering as it were to the very heavens, was revealed to his gaze. An indescribable glory emanated from a personage on the throne, and His train filled the temple, as His glory will finally fill the earth. Cherubim were on either side of the mercy seat, . . . and they glowed with the glory that enshrouded them from the presence of God. . . . These holy beings sang forth the praise and glory of God with lips unpolluted with sin.

The contrast between the feeble praise which he had been accustomed to bestow upon the Creator and the fervid praises of seraphim astonished and humiliated the prophet. He had, for the time being, the sublime privilege of appreciating the spotless purity of Jehovah's exalted character. . . . In the light of this matchless radiance, that made manifest all he could bear in the revelation of the divine character, his own inward defilement stood out before him with startling clearness. His very words seemed vile to him.

Thus when the servant of God is permitted to behold the glory of the God of heaven, as He is unveiled to humanity, and realizes to a slight degree the purity of the Holy One of Israel, he will make startling confessions of the pollution of his soul, rather than proud boasts of his holiness. In deep humiliation Isaiah exclaimed, ''Woe is me! for I am undone; because I am a man of unclean lips.'' . . .

This is not that voluntary humility and servile self-reproach that so many seem to consider it a virtue to display. This vague mockery of humility is prompted by hearts full of pride and self-esteem. There are many who demerit themselves in words, who would be disappointed if this course did not call forth expressions of praise and appreciation from others. But the conviction of the prophet was genuine. . . . How could he go and speak to the people the holy requirements of Jehovah? . . .

While Isaiah was trembling and conscience-smitten, because of his impurity in the presence of this unsurpassed glory, he says, ''Then flew one of the seraphims unto me, having a live coal in his hand, which he had taken with the tongs from off the altar: and he laid it upon my mouth, and said, Lo, this hath touched thy lips; and thine iniquity is taken away, and thy sin purged. Also I heard the voice of the Lord, saying, Whom shall I send, and who will go for us? Then said I, Here am I; send me.''—*Review and Herald,* Oct. 16, 1888.

JOHN CALLS FOR REPENTANCE

Repent ye: for the kingdom of heaven is at hand. Matt. 3:2.

John the Baptist in his desert life was taught of God. He studied the revelations of God in nature. Under the guiding of the Divine Spirit, he studied the scrolls of the prophets. By day and by night, Christ was his study, his meditation, until mind and heart and soul were filled with the glorious vision.

He looked upon the King in His beauty, and self was lost sight of. He beheld the majesty of holiness and knew himself to be inefficient and unworthy. It was God's message that he was to declare. It was in God's power and His righteousness that he was to stand. He was ready to go forth as Heaven's messenger, unawed by the human, because he had looked upon the Divine. He could stand fearless in the presence of earthly monarchs because he had bowed before the King of kings.

With no elaborate arguments or finespun theories did John declare his message. Startling and stern, yet full of hope, his voice was heard from the wilderness: "Repent ye: for the kingdom of heaven is at hand." With a new, strange power it moved the people. The whole nation was stirred. Multitudes flocked to the wilderness.

Unlearned peasants and fishermen from the surrounding country; the Roman soldiers from the barracks of Herod; chieftains with their swords at their sides, ready to put down anything that might savor of rebellion; the avaricious tax gatherers from their toll booths; and from the Sanhedrin the phylacteried priests—all listened as if spellbound; and all, even the Pharisee, and the Sadducee, the cold, unimpressible scoffer, went away with the sneer silenced and cut to the heart with a sense of their sins. Herod in his palace heard the message, and the proud, sin-hardened ruler trembled at the call to repentance.

In this age, just prior to the second coming of Christ in the clouds of heaven, such a work as that of John is to be done. God calls for men who will prepare a people to stand in the great day of the Lord. . . . As a people . . . we have a message to bear—"Prepare to meet thy God" (Amos 4:12). Our message must be as direct as was the message of John. He rebuked kings for their iniquity. Notwithstanding that his life was imperiled, he did not hesitate to declare God's Word. And our work in this age must be done as faithfully.

In order to give such a message as John gave, we must have a spiritual experience like his. The same work must be wrought in us. We must behold God, and in beholding Him lose sight of self. John had by nature the faults and weaknesses common to humanity; but the touch of divine love had transformed him.—*Testimonies,* vol. 8, pp. 331-333.

JESUS SHOWED US HOW TO LIVE

I received mercy for this reason, that in me, . . . Jesus Christ might display his perfect patience for an example to those who were to believe in him for eternal life. 1 Tim. 1:16, R.S.V.

He [Jesus] was a teacher, such an educator as the world never saw or heard before. He spake as one having authority, and yet He invites the confidence of all. "Come unto me, all ye that labour and are heavy laden, and I will give you rest. Take my yoke upon you, and learn of me; for I am meek and lowly in heart: and ye shall find rest unto your souls. For my yoke is easy, and my burden is light" (Matt. 11:28-30).

The only-begotten Son of the infinite God has, by His words, His practical example, left us a plain pattern which we are to copy. By His words He has educated us to obey God, and by His own practice He has showed us how we can obey God. This is the very work He wants every man to do, to obey God intelligently, by precept and example teach others what they must do in order to be obedient children of God.

Jesus has helped the whole world to an intelligent knowledge of His divine mission and work. He came to represent the character of the Father to our world, and as we study the life, the words, and works of Jesus Christ, we are helped in every way in the education of obedience to God; and as we copy the example He has given us, we are living epistles known and read of all men. We are the living human agencies to represent in character Jesus Christ to the world.

Not only did Christ give explicit rules showing how we may become obedient children, but He showed us in His own life and character just how to do those things which are right and acceptable with God, so there is no excuse why we should not do those things which are pleasing in His sight. . . .

The great Teacher came to our world to stand at the head of humanity, to thus elevate and sanctify humanity by His holy obedience to all of God's requirements, showing it is possible to obey all the commandments of God. He has demonstrated that a lifelong obedience is possible. Thus He gives chosen, representative men to the world, as the Father gave the Son, to exemplify in their life the life of Jesus Christ.—Manuscript 1, 1892.

In Him was found the perfect ideal. To reveal this ideal as the only true standard for attainment; to show what every human being might become; what, through the indwelling of humanity by divinity, all who received Him would become—for this, Christ came to the world. He came to show how men are to be trained as befits the sons of God; how on earth they are to practice the principles and to live the life of heaven.—*Education,* pp. 73, 74.

THE ENORMOUS HARVEST OF
A SINGLE ACT

And there came a certain poor widow, and she threw in two mites. . . . And he called unto him his disciples, and saith unto them, Verily I say unto you, . . . they did cast in of their abundance; but she of her want did cast in all that she had, even all her living. Mark 12:42-44.

By the laws of God in nature, effect follows cause with unvarying certainty. The reaping testifies to the sowing. Here no pretense is tolerated. Men may deceive their fellow men, and may receive praise and compensation for service which they have not rendered. But in nature there can be no deception. On the unfaithful husbandman the harvest passes sentence of condemnation.

And in the highest sense this is true also in the spiritual realm. It is in appearance, not in reality, that evil succeeds. The child who plays truant from school, the youth who is slothful in his studies, the clerk or apprentice who fails of serving the interests of his employer, the man in any business or profession who is untrue to his highest responsibilities, may flatter himself that, so long as the wrong is concealed, he is gaining an advantage. But not so; he is cheating himself. The harvest of life is character, and it is this that determines destiny, both for this life and for the life to come.

The harvest is a reproduction of the seed sown. Every seed yields fruits after its kind. So it is with the traits of character we cherish. Selfishness, self-love, self-esteem, self-indulgence, reproduce themselves, and the end is wretchedness and ruin. . . . Love, sympathy, and kindness yield fruitage of blessing, a harvest that is imperishable.

In the harvest the seed is multiplied. A single grain of wheat, increased by repeated sowings, would cover a whole land with golden sheaves. So widespread may be the influence of a single life, of even a single act.

What deeds of love the memory of that alabaster box broken for Christ's anointing has through the long centuries prompted! What countless gifts that contribution, by a poor unnamed widow, of "two mites, which makes a farthing" (Mark 12:42), has brought to the Saviour's cause! . . .

"He which soweth bountifully shall reap also bountifully.". . . By casting it away the sower multiplies his seed. So by imparting we increase our blessings. God's promise assures a sufficiency, that we may continue to give.

More than this: as we impart the blessings of this life, gratitude in the recipient prepares the heart to receive spiritual truth, and a harvest is produced unto life everlasting.—*Education,* pp. 108-110.

THOUGH SUFFERING, PAUL AND SILAS SING

At midnight Paul and Silas prayed, and sang praises unto God: and the prisoners heard them. And suddenly there was a great earthquake, so that the foundations of the prison were shaken: and immediately all the doors were opened, and every one's bands were loosed. Acts 16:25, 26.

As the messengers of the cross went about their work of teaching, a woman possessed of a spirit of divination followed them, crying, "These men are the servants of the most high God, which shew unto us the way of salvation. And this did she many days." . . .

Under the inspiration of the Holy Ghost Paul commanded the evil spirit to leave the woman. . . . Restored to her right mind, the woman chose to become a follower of Christ. Then her masters were alarmed for their craft. They saw that all hope of receiving money from her divinations and soothsayings was at an end and that their source of income would soon be entirely cut off. . . .

Stirred by a frenzy of excitement, the multitude rose against the disciples. A mob spirit prevailed and was sanctioned by the authorities, who tore the outer garments from the apostles and commanded that they should be scourged. "And when they had laid many stripes upon them, they cast them into prison, charging the jailor to keep them safely." . . .

With astonishment the other prisoners heard the sound of prayer and singing issuing from the inner prison. They had been accustomed to hear shrieks and moans, cursing and swearing, breaking the silence of the night. . . .

But while men were cruel and vindictive, or criminally negligent of the solemn responsibilities devolving upon them, God had not forgotten to be gracious to His servants. All heaven was interested in the men who were suffering for Christ's sake, and angels were sent to visit the prison. At their tread the earth trembled. The heavily bolted prison doors were thrown open; the chains and fetters fell from the hands and feet of the prisoners; and a bright light flooded the prison. . . . The jailer had fallen into a sleep from which he was awakened by the earthquake and the shaking of the prison walls.

Starting up in alarm, he saw with dismay that all the prison doors were open, and the fear flashed upon him that the prisoners had escaped. . . . Drawing his sword, he was about to kill himself, when Paul's voice was heard in the words of cheer, "Do thyself no harm: for we are all here." Every man was in his place, restrained by the power of God exerted through one fellow prisoner. . . .

The jailer dropped his sword. . . . Then, bringing them out into the open court, he inquired, "Sirs, what must I do to be saved?"—*The Acts of the Apostles,* pp. 212-216.

LYDIA'S HOSPITALITY

A certain woman named Lydia, a seller of purple, . . . heard us. . . . And when she was baptized, and her household, she besought us, saying, If ye have judged me to be faithful to the Lord, come into my house, and abide there. And she constrained us. Acts 16:14, 15.

"On the Sabbath," Luke [declared], "we went out of the city by a river side, where prayer was wont to be made; and we sat down, and spake unto the women which resorted thither. And a certain woman named Lydia, a seller of purple, of the city of Thyatira, which worshipped God, heard us: whose heart the Lord opened." Lydia received the truth gladly. She and her household were converted and baptized, and she entreated the apostles to make her house their home.—*The Acts of the Apostles,* p. 212.

God's Spirit can only enlighten the understanding of those who are willing to be enlightened. We read that God opened the ears of Lydia, so that she attended to the message spoken by Paul. To declare the whole counsel of God and all that was essential for Lydia to receive—this was the part Paul was to act in her conversion; and then the God of all grace exercised His power, leading the soul in the right way. God and the human agent cooperated, and the work was wholly successful.—*The SDA Bible Commentary,* vol. 6, p. 1062.

[The authorities] visited the prison, apologized to the apostles for their injustice and cruelty, and themselves conducted them out of the prison, and entreated them to depart out of the city. . . . The apostles would not urge their presence where it was not desired. They complied with the request of the magistrates, but did not hasten their departure. . . . They went rejoicing from the prison to the house of Lydia, where they met the new converts to the faith of Christ, and related all the wonderful dealings of God with them. They related their night's experience, and the conversion of the keeper of the prison, and of the prisoners.

The apostles viewed their labors in Philippi as not in vain. They there met much opposition and persecution; but the intervention of Providence in their behalf, the conversion of the jailer and all his house, more than atoned for the disgrace and suffering they had endured. The Philippians saw represented in the deportment and presence of mind of the apostles the spirit of the religion of Jesus Christ. . . .

The news of their unjust imprisonment and miraculous deliverance was noised about through all that region, and brought the apostles and their ministry before the notice of a large number who would not otherwise have been reached. Christianity was placed upon a high plane, and the converts to the faith were greatly strengthened.—*The Spirit of Prophecy,* vol. 3, pp. 385, 386.

PAUL WARNS AGAINST "TRADITION" AND "PHILOSOPHY"

Beware lest any man spoil you through philosophy and vain deceit, after the tradition of men, after the rudiments of the world, and not after Christ. Col. 2:8.

Surrounded by the practices and influences of heathenism, the Colossian believers were in danger of being drawn away from the simplicity of the gospel, and Paul, in warning them against this, pointed them to Christ as the only safe guide. . . . "As ye have therefore received Christ Jesus the Lord, so walk ye in him: rooted and built up in him, and stablished in the faith, as ye have been taught, abounding therein with thanksgiving." . . .

Christ had foretold that deceivers would arise, through whose influence "iniquity" should "abound," and "the love of many" should "wax cold" (Matt. 24:12). He had warned the disciples that the church would be in more danger from this evil than from the persecution of her enemies. Again and again Paul warned the believers against these false teachers. This peril, above all others, they must guard against; for by receiving false teachers, they would open the door to errors by which the enemy would dim the spiritual perceptions and shake the confidence of those newly come to the faith of the gospel.

Christ was the standard by which they were to test the doctrines presented. All that was not in harmony with His teachings they were to reject. Christ crucified for sin, Christ risen from the dead, Christ ascended on high—this was the science of salvation that they were to learn and teach.

The warnings of the Word of God regarding the perils surrounding the Christian church belong to us today. As in the days of the apostles men tried by tradition and philosophy to destroy faith in the Scriptures, so today, by the pleasing sentiments of higher criticism, evolution, spiritualism, theosophy, and pantheism, the enemy of righteousness is seeking to lead souls into forbidden paths. To many the Bible is as a lamp without oil, because they have turned their minds into channels of speculative belief that bring misunderstanding and confusion.

The work of higher criticism, in dissecting, conjecturing, reconstructing, is destroying faith in the Bible as a divine revelation. It is robbing God's Word of power to control, uplift, and inspire human lives. By spiritualism, multitudes are taught to believe that desire is the highest law, that license is liberty, and that man is accountable only to himself. . . . The power of a higher, purer, nobler life is our great need.—*The Acts of the Apostles,* pp. 473-478.

THE ESSENTIAL QUALIFICATION
FOR SERVICE

Jesus saith to Simon Peter, Simon, son of Jonas, lovest thou me more than these? He said unto him, Yea, Lord; thou knowest that I love thee. He saith unto him, Feed my lambs. John 21:15.

Little mention is made in the book of Acts of the later work of the apostle Peter. . . . As the number of believers multiplied in Jerusalem and in other places visited by the messengers of the cross, the talents possessed by Peter proved of untold value to the early Christian church. The influence of his testimony concerning Jesus of Nazareth extended far and wide. Upon him had been laid a double responsibility. He bore positive witness concerning the Messiah before unbelievers, laboring earnestly for their conversion; and at the same time he did a special work for believers, strengthening them in the faith of Christ.

It was after Peter had been led to self-renunciation and entire reliance upon divine power, that he received his call to act as an undershepherd. Christ had said to Peter, before his denial of Him, "When thou art converted, strengthen thy brethren" (Luke 22:32). These words were significant of the wide and effectual work which this apostle was to do in the future for those who should come to the faith.

For this work, Peter's own experience of sin and suffering and repentance had prepared him. Not until he had learned his weakness, could he know the believer's need of dependence on Christ. Amid the storm of temptation he had come to understand that man can walk safely only as in utter self-distrust he relies upon the Saviour. . . .

Christ mentioned to Peter only one condition of service—"Lovest thou me?" This is the essential qualification. . . . The love of Christ is not a fitful feeling, but a living principle, which is to be made manifest as an abiding power in the heart. . . .

The Saviour's manner of dealing with Peter had a lesson for him and his brethren. Although Peter had denied his Lord, the love which Jesus bore him had never faltered. And as the apostle should take up the work of ministering the Word to others, he was to meet the transgressor with patience, sympathy, and forgiving love. Remembering his own weakness and failure, he was to deal with the sheep and lambs committed to his care as tenderly as Christ had dealt with him. . . .

Ever he exalted Jesus of Nazareth as the Hope of Israel, the Saviour of mankind. He brought his own life under the discipline of the Master Worker. By every means within his power he sought to educate the believers for active service.—*The Acts of the Apostles, pp. 514-516.*

THOSE WHO RETURN TO THE OLD PATHS

And the ransomed of the Lord shall return, and come to Zion with songs and everlasting joy upon their heads: they shall obtain joy and gladness, and sorrow and sighing shall flee away. Isa. 35:10.

The world is full of men and women who manifest no sense of obligation to God for their entrusted gifts. They do not realize that God has entrusted them with talents, not for self-glorification, but for His own name's glory. They are eager for distinction. . . .

There are men whom God has qualified with more than ordinary ability. They are deep thinkers, energetic, and thorough. But many of them are bent upon the attainment of their own selfish ends, without regard to the honor and glory of God. Some of these have seen the light of truth, but because they honored themselves, and did not make God first and last and best in everything, they have wandered away from Bible truth into skepticism and infidelity. When these are arrested by the chastisements of God, and through affliction are led to inquire for the old paths, the mist of skepticism is swept from their minds. Some of them repent, return to the old love, and set their feet in the way cast up for the ransomed of the Lord to walk in. No longer are they actuated by the love of money or by selfish ambition. The Spirit of God working upon the heart is valued by them more highly than gold or the praise of men. When this amazing change is wrought, the thoughts are directed by the Spirit of God into new channels, the character is transformed, and the aspirations of the soul reach out toward heavenly things.

True religion has power today. It enables men to overcome the stubborn influence of pride, selfishness, and unbelief, and in the simplicity of true godliness to reveal a living connection with heaven. The grace which Christ imparts makes it possible for men to rise superior to all the infatuating temptations of Satan. It will lead them to the cross of Jesus as active, devoted, loyal workers for the advancement of the truth of heaven.

Fidelity to God has marked the heroes of faith from age to age. As they have been brought conspicuously before the world their light has shone forth. Their obedience to the command of Christ, ''Go forward,'' has led others to glorify God.

There are today moral heroes, men and women who are living noble lives of self-denial. They have no ambition for worldly fame. Their will is subordinate to the will of God. The love of God inspires their ministry. To do good and to save souls is their highest aim.

These have gained genuine knowledge, even the knowledge set forth by Christ in the words, ''This is life eternal, that they might know thee the only true God, and Jesus Christ, whom thou hast sent'' (John 17:3).— Manuscript 51, 1900.

REVEALING THE TRIUMPHS OF GRACE

Ye are my witnesses, saith the Lord, that I am God. Isa. 43:12.

The faithful ambassador of Christ is not ashamed of the banner of truth. He does not cease from proclaiming the truth, however unpopular it may be. In all places, in season, out of season, he heralds the glad tidings of salvation. Missionaries for God are called to face dangers, endure privations, and suffer reproach for the truth's sake, yet amid dangers, hardships, and reproach they are still to hold the banner aloft.

The third angel proclaims his message in no whispered tones, in no hesitant manner. He cries with a loud voice, while flying swiftly through the midst of heaven. This shows that the work of God's servants is to be earnest and rapidly performed. They must be brave witnesses for the truth. With no shame upon their countenances, with uplifted heads, with the bright beams of the Sun of Righteousness shining upon them, with rejoicing that their redemption draweth nigh, they go forth declaring the last message of mercy to the world.

These last-day witnesses are bold soldiers of Jesus Christ. They have tasted of the powers of the world to come. Their feet are not on sliding sand, but on solid rock. They are not easily moved away from the faith once delivered to the saints. These will be strengthened by their leader to cope with difficulties. They are messengers of righteousness, representatives of Christ, revealing the triumphs of grace.

From these chosen men of God the truth will shine forth. It will be heard from their lips, reflected in their countenances, and demonstrated in their lives. They will be marked by purity and uncorruptness. The grace of Christ has a refining, ennobling influence on the character. Many men and women of ability, refinement, and education will throw their all on the Lord's side. Many will part with friends and will sacrifice every worldly interest in order to proclaim the unsearchable riches of Christ. Their lives give evidence to the world of the power of Christianity. They witness that the gospel is what it purports to be, the power of God unto salvation. Bright beams of gospel truth are flashed from them upon the path of those who are in darkness. Their unswerving fidelity is registered in the books of heaven.—Manuscript 51, 1900.

Those who walk even as Christ walked, who are patient, gentle, kind, meek, and lowly in heart, those who yoke up with Christ and lift His burdens, who yearn for souls as He yearned for them—these will enter into the joy of their Lord. They will see with Christ the travail of His soul, and be satisfied. Heaven will triumph, for the vacancies made in heaven by the fall of Satan and his angels will be filled by the redeemed of the Lord.—*Review and Herald,* May 29, 1900.

GOD'S PEOPLE TO REVEAL PRINCIPLES

As thou hast sent me into the world, even so have I also sent them into the world. John 17:18.

It is God's purpose to manifest through His people the principles of His kingdom. That in life and character they may reveal these principles, He desires to separate them from the customs, habits, and practices of the world. He seeks to bring them nearer to Himself, that He may make known to them His will.

His purpose for His people today is the same that He had for Israel when He brought them forth from Egypt. By beholding the goodness, the mercy, the justice, and the love of God revealed in His church, the world is to have a representation of His character. And when the law of God is thus exemplified in the life, even the world will recognize the superiority of those who love and fear and serve God above every other people in the world.

Seventh-day Adventists, above all people, should be patterns of piety, holy in heart and in conversation. To them have been entrusted the most solemn truths ever committed to mortals. Every endowment of grace and power and efficiency has been liberally provided. They look for the near return of Christ in the clouds of heaven. For them to give to the world the impression that their faith is not a dominating power in their lives, is greatly to dishonor God.

Because of the increasing power of Satan's temptations, the times in which we live are full of peril for the children of God, and we need to learn constantly of the Great Teacher, that we may take every step in surety and righteousness. Wonderful scenes are opening before us; and at this time a living testimony is to be borne in the lives of God's professed people, so that the world may see that in this age, when evil reigns on every side, there is yet a people who are laying aside their will and are seeking to do God's will—a people in whose hearts and lives God's law is written.

God expects those who bear the name of Christ to represent Him. Their thoughts are to be pure, their words noble and uplifting. The religion of Christ is to be interwoven with all that they do and say. They are to be a sanctified, purified, holy people, communicating light to all with whom they come in contact. It is His purpose that by exemplifying the truth in their lives, they shall be a praise in the earth.

The grace of Christ is sufficient to bring this about. But let God's people remember that only as they believe and work out the principles of the gospel can they fulfill His purpose. Only as they yield their God-given capabilities to His service will they enjoy the fullness and the power of the promise whereon the church has been called to stand.—*Counsels to Parents and Teachers,* pp. 321, 322.

GOD LEADS US TO PERFECT TRUST

He shall sit as a refiner and purifier of silver: and he shall purify the sons of Levi, and purge them as gold and silver, that they may offer unto the Lord an offering in righteousness. Mal. 3:3.

The refining process is hard for human nature to endure; but only by it can the dross be purged from the character. In the furnace of trial we are purified from the dross that prevents us from reflecting the image of Christ. God measures every trial; He watches the furnace fire that must test every soul.

Through trial God leads His children to perfect trust. "In the world ye shall have tribulation," Christ says; "but in Me ye shall have peace." It is through much tribulation, that we are to enter the kingdom of God. . . .

No cross, no crown. How can we be strong in the Lord without trial? To have physical strength, we must have exercise. To have strong faith, we must be placed in circumstances where our faith will be tried. Every temptation resisted, every trial bravely borne, gives us a new experience, and advances us in the work of character building. Our Saviour was tried in every way, yet He triumphed in God constantly. It is our privilege under all circumstances to be strong in the strength of God, and to glory in the cross of Christ.

Through affliction God reveals to us the plague spots in our characters, that by His grace we may overcome our faults. Unknown chapters in regard to ourselves are opened to us, and the test comes, whether we will accept the reproof and the counsel of God. When brought into trial, we are not to fret and worry. We should not rebel, or worry ourselves out of the hand of Christ. We are to humble the soul before God.

The ways of the Lord are obscure to him who desires to see things in a light pleasing to himself. They appear dark and joyless to our human nature. But God's ways are ways of mercy and the end is salvation.

Elijah knew not what he was doing when in the desert he said that he had had enough of life, and prayed that he might die. The Lord in His mercy did not take him at His word. There was yet a great work for Elijah to do; and when his work was done, he was not to perish in discouragement and solitude in the wilderness. Not for him the descent into the dust of earth, but the ascent in glory, with the convoy of celestial chariots to the throne on high. . . .

"Happy is the man whom God correcteth. . . . He maketh sore, and bindeth up; he woundeth, and his hands make whole." . . . To every stricken one, Jesus comes with the ministry of healing. The life of bereavement, pain, and suffering may be brightened by precious revealings of His presence.—*Signs of the Times,* Feb. 5, 1902.

WE REJOICE IN TRIBULATION

For we have not an high priest which cannot be touched with the feelings of our infirmities; but was in all points tempted like as we are, yet without sin. Heb. 4:15.

Praise the Lord, that we have a compassionate, tender High Priest that can be touched with the feelings of our infirmities. We do not expect rest here. No, no. The way to heaven is a cross-bearing way; the road is straight and narrow, but we will go forward with cheerfulness knowing that the King of glory once trod this way before us.

We will not complain of the roughness of the way, but will be meek followers of Jesus, treading in His footsteps. He was a man of sorrows and acquainted with grief. He for our sakes became poor that we through His poverty might be made rich. We will rejoice in tribulation and keep in mind the recompense of reward, the "far more exceeding and eternal weight of glory."

We will not have a murmuring thought because we have trials. God's dear children always had them, and every trial well endured here, will only make us rich in glory. I crave the suffering part. I would not go to heaven without suffering if I could, and see Jesus who suffered so much for us to purchase for us so rich an inheritance; and to see the martyrs who laid down their lives for the truth, and the sake of Jesus. No, no. Let me [be] perfected through sufferings. I long to be a partaker with Christ of His sufferings, for if I am, I know I shall be a partaker with Him of His glory. Jesus is our pattern. Let us study to have our lives as near like Christ's as possible.

My soul cries out after the living God. My very being longs after Him. Oh, for to reflect His lovely image perfectly! Oh, for to be wholly consecrated to Him! Oh, how hard it is for dear self to die. We can rejoice in a whole Saviour; one who saves us from all sin. We can be shut in with God where we can daily say, "I live; yet not I, but Christ liveth in me" "to will and to do of his good pleasure." Glory be to God. I know that my life is hid with Christ in God.

The curtain has been lifted. I have seen the rich reward laid up for the saints. I have had a taste of the joys of the world to come, and it has spoiled this world for me. My affections, my interests, hopes, my *all* is in heaven. I long to see the King in His beauty, Him whom my soul loveth. Heaven, sweet heaven. "I long to be there; and the thought that 'tis near, makes me almost impatient for Christ to appear." Praise the Lord for a good hope through Jesus Christ of immortality and eternal life.—Letter 9, 1851.

GOD HAS A TENDER CARE FOR HIS PEOPLE

The eyes of the Lord are upon the righteous, and his ears are open unto their cry. Ps. 34:15.

You must not sink down discouraged. The fainthearted will be made strong; the desponding will be made to hope. God has a tender care for His people. His ear is open unto their cry. I have no fears for God's cause. He will take care of His own cause. Our duty is to fill our lot and place, live . . . humble at the foot of the cross, and live faithful, holy lives before Him. While we do this we shall not be ashamed, but our souls will confide in God with holy boldness.

God has released us from burdens; He has set us free. . . . Our enemies may triumph. They may speak lying words, and their slandering tongue frame slander, deceit, guile; yet will we not be moved. We know in whom we believe. We have not run in vain, neither labored in vain. Jesus knows us. . . . A reckoning day is coming and all will be judged according to the deeds that are done in the body. . . .

It is true the world is dark. Opposition may wax strong. The trifler and scorner may grow bolder and harder in their iniquity. Yet, for all this, we will not be moved. We have not run as uncertain. No, no. My heart is fixed, trusting in God. We have a whole Saviour. We can rejoice in His rich fullness. I long to be more devoted to God, more consecrated to Him. This world is too dark for me. Jesus said He would go away and prepare mansions for us, that where He is we may be also. Praise God for this. My heart leaps with joy at the cheering prospect.

Religion is made to dwell too much in an iron case. Pure religion and undefiled leads us to a childlike simplicity. We want to pray and talk with humility, having a single eye to the glory of God. There has been too much of a form of godliness without the power. The outpouring of the Spirit of God will lead to a grateful acknowledgment of the same; and while we feel and realize the wondrous love of God, we shall not hold our peace, we shall sacrifice to God with the voice of thanksgiving and make melody to Him with our hearts and voices. Let us plant our feet upon the Rock of Ages and then we will have abiding support and consolation. Our soul will repose in God with unshaken confidence.

Why do we so seldom visit the fountain when it is full and free? Our souls often need to drink at the fountain in order to be refreshed and flourish in the Lord. Salvation we must have. Without vital godliness our religion is vain. A form will be of no advantage to us. We must have the deep workings of the Spirit of God.—Letter 2a, 1856.

WE FIGHT LIFE'S BATTLES IN CHRIST'S STRENGTH

Take unto you the whole armour of God, that ye may be able to withstand in the evil day, and having done all, to stand. Eph. 6:13.

Let everyone who names the name of Christ read this scripture again and again, and then inquire, Am I clothed with the whole armor of God, that I may be a successful colaborer with Christ? The more we know of ourselves, the more we probe our motives and desires, the more heartfelt will be our consciousness of our utter inability to fight the battle of the Lord in our own strength. . . .

Stablish your hearts in the belief that God knows of all the trials and difficulties you will encounter in the warfare against evil; for God is dishonored when any soul belittles His power by talking unbelief.

This world is God's great field of labor; He has purchased those that dwell on it with the blood of His only-begotten Son, and He means that His message of mercy shall go to everyone. Those who are commissioned to do this work will be tested and tried, but they are always to remember that God is near to strengthen and uphold them. He does not ask us to depend upon any broken reed. We are not to look for human aid. God forbid that we should place man where God should be. . . . The Lord Jehovah is "everlasting strength."

A lesson of faith is given us in the experience of Christ with the disciples of John the Baptist. Imprisoned in the lonely dungeon, John had fallen into discouragement, and he sent his disciples to Jesus, asking, "Art thou he that should come, or do we look for another?" Christ knew on what errand these messengers had come, and by a mighty demonstration of His power He gave them unmistakable evidence of His divinity. Turning to the multitude, He spoke, and the deaf heard His voice. He spoke again, and the eyes of the blind were opened to behold the beauties of nature. . . . He put forth His hand, and at His touch the fever left the afflicted ones. At His command demoniacs were healed, and falling at His feet, worshiped Him. Then turning to the disciples of John, He said, "Go and shew John again those things which ye do hear and see."

That same Jesus who wrought those mighty works, is our Saviour today, and is as willing to manifest His power on our behalf as He was in the behalf of John the Baptist. When we are hedged about by adverse circumstances, surrounded by difficulties which it seems impossible for us to surmount, we are not to murmur, but to remember the past loving kindnesses of the Lord. Looking unto Jesus, the Author and Finisher of our faith, we may endure as seeing Him who is invisible, and this will keep our minds from being clouded by the shadow of unbelief.—*Signs of the Times,* Sept. 17, 1896.

GOD TESTS OUR LOYALTY TO HIM

And all the congregation of the children of Israel . . . pitched in Rephidim: and there was no water for the people to drink. Ex. 17:1.

By the command of God, the children of Israel were brought to Rephidim, a place destitute of water. He who was enshrouded in the pillar of cloud was leading them, and it was by His express command that they were encamped at this place. God knew of the lack of water at Rephidim, and He brought His people hither to test their faith; but how poorly they proved themselves to be a people whom He could trust!

Again and again He had manifested Himself to them. He had slain the firstborn of all the families in Egypt to accomplish their deliverance, and had brought them out of the land of their captivity with a high hand; He had fed them with angels' food, and had covenanted to bring them into the Promised Land. But now, when difficulty rose before them, they broke into rebellion, distrusted God, and complained that Moses had brought them and their children out of Egypt only that they might die of thirst in the wilderness. . . .

Many today think that when they begin their Christian life they will find freedom from all want and difficulty. But everyone who takes up his cross to follow Christ comes to a Rephidim in his experience. Life is not all made up of green pastures and cooling streams. Disappointment overtakes us, privations come, circumstances occur which bring us into difficult places. As we follow in the narrow way, doing our best, as we think, we find that grievous trials come to us. . . . Conscience stricken, we reason, if we had walked with God, we would never have suffered so. . . .

But of old the Lord led His people to Rephidim, and He may choose to bring us there also, in order to test our faithfulness and loyalty to Him. In mercy to us, He does not always place us in the easiest places; for if He did, in our self-sufficiency we would forget that the Lord is our helper in time of necessity. But He longs to manifest Himself to us in our emergencies, and reveal the abundant supplies that are at our disposal, independent of our surroundings; and disappointment and trial are permitted to come upon us that we may realize our own helplessness, and learn to call upon the Lord for aid, as a child, when hungry and thirsty, calls upon its earthly father.

Our heavenly Father has the power of turning the flinty rock into life-giving and refreshing streams. We shall never know, until we are face to face with God, . . . how many burdens He has borne for us, and how many burdens He would have been glad to bear if, with childlike faith, we had brought them to Him.—*Signs of the Times,* Sept. 10, 1896.

INSTEAD OF MURMURING, LET US EXERCISE FAITH

Philip saith unto him, Lord, shew us the Father, and it sufficeth us. John 14:8.

Shortly before Christ's ascension, Philip said to Him, "Lord, shew us the Father, and it sufficeth us." Grieved at his unbelief, Christ turned to him, saying, "Have I been so long time with you, and yet hast thou not known me, Philip?" Is it possible that I have walked with you, and talked with you, and fed you by miracles, and yet you have not comprehended that I was the Sent of God, "the way, the truth, and the life," that I came from heaven to represent the Father?

"Believest thou not that I am in the Father, and the Father in me? The words that I speak unto you I speak not of myself, but the Father that dwelleth in me, he doeth the works." "He that hath seen me hath seen the Father," for I am the brightness of His glory, and the express image of His person." . . .

Too often we grieve the heart of Jesus by our unbelief. Our faith is shortsighted, and we allow trials to bring out our inherited and cultivated tendencies to wrong. When brought into strait circumstances, we dishonor God by murmuring and complaining. Instead of this we should show that we have learned in the school of Christ, by helping those that are worse off than ourselves, those who are seeking for light, but are unable to find it. Such have a special claim upon our sympathy, but instead of trying to uplift them, we pass by on the other side, intent on our own interests or trials. If we do not show decided unbelief, we manifest a murmuring, complaining spirit.

"O thou of little faith, wherefore didst thou doubt?" Christ has already proved Himself to be our ever-present Saviour. He knows all about our circumstances, and in the hour of trial can we not pray that God will give us His Holy Spirit to bring to our minds His many manifestations of power in our behalf? Can we not believe that He is as willing to help us as on former occasions? His past dealings with His servants are not to fade from our minds, but the remembrance of them is ever to strengthen and uphold us.

No amount of tribulation can separate us from Christ. If He leads us to Rephidim, it is because He sees that it is for our good and for His name's glory. If we will look to Him in trusting faith, He will, in His own time, turn the bitterness of Marah into sweetness. He can open the flinty rock, and cause cooling streams to flow forth. Then shall we not lift our voices in praise and thanksgiving for past mercies, and go forward with full assurance that He is an ever-present help in time of trouble?—*Signs of the Times,* Sept. 17, 1896.

GOD'S GRACE SWEETENS EVERY AFFLICTION

I am the true vine, and my Father is the husbandman. Every branch in me that beareth not fruit he taketh away: and every branch that beareth fruit, he purgeth it, that it may bring forth more fruit. John 15:1, 2.

"Now ye are clean through the word which I have spoken unto you. Abide in me, and I in you." The very same sap and nourishment that nourishes the parent stock, nourishes the branch abiding in the vine. Christ is represented by the vine that imparts the nourishment, the vitality, the life, the spirit, the power, that the branch can bear fruit, and then when affliction and disappointment come, you are to show altogether a different character of fruit than the world. There is the evidence that you are connected with Jesus Christ, and that there is a power that sustains you in all your afflictions and disappointments and trials; and this power and this grace sweetens every affliction. [When] the cup of suffering may be placed to your lips, there is a Comforter and Helper. The cup of consolation is placed in the hand, and it may be the happiest period of your life.

"Abide in me, and I in you. As the branch cannot bear fruit of itself, except it abide in the vine; no more can ye, except ye abide in me." . . . Here are the most precious jewels of truth for every individual soul of us. Here is the only election in the Bible, and you can prove yourself elected of Christ by being faithful; you can prove yourself the chosen of Christ by abiding in the vine. . . .

Christ tells us plainly that the whole power, the whole fruit-bearing quality, is in the parent vine stock. Then let them be abiding in Christ, and drawing the nourishment from Christ, and what shall we see? We shall see something, the world will see something. There is a clear line of distinction between the believing and the unbelieving, between those that obey God, and those that disobey Him; there is a decided and marked difference in the fruit they bear. . . . The fruit is the character. . . .

Every ability that you have, every power that you have, your reasoning powers, every talent that you have, every capability that you have, is to be brought right into the religious life, and the kindness, the compassion, the pitifulness, the love of God, is the fruit borne upon the branch that is grafted into the living Vine. And then as the rich clusters . . . bow down that branch, showing that those that bear the most fruit, the richest clusters, have the true humility of lowliness, like Christ. He says, Learn of Me. Come unto Me. Now let us everyone hear it. It is the invitation not from the speaker, but it is the invitation from Jesus Christ Himself.— Manuscript 43, 1894.

WHATEVER OUR TRIAL, CHRIST IS NEAR

Jesus went unto them, walking on the sea. And when the disciples saw him walking on the sea, they were troubled. . . . But straightway Jesus spake unto them, saying, Be of good cheer; it is I; be not afraid. Matt. 14:25-27.

We are to watch. Christ said, Watch unto prayer. He does not deceive any of us. He takes us to an eminence, shows us the confederacy of evil and the strength of the powers of darkness that are arrayed against all who would have faith in Jesus Christ, and tells us to count the cost; but He does more for us; He does not leave us there without still further encouragement. He does not show us trials and conflicts and leave us without help to fight the battles. But He tells us that God has His angels that minister unto those who shall be heirs of salvation. Round about His throne are thousands and thousands and ten times ten thousands of angels.

What is their work? It is to do the bidding of Jesus Christ their Master. And what do they do? They tell you that Christ chose you, that heavenly angels are with you, and they remain with you. You can have but little strength to war against principalities and powers and spiritual wickedness in high places, but here is One who points you to the help heaven sent, that every soul, however strong or weak, . . . may be [victorious]. . . .

We say we do believe that Jesus Christ died, but is He your personal Saviour? Here is the faith part of it. . . . Do you grasp Him by the living hand of faith? Do you reach out your hand to Him and say, as did Peter, "Save, Lord, or I perish"? He will save you. You remember there the disciples were toiling with the ship, and they gave up all hope of reaching the land. While in their dread peril they see One coming toward them, stepping on the foam-crested billows as He would on solid earth, and they were afraid and said, "It is a spirit"; but Christ says, "It is I, be not afraid."

Oh, how much "It is I" means! It means everything to us when we are in trouble or perplexities. Can you not hear His voice? Can you not hear Him saying, "It is I; be not afraid"? . . . He is addressing Himself to us. Whatever your weakness or trial, Christ is near you. He says, "It is I, be not afraid." . . .

Did ever anyone lift [his] hands to Jesus and say, "Save, Lord, or I perish," and He pass [him] by? Never, never! He is a Jesus that hears the faintest cry. We need none of us faint or cry or be discouraged. We need not faint, for like Peter, we may look to the darkness and trials around us. . . . The Lord took the hand of Peter and he was saved. And thus we have a Saviour and in every trial we are to trust in the Lord God of Israel and He will be our Helper.—Manuscript 10, 1891.

THE VALUE OF PAIN

For I reckon that the sufferings of this present time are not worthy to be compared with the glory which shall be revealed in us. Rom. 8:18.

In the experience of the apostle John under persecution, there is a lesson of wonderful strength and comfort for the Christian. God does not prevent the plottings of wicked men, but He causes their devices to work for good to those who in trial and conflict maintain their faith and loyalty. Often the gospel laborer carries on his work amid storms of persecution, bitter opposition, and unjust reproach. At such times let him remember that the experience to be gained in the furnace of trial and affliction is worth all the pain it costs. Thus God brings His children near to Him, that He may show them their weakness and His strength. He teaches them to lean on Him. Thus He prepares them to meet emergencies, to fill positions of trust, and to accomplish the great purpose for which their powers were given them.

In all ages God's appointed witnesses have exposed themselves to reproach and persecution for the truth's sake. Joseph was maligned and persecuted because he preserved his virtue and integrity. David, the chosen messenger of God, was hunted like a beast of prey by his enemies. Daniel was cast into a den of lions because he was true to his allegiance to heaven. Job was deprived of his worldly possessions, and so afflicted in body that he was abhorred by his relatives and friends; yet he maintained his integrity.

Jeremiah could not be deterred from speaking the words that God had given him to speak; and his testimony so enraged the king and princes that he was cast into a loathsome pit. Stephen was stoned because he preached Christ and Him crucified. Paul was imprisoned, beaten with rods, stoned, and finally put to death because he was a faithful messenger for God to the Gentiles. And John was banished to the Isle of Patmos ''for the word of God, and for the testimony of Jesus Christ.''

These examples of human steadfastness bear witness to the faithfulness of God's promises—of His abiding presence and sustaining grace. They testify to the power of faith to withstand the powers of the world. . . .

They bore witness to the power of One mightier than Satan. . . . Through trial and persecution the glory—the character—of God is revealed in His chosen ones. The believers in Christ, hated and persecuted by the world, are educated and disciplined in the school of Christ. On earth they walk in narrow paths; they are purified in the furnace of affliction.—*The Acts of the Apostles,* pp. 574-576.

GOD TEACHES SELF-DISTRUST THROUGH TRIALS

My thoughts are not your thoughts, neither are your ways my ways, saith the Lord. Isa. 55:8.

The worker for God often regards the activities of life as essential for the advancement of the work. He looks upon himself as a necessity, and self is mingled with all that is said and done. Then God interposes. He draws His child away from the earthly, which holds his attention, that he may behold His glory. He says: "This poor soul has lost sight of Me and My sufficiency. His eye is not fixed upon his Lord. I must throw My light and My vitalizing power into his heart, and thus prepare him to work in right lines. By anointing his eyes with the heavenly eyesalve I will prepare him to receive truth."

The Lord is compelled to fortify the soul against self-sufficiency and self-dependence, in order that the worker shall not regard his failings as virtues, and thus be ruined by self-exaltation. Sometimes the Lord makes His path to the soul by a process that is painful to humanity; the work of purifying is a great work, and will always cost man suffering and trial. But he must pass through the furnace until the fires have consumed the dross, and he can reflect the divine image.

Those who follow their own inclinations are not good judges of what the Lord is doing, and they are filled with discontent. They see failure where there is triumph, loss where there is gain. Like Jacob, they are ready to exclaim, "All these things are against me," when the very things whereof they complain are working together for their good. "My thoughts are not your thoughts, neither are your ways my ways, saith the Lord." . . .

Let us consider the experience of Paul for a little. At the very time when it seemed that the apostle's labors were most needed to strengthen the tried and persecuted church, his liberty was taken away, and he was bound in chains. But this was the time for the Lord to work, and precious were the victories won.

When to all appearance Paul was able to do the least, then it was that the truth found an entrance into the royal palace. Not Paul's masterly sermons before these great men, but his bonds attracted their attention. Through his captivity he was a conqueror for Christ. The patience and meekness with which he submitted to his long and unjust confinement set these men to weighing character. Sending his last message to his loved ones in the faith, Paul gathers up with his words the greetings from these saints in Caesar's household to the saints in other cities.—*Signs of the Times,* Feb. 21, 1900.

MEEKNESS UNDER TRIAL

Because of my chains, most of the brothers in the Lord have been encouraged to speak the word of God more courageously and fearlessly. Phil. 1:14, N.I.V.

By his [Paul's] example, Christians were impelled to greater energy as advocates of the cause from the public labors of which Paul had been withdrawn. In these ways were the apostle's bonds influential, so that when his power and usefulness seemed cut off, and to all appearance he could do the least, then it was that he gathered sheaves for Christ in fields from which he seemed wholly excluded.

Before the close of that two years' imprisonment, Paul was able to say, "My bonds in Christ are manifest in all the palace, and in all other places" (Phil. 1:13), and among those who sent greetings to the Philippians he mentions chiefly them "that are of Caesar's household" (chap. 4:22).

Patience as well as courage has its victories. By meekness under trial, no less than by boldness in enterprise, souls may be won to Christ. The Christian who manifests patience and cheerfulness under bereavement and suffering, who meets even death itself with the peace and calmness of an unwavering faith, may accomplish for the gospel more than he could have effected by a long life of faithful labor. Often when the servant of God is withdrawn from active duty, the mysterious providence which our shortsighted vision would lament is designed by God to accomplish a work that otherwise would never have been done.

Let not the follower of Christ think, when he is no longer able to labor openly and actively for God and His truth, that he has no service to render, no reward to secure. Christ's true witnesses are never laid aside. In health and sickness, in life and death, God uses them still. When through Satan's malice the servants of Christ have been persecuted, their active labors hindered, when they have been cast into prison, or dragged to the scaffold or to the stake, it was that truth might gain a greater triumph. As these faithful ones sealed their testimony with their blood, souls hitherto in doubt and uncertainty were convinced of the faith of Christ and took their stand courageously for Him. From the ashes of the martyrs has sprung an abundant harvest for God. . . .

The apostle and his associate workers might have argued that it would be vain to call to repentance and faith in Christ the servants of Nero. . . . But Paul did not reason thus; in faith he presented the gospel to these souls, and among those who heard were some who decided to obey at any cost. Notwithstanding obstacles and dangers, they would accept the light, and trust God to help them let their light shine forth to others.—*The Acts of the Apostles,* pp. 464-466.

PAUL'S GODLY LIFE HAD IRRESISTIBLE POWER

Thou wilt keep him in perfect peace, whose mind is stayed on thee: because he trusteth in thee. Isa. 26:3.

Nero pronounced the decision that condemned Paul to a martyr's death. . . .

Few spectators were allowed to be present; for his persecutors, alarmed at the extent of his influence, feared that converts might be won to Christianity by the scenes of his death. But even the hardened soldiers who attended him listened to his words and with amazement saw him cheerful and even joyous in the prospect of death. To some who witnessed his martyrdom, his spirit of forgiveness toward his murderers and his unwavering confidence in Christ till the last proved a savor of life unto life. . . .

The heaven-born peace expressed on Paul's countenance won many a soul to the gospel. Paul carried with him the atmosphere of heaven. All who associated with him felt the influence of his union with Christ. The fact that his own life exemplified the truth he proclaimed gave convincing power to his preaching.

Here lies the power of truth. The unstudied, unconscious influence of a holy life is the most convincing sermon that can be given in favor of Christianity. Argument, even when unanswerable, may provoke only opposition; but a godly example has a power that it is impossible wholly to resist.

The apostle lost sight of his own approaching sufferings in his solicitude for those whom he was about to leave to cope with prejudice, hatred, and persecution. The few Christians who accompanied him to the place of execution he endeavored to strengthen and encourage by repeating the promises given for those who are persecuted for righteousness' sake. He assured them that nothing would fail of all that the Lord had spoken concerning His tried and faithful children.

For a little season they might be in heaviness through manifold temptations; they might be destitute of earthly comforts; but they could encourage their hearts with the assurance of God's faithfulness, saying, "I know whom I have believed, and am persuaded that he is able to keep that which I have committed unto him" (2 Tim. 1:12). Soon the night of trial and suffering would end, and then would dawn the glad morning of peace and perfect day.

The apostle was looking into the great beyond, not with uncertainty or dread, but with joyous hope and longing expectation. As he stands at the place of martyrdom he sees not the sword of the executioner or the earth so soon to receive his blood; he looks up through the calm blue heaven of that summer day to the throne of the Eternal.—*The Acts of the Apostles,* pp. 509-512.

PETER STRENGTHENED THOSE ENDURING TRIAL

That the trial of your faith, being much more precious than gold that perisheth, though it be tried with fire, might be found unto praise and honour and glory at the appearing of Jesus Christ. 1 Peter 1:7.

Human beings, themselves given to evil, are prone to deal untenderly with the tempted and the erring. They cannot read the heart; they know not its struggle and its pain. Of the rebuke that is love, of the blow that wounds to heal, of the warning that speaks hope, they have need to learn.

Throughout his ministry, Peter faithfully watched over the flock entrusted to his care, and thus proved himself worthy of the charge and responsibility given him by the Saviour. Ever he exalted Jesus of Nazareth as the Hope of Israel, the Saviour of mankind. He brought his own life under the discipline of the Master Worker. By every means within his power he sought to educate the believers for active service. His godly example and untiring activity inspired many young men of promise to give themselves wholly to the work of the ministry.

As time went on, the apostle's influence as an educator and leader increased; and while he never lost his burden to labor especially for the Jews, yet he bore his testimony in many lands and strengthened the faith of multitudes in the gospel.

In the later years of his ministry, Peter was inspired to write to the believers "scattered throughout Pontus, Galatia, Cappadocia, Asia, and Bithynia." His letters were the means of reviving the courage and strengthening the faith of those who were enduring trial and affliction, and of renewing to good works those who through manifold temptations were in danger of losing their hold upon God. These letters bear the impress of having been written by one in whom the sufferings of Christ and also His consolation had been made to abound; one whose entire being had been transformed by grace, and whose hope of eternal life was sure and steadfast.

At the very beginning of his first letter the aged servant of God ascribed to his Lord a tribute of praise and thanksgiving. "Blessed be the God and Father of our Lord Jesus Christ," he exclaimed, "which according to his abundant mercy hath begotten us again unto a lively hope by the resurrection of Jesus Christ from the dead, to an inheritance incorruptible, and undefiled, and that fadeth not away." . . .

In this hope of a sure inheritance in the earth made new, the early Christians rejoiced, even in times of severe trial and affliction.—*The Acts of the Apostles,* pp. 516-518.

TRIALS EDUCATE, PURIFY, AND STRENGTHEN

Beloved, think it not strange concerning the fiery trial which is to try you. . . . But rejoice, inasmuch as ye are partakers of Christ's sufferings; that, when his glory shall be revealed, ye may be glad also with exceeding joy. 1 Peter 4:12, 13.

Looking forward with prophetic vision to the perilous times into which the church of Christ was to enter, the apostle [Peter] exhorted the believers to steadfastness in the face of trial and suffering. "Beloved," he wrote, "think it not strange concerning the fiery trial which is to try you."

Trial is part of the education given in the school of Christ, to purify God's children from the dross of earthliness. It is because God is leading His children that trying experiences come to them. Trials and obstacles are His chosen methods of discipline, and His appointed conditions of success.

He who reads the hearts of men knows their weaknesses better than they themselves can know them. He sees that some have qualifications which, if rightly directed, could be used in the advancement of His work. In His providence He brings these souls into different positions and varied circumstances, that they may discover the defects that are concealed from their own knowledge. He gives them opportunity to overcome these defects and to fit themselves for service. Often He permits the fires of affliction to burn, that they may be purified.

God's care for His heritage is unceasing. He suffers no affliction to come upon His children but such as is essential for their present and eternal good. He will purify His church, even as Christ purified the temple during His ministry on earth. All that He brings upon His people in test and trial comes that they may gain deeper piety and greater strength to carry forward the triumphs of the cross.

There had been a time in Peter's experience when he was unwilling to see the cross in the work of Christ. When the Saviour made known to the disciples His impending sufferings and death, Peter exclaimed, "Be it far from thee, Lord: this shall not be unto thee" (Matt. 16:22). Self-pity, which shrank from fellowship with Christ in suffering, prompted Peter's remonstrance. It was to the disciple a bitter lesson, and one which he learned but slowly, that the path of Christ on earth lay through agony and humiliation. But in the heat of the furnace fire he was to learn its lesson. Now, when his once-active form was bowed with the burden of years and labors, he could write, "Beloved, think it not strange concerning the fiery trial which is to try you. . . . But rejoice, inasmuch as ye are partakers of Christ's sufferings."—*The Acts of the Apostles,* pp. 524, 525.

JOHN MET ERRORS UNFLINCHINGLY

This . . . is the message which we have heard of him, and declare unto you, that God is light, and in him is no darkness at all. 1 John 1:5.

John was not to prosecute his work without great hindrances. Satan was not idle. He instigated evil men to cut short the useful life of this man of God, but holy angels protected him from their assaults. . . . The church in its peril needed his testimony.

By misrepresentation and falsehood the emissaries of Satan had sought to stir up opposition against John and against the doctrine of Christ. In consequence dissensions and heresies were imperiling the church. John met these errors unflinchingly. He hedged up the way of the adversaries of truth. He wrote and exhorted, that the leaders in these heresies should not have the least encouragement.

There are at the present day evils similar to those that threatened the prosperity of the early church, and the teachings of the apostle upon these points should be carefully heeded. ''You must have charity'' is the cry to be heard everywhere, especially from those who profess sanctification. But charity is too pure to cover an unconfessed sin.

John's teachings are important for those who are living amid the perils of the last days. He had been intimately associated with Christ, he had listened to His teachings and had witnessed His mighty miracles. He bore a convincing testimony, which made the falsehoods of His enemies of none effect.

John enjoyed the blessing of true sanctification. But mark, the apostle does not claim to be sinless; he is seeking perfection by walking in the light of God's countenance. He testifies that the man who professes to know God, and yet breaks the divine law, gives the lie to his profession. ''He that saith, I know him, and keepeth not his commandments, is a liar, and the truth is not in him'' (1 John 2:4).

In this age of boasted liberality these words would be branded as bigotry. But the apostle teaches that while we should manifest Christian courtesy, we are authorized to call sin and sinners by their right names—that this is consistent with true charity. While we are to love the souls for whom Christ died, and labor for their salvation, we should not make a compromise with sin. We are not to unite with the rebellious, and call this charity.

God requires His people in this age of the world to stand, as did John in his time, unflinchingly for the right, in opposition to soul-destroying errors.—*The Sanctified Life,* pp. 64, 65.

CHRIST LIFTS US THROUGH SORROW

Happy is the man whom God correcteth. . . . He maketh sore, and bindeth up: he woundeth, and his hands make whole. He shall deliver thee in six troubles; yea, in seven there shall no evil touch thee. Job 5:17-19.

When tribulation comes upon us, how many of us are like Jacob! We think it the hand of an enemy; and in the darkness we wrestle blindly until our strength is spent, and we find no comfort or deliverance. To Jacob the divine touch at break of day revealed the One with whom he had been contending—the Angel of the covenant; and, weeping and helpless, he fell upon the breast of Infinite Love, to receive the blessing for which his soul longed. We also need to learn that trials mean benefit, and not to despise the chastening of the Lord nor faint when we are rebuked of Him. . . .

God would not have us remain pressed down by dumb sorrow, with sore and breaking hearts. He would have us look up and behold His dear face of love. The blessed Saviour stands by many whose eyes are so blinded by tears that they do not discern Him. He longs to clasp our hands, to have us look to Him in simple faith, permitting Him to guide us. His heart is open to our griefs, our sorrows, and our trials. He has loved us with an everlasting love and with loving-kindness compassed us about. We may keep the heart stayed upon Him and meditate upon His loving-kindness all the day. He will lift the soul above the daily sorrow and perplexity, into a realm of peace.

Think of this, children of suffering and sorrow, and rejoice in hope. "This is the victory that overcometh the world, even our faith" (1 John 5:4).

Blessed are they also who weep with Jesus in sympathy with the world's sorrow and in sorrow for its sin. In such mourning there is intermingled no thought of self. Jesus was the Man of Sorrows, enduring heart anguish such as no language can portray. His spirit was torn and bruised by the transgressions of men. He toiled with self-consuming zeal to relieve the wants and woes of humanity, and His heart was heavy with sorrow as He saw multitudes refuse to come to Him that they might have life.

All who are followers of Christ will share in this experience. As they partake of His love they will enter into His travail for the saving of the lost. They share in the sufferings of Christ, and they will share also in the glory that shall be revealed. One with Him in His work, drinking with Him the cup of sorrow, they are partakers also of His joy. . . . The Lord has special grace for the mourner, and its power is to melt hearts, to win souls.—*Thoughts From the Mount of Blessing,* pp. 11-13.

LOVE FOR JESUS MAKES SUFFERING SWEET

Our light affliction, which is but for a moment, worketh for us a far more exceeding and eternal weight of glory. 2 Cor. 4:17.

Jesus does not present to His followers the hope of attaining earthly glory and riches, and of having a life free from trial, but He presents to them the privilege of walking with their Master in the paths of self-denial and reproach, because the world knows them not. . . .

In an unpitying confederacy, evil men and evil angels arrayed themselves against the Prince of Peace. Though His every word and act breathed of divine compassion, His unlikeness to the world provoked the bitterest hostility. . . .

Between righteousness and sin, love and hatred, truth and falsehood, there is an irrepressible conflict. When one presents the love of Christ and the beauty of holiness, he is drawing away the subjects of Satan's kingdom, and the prince of evil is aroused to resist it. . . .

As men seek to come into harmony with God, they will find that the offense of the cross has not ceased. Principalities and powers and wicked spirits in high places are arrayed against all who yield obedience to the law of heaven. Therefore, so far from causing grief, persecution should bring joy to the disciples of Christ, for it is an evidence that they are following in the steps of their Master.

While the Lord has not promised His people exemption from trials, He has promised that which is far better. He has said, "As thy days, so shall thy strength be" (Deut. 33:25). . . . If you are called to go through the fiery furnace for His sake, Jesus will be by your side even as He was with the fait)ful three in Babylon. Those who love their Redeemer will rejoice at every opportunity of sharing with Him humiliation and reproach. The love they bear their Lord makes suffering for His sake sweet. . . .

They follow Christ through sore conflicts; they endure self-denial and experience bitter disappointments; but their painful experience teaches them the guilt and woe of sin, and they look upon it with abhorrence. Being partakers of Christ's sufferings, they are destined to be partakers of His glory.

In holy vision the prophet saw the triumph of the people of God. He says, "I saw as it were a sea of glass mingled with fire: and them that had gotten the victory . . . , stand on the sea of glass, having the harps of God. And they sing the song of Moses the servant of God, and the song of the Lamb, saying, Great and marvellous are thy works, Lord God Almighty" (Rev. 15:2, 3).—*Thoughts From the Mount of Blessing,* pp. 29-31.

AFFLICTION SPREADS KNOWLEDGE OF GOD

Take . . . the prophets, who have spoken in the name of the Lord, for an example of suffering affliction, and of patience. James 5:10.

There was never one who walked among men more cruelly slandered than the Son of man. He was derided and mocked because of His unswerving obedience to the principles of God's holy law. They hated Him without a cause. Yet He stood calmly before His enemies, declaring that reproach is a part of the Christian's legacy, counseling His followers how to meet the arrows of malice, bidding them not to faint under persecution.

While slander may blacken the reputation, it cannot stain the character. That is in God's keeping. So long as we do not consent to sin, there is no power, whether human or satanic, that can bring a stain upon the soul. A man whose heart is stayed upon God is just the same in the hour of his most afflicting trials and most discouraging surroundings as when he was in prosperity, when the light and favor of God seemed to be upon him. His words, his motives, his actions, may be misrepresented and falsified, but he does not mind it, because he has greater interests at stake. Like Moses, he endures as "seeing him who is invisible" (Heb. 11:27). . . .

In every age God's chosen messengers have been reviled and persecuted, yet through their affliction the knowledge of God has been spread abroad. Every disciple of Christ is to step into the ranks and carry forward the same work, knowing that its foes can do nothing against the truth, but for the truth. God means that truth shall be brought to the front and become the subject of examination and discussion, even through the contempt placed upon it. The minds of the people must be agitated; every controversy, every reproach, every effort to restrict liberty of conscience, is God's means of awakening minds that otherwise might slumber.

How often this result has been seen in the history of God's messengers! When the noble and eloquent Stephen was stoned to death at the instigation of the Sanhedrin council, there was no loss to the cause of the gospel. The light of heaven that glorified his face, the divine compassion breathed in his dying prayer, were as a sharp arrow of conviction to the bigoted Sanhedrist who stood by, and Saul, the persecuting Pharisee, became a chosen vessel to bear the name of Christ before Gentiles and kings and the children of Israel.—*Thoughts From the Mount of Blessing,* pp. 32-34.

WATCH, AND GIVE JESUS YOUR BURDEN

Watch ye therefore, and pray always, that ye may be accounted worthy to escape all these things that shall come to pass, and to stand before the Son of man. Luke 21:36.

In the solemn language of this scripture, a duty is pointed out which lies in the daily pathway of everyone, whether old or young. This is the duty of watchfulness, and upon our faithfulness here our destiny for time and for eternity depends. . . .

How many there are whose hearts are today aching under their load of care, and who are thinking, Oh, if there were only someone to help me bear my burdens! Well, there is Someone to help you bear your burdens; there is rest for you who are heavy laden. Jesus, the great Burden- bearer, invites, ''Come unto me, all ye that labour and are heavy laden, and I will give you rest.''

Here is the promise of the Master; but it is on condition. ''Take my yoke upon you,'' He says, ''and learn of me; for I am meek and lowly in heart; and ye shall find rest unto your souls.''

''For My yoke is grievous.'' Is that what He says? No. ''My yoke is easy, and my burden is light.'' The burden you are carrying which is so heavy, and which causes such weariness and perplexity, is your own burden. You desire to meet the world's standard; and in your eager efforts to gratify ambitious and worldly desires, you wound your consciences, and thus bring upon yourselves the additional burden of remorse.

When you do not want to be distinct from the world, but desire to mix up with it so that no difference is seen between you and the world, then you may know that you are drunken with the cares of this life. Oh, there are so many selfish interests, so many cords to bind us to this world! But we must keep cutting these cords, and be in a condition of waiting for our Lord.

The world has forced itself in between our souls and God. But what right have we to allow our hearts to become overcharged with the cares of this life? What right have we, through our devotion to the world, to neglect the affairs of the church and the interests of our fellow men? Why should we manufacture for ourselves burdens and cares that Christ has not laid upon us? . . .

''Watch ye therefore, and pray always.'' There is great need of watchfulness, not for our own sakes only, but also for the sake of our influence upon others. Our influence is far-reaching. . . . We should so speak and so walk that the Spirit of God may be in our hearts, and His blessing in our homes.—*Signs of the Times,* Jan. 7, 1886.

CHRISTIANS TO REPRESENT CHRIST IN EVERY ACT

But ye, brethren, be not weary in well doing. 2 Thess. 3:13.

What can we say to arouse those who profess to be the followers of Christ, to a sense of the solemn responsibilities resting upon them? Is there no voice that shall arouse them to work while the day lasts? Our divine Master gave His life for a ruined world. Who will deny self, and make some sacrifice to save souls for whom He died?

In every act of life, Christians should seek to represent Christ—seek to make His service appear attractive. Let none make religion repulsive by groans and sighs and a relation of their trials, their self-denials, and sacrifices. Do not give the lie to your profession of faith by impatience, fretfulness, and repining. Let the graces of the Spirit be manifested in kindness, meekness, forbearance, cheerfulness, and love. Let it be seen that the love of Christ is an abiding motive; that your religion is not a dress to be put off and on to suit circumstances, but a principle, calm, steady, unvarying. Alas that pride, unbelief, and selfishness, like a foul cancer, are eating out vital godliness from the heart of many a professed Christian! . . .

Love to Jesus will be seen, will be felt. It cannot be hidden. It exerts a wondrous power. It makes the timid bold, the slothful diligent, the ignorant wise. It makes the stammering tongue eloquent, and rouses the dormant intellect into new life and vigor. It makes the desponding hopeful, the gloomy joyous. Love to Christ will lead its possessor to accept responsibilities for His sake, and to bear them in His strength. Love to Christ will not be dismayed by tribulation, nor turned aside from duty by reproaches. . . .

Peace in Christ is of more value than all the treasures of earth. Let us seek the Lord with all our heart, let us learn of Christ to be meek and lowly, that we may find rest of soul. Let us arouse our dormant energies, and become active, earnest, fervent. The very example and deportment, as well as the words, of the Christian should be such as to awaken in the sinner a desire to come to the Fountain of life.

Then let us open our hearts to the bright beams of the Sun of Righteousness. Let us work cheerfully, joyfully, in the service of our Master. Let us praise Him, not only by our words in the congregation of His saints, but by a well-ordered life and godly conversation—a life of active, noble Christian effort. Let us give diligence to make our calling and election sure, remembering that we shall triumph at last, if we do not become weary in well doing.—*Signs of the Times,* June 24, 1886.

THE SCRIPTURES SAFEGUARD AGAINST DECEPTION

To the law and to the testimony: if they speak not according to this word, it is because there is no light in them. Isa. 8:20.

The people of God are directed to the Scriptures as their safeguard against the influence of false teachers and the delusive power of spirits of darkness. Satan employs every possible device to prevent men from obtaining a knowledge of the Bible; for its plain utterances reveal his deceptions. . . . So closely will the counterfeit resemble the true that it will be impossible to distinguish between them except by the Holy Scriptures. By their testimony every statement and every miracle must be tested.

Those who endeavor to obey all the commandments of God will be opposed and derided. They can stand only in God. In order to endure the trial before them, they must understand the will of God as revealed in His Word; they can honor Him only as they have a right conception of His character, government, and purposes, and act in accordance with them. None but those who have fortified the mind with the truths of the Bible will stand through the last great conflict. . . .

The apostle Paul declared, looking down to the last days: "The time will come when they will not endure sound doctrine" (2 Tim. 4:3). That time has fully come. The multitudes do not want Bible truth, because it interferes with the desires of the sinful, world-loving heart; and Satan supplies the deceptions which they love.

But God will have a people upon the earth to maintain the Bible, and the Bible only, as the standard of all doctrines and the basis of all reforms. The opinions of learned men, the deductions of science, the creeds or decisions of ecclesiastical councils, as numerous and discordant as are the churches which they represent, the voice of the majority—not one nor all of these should be regarded as evidence for or against any point of religious faith. Before accepting any doctrine or precept, we should demand a plain "Thus saith the Lord" in its support.

Satan is constantly endeavoring to attract attention to man in the place of God. He leads the people to look to bishops, to pastors, to professors of theology, as their guides, instead of searching the Scriptures to learn their duty for themselves. Then, by controlling the minds of these leaders, he can influence the multitudes according to his will.

When Christ came to speak the words of life, the common people heard Him gladly; and many, even of the priests and rulers, believed on Him.—*The Great Controversy,* pp. 593-595.

GOD WORKS MIGHTILY FOR HIS CHOSEN ONES

When thou passest through the waters, I will be with thee; and through the rivers, they shall not overflow thee: when thou walkest through the fire, thou shalt not be burned; neither shall the flame kindle upon thee. Isa. 43:2.

The three Hebrews declared to the whole nation of Babylon their faith in Him whom they worshiped. They relied on God. In the hour of their trial they remembered the promise, "When thou passest through the waters, I will be with thee; . . . when thou walkest through the fire, thou shalt not be burned; neither shall the flame kindle upon thee." And in a marvelous manner their faith in the living Word had been honored in the sight of all. The tidings of their wonderful deliverance were carried to many countries by the representatives of the different nations that had been invited by Nebuchadnezzar to the dedication. Through the faithfulness of His children, God was glorified in all the earth.

Important are the lessons to be learned from the experience of the Hebrew youth on the plain of Dura. In this our day, many of God's servants, though innocent of wrongdoing, will be given over to suffer humiliation and abuse at the hands of those who, inspired by Satan, are filled with envy and religious bigotry. Especially will the wrath of man be aroused against those who hallow the Sabbath of the fourth commandment; and at last a universal decree will denounce these as deserving of death.

The season of distress before God's people will call for a faith that will not falter. His children must make it manifest that He is the only object of their worship, and that no consideration, not even that of life itself, can induce them to make the least concession to false worship. To the loyal heart the commands of sinful, finite men will sink into insignificance beside the word of the eternal God. Truth will be obeyed though the result be imprisonment or exile or death.

As in the days of Shadrach, Meshach, and Abednego, so in the closing period of earth's history the Lord will work mightily in behalf of those who stand steadfastly for the right. He who walked with the Hebrew worthies in the fiery furnace will be with His followers wherever they are. His abiding presence will comfort and sustain.

In the midst of the time of trouble—trouble such as has not been since there was a nation—His chosen ones will stand unmoved. Satan with all the hosts of evil cannot destroy the weakest of God's saints. Angels that excel in strength will protect them, and in their behalf Jehovah will reveal Himself as a "God of gods," able to save to the uttermost those who have put their trust in Him.—*Prophets and Kings,* pp. 512, 513.

WRESTLING WITH GOD TO VICTORY

Though Noah, Daniel, and Job, were in it, as I live, saith the Lord God, they shall deliver neither son nor daughter; they shall but deliver their own souls by their righteousness. Eze. 14:20.

Satan leads many to believe that God will overlook their unfaithfulness in the minor affairs of life; but the Lord shows in His dealings with Jacob that He will in no wise sanction or tolerate evil. All who endeavor to excuse or conceal their sins, and permit them to remain upon the books of heaven, unconfessed and unforgiven, will be overcome by Satan. The more exalted their profession and the more honorable the position which they hold, the more grievous is their course in the sight of God. . . .

Jacob's history is also an assurance that God will not cast off those who have been deceived and tempted and betrayed into sin, but who have returned unto Him with true repentance. While Satan seeks to destroy this class, God will send His angels to comfort and protect them in the time of peril.

The assaults of Satan are fierce and determined, his delusions are terrible; but the Lord's eye is upon His people, and His ear listens to their cries. Their affliction is great, the flames of the furnace seem about to consume them; but the Refiner will bring them forth as gold tried in the fire. God's love for His children during the period of their severest trial, is as strong and tender as in the days of their sunniest prosperity; but it is needful for them to be placed in the furnace of fire; their earthliness must be consumed, that the image of Christ may be perfectly reflected.

The season of distress and anguish before us will require a faith that can endure weariness, delay, and hunger—a faith that will not faint, though severely tried. The period of probation is granted to all to prepare for that time. Jacob prevailed because he was persevering and determined. His victory is an evidence of the power of importunate prayer. All who will lay hold of God's promises, as he did, and be as earnest and persevering as he was, will succeed as he succeeded. Those who are unwilling to deny self, to agonize before God, to pray long and earnestly for His blessing, will not obtain it.

Wrestling with God—how few know what it is! How few have ever had their souls drawn out after God with intensity of desire until every power is on the stretch. When waves of despair which no language can express sweep over the suppliant, how few cling with unyielding faith to the promises of God. . . .

If the messengers who bear the last solemn warning to the world would pray . . . fervently and in faith, as did Jacob, they would find many places where they could say: "I have seen God face to face, and my life is preserved" (Gen. 32:30). They would be accounted of heaven as princes, having power to prevail with God and men.—*The Great Controversy,* pp. 620-622.

GOD'S PEOPLE PROTECTED

The Lord is thy keeper: the Lord is thy shade upon thy right hand. The sun shall not smite thee by day, nor the moon by night. The Lord shall preserve thee from all evil: he shall preserve thy soul. Ps. 121:5-7.

When Christ ceases His intercession in the sanctuary, the unmingled wrath threatened against those who worship the beast and his image and receive his mark (Rev. 14:9, 10) will be poured out. The plagues upon Egypt when God was about to deliver Israel were similar in character to those more terrible and extensive judgments which are to fall upon the world just before the final deliverance of God's people. . . .

These plagues are not universal, or the inhabitants of the earth would be wholly cut off. Yet they will be the most awful scourges that have ever been known to mortals. All the judgments upon men, prior to the close of probation, have been mingled with mercy. The pleading blood of Christ has shielded the sinner from receiving the full measure of his guilt; but in the final judgment, wrath is poured out unmixed with mercy. . . .

The people of God will not be free from suffering; but while persecuted and distressed, while they endure privation and suffer for want of food, they will not be left to perish. That God who cared for Elijah will not pass by one of His self-sacrificing children. He who numbers the hairs of their head will care for them, and in time of famine they shall be satisfied. While the wicked are dying from hunger and pestilence, angels will shield the righteous and supply their wants. To him that ''walketh righteously'' is the promise: ''Bread shall be given him; his waters shall be sure'' (Isa. 33:15, 16). ''When the poor and needy seek water, and there is none, and their tongue faileth for thirst, I the Lord will hear them, I the God of Israel will not forsake them'' (chap. 41:17).

''Although the fig tree shall not blossom, neither shall fruit be in the vines,''. . . yet shall they that fear Him ''rejoice in the Lord'' and joy in the God of their salvation (Hab. 3:17, 18). . . .

''The sun shall not smite thee by day, nor the moon by night. The Lord shall preserve thee from all evil: he shall preserve thy soul'' (Ps. 121:6, 7). ''He shall deliver thee from the snare of the fowler, and from the noisome pestilence. He shall cover thee with his feathers, and under his wings shalt thou trust. . . . Because thou hast made the Lord, which is my refuge, even the most High, thy habitation; there shall no evil befall thee, neither shall any plague come nigh thy dwelling'' (Ps. 91:3-10).—*The Great Controversy,* pp. 627-630.

Those who receive the seal of the living God and are protected in the time of trouble must reflect the image of Jesus fully.—*Early Writings,* p. 71.

"GLORY TO GOD IN THE HIGHEST"

And suddenly there was with the angel a multitude of the heavenly host praising God, and saying, Glory to God in the highest, and on earth peace, good will toward men. Luke 2:13, 14.

I entreat you, my brethren and sisters, to make . . . Christmas a blessing to yourselves and others. [The birth of Jesus] was celebrated by the heavenly host. Angels of God, in the appearance of a star, conducted the Wise Men on their mission in search of Jesus. They came with gifts and costly offerings of frankincense and myrrh, to pay their oblation to the infant King foretold in prophecy. They followed the brilliant messengers with assurance and great joy.

The angels . . . appeared to the humble shepherds, guarding their flocks by night, upon Bethlehem's plains. One angel first appeared, clothed with the panoply of heaven; and so surprised and so terrified were the shepherds that they could only gaze upon the wondrous glory of the heavenly visitant with unutterable amazement. The angel of the Lord came to them and said, "Fear not: for, behold, I bring you good tidings of great joy. . . . For unto you is born this day in the city of David a Saviour, which is Christ the Lord." . . .

No sooner had their eyes become accustomed to the glorious presence of the one angel, than, lo! the whole plain was lighted up with the wondrous glory of the multitude of angels that peopled the plains of Bethlehem. The angel quieted the fears of the shepherds before opening their eyes to behold the multitude of the heavenly host, all praising God, and saying, "Glory to God in the highest, and on earth, peace, good will toward men."

Then was the melody of heaven heard by mortal ears, and the heavenly choir swept back to heaven as they closed their ever memorable anthem. The light faded away and the shadows of the night once more fell on the hills and plains of Bethlehem; but there remained in the hearts of the shepherds the brightest picture mortal man had ever looked upon, and the blessed promise and assurance of the advent to our world of the Saviour of men, which filled their hearts with joy and gladness, mingled with faith and wondrous love to God.—*Review and Herald,* Dec. 9, 1884.

Those who love God should feel deeply interested in the children and youth. To them God can reveal His truth and salvation. Jesus calls the little ones that believe on Him the lambs of His flock. He has a special love for and interest in the children. . . . The most precious offering that the children can give to Jesus, is the freshness of their childhood.—*Ibid.,* Dec. 17, 1889.

THE REDEEMED SING, "WORTHY IS THE LAMB!"

To give unto them beauty for ashes, the oil of joy for mourning, the garment of praise for the spirit of heaviness. Isa. 61:3.

Millions went down to the grave loaded with infamy because they steadfastly refused to yield to the deceptive claims of Satan. . . . But now "God is judge himself" (Ps. 50:6). Now the decisions of earth are reversed. . . . They are no longer feeble, afflicted, scattered, and oppressed. Henceforth they are to be ever with the Lord.

They stand before the throne clad in richer robes than the most honored of the earth have ever worn. They are crowned with diadems more glorious than were ever placed upon the brow of earthly monarchs. The days of pain and weeping are forever ended. The King of glory has wiped the tears from all faces; every cause of grief has been removed. Amid the waving of palm branches they pour forth a song of praise, clear, sweet, and harmonious; every voice takes up the strain, until the anthem swells through the vaults of heaven: "Salvation to our God which sitteth upon the throne, and unto the Lamb." . . .

In this life we can only begin to understand the wonderful theme of redemption. . . . Yet with the utmost stretch of our mental powers we fail to grasp its full significance. The length and the breadth, the depth and the height, of redeeming love are but dimly comprehended. The plan of redemption will not be fully understood, even when the ransomed see as they are seen and know as they are known; but through the eternal ages, new truth will continually unfold to the wondering and delighted mind. Though the griefs and pains and temptations of earth are ended and the cause removed, the people of God will ever have a distinct, intelligent knowledge of what their salvation has cost.

The cross of Christ will be the science and the song of the redeemed through all eternity. In Christ glorified they will behold Christ crucified. . . . As the nations of the saved look upon their Redeemer and behold the eternal glory of the Father shining in His countenance; as they behold His throne, which is from everlasting to everlasting, and know that His kingdom is to have no end, they break forth in rapturous song: "Worthy, worthy is the Lamb that was slain, and hath redeemed us to God by His own most precious blood!" . . .

Mercy, tenderness, and parental love are seen to blend with holiness, justice, and power. While we behold the majesty of His throne, high and lifted up, we see His character in its gracious manifestations, and comprehend, as never before, the significance of that endearing title, "Our Father."—*The Great Controversy,* pp. 650-652.

THE DELIVERANCE OF GOD'S PEOPLE

For in the time of trouble he shall hide me in his pavilion: in the secret of his tabernacle shall he hide me; he shall set me up upon a rock. Ps. 27:5.

With earnest longing, God's people await the tokens of their coming King. As the watchmen are accosted, ''What of the night?'' the answer is given unfalteringly, '' 'The morning cometh, and also the night' (Isa. 21: 11, 12). Light is gleaming upon the clouds above the mountaintops. Soon there will be the revealing of His glory.'' . . . The heavens glow with the dawning of eternal day, and like the melody of angel songs the words fall upon the ear: ''Stand fast to your allegiance. Help is coming.'' . . .

The precious Saviour will send help just when we need it. The way to heaven is consecrated by His footprints. Every thorn that wounds our feet has wounded His. Every cross that we are called to bear He has borne before us. The Lord permits conflicts, to prepare the soul for peace. The time of trouble is a fearful ordeal for God's people; but it is the time for every true believer to look up, and by faith he may see the bow of promise encircling him. . . .

The eye of God, looking down the ages, was fixed upon the crisis which His people are to meet, when earthly powers shall be arrayed against them. Like the captive exile, they will be in fear of death by starvation or by violence. But the Holy One who divided the Red Sea before Israel, will manifest His mighty power and turn their captivity. ''They shall be mine, saith the Lord of hosts, in that day when I make up my jewels; and I will spare them, as a man spareth his own son that serveth him'' (Mal. 3:17).

If the blood of Christ's faithful witnesses were shed at this time, it would not, like the blood of the martyrs, be as seed sown to yield a harvest for God. Their fidelity would not be a testimony to convince others of the truth; for the obdurate heart has beaten back the waves of mercy until they return no more. If the righteous were now left to fall a prey to their enemies, it would be a triumph for the prince of darkness. Says the psalmist: ''In the time of trouble he shall hide me in his pavilion: in the secret of his tabernacle shall he hide me.''

Christ has spoken: ''Come, my people, enter thou into thy chambers, and shut thy doors about thee: hide thyself as it were for a little moment, until the indignation be overpast. For, behold, the Lord cometh out of his place to punish the inhabitants of the earth for their iniquity'' (Isa. 26:20, 21). Glorious will be the deliverance of those who have patiently waited for His coming and whose names are written in the book of life.—*The Great Controversy,* pp. 632-634.

PAUL'S TRIUMPHANT TESTIMONY

I have fought a good fight, I have finished my course, I have kept the faith: henceforth there is laid up for me a crown of righteousness, which the Lord, the righteous judge, shall give me at that day. 2 Tim. 4:7, 8.

This man of faith [Paul] beholds the ladder of Jacob's vision, representing Christ, who has connected earth with heaven, and finite man with the infinite God. His faith is strengthened as he calls to mind how patriarchs and prophets have relied upon the One who is his support and consolation, and for whom he is giving his life.

From these holy men who from century to century have borne testimony for their faith, he hears the assurance that God is true. His fellow apostles, who, to preach the gospel of Christ, went forth to meet religious bigotry and heathen superstition, persecution, and contempt, who counted not their lives dear unto themselves that they might bear aloft the light of the cross amidst the dark mazes of infidelity—these he hears witnessing to Jesus as the Son of God, the Saviour of the world.

From the rack, the stake, the dungeon, from dens and caves of the earth, there falls upon his ear the martyr's shout of triumph. He hears the witness of steadfast souls, who, though destitute, afflicted, tormented, yet bear fearless, solemn testimony for the faith, declaring, ''I know whom I have believed.'' These, yielding up their lives for the faith, declare to the world that He in whom they have trusted is able to save to the uttermost.

Ransomed by the sacrifice of Christ, washed from sin in His blood, and clothed in His righteousness, Paul has the witness in himself that his soul is precious in the sight of his Redeemer. His life is hid with Christ in God, and he is persuaded that He who has conquered death is able to keep that which is committed to His trust. His mind grasps the Saviour's promise, ''I will raise him up at the last day'' (John 6:40). His thoughts and hopes are centered on the second coming of his Lord. And as the sword of the executioner descends and the shadows of death gather about the martyr, his latest thought springs forward, as will his earliest in the great awakening, to meet the Life-giver, who shall welcome him to the joy of the blest. . . .

Like a trumpet peal his voice has rung out through all the ages since, nerving with his own courage thousands of witnesses for Christ, and wakening in thousands of sorrow-stricken hearts the echo of his own triumphant joy: . . . ''I have fought a good fight, I have finished my course, I have kept the faith: henceforth there is laid up for me a crown of righteousness, which the Lord . . . shall give me at that day.''—*The Acts of the Apostles,* pp. 512, 513.

OUR GLORIOUS DESTINY

Eye hath not seen, nor ear heard, neither have entered into the heart of man, the things which God hath prepared for them that love him. 1 Cor. 2:9.

Through the gospel, souls that are degraded and enslaved by Satan are to be redeemed to share the glorious liberty of the sons of God. God's purpose is not merely to deliver from the suffering that is the inevitable result of sin, but to save from sin itself. The soul, corrupted and deformed, is to be purified, transformed, that it may be clothed in "the beauty of the Lord our God," "conformed to the image of his Son." "Eye hath not seen, nor ear heard, neither have entered into the heart of man, the things which God hath prepared for them that love him" (Ps. 90:17; Rom. 8:29; 1 Cor. 2:9). Eternity alone can reveal the glorious destiny to which man, restored to God's image, may attain.

In order for us to reach this high ideal, that which causes the soul to stumble must be sacrificed. It is through the will that sin retains its hold upon us. . . . Often it seems to us that to surrender the will to God is to consent to go through life maimed or crippled. But it is better, says Christ, for self to be maimed, wounded, crippled, if thus you may enter into life. That which you look upon as disaster is the door to highest benefit.

God is the fountain of life, and we can have life only as we are in communion with Him. Separated from God, existence may be ours for a little time, but we do not possess life. . . . Only through the surrender of our will to God is it possible for Him to impart life to us. Only by receiving His life through self-surrender is it possible, said Jesus, for these hidden sins . . . to be overcome. It is possible that you may bury them in your hearts and conceal them from human eyes, but how will you stand in God's presence? . . . To sin, wherever found, God is a consuming fire. . . .

It will require a sacrifice to give yourself to God; but it is a sacrifice of the lower for the higher, the earthly for the spiritual, the perishable for the eternal. God does not design that our will should be destroyed, for it is only through its exercise that we can accomplish what He would have us do. Our will is to be yielded to Him, that we may receive it again, purified and refined, and so linked in sympathy with the Divine that He can pour through us the tides of His love and power. However bitter and painful this surrender may appear to the willful, wayward heart, yet "it is profitable for thee."

Not until he fell crippled and helpless upon the breast of the covenant angel did Jacob know the victory of conquering faith and receive the title of a prince with God.—*Thoughts From the Mount of Blessing,* pp. 60-62.

THE PURE IN HEART TO REFLECT CHRIST

He who loves purity of heart, and whose speech is gracious, will have the king as his friend.—Prov. 22:11, R.S.V.

Into the City of God there will enter nothing that defiles. All who are to be dwellers there will here have become pure in heart. In one who is learning of Jesus, there will be manifest a growing distaste for careless manners, unseemly language, and coarse thought. When Christ abides in the heart, there will be purity and refinement of thought and manner.

But the words of Jesus, "Blessed are the pure in heart," have a deeper meaning—not merely pure in the sense in which the world understands purity, free from that which is sensual, pure from lust, but true in the hidden purposes and motives of the soul, free from pride and self-seeking, humble, unselfish, childlike. . . .

To hearts that have become purified through the indwelling of the Holy Spirit, all is changed. These can know God. Moses was hid in the cleft of the rock when the glory of the Lord was revealed to him; and it is when we are hid in Christ that we behold the love of God.

"He that loveth pureness of heart, for the grace of his lips the king shall be his friend" (Prov. 22:11). By faith we behold Him here and now. In our daily experience we discern His goodness and compassion in the manifestation of His providence. . . . The pure in heart see God in a new and endearing relation, as their Redeemer; and while they discern the purity and loveliness of His character, they long to reflect His image. They see Him as a Father longing to embrace a repenting son, and their hearts are filled with joy unspeakable and full of glory.

The pure in heart discern the Creator in the works of His mighty hand, in the things of beauty that comprise the universe. In His Written Word they read in clearer lines the revelation of His mercy, His goodness, and His grace. . . .

The beauty and preciousness of truth, which are undiscerned by the worldly-wise, are constantly unfolding to those who have a trusting, childlike desire to know and to do the will of God. We discern the truth by becoming, ourselves, partakers of the divine nature.

The pure in heart live as in the visible presence of God during the time He apportions them in this world. And they will also see Him face to face in the future, immortal state, as did Adam when he walked and talked with God in Eden. "Now we see through a glass, darkly; but then face to face" (1 Cor. 13:12).—*Thoughts From the Mount of Blessing,* pp. 24-27.

CHRISTIANS TO REFLECT THE LIGHT OF HEAVEN

A city that is set on an hill cannot be hid. Neither do men light a candle, and put it under a bushel, but on a candlestick; and it giveth light unto all that are in the house. Matt. 5:14, 15.

''Ye are the light of the world,'' said Christ to His disciples. As the sun goes forth in the heavens, dispelling the shades of night, and filling the world with brightness, so must the followers of Jesus let their light shine to dispel the moral darkness of a world lying in sin. But they have no light of themselves; it is the light of Heaven which they are to reflect to the world.

''A city that is set on a hill cannot be hid.'' Our thoughts and purposes are the secret springs of action, and hence determine the character. The purpose formed in the heart need not be expressed in word or deed in order to make it sin, and bring the soul into condemnation. Every thought, feeling, and inclination, though unseen by men, is discerned by the eye of God. But it is only when the evil that has taken root in the heart reaches its fruition in the unlawful word or deed that man can judge the character of his fellowman.

The Christian is Christ's representative. He is to show to the world the transforming power of divine grace. He is a living epistle of the truth of God, known and read of all men. The rule given by Christ by which to determine who are His true followers is, ''By their fruits ye shall know them.'' . . .

The Christian's godly life and holy conversation are a daily testimony against sin and sinners. But he must present Christ, not self. Christ is the great remedy for sin. Our compassionate Redeemer has provided for us the help we need. He is waiting to impute His righteousness to the sincere penitent, and to kindle in his heart such divine love as only our gracious Redeemer can inspire. Then let us who profess to be His witnesses on earth, His ambassadors from the court of heaven, glorify Him whom we represent, by being faithful to our trust as light bearers to the world.

Everyone who at last secures eternal life will here manifest zeal and devotion in the service of God. He will not desert the post of duty at the approach of trial, hardship, or reproach. He will be a diligent student of the Scriptures, and will follow the light as it shines upon his pathway. When some plain, scriptural requirement is presented he will not stop to inquire, What will my friends say, if I take my position with the people of God? Knowing his duty, he will do it heartily and fearlessly.

Of such truehearted followers Jesus declares that He is not ashamed to call them brethren. The God of truth will be on their side, and will never forsake them. All apparent losses for Christ's sake will count to them as infinite gain.—*Signs of the Times,* March 25, 1886.

SCRIPTURE INDEX

ZEPHANIAH

1:14 .... July 6
2:3 .... Sept. 6

MALACHI

3:3 .... Dec. 1
3:16 .... July 25

MATTHEW

1:23 .... Jan. 1
3:2 .... Nov. 21
4:10 .... Feb. 15
4:16 .... Aug. 28
5:3 .... Feb. 16
5:7 .... Aug. 1
5:9 .... Jan. 24
5:13 .... July 10
5:14 .... Oct. 1
5:14, 15 .... Dec. 31
5:16 .... Nov. 1
5:17 .... Feb. 22
5:19 .... Feb. 9
5:34-36 .... Feb. 26
5:44 .... Feb. 27
5:48 .... Jan. 10
6:20, 21 .... Sept. 9
6:24 .... Feb. 20
8:17 .... Jan. 5
11:28, 29 .... June 6
14:25-27 .... Dec. 8
16:24 .... Aug. 4
18:4 .... Sept. 4
18:7 .... Sept. 26
20:28 .... Aug. 20
25:4 .... July 16
25:6 .... July 14
25:40 .... Aug. 21

MARK

1:35 .... Apr. 14
2:15 .... Jan. 17
12:30, 31 .... Feb. 6
12:42-44 .... Nov. 23
16:18 .... Aug. 12
16:20 .... July 30

LUKE

2:13, 14 .... Dec. 25
2:52 .... Jan. 23
5:4-6 .... Aug. 11
6:37 .... July 8
9:56 .... Mar. 20
10:36, 37 .... Aug. 3
12:12 .... July 21
14:13, 14 .... Aug. 31
16:10 .... Oct. 22

17:26, 27 .... Nov. 3
18:1 .... Apr. 17
19:10 .... Aug. 24
21:3 .... Sept. 11
21:36 .... Dec. 19
22:27 .... Aug. 27
23:42 .... Jan. 20
24:15-32 .... Aug. 13

JOHN

1:4 .... Jan. 21
1:29 .... Jan. 12
3:3 .... Apr. 21
3:7 .... July 13
3:16 .... Jan. 9
4:14 .... Apr. 5
4:35 .... Aug. 16
5:39 .... Apr. 24
7:37, 38 .... Jan. 4
7:46 .... Jan. 18
8:12 .... June 2
9:4 .... July 9
9:5 .... July 2
10:30 .... Jan. 25
12:31, 32 .... Feb. 5
12:36 .... June 3
14:6 .... Jan. 22
14:8 .... Dec. 6
14:12 .... Jan. 30
14:14 .... Apr. 18
14:26 .... Apr. 25
14:27 .... Sept. 21
15:1, 2 .... Dec. 7
15:8 .... Mar. 24
16:7 .... Jan. 8
16:8 .... Apr. 27
17:3 .... Apr. 4
17:11 .... July 4
17:18 .... Nov. 30
17:19 .... Mar. 28
17:21 .... July 5
20:21 .... Oct. 3
21:15 .... Nov. 27

ACTS

1:8 .... Apr. 26
4:13 .... Jan. 28
4:31 .... Aug. 15
5:32 .... July 18
10:34 .... Jan. 15
10:35 .... Jan. 14
13:47 .... Aug. 10
16:14, 15 .... Nov. 25
16:17 .... July 23
16:25, 26 .... Nov. 24
20:20, 21 .... Aug. 19

ROMANS

3:23, 24 .... Mar. 4
3:25, 26 .... Mar. 5
5:1, 2 .... Oct. 11
5:19, 20 .... Feb. 11
6:13 .... Oct. 10
7:12 .... Feb. 1
8:3, 4 .... Feb. 2
8:18 .... Dec. 9
8:34 .... Jan. 19
12:9, 10 .... June 25
12:10, 11 .... Sept. 29
13:10 .... Feb. 13
14:19 .... Aug. 22
15:13 .... Apr. 30

1 CORINTHIANS

1:30 .... Mar. 30
2:9 .... Dec. 29
2:12 .... Apr. 29
3:9 .... July 3
3:21-23 .... Apr. 20
6:18 .... May 16
6:19 .... May 6
6:20 .... May 4
9:25 .... May 12
9:27 .... Oct. 25
10:31 .... May 17
13:4, 5 .... Oct. 18
13:5-7 .... Oct. 19
15:57 .... Mar. 26
15:58 .... Mar. 29

2 CORINTHIANS

3:18 .... Jan. 6
4:6 .... Apr. 2
4:17 .... Dec. 17
5:15 .... May 31
5:15 .... Aug. 18
6:1 .... July 7
6:16 .... Oct. 23
6:17 .... May 5
9:6 .... Aug. 30
10:5 .... Oct. 21

GALATIANS

2:20 .... Apr. 3
4:4, 5 .... Jan. 2
5:1 .... Apr. 10
6:8 .... May 10
6:9 .... Sept. 30
6:14 .... Sept. 3

EPHESIANS

2:4-6 .... Oct. 31
2:13, 14 .... Jan. 13
2:19, 20 .... July 29

381

3:14-16	July 19
3:17-19	July 20
4:7, 8	Apr. 28
4:23, 24	May 30
5:1	Jan. 26
6:1	June 7
6:2, 3	June 19
6:4	June 9
6:6, 7	Aug. 17
6:13	Dec. 4
6:16	Apr. 22

PHILIPPIANS

1:14	Dec. 11
2:5	Oct. 16
2:7	Aug. 6
2:13	Oct. 4
2:15	Aug. 5
3:14	Oct. 12

COLOSSIANS

2:8	Nov. 26
2:9	Jan. 31
3:3, 4	Jan. 27
3:16	Apr. 11
3:23, 24	Oct. 2
4:6	Sept. 25

1 THESSALONIANS

1:8	Sept. 5
4:2, 3	Mar. 25
4:8	July 22
5:23	Mar. 11
6:17	June 18

2 THESSALONIANS

3:13	Dec. 20

1 TIMOTHY

1:16	Nov. 22
3:16	Mar. 9

2 TIMOTHY

1:7	May 15
2:15	June 16
2:19	Mar. 10
2:24	Oct. 13
4:7, 8	Dec. 28

TITUS

2:11, 12	Oct. 9
2:13, 14	Sept. 1
3:2	Sept. 19

HEBREWS

2:9	Jan. 3
2:11	Mar. 7
4:12	Apr. 7
4:15	Dec. 2
9:24	Mar. 2
10:9	Aug. 2
10:16, 17	Feb. 23
10:24	Aug. 9
11:1	Apr. 23
11:5	Nov. 2
11:24, 25	Nov. 9
12:2	Sept. 20
12:13	Aug. 23

JAMES

1:27	Aug. 26
2:12	Feb. 17
2:21, 22	Mar. 6
3:17, 18	Mar. 31
5:10	Dec. 18

1 PETER

1:7	Dec. 13
1:13	Oct. 24
1:15, 16	May 23
2:4, 5	Sept. 16
2:6	July 28

2:9	July 1
3:3, 4	Sept. 8
3:8	Jan. 16
4:7	Oct. 8
4:12, 13	Dec. 14

2 PETER

1:2	Mar. 27
1:10	Oct. 28
1:16	July 26
3:14	Oct. 26

1 JOHN

1:5	Dec. 15
1:7	July 17
1:9	Mar. 3
2:1, 2	Mar. 1
2:5	Feb. 10
2:6	Mar. 8
2:10	July 27
2:17	Oct. 7
3:3	Oct. 17
3:4	Feb. 4
3:4, 5	Feb. 21
3:7	Feb. 14
3:16	Oct. 30
3:18	Aug. 8
4:7	Mar. 19
4:10, 11	Oct. 29
4:12	Feb. 28
5:4	Jan. 7
5:12	Mar. 21

3 JOHN

2	May 11

REVELATION

1:10	Mar. 22
3:4	Sept. 10